ONE DAY AT A TIME

BY DAVID TOSSELL

fairfield books

First published by Fairfield Books in 2023

fairfield books

Fairfield Books
Bedser Stand
Kia Oval
London
SE11 5SS

Typeset in Garamond and Proxima Nova
Typesetting by Rob Whitehouse
Photography by Getty Images unless stated

© 2023 David Tossell
ISBN 978-1-915237-23-1

A CIP catalogue record for is available from the British Library

Printed by CPI Group (UK) Ltd

ONE DAY AT A TIME

THE HISTORY OF LIMITED-OVERS CRICKET IN 25 MATCHES

DAVID TOSSELL

CONTENTS

PREFACE

It began at 65 overs. Then 60, reducing to 55 or 50. There was 40 overs, too, which begat 20. There has been some dabbling with ten overs and now, as England's cricket authorities look for ways to repackage their sport, especially for inflexible television schedulers, they have done away with overs completely. It's all balls now. One hundred of them.

The common theme is that over the past 60 years, whenever cricket needed to make itself more popular, it seemed there was only ever one solution: to make the game shorter. Package a complete match into a single day, then an afternoon, now a couple of hours after work and still be back in the local in time for last orders.

As 2023 marks the 60th anniversary of professional cricket's first formalised one-day competition and the latest version of the World Cup, it is worth celebrating the short game. This book aims to do exactly that by tracing the history of limited-overs cricket through its most significant matches.

Some are included because they are undeniable milestones on cricket's evolutionary path or triggered subsequent events that impacted on the sport most deeply. Others have secured their place because they have achieved iconic status – for reasons pertaining to on-field or off-field matters – or feature remarkable individual achievements that have helped to define cricket's history. Trends and developments will be examined along the way, but the final choice of matches, inevitably in a book of this nature, is subjective. One can make valid arguments for different games.

Some of the selections are a product of my own geography and nationality. As someone who listened to England's collapse against Australia in the inaugural men's World Cup semi-final via an earpiece leading from a radio concealed in my school desk, I had no second thoughts about including a final chapter that spotlights the moment when the nation that properly launched limited-overs cricket finally reached its pinnacle. Meanwhile, there will be those in Australia who might have used the 2020 Women's World T20 final in front of 84,000-plus at the Melbourne Cricket Ground to discuss the recent growth of the women's game rather what I felt was a more symbolic, and dramatic, 2017 World Cup final at a packed Lord's.

Note that throughout the book I have used contemporaneous names and terminology in order to better represent the time, for example referring to Calcutta and Madras before their name changes and describing 'batsmen' rather than the modern adoption of 'batter' in both the men's and women's game.

Such evolution in nomenclature reflects the development of society as surely as I hope the matches featured here will chart the journey of a sport that, while historically accused of being hidebound by tradition and prejudice, has proved itself able to modernise and innovate over the course of six decades.

1

'THE STUFF THE DOCTOR ORDERED'

*Sussex v Worcestershire, Gillette
Cup Final, 1963, Lord's*

Ted Dexter got it immediately. He might have been a flamboyant, hard-hitting batsman who could lift crowds to a peak of excitement; and his passion for racehorses meant his tendency towards gambling extended far beyond his time at the crease. But when it came to this new kind of cricket, played to a finish in one day, he was a realist. Until recently an amateur, he now exhibited the ruthlessness of a professional hit man, let alone someone paid to play his chosen sport.

Just what lengths Dexter was prepared to go to in order to win a limited-overs match were obvious to Worcestershire batsman Roy Booth as he looked around Lord's. Spaced out along the boundary – behind which a raucous crowd of 23,000 had been enjoying cricket's first major knockout final – Sussex fielders were intent on defending their team's modest total. The overs and partners were running out on Booth, who made a pointed gesture of counting the fielders now defending the rope, his contempt at such tactics obvious. Nine.

Not for the first time during this historic season, Dexter's approach brought disapproval. But no letters of protest from county committees, unfavourable comments by journalists or the jeers of opposition crowds were ever going to divert him from his ambition. They were dismissed by the England captain with the same contempt he showed for wide half-volleys.

Dexter was equally as scornful of those fellow professionals who had been slow to realise the importance of a competition that had been one of sport's talking points during an English summer dominated by the Profumo Affair, the Great Train Robbery and the relentless ascent of The Beatles. 'At least the game was being taken seriously by that stage of the season,' he recalled. 'Earlier it had been treated with a cross between mild amusement and palpable disdain by some of the old school players.' Such an attitude, he felt, betrayed 'a basic misunderstanding of the history and origins of cricket'.

Not only were the sport's historical roots in single-innings contests, but the idea of a knockout event in cricket had been around for almost as long as the FA Cup. As early as 1893, a couple of decades after the launch of football's oldest competition, MCC had canvassed counties about such a tournament. Few had wanted it; six teams agreed to trial it; and, after one initial game between Kent and Sussex at Lord's, everyone abandoned it.

In 1943, with an end to war in Europe now in the foreseeable future, the MCC's Advisory County Cricket Committee raised the possibility of a knockout competition as a way of boosting interest and generating money when competitive sport resumed. It was agreed, however, that any such initiative should feature three-day cricket, because single-innings contests would be 'detrimental to the art and character of the game' and that 'a captain will be drawn towards placing his field and using his bowler not to take wickets, but to keep runs down'. Officially, the idea remained a live one until being scrapped until 1957.

In the meantime, a new reality had begun to descend on the game. More than 2.2 million fans had watched county cricket in 1947, mirroring the boom in football attendance as the British public welcomed the return of high-level organised national sport. By 1951 that number had decreased to 1.8 million and was on its way to sinking to around 700,000 in the early years of the next decade. When *Wisden* looked ahead to the summer of 1963, writer John Solan acknowledged that 'county cricket is already being forced to move with the times' and accepted that cricket 'as a game for the spectator on anything like the scale of 20 years ago ... seems to have had its day'.

Where post-war austerity had placed going to the cricket or football high on the average person's list of recreational options, the greater prosperity of the 1950s presented more varied choices. Sitting in front of the family's new television set; eating in restaurants; venturing further afield than Blackpool or Clacton on holiday; or putting money towards the greater range of affordable consumer goods – all had become the enemy of county committees looking to fill their grounds. 'If I were not a player,' stated Middlesex and England spinner Fred Titmus, 'I wouldn't find time very often to spend a whole day at a county game' – although it is fair to note that football was also seeing a downward trend in attendance by this time, albeit not as drastic.

Simultaneously, county finances had been impacted by the effects of two world wars, which meant that families hitherto rich enough to offer patronage to their local clubs faced depleted funds and often crippling death duties. Between 1955 and 1960, counties' expenditure had exceeded their cricket income by an average of £120,000 per year. The product on the field was also not thought to be helping. Whereas only 25 per cent of County Championship games had been drawn in 1938, the number had climbed to 50 per cent by early in the 1950s.

In 1956, MCC began a fresh look at arresting the decline in attendance at first-class cricket and in 1960 the counties asked the sport's administrators to re-examine the notion of a cup-style tournament. Affirming the view that a three-day competition was not workable – what happened in the event of a draw? – MCC this time took a positive view of a one-innings format and in December 1961 the Advisory Committee narrowly passed a motion to introduce a knockout cup in 1963.

In his essential book, *A Social History of English Cricket*, author Derek Birley suggested that any objections 'reflect a more fastidious age, both culturally and morally … when splitting infinitives was a serious crime, "gay" meant light-hearted and "ecstasy" meant joy, actors kept their clothes on, four-letter words were gutter language and the new premium bonds were thought a "squalid raffle"'.

A kind of trial run was staged in 1962, at the suggestion of Leicestershire's far-sighted secretary, Mike Turner. The Midlands Knockout Cup was contested by Derbyshire, Leicestershire, Northamptonshire and Nottinghamshire and played over two Wednesdays in early May. 'I saw some gaps in the fixture list and phoned around,' said Turner. 'My opposite numbers jumped at the chance.'

Turner managed to secure television coverage on ATV, the ITV franchise for the Midlands region, although the action had to share air time with the 2,000 Guineas race meeting from Newmarket and schools programming, before giving way completely to shows such as *Zoo Time* and *Robin Hood* by the time young viewers were back home for tea. The weather was bitterly cold and attendance was sparse. 'The crowds are not exactly flooding in,' wrote the *Daily*

Mirror's Brian Chapman. 'But I believe they will when they realise the idea does produce bright and challenging cricket.'

The final saw Northants beat Leicestershire at Grace Road, with seamer Gordon Williamson taking five wickets in 18.2 overs, no restrictions having yet been placed on bowlers' workload. 'As a day's cricket it was interesting for what it was,' reported *The Times* Cricket Correspondent John Woodcock on a game that was evenly contested for the most part, before Northants got home by five wickets with a little more than five of their 65 overs remaining. Woodcock added, 'The very idea of one-day cricket is, of course, the cynics' delight. A catchpenny scheme, they call it.' Observing that seamers were likely to dominate such games in the future but predicting a positive effect on 'English batsmanship', he was open-minded enough to add, 'One can imagine, with a more important cup at stake, a county's supporters thoroughly enjoying the change from the routine of three-day cricket.' He concluded, 'As a diversion, next year's competition could be a real success.'

A measure of achievement would be the generation of income, which was where the Gillette Safety Razor Company came in. The Massachusetts-based organisation's involvement in sport dated back to baseball's World Series in 1939, when it paid for its advertisements to air during the broadcasts of the games. In the 1950s, it had sponsored a popular sports show on Radio Luxembourg. Meanwhile, sponsorship was becoming visible in British sport, most notably in horse racing.

When Gillette's representatives approached MCC in 1962 to ask about ways to get involved in cricket, discussion revolved around coaching films, the provision of artificial pitches and the promotion of the Lord's museum. Almost as an afterthought, MCC assistant secretary Jim Dunbar mentioned the forthcoming competition. A series of follow-up correspondence ensued, in which Gillette offered to provide a trophy and prizemoney. The MCC asked how much – and Gillette responded by asking them to name a price that would insure them against a loss in each match. The resulting deal saw Gillette putting up £6,500 a year, plus promotional investment 'for the purposes of identification with the competition', which was itemised as including the purchase of trophies, printing and entertainment costs. A three-year deal, with the option of an annual renewal thereafter, was voted through – not because MCC expected one-day cricket to recreate the post-war boom, but as an acknowledgement that a match offering a guarantee of a definite result at the end of the day could entice spectators back to the grounds.

The 65-over competition's cumbersome title of the First-Class Counties Knockout Competition for the Gillette Cup gave traditionalist publications such as *Wisden* and *The Times* the opportunity to ignore the sponsor and refer simply to the Knockout Competition, despite a quarter-page advert in the latter on the first full day of competition on 22 May 1963 with 'The Gillette Cup' in dominant lettering. Underneath was the wording, 'MCC announce the first round of the County Cricket Competition for the Gillette Cup,' and a summary of the rules – which included a 15-over restriction per bowler – and that day's eight fixtures.

The first game had actually been played three weeks earlier, when Lancashire hosted Leicestershire in a preliminary contest designed to bring a 17-team competition down to the 16 needed for knockout cricket. Perhaps inevitably, the Manchester weather played its part, forcing the two innings of the game between the previous season's bottom two clubs in the County Championship to be split over two days. Lancashire won after posting 304 for 9, the kind of score that would not become common in this form of cricket for a number of decades. Peter Marner won the tournament's first £50 Man-of-the-Match Award for his 121 runs and three wickets.

Much reportage of the early matches adopted the tone of theatre reviews, assessing the quality and value of what was being laid in front of the audience before concerning itself with the details of the action. After the first day at Old Trafford, *The Times* noted, 'The day's play augurs well for the competition as a whole, for Marner's vintage innings of 121 would stand on its own in any form of cricket.' Note the implication that the worth of the performance was that it replicated 'proper cricket'. One wonders if the unnamed correspondent would have been as impressed had the all-rounder slogged his runs off 60 deliveries. Significantly, the first-round victory of the eventual inaugural winners was presented with a headline reading, 'Sussex relish new conditions,' after they beat Kent by 72 runs at Tunbridge Wells.

A few weeks after acceptance of the Gillette proposal, the distinction between amateurs and professionals – gentlemen and players – had been abolished. That in turn increased the need for cricket to generate additional income, given that the number of professionals was increasing from around 220 to 300. *Wisden* lamented the possible loss of leadership qualities that the amateurs were perceived to offer and warned, 'By doing away with the amateur, cricket is in danger of losing the spirit of freedom and gaiety which the best amateur players brought to the game.'

Dexter had been one such man, although it was his desire to bring Sussex its first trophy that informed his pragmatic approach to one-day cricket, not any diminishing of his own sense of liberty because he was now an employee. His realisation that games could not be approached merely as a shorter version of first-class cricket put Sussex a step ahead of most other counties. While other teams kept fielders in catching positions rather than on the boundary, Dexter understood that this was a different game, wasting little time before dispatching men to the deep. 'The need for far-flung field placings, with never a slip catcher to be seen, is a mathematical and geometrical fact of life unless there is express legislation to prevent it,' he would say.

While other captains did their best to appease *Wisden* by keeping the Corinthian spirit alive, attacking throughout and generously leaving swathes of boundary rope unattended, Dexter instructed his team to bowl full and straight. His goal was to deny batsmen the opportunity to score square of the wicket and to set his fields to combat straight hitting. 'Any ball that wasn't going to hit the stumps was a bad ball,' he explained. 'The same could be said of a short ball which was likely to pass over the top of the stumps. The only way that might get a batsman out was with an edge to the wicketkeeper and there are too many scoring opportunities from nudges through the area of the slips.'

He told Sky Sports many years later, 'There were some very odd ideas flying about on how to stop people scoring. I remember Trevor Bailey saying, "If I bowl short of a length at the body no one is ever going to score more than two an over off me." I think we took him for 10 an over.'

In the modern age of musclebound Twenty20, variations are perceived to be the key to a successful bowler, but Dexter's view was, 'With the bowlers aiming at the stumps, it was my job to set the field according to the batsman. I felt if you bowled the ball in the same place all the time it was the best way to stop batsmen scoring because you could set a field accordingly.'

Such an approach seems outdated six decades on, but Dexter possessed the same ability to think about, relish and respond to the challenges before him that the best Twenty20 captains would demonstrate in the future. With his charismatic personality and tactical acumen, not to mention his often breathtaking strokeplay, how successful might he have been as an Indian Premier League skipper?

Even at the age of only 28, Dexter had – like many international cricketers – begun to tire of returning to the treadmill of county cricket, with its endless travelling and a three-day format whose biggest challenge to captains was often how they could contrive enough declarations to set up a meaningful final day. 'One-day cricket was his kind of game,' said Sussex fast bowler John Snow. 'It was instant and aggressive and its atmosphere brought out the best in him. He really became involved, more so than in county games. Ted was a man of moods, often caught up in theories, keen when the action was hot, disinterested when the game was dull. Probably his moods were reflected in our performances.'

'We were just lucky that we had a captain in Ted Dexter who had worked out how to play it,' recalled batsman and wicketkeeper Jim Parks, who biffed a quick 59 late in Sussex's 314 for 7 in their opening game against Kent after Ken Suttle scored the second official limited-overs (List A) century. 'We'd done our homework. I was vice-captain and we had sat down and worked out what we were going to do. When they batted, Ted had players scattered all over the field.'

Kent skipper Colin Cowdrey – who had lost the England leadership to Dexter – persevered with slip fielders after asking Sussex to bat. So little did he think about keeping the score down that left-armer Derek Underwood, who would earn his reputation as one of the hardest bowlers to get away, went for 87 in 11 wicketless overs.

Kent were two down and approaching 100, with Cowdrey and the increasingly fluent Peter Richardson at the crease, when Dexter's approach revealed itself. He took the sensible precaution of setting the field back when Richardson was on strike, thereby cutting off boundaries and allowing him to take singles. Trying to get him out was less important than keeping him away from the strike. For all the jeers that the Nevill Road crowd directed at Dexter, you'd have thought he'd set a bear trap on the wicket. 'Everyone thought it was a rotten thing to do,' he recalled. 'I had shown people what they could be let in for.'

Richardson went on to score 127, but Kent never threatened to get close. Dexter felt that naming Richardson Man of the Match was an attempt to 'placate' an angry home crowd. Kent's committee sent a letter to Sussex complaining that Dexter's tactics had gone against the 'spirit of cricket'. In defence of his skipper, Parks said, 'Defensive fields may be unattractive, but it is often the way to win. How can one criticise successful captaincy?'

There was a certain irony in Sussex leading the way in this practical approach to getting the job done. Not only had Dexter always seemed the personification of the noble amateur cricketer – nicknamed 'Lord Ted', he would even stand unsuccessfully for Parliament in 1964 – but Sussex had also provided a cricketing home for Indian aristocracy such as Ranjitsinhii, Duleepsinhji and the ninth Nawab of Pataudi, 'Tiger' as he was known around the sport. 'We were blue bloods,' said Peter Graves, who would soon be joining the Sussex batting line-up. 'We were probably tainted as being the worst county for the gentleman player bit.'

In the quarter-finals, Sussex thrilled a Hove crowd of 15,000 with a 22-run win against Yorkshire. 'No one could remember seeing more people on the County Ground,' noted *The Times* after Parks scored a dashing 90 in another big total. 'I did like to lift the ball,' he remembered, describing 'putting Tony Nicholson four times over the square cover boundary for six'.

The Times noted the field placings in the game as 'largely defensive, often shamelessly so'. But an exciting finish appeared to have won over Woodcock, who rejoiced in the 562 runs scored on the day. Yorkshire were in the hunt until their young, bespectacled number six, Geoffrey Boycott, was run out for 71. 'Ian Thomson made a spectacular throw from the boundary right into my gloves,' Parks remembered. 'I didn't have to move an inch.'

Another big crowd – 8,000 – at Northampton saw Dexter (115) and Parks (71) share a partnership of 160 as Sussex matched their 292 total of the previous round and beat the home team easily to reach the final. It was almost two months before the final arrived, but far from diluting interest in a competition that had captured the imagination of the cricketing public and enticed many to county grounds for the first time, the wait only seemed to heighten anticipation. On the first Saturday in September, cricket's first all-ticket crowd, paying a uniform seven shillings and sixpence (37.5 pence) each, packed Lord's. With 8,000 travelling from Sussex and 5,000 from Worcester, the favoured narrative of the newsreels when reporting on FA Cup finals – that of happy out-of-towners enjoying their big day in the bright lights of London – was easily transplanted. 'Supporters wore favours,' reported *Wisden*, 'and banners were also in evidence, the whole scene resembling an Association Football final more than the game of cricket.' The *Daily Mirror* described the scene as 'a reasonable replica of Wembley'. It was not enough, however, to tempt Worcestershire seamer Jim Standen, who was instead playing in goal for West Ham United in their Division One game against Sheffield United. He had taken 7 for 22 in 18 overs in his previous two games in the tournament.

Sussex had reached the final by batting first on three occasions and chose to do so again after Dexter won the toss at Lord's. The expectation at the start of the tournament had been that teams would universally opt to bat second in order to know the pace at which they needed to score, but only four of the matches leading up to the final had witnessed successful run chases. Again, Dexter was an early adopter, realising that the team batting first could better dictate proceedings.

The Sussex skipper, for whom playing in front of a full house at cricket headquarters was a regular occurrence, gave no thought to going round his young team to offer counsel and comfort. He trusted that everyone knew their job and would carry it out. They did, but it was not that easy; at least not for batsmen faced with damp late-summer conditions after rain had fallen on London.

Despite the common consent that limited-overs was a game for seamers, Worcester chose three spinners, including left-armer Norman Gifford, making his debut in the tournament. 'I wouldn't have picked me,' said the man who would become a rival to Underwood in the England set-up. 'Spinners were seen as a bit of a risk then, but the pitch was damp and looked as if it would turn a bit. As it transpired, nearly half the wickets fell to spin.'

Worcester skipper Don Kenyon posted two slips, a gully and a short leg, seemingly intent on proving that an orthodox attacking field could bring rewards even in the shortened game. Oakman and Richard Langridge began well enough, grafting their way to a partnership of 62 before Gifford removed them both in the same over. From then on, there was a steady stream of wickets. Dexter made only three before being given out caught at slip off bat and pad, an occurrence that prompted a hunting horn to be blown among the Worcester fans. Such behaviour provoked disapproval from the *Daily Mirror*, whose reporter also blanched when 'a couple of players slapped the catcher on the shoulders in a soccer-like excess of enthusiasm'.

Gifford took two wickets either side of lunch, removing Suttle and Les Lenham, and it was left to Parks alone to reproduce the batting form of the earlier rounds. 'We had to bat properly that day,' he remembered. Driving powerfully on the slow turning track and hitting Slade over extra cover for the day's only six, he forced his way to 57, helping Sussex to a final total of 168 off 60.2 overs.

When the reliable Ian Thomson opened the bowling, Dexter decided that one slip fielder was the only close catcher he needed; three fewer than Worcester had begun with. Kenyon was bowled early on by a Tony Buss delivery that cut back at him and, at 38, Buss took a return catch to dismiss Horton. The partnership of Ron Headley and England's Tom Graveney appeared to hold the key to the outcome of the final, but Dexter had another trick up his sleeve. Hitherto unused in the tournament, off-spinner Oakman had been brought on as first change. Dexter's recollection in 1980 that 'the match was as good as lost when I threw to ball to [Oakman]' might have been an exaggeration created by the mists of time, but the fact that he was left with that impression is indicative of the significance of the move. The hunch that Oakman could be as effective as Gifford earlier in the day was spot on. Headley was held to 25 runs and two boundaries in more than two hours at the crease, the future West Indies opener consistently hitting the ball too fiercely at deep-lying fielders rather than taking weight off his shots and picking up singles.

Graveney scored more swiftly but fell for 27, his vital wicket captured by Oakman, whose 13 overs cost only 17. A frustrated

Headley eventually skied Don Bates to Snow, the young fast bowler making his first appearance in the Gillette Cup. As the light began to fade and drizzle descended, it was to Snow's pace that Dexter turned. 'It was obvious that Ted's tactics upset a few people,' said Snow, 'but he was within the regulations and he was playing to win.'

Snow had Robert Broadbent caught and then he bowled Slade and Gifford, leaving Worcester needing 36 off the final eight overs with the last pair together. Booth, a journeyman county wicketkeeper, looked for a time like he might be the hero of Lord's. As Dexter sent his men further afield, Booth, quick-footed in his shot-making and running between the wickets, edged his team closer to an unlikely victory. Yet with 16 runs needed off 11 balls, the batsmen attempted a second run and Suttle's throw beat Bob Carter. 'If the promoters had stage-managed the affair they could not have kept the crowd in a more savage state of suspense,' wrote *The Observer*'s John Arlott of the tense climax.

It was enough to prompt Kenyon to argue, 'The pressure would be too much for the players to play this type of game regularly.'

The crowd raced to the field and stayed below the pavilion balcony to watch Dexter receive the 14-inch, nine-carat gold and sterling silver trophy – as he would do again one year later, when Sussex chased for the first time in their tournament history to beat Warwickshire. 'We did well because we had a one-day side,' suggested Snow. 'We had the seamers to bowl teams out in the one-dayers and the strokemakers to get the runs.'

Sussex's prizemoney was £1,899, from which the players received a £9 bonus to add to their £5 match fee, a modest amount even when your annual salary was only £1,000, as it was for Sussex batsman Suttle. 'Not that you did it for the money,' he remarked. 'Walking out in front of a packed Lord's house – absolutely marvellous.' And let's not forget the leather toilet bag donated to each finalist by the sponsors, who understandably insisted that the tournament be called The Gillette Cup from here on.

The Sussex fans, celebrating the first trophy in their club's 134-year history, were unrestrained. They were somewhat surprised, though, when the Man of the Match prize was again handed to one of their vanquished opponents, Gifford. Even he admitted later, 'They should have given it to Jim [Parks]. It was a sticky wicket, as they only had one cover for the wicket and rain had got underneath, and he batted magnificently. He was perfect for one-day cricket. He was a player who was never afraid to hit over the top.'

In *The Times*, Woodcock was reserved in his appreciation of the whole occasion. The game, he reported, contained 'several of the best features of this type of cricket and a number of the worst'. Sussex had achieved success 'through attrition rather than attack', which was 'contrary to the aims of the competition'. He complained that Sussex bowled only 24 overs of spin in four matches and 'deployed their fielders with unremitting caution'. He called it a weakness of the competition, rather than attributing any deficiency to the teams unable to find a way to overcome such tactics. The *Daily Express*'s Brian Chapman aired similar views, claiming that 'the wrong team won' and warning, 'Ted Dexter's tactics, successful as they were, could eventually kill a great idea.'

Arlott was a little more generous. 'Perhaps it was not, strictly speaking, first-class cricket, but as entertainment it is with us for the foreseeable future,' he wrote. 'Let us be grateful for it.' In the *Daily Mirror*, Peter Wilson suggested, 'It may not have been cricket of the purists but, golly, it was the stuff the doctor ordered.' And even Woodcock's closing verdict was that the competition had been 'a happy diversion'.

It would quickly become apparent that it had diverted the whole course of cricket.

SUSSEX v WORCESTERSHIRE, Gillette Cup Final
7 September 1963, Lord's

Sussex		Balls	4s	6s
RL Langridge	b Gifford	34	-	3	
ASM Oakman	c Slade b Gifford	19	-	1	
KG Suttle	b Gifford	9	-		
*ER Dexter	c Broadbent b Horton	3	-		
†JM Parks	b Slade	67	-	4	1
LJ Lenham	c Booth b Gifford	7	-		
GC Cooper	lbw b Slade	0	-		
NI Thomson	lbw b Flavell	1	-		
A Buss	c Booth b Carter	3	-		
JA Snow	b Flavell	10	-	1	
DL Bates	not out	3	-		
Extras	(b 9, lb 10, nb 3)	22			
Total	(all out, 60.2 overs)	168			

Fall: 62, 67, 76, 98, 118, 123, 134, 142, 157, 168
Bowling: Flavell 14.2-3-31-2; Carter 12-1-39-1; Slade 11-2-23-2; Gifford 15-4-33-4; Horton 8-1-20-1

Worcestershire		Balls	4s	6s
*D Kenyon	lbw b Buss	1	-		
MJ Horton	c and b Buss	26	-	3	
RGA Headley	c Snow b Buss	25	-	2	
TW Graveney	c Dexter b Oakman	29	-	4	
DW Richardson	c Parks b Thomson	3	-		
RG Broadbent	c Bates b Snow	13	-	1	
†R Booth	not out	33	-	3	
DNF Slade	b Buss	3	-		
N Gifford	b Snow	0	-		
JA Flavell	b Snow	0	-		
RGM Carter	run out	2	-		
Extras	(b 8, lb 9, nb 2)	19			
Total	(all out, 63.2 overs)	154			

Fall: 7, 38, 80, 91, 103, 128, 132,133, 133, 154
Bowling: Thomson 13.2-4-35-1; Buss 15-2-39-3; Oakman 13-4-17-1; Suttle 5-2-11-0; Bates 9-2-20-1; Snow 8-0-13-3

Sussex won by 14 runs. **Toss:** Sussex. **Umpires:** FC Gardner, FS Lee.
Man of the Match: N Gifford. *Note: (-) indicates incomplete historical data.*

2

'TEN MINUTES TO NINE IN GATHERING GLOOM'

Lancashire v Gloucestershire, Gillette Cup semi-final, 1971, Old Trafford

If the ascent of the one-day game began with the inaugural Gillette Cup, then the summit – at the English domestic level anyway – was reached shortly before nine o'clock on a late July evening in Manchester in 1971. For a glorious couple of hours, BBC television schedulers gave themselves up to a gripping run chase and the nation stopped for a game of county cricket in a manner never since repeated.

The 60-over semi-final between Lancashire and Gloucestershire had already long since overrun its timeslot on BBC2, bumping an investigation into bankruptcy by the current affairs programme *Man Alive* off air. Commentator Jim Laker received a call from BBC1 programmers warning him to be ready if the game was still in progress at 8.50 p.m. It was. Instead of Robert Robinson's voice introducing a 10-minute show, *The Fifties*, to take the network up to the *Nine O'Clock News*, viewers saw a cricket scorebox appear on their screens and heard Laker break into his BBC2 commentary with a quick recap for the new BBC1 audience. 'Tremendous scenes here at Old Trafford, Lancashire,' he intoned and, as the picture moved to the field, he continued, 'Still out there, 11 wanted to win. There's certainly four of them there – a magnificent cover drive by Hughes. Ten minutes to nine in gathering gloom...'

It was eight years since the corporation's live coverage of the first final had come to an abrupt halt at 5 p.m. to accommodate the cartoon antics of *Deputy Dawg*. While televised matches were still interrupted for horse racing, schools programming and competing summer sports, the launch of BBC2 in 1964 had created greater capacity for cricket on British screens.

'An all-action formula that the masses enjoy,' had been the verdict of one of the Gillette Cup's first stars, Jim Parks, on the new, truncated version of the sport. 'It is cricket for the man in the street.' Quickly, many saw an opportunity to get that man off the street and into the ground – especially at weekends – or onto his couch in front of cricket on BBC's new station.

The International Cavaliers was an all-star team of Test and county cricketers thrown together on an *ad hoc* basis for occasional tours and to play benefit and charity matches. After two years of successful Gillette Cup competition, agent and promoter Bagenal Harvey – the man who turned Denis Compton into the 'Brylcream Boy' and helped Johnny Haynes become football's first £100 per week player – saw an opportunity to establish a formal programme of Sunday matches against English counties, beginning in 1965. Ted Dexter, another of his clients, assured him there would be no shortage of players fed up with 'travelling 150 miles to play in front of two men and a dog at some obscure outpost' who would willingly make the same journey for the thrill of a full house and extra pocket money.

Rothmans of Pall Mall, the cigarette company, agreed to sponsor the games, including provision of a 100 guineas purse, to be awarded to the host county's beneficiary, local cricket development programmes or a charity. BBC2 agreed to devote Sunday afternoons to the games, thanks to the persuasive manner of controller of programmes Huw Wheldon. Summoned to the BBC's board of governors to plead a case for the corporation to broadcast sport on the Sabbath, his roll-call of potential audience-inducing stars made a sufficiently convincing argument, as long as the 40-overs per team could be completed between 2 and 6.30 p.m. For that to happen, Dexter suggested that bowlers were restricted to 15-yard run-ups.

Brian Moore, later to become one of football's most iconic commentators after switching to ITV, joined Sir Learie Constantine and Brian Johnston behind the microphone for the first match against Worcestershire at Kidderminster on 2 May 1965. A Cavaliers team including Denis Compton, England players MJK Smith, John Murray, Fred Titmus and Tom Cartwright, Pakistan's Mushtaq Mohammed and a young West Indian all-rounder, Keith Boyce, lost by 23 runs. A week later, Parks stole the show by slamming a 16-minute half-century against Nottinghamshire and scoring all 72 runs of a fifth-wicket partnership with Alan Oakman. Parks would cement his Cavaliers legend by scoring the fastest fifty of the following season's games, although it took him a comparatively pedestrian 22 minutes to reach the milestone against Somerset at Bath.

Crowds responded with remarkable enthusiasm. 'When we went to Lord's for the first time [versus Middlesex in 1968] we told them to be ready, there'd be a big crowd,' Dexter remembered. 'They said, "No there won't." They sold out of everything … we took the place by storm.' It even led to Sunday play – also beginning at 2 p.m. – to be trialled in the County Championship in 1966.

Parks's verdict on the Cavaliers was, 'The combination of sponsorship, Sunday play and cup-tie cricket concentrated into matches that fans see concluded in one day seems to be irresistible.' He also insisted, 'Although the approach to these exhibition matches is light-hearted on the surface there is also an underlying determination to do one's best and not be beaten.' Given that Parks was making such comments in 1968 he might have been playing the role of good salesman and over-emphasising the seriousness of the games, although no professional wanted to look bad in front of the TV cameras.

One batsman who certainly appeared disinclined to toss his wicket away in a rush of frivolity was Geoffrey Boycott, whose first encounter with the Cavaliers saw him score an unbeaten 86 at Middlesbrough in 1966. The England opener was by then owner of a Gillette Cup winner's medal, having delivered one of the competition's greatest innings in the 1965 final as Yorkshire became the first team other than Sussex to win the trophy. His 146 against Surrey remained the highest individual score in the final of England's premier one-day tournament until Alex Hales hit a match-winning 187 not out for Nottinghamshire, also against Surrey, in 2017.

The counties realised that Sunday cricket's golden goose had enough eggs for everyone. Early in 1968, a new league was announced, to begin in 1969, aping the exact format of the Cavaliers games. Every county would play 16 games per season, with players earning an additional £6 10s (£6.50) per match, although winners' bonuses could take that up to £11. Imperial Tobacco offered £60,000 per year to attach their John Player brand to the event, enough to make cricket's rulers turn away from Rothmans. Unsurprisingly, BBC2 also opted for Player's County League action, fighting off the challenge of the ITV network under head of sport Jimmy Hill, who even took court action to claim that they had already been awarded the rights ahead of BBC in a legally binding agreement.

The Cavaliers, for all that they had given to the development of the modern game, found themselves begging for scraps when 1969 rolled around. The *International Cavaliers' World of Cricket*, published in 1970, would feature a retrospective on the team's summer of '69 that could not hide its tone of bitterness. 'Normal surroundings and regular opponents were conspicuous by their absence,' Dexter wrote, noting that the first game of the season 'found us manoeuvring our way shamefacedly into Scotland' to play in front of 1,000 people. With no counties to face, their season consisted of games against minor representative teams and invitation XIs – four of which received some coverage on ITV. When Rothmans concluded its involvement with the Cavaliers at the end of the year, time was running out on the venture and 1970 proved to be the final season in which the all-stars toured the country.

In the meantime, the John Player League, as it became known in its second year, had stormed through the door that the Cavaliers had pushed open. The introduction in 1968 of overseas players to English counties meant that the competition offered the roll-call of star names that was formerly the exclusive domain of the Cavaliers. And its condensed structure met the imperative identified by many to introduce more attacking batsmanship to the game.

Wisden editor Norman Preston had spoken in 1967 of 'the problems that have driven crowds from the County Championship', while guest writer Denis Compton predicted two years later that the potential of fuller houses would tease the best of intentions from the players. 'Because of the absence of crowds at county games in the past few seasons, some cricketers advance the argument that it is difficult to provide entertaining play in such an unreal atmosphere,' he argued. His hope was that the new impetus of Sunday competition would address 'the fact that a majority of players seem to have resigned themselves to playing unenterprising cricket'.

John Arlott predicted that the new tournament would 'present the county game in a fresh way, which may well recall the deserters, attract new and regular spectators from an entire fresh section of the population, and perhaps even achieve the financial solvency so lately tacitly regarded as impossible.'

Another heavyweight opinion, EW Swanton in *The Cricketer*, saw the promotion of the three-day game as the chief potential benefit of Sunday competition. He wondered 'what sort of fist the counties [will] make of the Sunday League which is introducing them through television to such a vast new public. What they must hope to do is not only to keep uppermost the more positive aspects of "instant cricket" but so to project themselves as men of wit and character that they will also bring new followers to the Championship.' He warned that the price of the new tournament would be too expensive if 'it simply whets unsophisticated appetites for the highly flavoured variant at the expense of the full game'. Swanton might have come across as a cricketing snob, but his attitude would find echoes when Twenty20 was introduced 34 years later at the expense, many feared, of the purer skills of 40- or 50-over cricket.

* * *

When *Wisden* published its verdict on the first John Player season, Preston enthused about its 'feverish tempo' and 'sense of urgency'. There was, of course, the usual warning that it was not first-class cricket and fears for the role of the spinner, but the overriding conclusion was that of 'instant success'. On the field, that success was monopolised by Lancashire, lifting the title in each of the league's first two seasons. With only one shared County Championship title, in 1950, to their name since 1934, most supporters and members had scant memory of any kind of achievement, but suddenly they had a team apparently designed perfectly for one-day cricket.

Their batting line-up included the hard-hitting Indian wicketkeeper Farokh Engineer and Guyanese left-hander Clive Lloyd. A West Indies Test player since 1966, Lloyd became the most destructive force in the shortened game for the best part of a decade; a man who, although he tended to stoop from his 6ft 4in, stood tallest on the biggest of occasions.

After veteran England seamer Ken Higgs departed Old Trafford following the 1969 season, young fast bowlers Peter Lever and Ken Shuttleworth stepped forward and were both judged good enough to make the Ashes tour of 1970-71. Engineer called the duo 'as good as anyone in the world; great bowlers, quick and a delight to keep wicket to'. His verdict on slow men David Hughes and 'Flat' Jack Simmons, who added vital late-order runs, was 'they were not the greatest of spin bowlers, [but] very, very good cricketers, excellent fielders and excellent all-rounders'. He continued, 'We had the perfect fielding side, the perfect batting side, the perfect bowling side'

It was entirely appropriate that Lancashire's first Sunday League game was against Sussex, their predecessors as one-day revolutionaries, on 27 April 1969. Parks proved his enduring power with 70 before Lloyd gave warning of feats to come by guiding Lancashire home with an unbeaten 59. They won the title with a Sunday to spare and repeated the feat in 1970, winning 13 games and clinching the title against Yorkshire. A crowd officially recorded as 27,549 but thought to be a little higher, attended that decider, which seemed to make mockery of *The Sunday Times* asking that day, 'Is cricket dead?' – although the paper dismissed one-day cricket as 'candyfloss'. It was left to Vernon Addison to point out in a book published that year, *Lancashire On Top*, 'All too often the phenomenon of one-day cricket has been begrudgingly acknowledged as an illegitimate son who turns out to be brilliant.'

There were, however, those eager to capitalise on the growing influence of the one-day game in England rather than poo-poo it. A new cricket board game, made by long-time manufacturer Ariel, arrived in 1970. *The Gillette Cup*, which had a generic cricket illustration on the box rather than a player endorsement, used batting and bowling cards and the placement of fielding figures on a cardboard field to reconstruct 60-overs matches. Perhaps with an unintentional eye to the future of limited-overs cricket, the rulebook did, however, suggest, 'When time does not permit a long game, a shortened version may be played by treating every batsmen's shot as in the air and, therefore, giving the fielders more opportunities of taking catches.'

Around 1976, another games company, Capri, would produce *Knockout Cricket*, which, as a card, dice and board-based game, followed some of the same principles as its predecessor. Cricket's first one-day international centurion, Dennis Amiss, featured on the box. Like *Gillette Cup*, it could be used to play games of any length, but it is notable that the branding and marketing push was again around limited-overs cricket.

As much as their victories, Lancashire's limited-overs team became known for another element of the modernisation of the sport, their fans. Reports of the early Gillette Cup finals made comparisons with the FA Cup, but it was the Red Rose followers on big one-day occasions who created the template for the football-style support that attached itself to many counties. Limited-overs matches grew as occasions and succeeded in attracting exactly the non-traditional audience its creators had desired. The kind of support that, by the 21st century, had transferred itself from counties to the England team's 'Barmy Army'. Looking back now on footage of England's early-1970s Test matches, with their often half-empty grounds, is a jarring experience – not only because of the stark contrast to the modern day, but also in comparison to the large and vibrant crowds at the top limited-overs county games of the period. In fact, a week after Old Trafford staged its full-to-the-rafters Gillette Cup semi-final of 1971, only 26,047 turned up for the five days of England's Test against Pakistan, the receipts of less than £11,000 failing to cover expenses.

Addison described 1970 as 'the year that the Kop came to cricket, the time when the youngsters rediscovered the game and flocked to support it'. Engineer, whose lodgings when he first arrived from India made him a neighbour of George Best, recalled, 'From our dressing room we could see, for those Gillette Cup matches or on a Sunday, the crowd pouring out of the station singing, "Lancashire, la la la,". We were the Manchester United of cricket.' Simmons described the crowd as 'unbelievable' and added, 'I spoke to them every opportunity I had. They knew you were giving your all, and we had a very good rapport.'

Writing in the *Daily Express*, James Lawton suggested Lancashire's fans at Lord's would 'look and sound as out of place as washboards in the Halle'. And he continued, 'These lads, whose fathers were brought up on League cricket, have discovered the joys of one-day cricket, as a young man might savour his first taste of good whisky. And if their manner of satisfaction should offend the establishment, well that is no concern of theirs.'

According to opener Barry Wood, such support lit a fire under his team. 'We responded to a big crowd,' he said. 'That is one of the reasons why we didn't win the Championship. I remember a pre-season meeting where I said that if we approached every match like a one-day game we would win hands down, but we didn't have that attitude for the three-day game. For a one-day game there would be a buzz around. I was always the first to arrive at the ground, but for one-day games we all arrived together at the same time.'

Their second Sunday title secured, Lancashire became the first county to complete a one-day double a week later, beating Sussex by six wickets in the Gillette Cup final. Chasing 185 to win, their victory was secured by 70 not out from the consistent Harry Pilling, the club's leading run-scorer in each of the first two Sunday campaigns. 'We used to call him Mr Reliable in the dressing room,' said Engineer of a man whose range of off-season jobs once included that of coffin salesman. 'We knew that whatever happened at one end, he would be at the other steadily going along making runs, whatever the wicket. He should have played for England.'

When it came to limited-overs cricket, Lancashire had the same intimidating presence that Leeds United brought to the football field in the same period. By the neutral fan, however, they were loved rather than reviled – and they never seemed to slip up in the late stages of tournaments in the manner of Don Revie's men.

In the Revie role at Lancashire, the man pulling the various elements together was Jack Bond, a modest middle-order batsman whose long career seemed to be petering out in the second eleven in 1967 before he was asked to step into the captain's role vacated by Brian Statham. 'When it came down to a close analysis of the needs of the moment and the demands of a membership and public who had grown tired of Lancashire's lack of success only a man in close touch with the players, the problems and the followers, could hope to succeed,' said *Wisden* when naming him one of its Cricketers of the Year in 1971 on the strength of his leadership. 'Bond fitted the bill. He had experience. He had earned the respect of the club officials.'

His greatest achievement was assimilating the new foreign imports into a team based largely on promising youngsters. He instilled unity of purpose and a sense of fun and togetherness. 'Jack was honest,' said opening batsman David Lloyd, 'and just genuinely wanted his young players to do well. He was almost a father figure to all of us.'

Simmons recalled that Bond 'created a very good dressing room'. He explained, 'He wasn't one who said, "You can't have a drink tonight." He would probably buy you one. He wanted everyone to be part of a family and that is how I believe he created that determination to succeed. His man-management created that respect. At times, if the wicket was very good and we had got five wickets down, he would allow me or David Hughes to go in ahead of him, but if the wicket was indifferent and wasn't easy he would always go in before us.'

Bond was also one of the first captains to stress the importance of one-day cricket and to recognise what it took to win. 'Lancashire and one or two others were ahead of everyone else at that time,' said Wood. 'That was down mainly to Bondy, who was a very shrewd tactician.'

He also recognised the importance of fielding in the shortened game, even introducing some practice drills before Sunday games. 'He said that in one-day cricket fielding will win us games,' remembered Simmons. 'He insisted that when we went out there we had to dive for the ball. He said that if you save one, that's one less we have to score. If everyone does it two or three times, that is 20 to 25 runs, and that is a big difference between winning and losing a one-day game.'

Wood continued, 'I remember the older players saying it was a younger man's game. I said, "No, it's a fitter man's game. You have got to improve your fitness." I was also a semi-pro footballer so maintained a higher level of fitness than most county players, but we were all naturally fit and didn't have too many injuries.'

Wisden's citation of Bond suggested that before he became captain 'Lancashire had got into the habit of playing cricket the professional way – efficiently but with no apparent enjoyment'. A deeply religious man, the description of him by cricket's bible was that 'he may not be cricket's most talented captain, but he is certainly the game's most enthusiastic leader'.

Author and Lancashire observer Brian Bearsaw wrote, 'Bond has always been a team man, unselfish to a remarkable degree ... He plays for them and believes in them and is prepared to put every one of the remaining ten before himself. Personal success means absolutely nothing to Bond.' Engineer summarised his skipper in similar tones when he said, 'None of us remember Bondy doing a thing, except marshalling the team.'

Although Engineer did admit, 'He did one thing. At Lord's he held that catch to dismiss Asif Iqbal. My word, he flew like a rocket and held that catch and that catch won us the Gillette Cup that year because Kent were cruising it.' It was indeed Bond's flying grab at extra cover to dismiss the Pakistan all-rounder that brought Lancashire their second successive Gillette Cup triumph in 1971.

Yet it is that year's semi-final that has gone down in history. A crowd of 23,250 was recorded at Old Trafford, although witnesses to non-paying fans climbing over fences and sneaking past turnstile operators reckon there might have been closer to 30,000 in the ground. Many fans were directed to the grass behind the boundary ropes. Rows of children, mostly boys, who were enjoying the first week of school holidays, were allowed to sit in front of the sightscreens. It contributed to the theatre of an occasion that Laker recalled by noting five years later, 'For as long as I watch one-day cricket I cannot seriously believe I shall see a more dramatic day's cricket.'

It began benignly enough, with Gloucestershire captain Tony Brown calling incorrectly and being asked to bat on an easy-paced track. Former Lancashire opener David Green and partner Ron Nicholls took the score to 57 before Green was run out by Clive Lloyd, one of the most feared fielders in the game. Unperturbed, Nicholls eased towards a half-century and lunch was reached at 87 for 1 from 33 overs, a solid foundation rather than the fatally pedestrian progress that such a score would represent in later years. When the resumption was delayed for an hour by rain, no one could have foreseen that the revised timeline would propel the match into folklore.

The entry of the fair-haired South African, Mike Procter, injected some urgency. Denied the opportunity to continue in Test cricket by his country's exclusion from international cricket a year earlier because of its apartheid policies, no one revelled in big cup occasions more than Procter, whose uncomplicated approach was to hit as far and bowl as fast as possible. Driving magnificently, he thrashed nine fours and a leg-side six in his 65. He brought up his fifty by blasting Hughes for the third time in quick order through the covers, with still no man back on the boundary. Simmons stemmed the flow of runs with a 12-over spell of off-spin that cost only 25, and it needed the belligerence of Mike Bissex to take Gloucester to 229 after a score of 250-plus looked likely before Procter departed.

David Lloyd and Wood compiled a 50-partnership by the 17th over of Lancashire's reply. At 61, Brown dismissed Lloyd, but the 5ft

3in Pilling – a man whose name Laker seemed contractually obliged to preface with 'little' at every mention – helped to carry the score into three figures before another wicket fell. Clive Lloyd, scorer of a quarter-final century against Essex, appeared ready to unleash his brand of brutality, pulling Procter in front of midwicket and clubbing down on the ball to force it straight for another boundary. Procter responded with a bouncer outside off stump, going across left-hander Lloyd's body, but the batsman was on it quickly enough to whip it wide of mid-on for two. Procter unleashed the same ball and this time Lloyd swayed back and let it fly through to keeper Barrie Meyer. Wood set off, thinking he had time to complete a bye, but was run out for 50, leaving Lancashire 136 for 3 in the 39th over. 'It was a painstaking 50,' Wood admitted. 'I batted us into a crisis.'

John Sullivan went down on one knee to launch what would in later years be known as a slog sweep. It went for four over a boundary rope that young fans, energised by their fizzy drinks and sweets, seemed to be nudging ever closer to the middle. But the long-striding left-arm seamer Jack Davey took out Sullivan's stumps, and then off-spinner John Mortimore held one back to Lloyd, who advanced to hit it to the leg side and was bowled. Engineer played back to push Mortimore towards mid-on, only for his foot to slip under him and knock off the leg bail. With fewer than 14 overs left, Lancashire were 163 for 6, still needing 67. 'This enormous and vibrant crowd that had been cheering every run went quiet,' Laker recalled solemnly.

It was now gone 8 p.m. – which was already a late, late finish – and the light had dimmed irretrievably. Umpires Dickie Bird and Arthur Jepson conferred before deciding to play on. Not that it would have been part of their considerations, but a big audience was growing after work on BBC2 and no one – except maybe fans of *Man Alive* – wanted them to pull stumps and return the following morning.

Bond and Simmons, respectively 39 and 30 years old, had seen enough in their careers not to be panicked. They pushed along to 188 for 6 from 50 overs, at which point Procter, with four overs left to bowl, was asked to reintroduce his windmill deliveries from the Warwick Road End. He hit Simmons on the pad with a leg-stump yorker and Bird marched towards square leg to talk to Jepson. Laker

31

commented, 'I can't think they'll stay out there.' Yet Bond's intentions were clear, tapping his bat on the ground as though planting a flag. And he had an ally. Simmons recalled, 'As Dickie approached him, Arthur shouted out, "Bugger off, Dick, we are continuing."' There was, however, a consultation that cost another three minutes. In the pavilion, Wood recalled, 'We wanted to finish it, knowing if we came back the following day there would be no bugger there watching.'

Simmons thick-edged the next ball past third man for four and Procter came back with a short delivery that the Lancashire man, through instinct rather than visual guidance, hooked for a single. In the 53rd over Bond squeezed Procter behind the wicket to bring up the 200.

With seven overs remaining, 27 were needed, but Simmons swished across the first ball of Mortimore's 10th over and was bowled. Schoolboys raced out to greet him and jostle him back to the pavilion. Even with only three wickets remaining, the target seems comfortable when viewed through modern eyes, although these were the days before captains were restricted in their choice of field placings and tailenders were not trained to club sixes. And it was effectively night time.

Player silhouettes were just about discernible in the far reaches of the outfield, but it was electricity from the pavilion and the railway station beyond Procter's bowling marker that was casting shadows, rather than any semblance of daylight. 'The lights on the scoreboard and in the station were flashing like headlights,' said Simmons. Even at this late stage, a word from Bond would likely have ended the day. Yet he was concerned for the crowd on the edges of their seats and aware that seeing the ball was just as difficult for Gloucestershire, who had been in the field for more than three hours since tea. Why allow a refreshed Procter to bowl after a night's rest?

Hughes descended the pavilion steps, having been playing nervous air shots in the dressing room and visualising where he could pick up quick singles. Eventually he'd settled down and waited his turn to bat. 'Because I had been sitting in a dark corner of the dressing room it seemed quite light out in the middle,' he explained. 'The atmosphere was electric.' Behind him, the clock next to the players' balcony showed 8.45 p.m.

'Let's look for the singles,' suggested Bond.

'If I can see them, skipper, I think I can hit them,' was Hughes's reply.

At 204 for 7 and six overs to bowl, Procter was replaced by Davey, the superstar's final two overs being saved for the climax. Hughes nudged a single behind square leg, but Bond could score no more in the over. Still 25 needed from five overs, two of which would be Procter's and, therefore, virtually unseeable. As Mortimore prepared for his final six balls, Hughes told Bond, 'We have maybe got to have a go at this fellow now.'

According to Simmons, 'Tony Brown's mistake was keeping Mortimore on for one more over after he'd got me out. David didn't want to face Procter in that light, but he could always hit the spinners.'

Hughes recalled, 'I cursed having no sightscreens. They had been taken down to allow more people to get in.' Determining to hit as straight as possible, Hughes backed away to leg and sent the first ball over extra cover for four. Jeers greeted Mortimore as he slowly adjusted his field, waving reinforcements over to the off side. The batsman's response was to hammer his next delivery into a now feverish crowd beyond long-on. 'I noticed the kids had shoved the rope in about 20 yards, so what you might have thought were big hits I only just cleared the square with them,' he said, using some artistic licence. Some of those same youngsters galloped out to the square. Seeing more seconds wasted, Hughes waved them away, while Bird moved towards them like an impatient sheepdog tired of his unruly herd.

A sliced drive through the off side produced two more runs, at which point Lancashire's players tried to make themselves seen and heard from the dressing room, reminding their teammate that he was close enough now to get them in singles. Hughes had other ideas. He hacked wide of mid-on for two and BBC1 viewers joined the action in time to see the fifth ball dispatched for another four, driven square along the ground. And then the final flourish. Modern observers would be screaming for Mortimore to fire the ball in flatter at leg stump, instead of bowling 'normal' deliveries that were effectively in the slot. Sure enough, Hughes advanced and took the ball from middle and leg to send it soaring over long-on for six. Bond hugged Hughes, although the batsmen released their embrace to wave angry bats at the youngsters dancing around them. Hughes paced around, blew out a deep breath and removed his gloves as though he could barely believe what he had just achieved.

The 24-run over had come out of nowhere, not just in the context of the match, but of the entire era. It is hard to convey the unique nature of such hitting for its time, especially when one factors in the atmosphere, the audience, the pressure of a semi-final and the lateness of the hour. In the days when only a restricted number of games appeared on television – unlike the modern era of scheduled-for-broadcast World Cups and Indian Premier League campaigns – it was glorious good fortune that such a feat had been pulled off in a game designated for live coverage.

Just the formalities to complete. Procter elicited boos by bowling a bouncer at Bond and then threatened to throw down the stumps after the batsman played a yorker back down the wicket. Two more dot balls, before Bond slashed Procter's fifth delivery through the ring of off-side fielders into the approaching wave of fans. Hughes punched the air, made sure to ground his bat for the winning single and sprinted toward the pavilion. Instead of a last-over nail-biter, he had ensured victory with 19 balls to spare, earning man-of-the-match honours

Hughes had played, according to Laker, 'half a dozen shots worthy of being ranked with the greatest of our time,' which, if falling prey to hyperbole, was an indication of the frenzied, unprecedented nature of the occasion. Besides, Laker was perhaps in a state of frenzy himself by then. With his usual commentary companions down at Canterbury for the rain-hit contest between Kent and Warwickshire, he had been alone on the microphone without a bathroom break for the entirety of Lancashire's four-hour innings.

In contrasting understatement, Laker looked at the fans dancing and chanting on the field and noted, 'They have really gone for this Gillette Cup cricket in a big way.' Before dispersing, they demanded several curtain calls from the Lancashire players, who obliged by waving from the pavilion balcony. Hughes was photographed with 24 glasses of champagne to mark his miraculous over. Gloucestershire wicketkeeper Barrie Meyer, who recalled that his 'shell-shocked' teammates 'could not believe the sudden turnaround', added, 'The kindly meant gesture of the Lancashire players in sending in a tray of glasses filled with champagne only succeeded in rubbing salt into our wounds.'

The nation took a deep breath, composed itself and settled down to watch the news, with its far less compelling tale of Labour MPs and trade union leaders opposing Britain's proposed entry into the Common Market, as the European Union was then known. What they had witnessed was the zenith of televised one-day domestic cricket; a day that would be etched into the legend of the English game. Lancashire would win a third Gillette Cup final a year later against Warwickshire on the back of a brilliant Clive Lloyd century, but international competition was entering the limited-overs arena. County cricket would never have it so good again.

LANCASHIRE v GLOUCESTERSHIRE, Gillette Cup Semi-Final

28 July 1971, Old Trafford

Gloucestershire			Balls	4s	6s
RB Nicholls	b Simmons	53	-	-	
DM Green	run out	21	-	-	
RDV Knight	c Simmons b Hughes	31	-	-	
MJ Procter	c Engineer b Lever	65	-	9	1
DR Shepherd	lbw b Simmons	6	-		
M Bissex	not out	29	-	-	
*AS Brown	c Engineer by Sullivan	6	-		
HJ Jarman	not out	0	-		
Extras	(b2, lb14, nb1, w1)	18			
Total	(6 wickets, 60 overs)	229			

Fall: 57, 87, 113, 150, 201, 210
Did Not Bat: JB Mortimore, †BJ Meyer, J Davey
Bowling: Lever 12-3-40-1; Shuttleworth 12-3-33-0; Wood 12-3-39-0; Hughes 11-0-68-1; Simmons 12-3-35-2; Sullivan 1-0-6-1.

Lancashire			Balls	4s	6s
D Lloyd	lbw b Brown	31	-	-	
B Wood	run out	50	-	-	
H Pilling	b Brown	21	-	-	
CH Lloyd	b Mortimore	34	-	-	
J Sullivan	by Davey	10	-	-	
†FM Enginner	hit wicket b Mortimore	2	-		
*JD Bond	not out	16	-	-	
J Simmons	b Mortimore	25	-	-	
DP Hughes	not out	26	-	2	2
Extras	(b1, lb13, nb1)	19			
Total	(7 wickets, 56.5 overs)	230			

Fall: 61, 105, 136, 156, 160, 163, 203
Did Not Bat: P Lever, K Shuttleworth
Bowling: Procter 10.5-3-38-0; Davey 11-1-22-1; Knight 12-2-42-0; Mortimore 11-0-81-3; 12-0-32-2.

Lancashire won by 3 wickets. **Toss:** Lancashire. **Umpires:** HB Bird, A Jepson.
Man of the Match: DP Hughes. *Note: (-) denotes incomplete historical data.*

'JUST ANOTHER THREE GAMES OF CRICKET'

England v Australia, Prudential Trophy 1972, Old Trafford

This time it was for real. England versus Australia; no need for an 'XI' to be tagged on the end. And it was properly scheduled and promoted; not a rain-induced afterthought. John Snow, dark hair bobbing throughout his easy approach to the crease, dropped his first delivery short and wide. The pain of conceding four runs as Australian opener Keith Stackpole cut it contemptuously to the Old Trafford boundary was genuine enough. International limited-overs cricket had begun in earnest.

When the programme for the Australian team's Ashes tour of England in 1972 was devised, the desire for a three-match series of one-day internationals was irresistible. There was a sponsor ready to put up the money – the Prudential insurance company – and there was a free weekend after the conclusion of the fifth Test match during which it could be played. And there was precedent; both in the form of tentative similar ventures in the mid-Sixties, and in what was now recognised as the first official 'ODI' during England's most recent tour of Australia.

Once the success of the shorter format of the game was established at county level and had begun spreading to domestic cricket in other countries it was only a question of time before it came under the flag of international competition. Rothmans, buoyed by the popularity of their series of International Cavaliers games around the English counties, had been quick to see the potential. With the West Indies touring in 1966, they promoted a version of a 'World Cup' – never, of course, one likely to capture the imagination in the manner of the football version that same year. Lord's hosted a triangular series of games contested by a Rest of the World team, an England XI and a West Indian XI, the numerical qualification attached to signify the denial of full international status.

The announcement of the event, in March, was too late for it to be included in most of the season's printed schedules and its launch coincided with the headline-grabbing theft of football's World Cup, the Jules Rimet trophy, from an exhibition in Westminster Central Hall. The games, in what can be recognised now as a modernist approach, would consist of 50 overs per side. And the build-up included another very 21st-century element: a public vote.

The selection of the world team, to be led by Australia's Bobby Simpson, was left to the readers of the *Radio Times*. Players were short-listed in five categories: opening and middle-order batsmen, wicketkeepers, fast and slow bowlers. 'You must bear in mind that some of the famous names may well be better suited than others to this particular form of cricket,' wrote BBC commentator Denis Compton in the magazine, which printed voting slips and invited 'schoolboys home on holiday' to participate. The publication reported receiving entries from 'Egypt, the Bahamas and India', the end result being a line-up that read: Simpson, Hanif Mohammad (Pakistan), Grahame Thomas (Australia), Graeme Pollock (South Africa), Colin Bland (South Africa), 'Tiger' Pataudi (India), Mushtaq Mohammad (Pakistan), Deryck Murray (West Indies), Bapu Nadkarni (India), Peter Pollock (South Africa), Graham McKenzie (Australia). Australian all-rounder Doug Walters had been in the original selection, but was denied his place by the Australian government, who insisted he complete his military service.

Lacking in limited-overs experience, the Rest of the World overcame the International Cavaliers in a warm-up game, while West Indies beat Warwickshire at Edgbaston in front of a 10,000 crowd that eclipsed attendance at the tournament proper. Perhaps the public had World Cup fatigue after the heroics of Alf Ramsey's men or were too wrapped up in the new football season, but only 13,000 attended the three days of competition at Lord's, all of which were televised live by the BBC. According to presenter Peter West, the 'sorry lack of press publicity for the Lord's matches' was 'a sad thing for cricket when world-class cricketers were gathered at the headquarters of the game'. *The Times*, on the Monday after the opening England-Rest of the World game had taken place on the second Saturday in September, neglected to offer any kind of match report, focusing instead on the first day of the MCC's three-day game against Yorkshire at the Scarborough Festival. What the newspaper's readers missed – unless they also took *The Daily Telegraph* – was a description of John Edrich opening the England innings with a 12-ball duck before Jim Parks and Basil D'Oliveira both got into the 40s in a modest total of 201 for 7. The seam bowling of Lancashire's Ken Higgs (5 for 34) and Essex's Barry Knight (3 for 19) then shot out the World team for 119.

In a game that *The Times* did report – under the headline 'West Indians win an agreeable match' – the World team came up short once more, this time by only 18 runs. Seymour Nurse, who had scored more than 500 runs in the summer's Test matches, made 88 to set up a West Indies total of 254 for 7, before half-centuries by Hanif and Graeme Pollock kept the all-star side in contention. That left the next day's contest between England and West Indies as, in effect, a final.

Asked to bat, England began slowly, Edrich this time finding himself two not out after the first 12 overs, by which time his team's total had crept to 21 without loss. Scoring at close to six an over during the final 30, England rallied to 217 for 7. Injury to Colin Cowdrey while batting meant that England were led in the field by Ted Dexter, mastermind of Sussex's Gillette Cup triumphs but ignored during the Test series. Typically, Dexter adopted more defensive fields than Garry Sobers had considered. Higgs, a steady seamer once described by a reporter as possessing 'an arse that crossed two postcodes', again made the decisive contribution. His dismissal of Nurse for 58 was part of a three-wicket burst in two overs that left West Indies looking at a final total of 150. It rounded off a memorable summer for Higgs, who had taken 24 Test wickets and shared with Snow a last-wicket stand of 128 at The Oval, two short of a world record. Had he been born a decade later, he could have been a mainstay of England's one-day efforts. As it was, he concluded two decades of List A limited-overs cricket with a bowling average of 18.96 and an economy rate of 3.36. 'He did not have days when he sprayed it around,' said former Lancashire captain Bob Barber. 'He was just so consistent.'

There are those who argue that the England-West Indies finale should be recorded as the first one-day international. But those cursed Roman numerals took care of that. Not that it prevented an increasingly interested *Times* noting, 'A season which has seen English cricket at its lowest ebb for many years has ended for England on a high note.'

Writing in *The Cricketer*, Michael Melford concluded, 'I am not a devotee of one-day cricket as such and I think a little of it goes a long way, but I do believe such a tournament may be worthwhile when played by the best.' And, despite the disappointing attendance, the event reappeared in 1967, when the Rest of the World proved too strong for both England and the touring Pakistanis. Yet it could not be said to have created a clamour for official limited-overs competition at international level. That would have to wait for more than three more years and would depend on a deluge in Melbourne.

It is ironic that rain, the curse of limited-overs cricket – unless your name is Duckworth or Lewis – should represent the genesis of one-day internationals. After the first three days of England's third Ashes Test at Melbourne in 1970-71 were washed out and the game abandoned without a ball bowled, the Australian Cricket Board were left staring at a hole in their accounts. Their two solutions were to add a seventh match to the already-arduous six-game series, and to play a one-innings contest at the Melbourne Cricket Ground on 4 January, the scheduled fifth day of the Test. England's players, who threatened to go on strike because of the lack of consultation over the additional Test, were happier with the addition of a one-day game, seeing it as a chance to break the monotony of inaction. The ever-reliable Rothmans stepped in with £5,000 of sponsorship money and a £90 man-of-the-match award. The match was billed as an Australian XI against an England XI, but – unlike the 1966 games in England – this one lost its Roman numerals over the years and became recognised as one-day international number one. '[That] rather surprised me,' Aussie off-spinner Ashley Mallett would record. 'I thought, "Gee, it's part of history." That game we thought was a bit of a joke.' And England skipper Ray Illingworth remembered years later, 'I can't say we played with the same intensity as today.' Yet Sir Donald Bradman had the foresight to announce to the crowd at the end of the game, 'You have seen history made today.'

The game was billed by broadcaster ABC as an 'international knockout match' and commentator Alan McGilvray was called upon to pitch its merits to an audience who might not have seen any of Australia's own Gillette Cup, introduced the previous season. 'There's more tactical operations,' he explained. 'There's more alertness in the field, better running between the wickets. Generally, it's a spectacle that I've enjoyed in England very much.'

In front of a crowd of 46,000, Edrich scored the first official ODI half-century. Hitting five of his team's seven fours, he made 85 as England were bowled out for 190 in 39.4 of their 40 eight-ball overs. Part-time spinner Keith Stackpole took three wickets, causing Peter Lever to recall, 'We played badly. He took three wickets and he can't bowl.' Australia reached their target with six wickets and 42 deliveries in hand, repeating the success they'd achieved in Test cricket's first match 94 years earlier.

The response from public and media was positive, even though *Wisden* neglected to carry a match report in its chronicle of the tour in the 1972 edition and Greg Chappell would recall that 'everyone sort of saw one-day cricket as being an add-on and a bit of fun to be had on the side ... I don't think anyone really had any idea of what might grow out of it.' Yet the English newspapers foresaw more 'one-day Tests' – as they were often referred to – and England tour manager David Clark predicted a week of limited-overs cricket being part of Australia's 1972 programme in England.

* * *

The Test and County Cricket Board[1] had already agreed to add a third limited-overs competition to the 1972 summer schedule – the 55-over Benson and Hedges Cup, with its regional group games followed by knockout play. 'One-day cricket was a shot in the arm for county cricket; it was a bit in the doldrums and wanted tweaking,' recalled Dennis Amiss, who was poised to mark himself down in history when the logical step was taken to inaugurate formal international competition. Dexter, who needed little persuading of the potency of one-day cricket, described the new Prudential Cup between England and Australia as a 'bold and well-conceived plan'.

---

[1] The forerunner of the England and Wales Cricket Board, the TCCB had been established in 1968, taking over the functions of the former Advisory County Cricket Committee and Board of Control for Test Matches

Old Trafford staged the opening of the historic three-match series. After Snow's first ball had gone for four, Surrey's Geoff Arnold could not have been happier with his opening delivery as right-hander Graeme Watson was bowled behind his legs. Arnold, with his tip-toeing approach and upright delivery, was a master of moving the ball around off the seam, especially with conditions in his favour. In a 14-match ODI career he would concede fewer than three runs per over and take 19 wickets at an average cost of 17.84.

'Basically, you bowled like you did in a Test match,' he explained. 'We always discussed hitting the wicket hard and being positive about the lengths you were going to bowl and hitting the top of the splice. You bowled straight so they couldn't free their arms and that was it. You tried to get wickets early and if you had attacking fields, which we did, then it put the batsmen under pressure. We bowled yorkers at the end and I developed a slow off-cutter as well. Nowadays if they bowl four balls in the right area they have to change for the remaining two. We just continued to do the same. The batsmen didn't look to smack the ball as much as they do these days.'

Australian vice-captain Stackpole and skipper Ian Chappell rode a mixture of skill and fortune to survive an hour and take the score to 66 before Stackpole lofted Tony Greig to D'Oliveira at mid-on. 'To us it was just another three games of cricket,' said Chappell. 'You bowl to get people out; you bat to score runs as quickly as possible. We didn't approach them with the same intensity as the Tests, but we didn't want to be beaten. I offered to stand down as captain because I wasn't going to employ any ultra-defensive tactics, but Stacky said he would take the same approach as me.'

Meanwhile, batsman Ross Edwards remembered the Australians' practices as 'farcical,' saying, 'Everybody just slogged as much as they could.'

While Australia had been forced to pick the most suitable players from their Ashes squad, naming 10 of those who had won the fifth Test, England showed an awareness of the need for specialists that would not always be a part of their selection policy in coming years. Their line-up showed five changes from the conclusion of a series that had seen them retain the Ashes with a 2-2 draw. Amiss and another discarded Test batsman, Keith Fletcher, were considered more suitable options than Edrich and Middlesex's Peter Parfitt, while Bob Woolmer was included at number nine on the strength of his nagging medium pacers in Kent's fine one-day unit. The absence of injured Test skipper Ray Illingworth meant England fielded a seam-only attack, while the surprising choice of leader was 41-year-old former captain Brian Close, who had last represented his country in 1967. Since then he had been released by Yorkshire, partly because he was not considered to be taking one-day cricket seriously enough. But now he was earning praise for the way in which he had invigorated a perennially underachieving Somerset team, both as a player and, during this latest season, as captain.

England squad member Barry Wood explained, 'We had a team talk before the first game and it was all about Man of the Match awards. Closey was asking, "Do we share it or do we keep it?" Everybody barring one man agreed that it should be shared. The astonishing thing was that Closey disregarded all the other buggers and went with Boycs [Geoffrey Boycott], so we didn't share it.'[2]

By lunch,[3] Woolmer had taken his first international wicket by bowling Ian Chappell for 53, but Australia looked well set for a considerable score by the standards of the day. The Kent man struck again, bowling Greg Chappell for 40 with a yorker on his way to figures of 3 for 33 in his 10 overs. Only Ross Edwards, eventually run out for 57, made any further significant contribution. Paul Sheahan and Walters fell to Arnold and Woolmer respectively and Marsh gave Snow his first victim when caught by Close. A final total of 222 for 8 from 55 overs was modest after being 156 for 3.

The 15,000 Old Trafford crowd had been disappointed that their own opener, Wood, had been left on the sidelines after scoring 90 on debut in the final Test match. They were also taken aback to see Dennis Lillee delivering at less than full pace off a shortened run-up rather than the full, rampaging charge of more than 20 strides that

---

2 According to Wood's Lancashire colleague, David Lloyd, 'That was very common; it wasn't just Geoffrey Boycott. There were quite a number of players who opted out of the pool in county cricket. At the time, the first to 100 wickets, or something like that, got a Ford Capri and the idea was this car would be sold and pooled. But a number of bowlers said, "No, that is my car. I'm having that."'

3 One-day cricket was still following the usual mealtime conventions of lunch at around 1 p.m. and tea in late afternoon, regardless of where that fell within the respective innings.

had brought him 31 Ashes wickets. Boycott took advantage of the additional time he was afforded to hook to the boundary twice and force another four off his legs. Bob Massie, the 16-wicket hero of his debut Test at Lord's, was just as ineffective. 'The main approach was to keep wickets in hand until the last 10 or 15 overs,' said Amiss. 'If they bowled a bad ball early you smacked it for four but you didn't have targets for 10 overs or anything. We tried to see off Lillee and you knew that your tempo had to be smarter than a Test, but you went along smoothly and aimed to go mad at the end. It was hard on the batsmen down the order but nice for the openers, who could take their time.'

England's opening partnership reached 48 before Boycott was acrobatically caught behind by Marsh. Then Amiss and Fletcher, both buoyed by selection for England's winter tour of India and Pakistan, carried the score to 107 for 1 off 23 overs by tea. They drove well against mediocre bowling and found gaps on the leg side, continuing on their comfortable way after the break with a further 66 runs in 14 overs. 'We might have practised one or two shots, hitting over the top or going down the wicket and playing with more urgency than usual,' Amiss continued, 'but nothing like the intensity you see today.'

When Fletcher was bowled for 60, which included eight boundaries, the pair had combined for 125 in 26.4 overs, although it was still more common for such deeds to be reported in terms of minutes taken, which in this case was 86. With only 50 more needed to win, interest focused on whether Amiss could record the format's first century. After Close was run out at the non-striker's end via an unlucky deflection and John Hampshire helped himself to 10 off Lillee's final over, the Warwickshire man reached the landmark against the occasional spin of Stackpole. He fell shortly after to Watson for 103, made off 134 balls and including nine fours, but England reached their target with 5.5 overs in hand.

Two days later at Lord's, Lillee decided he had seen England's openers score enough runs. Chappell explained, 'I told Dennis he could bowl off a short run in the ODIs if he wanted to – he'd had a gruelling Test series. But when Dennis Amiss made a century he said, "I am going back on the long one."' He duly set the tone for the match by ripping out Boycott's middle stump and an England total of 236 for 9 never looked like being enough on a good track. Half-centuries by Stackpole and Sheahan and 48 by Greg Chappell saw Australia home with 21 balls in hand.

The closest finish in the brief history of ODIs was played out before a Bank Holiday Monday crowd at Edgbaston, where Arnold was at his nagging best to return figures of 4 for 27 and Wood, given a chance at last, chipped in with a pair of wickets. Chasing only 180 to win, Boycott and Amiss shared an opening stand of 76, but both fell in the 40s as England lost four quick wickets. After Fletcher and Wood put England back on track, another rush of wickets left them at a precarious 172 for 8, before Greig drove and edged Mallett for two fours to secure England's series victory.

Did the players leave the field with a sense of what had been created? Probably not, according to Chappell. 'I haven't found cricketers to be all that good at visualising the future,' he admitted, while Wood recalled, 'The idea of international one-day cricket certainly got me excited. But as for the others, maybe not as much as it should have.' Yet former Australia batsman Jack Fingleton had previewed the series in *The Cricketer* by writing, 'As tours are now such time-consuming affairs, it is inevitable that one-day games will become more fashionable in future, taking over from the four-day ones in many instances.'

The TCCB needed little convincing. Even before the on-field success of the series, they'd enjoyed counting the value of Prudential's £40,000 sponsorship. Once the Australians were given their £2,500, and £4,000 was set aside for prizemoney, the TCCB were able to demonstrate their largesse by giving £950 to each of the 17 first-class counties, with an additional identical amount to the three host grounds. The Prudential Cup series was back in 1973 and 1974, with a pair of games scheduled between England and each of the two touring teams during those summers.

The International Cricket Conference, as the ICC was known then, was equally quick to see the potential, determining in 1972 to stage a World Cup 'as soon as practicable'. The following summer, ironically a few days before the final of the inaugural women's version, the ICC confirmed that 1975 would see the first men's World Cup staged in England.

ENGLAND v AUSTRALIA, Prudential Trophy, 1st One-Day International

24 August 1972, Old Trafford

Australia			Balls	4s	6s
KR Stackpole	c D'Oliveira b Greig	37	62	6	
GD Watson	b Arnold	0	1		
*IM Chappell	b Woolmer	53	75	5	
GS Chappell	b Woolmer	40	66	5	
R Edwards	run out	57	84	6	
AP Sheahan	b Arnold	6	9		
KD Walters	lbw b Woolmer	2	7		
†RW Marsh	c Close b Snow	11	17	1	
AA Mallett	not ou	6	15		
Extras	(b 2, lb 3, nb 5)	10			
Total	(8 wickets, 55 overs)	222			

Fall: 4, 66, 125, 156, 167, 170, 205, 222
Did Not Bat: DK Lillee, RAL Massie
Bowling: Snow 11-1-33-1; Arnold 11-0-38-2; Greig 11-0-50-1; Woolmer 10-1-33-3; D'Oliveira 9-0-37-0; Close 3-0-21-0

England			Balls	4s	6s
G Boycott	c Marsh b Watson	25	38	3	
DL Amiss	b Watson	103	134	9	
KWR Fletcher	b Massie	60	76	8	
*DB Close	run out	1	1		
JH Hampshire	not out	25	41	5	
BL D'Oliveira	not out	5	5	1	
Extras	(b 1, lb 6)	7			
Total	(4 wickets, 49.1 overs)	226			

Fall: 48, 173, 174, 215
Did Not Bat: AW Greig, APE Knott, RA Woolmer, JA Snow, GG Arnold
Bowling: Lillee 11-2-49-0; Massie 11-1-49-1; Watson 8-1-28-2; Mallett 11-1-43-0; GS Chappell 3-0-20-0; Walters 3-1-16-0; Stackpole 2.1-0-14-0

England won by 6 wickets. **Toss:** Australia. **Umpires:** CS Elliott, AEG Rhodes.
Man of the Match: DL Amiss.

4

'IT'S ABSOLUTE CHAOS OUT THERE'

Australia v West Indies, World Cup Final, Lord's, 1975

Two weeks, eight teams, 15 matches, 160,000 spectators, and one hell of a final, lasting almost ten hours. So reads the ledger of the first men's cricket World Cup, staged in England in June 1975. The numbers, however, do the tournament no more justice than casual mention of Clive Lloyd's 102 or three Viv Richards run-outs adequately describe one of the most memorable days that even Lord's had ever witnessed.

Once the ICC had decided to advance its plans to bring the globe's major cricketing nations together, two critical issues remained to be resolved. The first was taken care of by Prudential, who paid £100,000 to become the tournament's sponsor. The second was beyond the reach of mere money: how to get India and Pakistan comfortable with playing together given that conflict between the two countries had prevented them facing each other in Test cricket since 1961. The solution was relatively simple. Keep them apart in the draw for the group stage and let the on-field chips fall where they may.

Without anyone suggesting foul play, there was no doubt that the draw was conveniently kind to the host nation. While England were put in a group with India and New Zealand, neither of whom had any notable limited-overs experience, Australia, Pakistan and West Indies – all considered potential winners – had to scrap over two semi-final berths. Even Sri Lanka, the better of the non-Test participants, were shoved into that group, while England's pool received the scratch team from East Africa. Only South Africa, banned from international cricket since 1970, were absent from the sport's first global gathering, an event momentous enough to merit pre-tournament cocktails at Buckingham Palace and a photo opportunity for all the teams with the Queen, Prince Philip and Prince Charles. There was even the involvement of cartoon royalty, with Disney character Jiminy Cricket the competition's marketing mascot.

Shell-shocked from a winter Ashes offensive delivered by the destructive partnership of Dennis Lillee and Jeff Thomson, England had been subjected to reports of disunity among the selection committee over who should lead them into the tournament. While chairman Alec Bedser proposed retaining Mike Denness, despite the 4-1 defeat in Australia, there was also support for South African-born all-rounder Tony Greig. The chairman's casting vote saved Denness, who saw his team make the most of their fortuitous draw.

With Geoffrey Boycott declaring himself unavailable for the summer's internationals, having found 'peace and contentment' since standing down the previous year, it was Dennis Amiss, already ODI cricket's first centurion, who now achieved the distinction of reaching the first World Cup hundred. In the competition's opening game – only the sport's 19th ODI – his well-constructed 137 set up a 60-over total of 334 for 4 against an Indian attack that had left out Bishan Bedi for a fourth seamer. 'We didn't have any chance of winning any game,' admitted Indian bowler Madan Lal. 'We were not prepared.'

India's premier batsman, opener Sunil Gavaskar, then plodded through his team's reply for an unbeaten 36 off 174 balls in a total of 132 for 3. At one point, an Indian fan – unbuttoned shirt and bare torso above fashionable high-waisted flared trousers; leather coat slung over his shoulder – strode to the middle to berate and gesture at Gavaskar. 'We just couldn't believe it and the crowd couldn't believe it,' said Amiss of his Indian counterpart. 'He was just protesting that we had got too many runs.'

Commentator Tony Lewis, a former England captain, called it 'an act of senseless perversity' and there was a suggestion, later denied, that Gavaskar had been protesting against the appointment of Srinivas Venkataraghavan as captain. Team manager Gulabrai Ramchand released a statement condemning his own player, but added, 'He will not be disciplined.'

Gavaskar put it down to lack of form rather than any kind of petulance, calling it 'by far the worst innings I have ever played'. He said, 'Right from the start we knew that the chase was out of the question. Even my attempts to take a single and give the strike to the other batsman failed. There was a complete mental block as far as I was concerned.' Despite his manager's assurance, there was a further demand by the Board of Control for Cricket in India after the tournament for him to explain his actions, before the matter was eventually dropped.

Meanwhile, England qualified comfortably for a semi-final that sent shivers through their batting line-up; a reacquaintance with Australia. Yet under Headingley's hazy cloud and on a green pitch, it was not Lillee and Thomson from whom they had to run for cover. Instead, left-arm swing bowler Gary Gilmour had the game of his life, striking six times to leave the host team 36 for 6. 'It was as black as arseholes and you couldn't see anything,' said England opener Barry Wood. 'At Headingley they had no sightscreen for Test matches and big one-day matches. They did for county matches, but for big games they took them away. Frank Hayes and I were both out offering no shot because we hadn't seen the ball.'

Gilmour had little sympathy for the old enemy. 'They must have experienced those conditions before,' he told an ICC film crew before his death in 2014. 'All should have been experienced in what was going to happen on that morning. They failed the test.' England limped to 93 all out and then, astonishingly, John Snow and Chris Old reduced Australia to 39 for 6. It was Gilmour's day, though, and his unbeaten 28 saw his team home without further loss.

As pleased as Australia were to be in the final, it had barely registered on their list of ambitions for their summer in England. 'One-day cricket was in its infancy and for us it was no big deal,' remembered Ross Edwards. 'OK, so it was the World Cup, but we were just going to go out there and have a bit of a slog. We had a bit of luck and got to the final, but this was only a prelude, a bit of a carnival before the important stuff, playing for the Ashes. We didn't take it that seriously.'

They would now face West Indies, for whom the tournament carried greater significance and who had already beaten them once on their way to the final. Left-hander Alvin Kallicharran had destroyed Lillee in an innings of 78 as his team won by seven wickets at The Oval in the Group B decider. Hooking anything short and skipping into flamboyant off-side drives when the ball was pitched up, Kallicharran produced a 10-ball sequence that read: 4, 4, 4, 4, 4, 1, 4, 6, 0, 4.

Yet it was their game against Pakistan at Edgbaston three days earlier that skipper Lloyd would come to recognise, not only as a turning point in this tournament, but in his leadership of the team and its development into the behemoth that would dominate the sport for more than a decade. Lloyd had been appointed West Indies captain for the previous winter's tour of India, meeting the selectors' desire for a young skipper to succeed Rohan Kanhai. The most experienced of the younger group of players in the side, Lloyd had occasionally led Lancashire and he now revelled in the responsibility of uniting a dressing room that, following the example of the selectors themselves, could too often be riven by inter-island politics and jealousies.

'Clive and the West Indies were lucky that the young team gelled together and we didn't have to worry about selection policies or arguments for years,' said Kallicharran. 'It was same team formula and, as that progressed, so Clive's captaincy progressed.' It would mean that Lloyd's voice in matters of selection made others look beyond the parochialism pervading a cricketing nation that has never been a nation at all. 'All islands have their own flags, currencies and accents,' said the great spinner Lance Gibbs. 'Other than cricket, nothing brings us together. There's no sense of unity.'

Lloyd acknowledged, 'We come from different countries, with equally different backgrounds. But at the same time, we should think of togetherness.' And he understood the importance of his team to the way its fans viewed their place in the world, telling biographer Trevor McDonald, 'It's much more than a game. It carries with it all sorts of aspirations and hopes of West Indian people. The key to the West Indian captaincy is realising all that.'

Yet all of that might have been undermined but for a remarkable recovery at Edgbaston, where a partnership of 64 between wicketkeeper Deryck Murray and fast bowler Andy Roberts, still a tournament record for the last wicket, clawed them to a target of 267 with two balls remaining. 'The game was done and dusted and Pakistan were celebrating,' said Murray. 'It defined the World Cup for the West Indies. It was great to eke out those runs.' Roberts eventually won the game with a delicate push into the leg side and a quickly run single. According to bowler Vanburn Holder, 'Even the senior players were jumping up and down, hugging each other and crying.'

Indifferent Test results and the absence of veteran Garry Sobers through injury meant that the West Indians had not considered themselves favourites, despite their collective experience of one-day cricket in England. 'We had a bit of youth and we had some experience,' said Lloyd. 'The best team at the time was Australia. We were probably about fourth in line. We weren't favourites because don't forget we had just come off a run of losing Test matches.'

West Indian journalist Tony Cozier felt differently. 'The fact they had played in English county cricket and played the one-day version of the game; most of those players knew what it was all about.'

Yet according to Murray, 'We were just hopeful that we would do well. We had the reputation of having the batsmen who could thrill a crowd, score relatively quickly, so we were really excited, looking forward to it.' But there were doubts. 'Will we get our tactics right? Will we bowl the right bowlers at the right time?'

That, of course, was down to Lloyd. 'He is a charismatic leader, leads by example, gelling the team together and making sure all the parts worked,' Murray continued. 'When you have got bowlers like Andy Roberts, Bernard Julien, Vanburn Holder, Keith Boyce, they want to get wickets. So the captain may be thinking, "Look, contain them and I will set a field on the off side," [but] they wanted to be bowling in-swingers and out-swingers and everything else. It was interesting trying to hold it all together.'

Yet the Pakistan victory created the confidence that all would work out. Lloyd recalled, 'Once we won that game, we realised we could do anything. We knew after that game we had to win this tournament.'

A routine semi-final victory against New Zealand left West Indies one game away from that ambition and it was obvious from the early hours of Saturday 21 June that it would be a largely Caribbean crowd at Lord's to witness them achieving their destiny. 'The atmosphere,' Gilmour recalled with an air of awe. 'Lord's packed to capacity – 99 per cent West Indian, one per cent English and Australian. It was a great day.' Australian captain Ian Chappell added, 'We all got off the bus and there was a lot of West Indian supporters all milling around behind the pavilion there. They were terrific.'

This was a golden era in the experience of the West Indian cricket fan in England. Their boisterous, exuberant hordes of fans would define their matches in England throughout the team's dominance of the 1970s and 1980s – until familial links with the Caribbean became more distant and a general resurgence of demand for international tickets in England allowed the authorities to put prices up to unrealistic levels for many. West Indies' first win on English soil had come in 1950, only two years after the converted troop ship, *Empire Windrush*, had docked at Tilbury to signal the real beginning of the post-war migration of large numbers of Caribbean citizens to the British Isles. Support for West Indies had grown as more immigrants found their way to Britain and by the time their team was being beaten in England in 1957, the number of West Indians in Britain was approaching 200,000.

The Tests of the late 1950s and early and mid '60s had a backdrop of the Caribbean territories' successful quest for independence from their historical rulers and, in England, worsening relations between white and black communities. The West Indians' duplication of their distinct homeland culture had unsettled many of their new countrymen. As Britain headed into economic recession in the late 1950s, racial tension was exacerbated, leading to discrimination when it came to finding jobs and housing and escalating into riots in Nottingham and Notting Hill.

The West Indies' Test series victories of 1963 and 1966 made heroes of the likes of Wes Hall, Charlie Griffith, Kanhai and Sobers within Britain's Caribbean diaspora. Sir Bill Morris, who eventually became head of the Transport and General Workers Union after arriving in England in 1954, explained, 'Recognising that Caribbean people living in England hadn't got many heroes to look up to ... for us, cricket fulfilled that role.'

West Indies cricket brought the displaced Caribbean islanders together in a state of shared identity – a state of affairs equally applicable to fans and players, many of whom were soon dominating the English domestic game. 'Most of them were playing in England in the County Championship,' noted Cozier, 'so they were identified in England as West Indians, not as Trinidadians or Barbadians or Guyanese. They were supported by a West Indian crowd, not a Trinidadian crowd or a Barbadian crowd. There was none of the insular divisions we have in the West Indies to affect them.'

Incidents such as Conservative MP Enoch Powell's infamous 'river of blood' speech in 1968 – following the arrival of large numbers of Kenyan Asians in the UK – and the blame many placed on the immigrant community for the country's economic and social problems, made those bonds even closer, the importance of cricket even greater. Former England Test bowler Gladstone Small, a mid-1970s arrival from Barbados, recalled the homeland connection offered by cricket. 'It was all you had. My parents were very much West Indians. Cricket linked them to the culture they knew and remembered and had brought from home. West Indies cricket was probably the biggest product to leave the Caribbean. It brought the islands together and was a big source of identity for the West Indians who lived in the UK.'

The atmosphere created by West Indian fans at World Cup games and Test matches could become stifling for opposition. England bowler Chris Old recalled, 'The West Indian fans would keep up their chants and rhythms all day, every day, anxious to contribute in any way possible on behalf of their team. If you were doing well you could shut out the noise, but when you were not doing well or feeling great it could get to you. Your mind was slightly distracted and everything going on in the background came more into it.'

Kallicharran confirmed, 'The support for the West Indies in England was immense. That played a big part in our success. Cricket was their identity and they were desperate to have a successful team in England. Cricket was all they had and that helped us.' Ian Chappell remembered the crowds for the final being 'boisterous, but respectful', while Greg Chappell described the crowd at The Oval for the group game as reminiscent of Trinidad, with its 'calypso music, the colourful costumes and the carnival atmosphere'.

When the day of the final arrived, the condensed timetable of the tournament and the norms of the era meant that Chappell's Australians 'didn't feel the need to do much pre-match planning'. According to Gilmour, 'It was new and we didn't know what to do. Ian Chappell used to say to us if we get through the first 15 overs and we have got 30 runs on the board without the loss of a wicket we have done well.'

On this occasion, Chappell won the toss. 'I sent them in because of the early start,' he explained. 'I thought if there was going to be any movement it would happen early.' The breakthrough he desired came via a route he couldn't have anticipated. With 12 on the board, Lillee, charging in from the Nursery End, unleashed a bouncer that a swivelling Roy Fredericks swing high into the Tavern Stand. Then the left-hander realised that his hurried pirouette had dislodged the bails, leaving him swatting the air with his bat on his frustrated walk back to the pavilion.

The in-form Kallicharran, who had got into the 70s again in the semi-final, announced his arrival by taking Gilmour for two fours – a cover drive and a flamboyant hook. But then he flashed outside the off stump and edged to Marsh with the score on 27. Gordon Greenidge's uncharacteristically tentative innings ended at 13, bringing Lloyd to the crease at 50 for 3.

As fans of Lancashire had witnessed so often, Lloyd could turn the course of a one-day game in the briefest passage of play. It meant that, having hooked Lillee into the Tavern for six, Australia must have feared the worst when Lloyd, on 26, mistimed a hurried attempt to repeat the feat and Ross Edwards could not cling on at midwicket. 'After that the ball just started hitting the bat rather sweetly,' said Lloyd with an understatement that hints at the apparent effortless of his innings. 'I thought this must be my day. I had Rohan Kanhai at the other end, as a senior person, someone I had a lot of respect for. He was playing some terrific shots and I was sort of just hitting them in the middle and it just went on and on and the crowd was getting more excited.'

When Lloyd flicked Thomson off his legs for four it brought up a 50 partnership in only 49 minutes. Kanhai had contributed a mere six runs, yet the former skipper's efforts were not being underestimated, even though he went from the 23rd over to the 34th without scoring. Thomson, whose tournament had begun with a dozen no-balls against Pakistan at Headingley, thought he'd had Kanhai caught early in his innings, only to have over-stepped once again. 'I knew Rohan was a bloody good player,' said Ian Chappell. 'He doesn't get much kudos really. Lloydy gets all the kudos for making a hundred, but [Rohan] really steadied things after we got some early wickets and then Lloydy just came in and blasted us.'

Max Walker, who had bowled seven economical overs in the morning, saw the first ball of his eighth clubbed past him for Lloyd to reach his 50. Australia twice came close to dismissing Kanhai, when first Edwards and then Lillee could not quite make enough ground to catch him in the deep, but it was what was happening at the other end that was threatening to put the game beyond the

Aussies. Lloyd lifted a good length good ball from Walker into the Grand Stand for six and then slashed to an unguarded cover boundary for four. 'There is no way you can bowl at a man like Clive Lloyd when he is in this sort of form,' commentator Jim Laker observed. He reached 99 by flicking Gilmour through midwicket and drove square for a single to reach three figures. According to John Woodcock in *The Times* it was an innings that 'will always be talked about while those who saw it are still alive'. When Lloyd lifted his Duncan Fearnley bat to the crowd it looked like an ice lolly stick in the hands of the sport's undisputed giant, and Woodcock went as far as saying, 'Lloyd made the pitch and the stumps and the bowlers and the ground all seem much smaller than they were.' The quietly unimposing Kanhai was soon offering a peremptory lift of his cap to reveal his grey hair and mark his half-century after bashing a Doug Walters half-volley through the covers.

At 199 for 3, Lloyd chased one down the leg side from Gilmour, and Marsh stuck out a right glove to grab the ball just above the ground. Lloyd was gone for 102 off 85 balls and then Gilmour bowled Kanhai and Viv Richards in quick succession, meaning three wickets had gone for ten runs. But there was further brisk hitting to come from fast bowlers Keith Boyce and Bernard Julien and keeper Murray, who eventually gave Gilmour his fifth wicket with a return catch. A final total of 291 for 8 left Australia needing to achieve a total that no team batting second in limited-overs cricket in England had ever managed.

'Even though we were chasing a big total I thought we had a chance of getting it,' recalled Ian Chappell, who was called to the crease at 25 after Boyce had Rick McCosker caught at second slip. Keen to drive whenever the ball was pitched up, Chappell forced Julien through extra cover before getting away with a return chance offered to Boyce.

He and Turner had taken the score to 81 when Lloyd introduced his loopy medium pace. Chappell nudged the ball into the leg side and ran. Turner hesitated and became the first of Australia's run-out victims when Richards scooped the ball up at midwicket and threw down the stumps at the keeper's end. 'The first one I don't think was out,' Chappell argued. 'If you look at the photo he is level with the stumps and the bails are not very far off. I remember looking back.

There was an easy run there, but he was a bit slow out of the blocks, so I looked back to see how he was going and even just looking back I thought that is not out.' Dickie Bird thought otherwise.

By the 28th over Chappell, having punished a Lloyd long hop and flicked Roberts to the rope at fine leg, had moved to 48. He pushed Roberts into the off side and a clear shout of 'no' could be heard on the TV coverage, followed by a more tentative 'yes' after Julien overran the ball coming in from point. Richards picked up and this time it was Greg Chappell who was left stranded, regretting that he had not simply taken a chance as soon as the ball had been struck. 'If Greg didn't think there was a run he would have sent me back,' said brother Ian. 'He said afterwards he thought there was a run there but Viv threw them down from side on.' Richie Benaud's verdict for the viewers was, 'That's a tragedy for Australia,'

Putting it behind him, the elder Chappell hacked Roberts back towards the Nursery End, running three to reach his half-century. Walters, meanwhile, began scoring freely, taking fours off Holder on either side of the wicket. At 162 for 3, Australia needed another 130 off 22 overs and, with two men on the leg-side boundary, Chappell pushed gently towards midwicket and set off for what looked like an easy run. Astonishingly, Richards – making the kind of impact in the field that he would make in future with his bat – struck again, throwing over the top of the stumps for Lloyd to remove the bails and dismiss Chappell for 62, scored from 93 balls. 'We realised that the Australians were not great runners between the wickets,' Lloyd recalled. 'We realised that quite early actually. We realised that we can get a couple of them run out because they were a bit suicidal at times.'

Once Walters had been bowled for 35, trying to whip Lloyd through the leg side, and Marsh went in similar fashion against Boyce, Australia's hopes seemed to be over at 195 for 6. After some vigorous blows by Edwards and Gilmour, who both eventually fell to skied catches, Holder's direct throw made Walker the fourth man to be run out, leaving Australia 233 for 9. Now it was just a matter of time, wasn't it? The West Indian fans certainly thought so, standing on the boundary rope around the entire ground, except for the area in front of the pavilion, as they waited for the wicket that would make them world champions.

Yet Lillee and Thomson had other ideas, hitting boundaries and scampering singles as their partnership grew and night time descended. Thank heavens this was the summer solstice. The game needed every minute of available daylight as the clock headed towards 9 p.m. The 250 mark was reached with an overthrow, but when Thomson chipped Holder to Fredericks at cover it seemed to be game over. The crowd stampeded, yet Tom Spencer, officiating at the Pavilion End, had signalled for a no-ball. By the time Fredericks had missed with his throw at the stumps there were fans and police on the square and the batsmen were charging up and down for overthrows. 'It's absolute chaos out there,' Laker chuckled. 'Nobody knows what's happened. Lillee says, "Keep on going we can run 10 here."' Once the scene had been cleared, two runs were awarded.

Australia had got to within 17 runs of their opponents' score with nine balls left when Thomson swiped at Holder. The ball missed the leg stump, Thomson took a couple of steps down the wicket and was thrown out by Murray as he turned in a desperate attempt to get back. It was ruled as a fifth run-out rather than a stumping. Either way, West Indies had won and Murray was even more impressive in gathering up all three stumps and running full pelt to the safe zone at the pavilion steps ahead of the spectators' charge. Boyce was lost somewhere in the crowd. 'Unforgettable scenes here at Lord's Cricket Ground at the end of one of the greatest one-day matches one could possibly have wished for,' was Laker's succinct and indisputable summary.

Lloyd completed his work by accepting the gold trophy from the Duke of Edinburgh. No wonder he called it 'one of the finest days' of his career. 'Any cricket enthusiast would have enjoyed that final because there was great cricket on both sides.. You can't beat something like that.'

Even the umpires had been swept along by the excitement and drama of the day. 'It was the finest game of cricket I ever stood in,' said Bird. 'It had everything. I was at the ground at half past seven the morning, we came off the field at nine o clock at night and it was a magnificent day. I think that is when one-day cricket really took off.'

Richards was one of the men who would use that launchpad to reach the greatest heights in the format. 'I sensed then cricket was on the move,' he recalled. 'Leisurely three-day matches in England played before a handful of spectators were being overtaken. As cricketers from the different countries talked together at the World Cup they knew that the restructuring of the game would continue.'

They did not know the half of it.

AUSTRALIA v WEST INDIES, World Cup Final
21 June 1975, Lord's

West Indies			Balls	4s	6s
RC Fredericks	hit wicket b Lillee	7	13		
CG Greenidge	c Marsh b Thomson	13	61	1	
AI Kallicharran	c Marsh b Gilmour	12	18	2	
RB Kanhai	b Gilmour	55	105	8	
*CH Lloyd	c Marsh b Gilmour	102	85	12	2
IVA Richards	b Gilmour	5	11	1	
KD Boyce	c GS Chappell b Thomson	34	37	3	
BD Julien	not out	26	37	1	
†DL Murray	c and b Gilmour	14	10	1	
VA Holder	not out	6	2	1	
Extras	(lb 6, nb 11)	17			
Total	(9 wickets, 60 overs)	291			

Fall: 12, 27, 50, 199, 206, 209, 261, 285.
Did Not Bat: AME Roberts
Bowling: Lillee 12-1-55-1; Gilmour 12-2-48-5; Thomson 12-1-44-2; Walker 12-1-71-0; GS Chappell 7-0-33-0; Walters 5-0-23-0

Australia			Balls	4s	6s
A Turner	run out	40	54	4	
RB McCosker	c Kallicharran b Boyce	7	24	1	
*IM Chappell	run out	62	93	6	
GS Chappell	run out	15	23	4	
KD Walters	b Lloyd	35	51	5	
†RW Marsh	b Boyce	11	24		
R Edwards	c Fredericks b Boyce	28	37	2	
GJ Gilmour	c Kanhai b Boyce	14	11	2	
MHN Walker	run out	7	9	1	
JR Thomson	run out	21	21	2	
DK Lillee	not out	16	19	1	
Extras	(b 2, lb 9, nb 7)	18			
Total	(58.4 overs)	274			

Fall: 25, 81, 115, 162, 170, 195, 221, 231, 233, 274.
Bowling: Julien 12-0-58-0; Roberts 11-1-45-0; Boyce 12-0-50-4; Holder 11.4-1-65-0; Lloyd 12-1-38-1.

West Indies won by 17 runs. **Toss:** Australia. **Umpires:** HD Bird, TW Spencer.
Man of the Match: CH Lloyd.

5

'BIG BOYS PLAY AT NIGHT'

WSC Australia v WSC West Indies, International Cup, Sydney, 1978

Australia remained in England after the inaugural World Cup to retain the Ashes in a four-match series. When they returned two years later, they brought with them a time bomb that was to blow the cricket authorities out of their bunker of complacency and change limited-overs cricket for good. In fact, much of what is familiar about the modern one-day game stems from a garden party in Hove on 7 May 1977.

Tony Greig, who had inherited the England captaincy during the summer of 1975, was hosting the tourists at his home on the Saturday night of their three-day warm-up game against his county side, Sussex. Along with most of the Australian players, Greig was part of a small group who knew about the negotiations and deliberations that had been going on since that March's Centenary Test in Melbourne.

Australian journalists Peter McFarline, writing for *The Age*, and Alan Shiell, of *The Australian*, were also present, having used the rain that had ruined that day's play to check on rumours coming from home of an unofficial international series to be played during the next southern hemisphere summer. When McFarline shared with John Snow details of the story they were filing, the fast bowler informed Greig. He hit the phone, calling Kerry Packer, the Australian media mogul who had become a central figure in his life and those of the various English and overseas cricketers with whom he had been sharing Packer's plans. Then Greig and his agent, Reg Hayter, issued a statement. 'There is a massive cricket project involving most of the world's top players due to commence in Australia this winter,' he said. 'I am part of it, along with a number of English players. Full details and implications of the scheme will be officially announced in Australia later this week.'

The Australian team that had almost won the first World Cup was a collection of bankers, architects, engineers and insurance salesmen, underappreciated and underpaid by officialdom and able to represent their country only via the grace of employers who rather liked the idea of having a national folk hero on the payroll. Rodney Marsh reckoned that his various salary streams totalled one-tenth of the annual income of his brother Graham, a professional golfer with a fraction of his public profile.

Their growing discontent was a godsend to Packer, head of the Consolidated Press Holdings media group built by his father Frank. A fearsome bear of a man, he had resolved to bring live cricket to his Channel 9 commercial television network, but when finally granted a meeting with the Australian Cricket Board (ACB) he was told a verbal deal had been agreed with their long-time partners at the Australian Broadcasting Corporation (ABC). 'Come on now, we are all harlots,' he told the board members sitting across the room. 'I know you haven't signed your contracts. What's your price?'

ACB chairman Bob Parish had shaken hands on a deal worth $210,000 over three years. Packer responded by offering $1.5 million for a three-year period beginning at the end of the new ABC deal. When Parish could do no better than to say it would be considered in three years' time, Packer went away and registered the name of World Series Cricket Pty Ltd with a view to filling his airtime with something similar to the International Cavaliers matches that had proved popular in England in the 1960s. His first thought was an Australia versus World XI series that could co-exist with the official Tests against India. In a series of private meetings during the home series against Pakistan and the Centenary Test against England that followed, most of the key Australian players were signed. Ian Chappell's protestations to Packer that it was his younger brother, Greg, who was now captain of Australia and should therefore select and lead this new team was greeted with, 'You think this is a fucking democracy, do you?'

For someone like 36-year-old Ian Redpath, who had turned down overseas tours, including the first World Cup, and eventually been forced into early retirement because of the need to earn a living through his antiques business, this was 'a bonus I had not expected'. He explained, 'I had been out of cricket for a year but, as I said to my dear wife, "I just cannot afford not to be involved." I had a contract. You could make plans and it was much better money than we had received playing for the national side, so it wasn't a hard decision because the money I'd received all through my married life was pretty rough.'

Such was their dedication to the pact of secrecy to which they had sworn, no player was aware which others had been approached.

Having led his team in a memorable Centenary Test in Melbourne, Greig set off to meet Packer. There was no cricketer more aware of his commercial value and of the limited timescale in which to capitalise upon it than Greig, who said, 'Cricket was wonderful fun, but I had to get into a serious job as some stage.' Believing they would be discussing a possible broadcasting career, Greig was stunned to be offered $90,000 over three years to captain a World team and act as a consultant and recruiter. 'It came as more than a shock to be propositioned with a plan that basically involved being bought up for a commercial purpose.'

As well as the money, Greig was conscious of the precarious status of an England captain, prone to be hounded by the media and discarded by selectors. Aware that reaction to World Series Cricket (WSC) 'was certain to be violent' – especially as Packer had now decided to schedule in direct competition to 'official' matches and deny Test cricket the services of his players – Greig admitted, 'I was worried least by the thought that the authorities were in for a shock. I believed it was overdue. They needed something like this to accelerate their progress towards a more business-like approach to the game. I did it for Tony Greig first and for my family. Secondly, I did it because the establishment deserved it.'

He helped to recruit English colleagues Snow, Underwood and Alan Knott, the latter recalling, 'Participation would mean playing cricket in Australia for three winters – with no restrictions on wives and families and that was the main reason why I eventually signed.' Greig also joined WSC's Austin Robertson in the Caribbean, where West Indies were playing Pakistan, whose quartet of Imran Khan, Majid Khan, Mushtaq Mohammad and Asif Iqbal were easily persuaded to sign.

Next in line was Clive Lloyd, whose offer of $90,000 for three years was a chance to secure the financial future that was denied to most West Indian cricketers. Viv Richards and Andy Roberts followed. Michael Holding's involvement was secured when Jamaican Prime

Minister Michael Manley, a fierce anti-apartheid campaigner, agreed that he could play alongside South Africans if they were already playing in county cricket – a strange distinction that meant the great batsman Graeme Pollock and leg-spinner Denys Hobson were unable to join Barry Richards, Eddie Barlow and Mike Procter on Packer's list of players.

'Tony Greig stood up and outlined the plan,' recalled Procter. 'It sounded great. We would get $25,000 a year plus bonus money for three years. If you were injured and couldn't play, you'd still get the full whack. We discussed the pros and cons and the English guys all realised it would probably mean the end of their Test careers.'

Snow, his England days already at an apparent end, was among the most receptive of recruits. 'If it hadn't been Packer then it would have been something else,' he said. 'The unrest was there. You don't get all the top players to sign unless something like that is needed. I was finishing up my career anyway, but it was a kick to the system. It needed some kind of large explosion to move the thing forward and change the mindset of the people running the game. We were getting frustrated knowing that for what we were getting paid for a Test match you could go and empty dustbins down Marylebone High Street and be finished by lunchtime.'

While the garden marquee at Greig's home was being dismantled, the story broke on both sides of the world. The *Daily Mirror*'s headline, 'Test Pirates,' summed up the tone of the media coverage, while John Arlott in *The Guardian* was among the first to describe the scheme as a 'circus', a label that infuriated Packer. His own publication, *The Bulletin*, revealed fully the plan for six five-day 'Supertests' and a series of one-day games between the Australian and World teams. By the time the first WSC season of 1977-78 was ready to begin, the unsettled Australian team had lost the Ashes 3-0; Greig had been stripped of the England captaincy but retained in the team throughout the series; and an entire West Indies squad had been signed, along with additional English batsmen Dennis Amiss and Bob Woolmer to swell the World team's ranks.

Venues, however, were more difficult to procure than players. Conflict with the sport's authorities meant that established cricket grounds closed their doors to Packer. Instead, matches were scheduled for VFL Park in Melbourne and Football Park in Adelaide, both Australian Rules football stadiums; Perth's Gloucester Park, a trotting track; and the Sydney Showground. Necessity, of course, leads to innovation, and the drop-in pitches that WSC was forced to use would in future years become a feature of cricket in multi-purpose arenas. And Packer's search for an audience led to experiments that would change the landscape of cricket.

The first of Packer's brand of one-day internationals, for the International Cup, attracted fewer than 1,700 to Football Park to watch Australia take on the World team. Four days later, the same teams took the field under the floodlights at VFL Park in Melbourne, where a white ball was used. The game was not billed as part of the WSC tournament but had far-reaching consequences. Greig and Australian captain Ian Chappell were cautious enough about this new environment to agree that bouncers – pretty much the stock delivery of the Supertests – would be outlawed. Greig was also wary enough about the effect of artificial light on batting conditions that he opted to bat first when he won the toss. The white ball proved easy enough to see, but there were concerns about its visibility against the players' white clothing – a problem that would be addressed in due course.

Chappell and Rick McCosker's century opening partnership helped chased down the World's all-out total of 204 and Greg Chappell followed his brother in making a half-century. The home team won by six wickets with three of their 40 eight-ball overs remaining. Inevitably, it was the antagonistic Greig who broke the bouncer ceasefire, being hooked for four by McCosker. 'If you want to bowl bouncers, Greigy, we'll turn the lights off for you,' Chappell responded.

The two former Ashes captains would clash constantly over the two years of World Series Cricket. 'There was a lot going on between Tony and Ian,' said Derek Underwood. 'It was a lot to do with Greigy being the senior figure to Chappell off the field. That didn't help their relationship.'

Greig admitted, 'I didn't like him and he didn't like me. As simple as that. I think maybe it goes back to the series in England when I became captain, but I have no idea.' Chappell explained, 'I respected him as a player because I thought he always got the best out of his ability. The problem I had with him during World Series Cricket was that he was off earning other money by doing ads and things like that while the rest of his team were training. I thought that was pretty ordinary and I lost a bit of respect for him. It led to a few of our ructions. Then, apart from for the money side, he wasn't worth his place in the team.'

There was a day late in November 1978, however, that would unite everyone involved in Packer's venture. The 6,442 attendance at for the first floodlit game had been an encouraging improvement on the daytime crowds and three more games were rescheduled as day-nighters, drawing a total of 50,000 spectators. It was a ray of light for Packer in a gloomy season that saw his savagely contested Supertests afflicted by poor attendance. It was also enough to convince the ACB, which had staged only two one-day internationals since that inaugural game in 1971, to introduce five such games as part of England's 1978-79 tour programme.

Going into his second season, one that would offer the opposition of an official Ashes series, Packer was convinced attendance would improve if he could break into the homes of mainstream cricket. The Sydney Cricket Ground, not the Sydney Showground, was the stage he craved. 'Those battles have to be fought and in order to get over those kinds of things you have a guy like Kerry Packer, who then starts to work the politics of the whole thing,' Greig would tell Sky Sports years later. 'Most of the grounds are owned by the state and slowly but surely he was able to get in there and change things. It became clear to us before it became clear to other people that the first season was going to be really tough, but when we got back for the second season things would change a bit.'

Politicians proved more sympathetic to Packer's cause than those in charge of cricket. Neville Wran, the Labour premier of New South Wales, became an ally – in return for Packer's support at election time – and his intervention forced the SCG Trustees to give WSC the keys to one of the country's most historic arenas. He also paved the way for six towers of floodlights to be erected.

As Australia's establishment team – was it the real one or a merely a second eleven? – set off on a summer that would see them overwhelmed 5-1 by Mike Brearley's England, World Series Cricket decided to lay claim to patriotism, as well as the top players. An aggressive promotional campaign was constructed around what was, in effect, its own national anthem. The irritatingly catchy

'C'mon, Aussie. C'mon' was soon at number one in the charts, further mocking the efforts of the ACB's overmatched official squad.

Attendance at the Ashes contests, while down on previous series, would still dwarf those of WSC's Supertests, but the battle for hearts and minds took a decisive turn on 28 November, under the new SCG lights. 'When Packer put the lights up at the SCG for the second year we were home and dry,' said Underwood.

At the start time of 2.15 p.m. there were around 5,000 inside the ground for Australia's WSC International Cup game against West Indies, although lines of fans were snaking back from the turnstiles. For the early arrivals, there was the bonus of the Australian players tossing white balls into the crowd, and then the sight of Dennis Lillee trapping opener Richard Austin lbw with the score on 12 and bowling Viv Richards second ball. Austin was playing because the West Indies had chosen to rest Roy Fredericks and Desmond Haynes, along with fast bowler Michael Holding, which left WSC susceptible to accusations that the deck was stacked in favour of the home victory that would most benefit the series.

Greg Chappell's medium pace was unexpectedly productive, Lawrence Rowe offering a catch to Marsh to become the first of his five victims. Yet it was Lillee who was striking the most significant blows, having Greenidge caught by David Hookes for 41 and bowling Lloyd within three runs of each other to leave West Indies 74 for 5. Jim Allen and Deryck Murray took the score into three figures, but then Chappell cleaned up to finish with figures of 5 for 19 as West Indies were dismissed for 128 in the 48th over.

Yet the most notable numbers were those being clocked up at the gate. By the innings break, there were officially 30,000 inside and plenty more still waiting to get in. Australian Test great Bill O'Reilly, columnist for the *Sydney Morning Herald*, described the 'buzz of excitement' when the lights were switched on and said that night cricket 'had swept Sydney off its feet'. When the count reached 44,477 and there were still crowds outside, Packer happily agreed to a police suggestion that, for the sake of safety, the gates should be opened. By most people's estimates there were 50,000 in the stadium by the end of the night.

Lillee, who had been invited into an executive box to look at the scenes outside, recalled, 'There were hordes of people and cars as far as the eye could see … As I looked out in the gloomy light I got a tingling feeling through my body.' Greg Chappell stood in the Members' Stand watching the crowds fighting to get in. Rodney Marsh turned to him and beamed, 'We're back.'

Redpath remembered, 'All the players had been bracketed with Ned Kelly because we sided with Packer and because of that we felt we were pretty tight-knit. The second year we got a bit more established and that one-day game at Sydney underlines it. It was electric. It was a taste of what was to come.'

Greig arrived late after fulfilling promotional commitments to a provincial game and 'choked back tears' when he saw the scenes. 'All the hard work had been worth it. WSC had been accepted,' he said, feeling personal vindication for his loyalty to Packer. His employer, meanwhile, was surprising everyone with his calm acceptance of what was going on, as though he'd never expected anything else.

Back on the field, Australia built on an opening partnership of 40 between Bruce Laird and Greg Chappell, with Ian Davis making an unbeaten 48 to see his team home by five wickets with 13 overs remaining. Most importantly, though, as Alan Lee pointed out in his book about that Australian summer, 'Packer had struck gold and found something that would arouse the envy of the traditional cricket authorities.' He had hit upon a formula that the masses would embrace; something that Adrian McGregor, writing in Australia's *Time*, described as 'the proletarianism of cricket'. O'Reilly called it an 'incredible performance' and said that Packer had won the first part of the battle for the Sydney public 'by the proverbial mile'. As Lillee recalled, 'From that moment we knew we would win … I knew Packer would get what he wanted.'

With the first Test between Australia and England starting at Brisbane three days later, the traditionalists were left to take comfort from news reports that spoke sniffily of the pitch invasions, the beer-induced fist fights on The Hill and the 13 arrests made by police unprepared for the size of the gathering. It meant that sales of alcohol were limited and security increased when the teams met again the next night.

Inevitably, the crowds diminished after that first triumph, and exact attendance figures for World Series Cricket games have proved elusive, especially given the number of tickets reportedly given away for free. But figures quoted by Richard Cashman in his 1984 book 'Ave A Go, Yer Mug! estimate that crowds for Packer's one-day internationals rose from an average of just over 9,000 to more than 17,000 from first season to second.

Another big attendance was achieved at the SCG a couple of months later when WSC solved the conundrum of making the white ball more visible against the players' uniforms. When Australia and West Indies took the field in front of a crowd that grew to more than 45,000, the first sight of the pastel yellow and coral pink uniforms prompted jeers and wolf-whistles.

Brearley, who had sought permission to go and watch WSC in action, recorded, 'With the yellow and strawberry colours, the game was more dramatic because one could see who was on which side'. He was not being facetious when he suggested that Packer should have gone as far as putting numbers on the players' backs to aid identification.

The kits might have been the main talking point of the game had the night not ended in such chaos that different newspapers ended up reporting different results. It was strange enough when Ian Chappell, angry at the crowd jeering him for his slowly-constructed 31, decided to stubbornly play out the final over of the innings for a maiden against the bowling of Colin Croft. But things would get weirder after rain delayed the West Indies reply. Having originally been set 150 to win at three per over, the revised target was now 48 off 16.

Despite losing early wickets, West Indies passed their target in the ninth over with four wickets down, at which point the crowd ran on to the field and the TV crews began to pack up. But the umpires' interpretation of the playing conditions was that 15 overs per side had to be bowled to constitute a game and that play should continue. By 10.25, five minutes before the local council insisted that the lights had to be turned off, only 12 overs had been bowled. At which point, more rain fell and the game came to an end. But what was the result? The Australians argued that it was a void game, their opponents claimed victory; and the fans were left to base their understanding on which newspaper they read the next day. Fortunately for the competition's integrity, either result ensured that West Indies qualified to face Australia in the finals. In the end they were officially recorded as winners of the match.

By the end of the season, Packer teams would be playing their day-night Supertest matches in their new outfits – light blue for the World XI – and players joined fans in sporting T-shirts bearing the slogan, 'Big Boys Play at Night'. It was safe to say that the rest of the world was now taking notice of WSC instead of dismissing it as a circus and mocking them for playing in 'pyjamas'.

'That was the biggest thing about Packer,' said Snow. 'The impact it was going to have on the organisation of cricket and the people running the game. It showed them what was possible, and maybe necessary, to carry cricket forward into the next era.'

Not that everyone suddenly began putting up floodlights. India needed the impetus provided to limited-overs cricket by its 1983 World Cup triumph before hosting a day-nighter against Australia in 1984, the first one-day international under lights outside of Australia. Television viewers in England had seen night cricket on their screens as early as 1952, when Arsenal played Middlesex in a benefit match for England spinner Jack Young on the football pitch at Highbury. Played with balls and stumps painted white, the game was considered enough of a novelty for BBC to interrupt its evening schedule to drop in on the action for half an hour at 7 p.m. and again at 10 p.m., by which time Young – who came out to bat in a miner's helmet – had already scored the winning runs. Middlesex batted on, however, for the benefit of the cameras.

With the long, light and often chilly evenings of an English summer not exactly lending themselves to the concept, it would be 1997 before Warwickshire hosted a game against Somerset in the Axa Life-sponsored 40-over league under temporary lights at Edgbaston in what was the nation's first official day-night game. That honour should have gone to Surrey a month earlier, but rain washed out their match against Nottinghamshire. By that time, Australia was already three years on from having experimented with day-night first-class matches in the Sheffield Shield.

World Series Cricket had brought colour to the sport and, literally, put it in the spotlight. Cricket's structure and calendar, in Australia at least, had been changed irrevocably and players' lives would never be the same again. But there was a storm coming.

WSC AUSTRALIA v WSC WEST INDIES, WSC International Cup

28 November 1978, Sydney Cricket Ground

WSC West Indies			Balls	4s	6s
RA Austin	lbw b Lillee		6	-	
CG Greenidge	c Hookes b Lillee		41	-	
IVA Richards	b Lillee		0	2	
LG Rowe	c Marsh b GS Chappell		2	-	
*CH Lloyd	b Lillee		21	-	
JC Allen	lbw b GS Chappell		21	-	
†DL Murray	b GS Chappell		17	-	
BD Julien	c and b GS Chappell		1	-	
AME Roberts	c Marsh b Walker		5	-	
J Garner	b GS Chappell		5	-	
CEH Croft	not out		1	-	
Extras	(lb 6, nb 1, w 1)		8		
Total	(47.3 overs)		128		

Fall: 12, 12, 37, 71, 74, 108, 110, 117, 125, 128
Bowling: Lillee 9-2-13-4; Malone 10-3-18-0; Gilmour 9-1-37-0;
GS Chappell 9.3.-3-19-5; Walker 10-2-33-1.

WSC Australia			Balls	4s	6s
BM Laird	run out		15	-	
GS Chappell	c Julien b Garner		22	-	
*IM Chappell	c Murray b Roberts		19	-	
IC Davis	not out		48	-	
DW Hookes	run out		3	-	
IR Redpath	b Roberts		1	-	
†RW Marsh	not out		6	-	
Extras	(b 2, lb 8, nb 4, w 1)		15		
Total	(5 wickets, 37 overs)		129		

Fall: 40, 53, 95, 99, 106
Did Not Bat: GJ Gilmour, DK Lillee, MHN Walker, MF Malone.
Bowling: Roberts 8-2-21-1; Julien 7-1-34-0; Croft 9-1-35-0; Garner 8-2-18-2;
Austin 5-0-6-0.

WSC Australia won by 5 wickets. **Toss:** No toss. **Umpires:** D Sang Hue, JR Collins.
Man of the Match: DK Lillee. *Note: (-) denotes incomplete historical data.*

6

'ONE OF THE WORST THINGS
I HAVE EVER SEEN'

Australia v New Zealand, World Series Cup, 1981, Melbourne

Had it really come to this? It was bad enough, some still believed, that the teams engaged in combat before their eyes wore, not white, but yellow and green and, in the inexplicable case of New Zealand, beige and brown. Even worse was that instead of a national crest over their left breasts, the players carried the red ball and black stumps of the World Series Cricket logo – as clear a sign of the war lost to Kerry Packer as if it had been the bloodstain of a bullet through the heart.

Yet surely the game had not so completely lost its soul, so totally abandoned any semblance of dignity, that it would allow the abomination that was about to happen in front of a then world-record one-day crowd of 52,990 at the Melbourne Cricket Ground and millions of television viewers. Needing merely to prevent a six being hit off the final ball to take a 2-1 lead in the best-of-five finals of the World Series Cup, Australia captain Greg Chappell had, according to all the evidence, instructed his brother Trevor to roll the ball along the ground underarm at the number 10 batsman, Brian McKechnie, who had just arrived at the crease. McKechnie might have been an All Blacks international rugby player, but according to Kim Hughes the Aussie view of him was, 'He couldn't hit the skin off a rice pudding.'

Greg Chappell had been sitting on the scorched grass with his head on his knees as McKechnie approached the crease. Rising to his feet he approached his younger brother and asked, 'How are you bowling your underarm?'

Trevor rolled his eyes and replied, 'I don't know.'

'Well, you're just about to find out because that's what you'll be bowling.'

Chappell instructed umpire Don Weser of his intention and the message was relayed down the wicket. Non-striker Bruce Edgar, wearied after batting through the innings for an unbeaten century, turned to the bowler. 'You are not serious, are you?' he challenged. 'It's a bloody stupid way to finish great game.' Four decades later, he admitted, 'It fell on deaf ears.'

'It looks to me as though they are going to bowl underarm off the last ball,' commentator Bill Lawry informed the TV audience. 'This is possibly a little bit disappointing.' McKechnie displayed his incredulity by dropping his bat to the ground, while, back in the New Zealand dressing room, vice-captain Mark Burgess hurled a coffee cup against the wall.

Behind the stumps, Rodney Marsh shook his head and called out, 'Don't do that, mate.'

'Don't tell me,' the bowler shouted back and, indicating the Australian captain, 'Tell him.'

But there was no telling Greg Chappell. His mind was made up. What was unknown at the time, and not revealed until he discussed it some years later, was the state that mind was in. And to understand that you need to go back to World Series Cricket and the fight for control of the sport in Australia.

When Ian Chappell's Australian team had thrashed England in the 1974-75 series, the tour was reckoned to have generated more than A$500,000 in profits for the Australian Cricket Board. It was the players' minimal percentage of such a windfall that made them so susceptible to the largesse of Kerry Packer. And when the replacement Australian team's 5-1 humiliation in the series four years later saw the ACB's revenue plummet to barely a quarter of that amount, it meant that the ACB was estimated to have lost A$800,000 over a two-year period of conflict with WSC.

Cricket had cost Packer A$6 million over two years, but he had deeper pockets than his rivals. And it was still a relatively inexpensive way for his television channel to meet the government-mandated quota of Australian-produced content. The ACB could not afford to continue to have Packer as an enemy. While the WSC Australian and West Indies teams were engaged in a five-match series in the Caribbean in April, Tony Greig declared, 'A compromise is imminent.' Within days, the ACB released a brief statement saying that Channel 9's bid for its television rights had been agreed. A deal duly signed the next month gave Packer's subsidiary company, PBL Sports Pty Ltd, exclusive promotional rights to Australian cricket for ten years for an annual payment to the ACB of A$1.7 million. As part of that, one-day internationals would be played under the World Series Cricket banner. Packer would cease his matches immediately and the sport would be united once more.

Packer paid his players the third year of their contracts and for the most part they celebrated, although for South Africans such as Mike Procter and Clive Rice, exiled from Test cricket, it meant the loss of a precious year of the elite competition they craved. Rice even cried upon hearing the news. England wicketkeeper Alan Knott, who'd had enough of touring with his country, said, 'It was the most continually competitive cricket in which I've been involved. I felt very disappointed when it was announced that it would not be continuing.'

Cricket's first summer of peace in Australia had a very different identity to anything seen before. The ACB had planned for India and England to tour in 1979-80 but now the Indians were paid off and replaced by West Indies for a summer programme that looked very much like Packer cricket played under the banner of officialdom.

Australia played three Tests against each of their visitors, with the opponents alternating, and the three teams also contested a series of 50-over internationals, weaved throughout the summer rather than staged in one block. England's conditions of participation were to refuse to play for the Ashes over a truncated Test series; or to wear coloured clothing in the one-dayers; or to allow the fielding restrictions that had been part of WSC and of which they had no experience. Their concession was wearing coloured pads and gloves and agreeing to use a white ball in day-night games.

'Australia and West Indies can play with green balls and hockey sticks if they like,' said captain Mike Brearley. 'Our agreement was to play under existing laws if there was any disagreement.' Brearley subsequently stationed all his fielders, including wicketkeeper David Bairstow, on the boundary for the final ball of a match in which West Indies needed three runs to win.

Freed from Packer's selectorial influence, Ian Chappell stepped down from the captaincy, playing one final season of international cricket under the leadership of brother Greg. When the 50-over World Series Cup began with the first official day-night ODI at the SCG – almost a year exactly since Packer's big night – the new skipper made an unbeaten 74 to take Australia beyond their target of 194. Yet Australia finished last in the standings after the 12 group matches were completed. England upset their WSC-hardened opponents, winning all four matches against the host nation.

Just as surprising as reaching the final series against West Indies, which they lost 2-0, was the identity of Geoffrey Boycott as their most potent batsman. Riled by a decision to leave him out of the first match, and the implication that his game was too inflexible for the demands of the format, he scored 68 and 105 when called up for games against Australia. His century at Sydney combined technique and innovation and the 39-year-old confessed, 'It felt as though a lot of years had slipped off my shoulders.' A year after a disappointing Ashes series, the rejuvenated Boycott averaged 85 and passed 50 in five of his six matches.

Without England's reticence to worry about, the ACB were able to go full-steam ahead into the 1980-81 season, with India and New Zealand donning coloured uniforms for a World Series Cup expanded to 15 qualifying games and a best-of-five final. The New Zealand players were shocked when they saw the beige and brown outfits that had been selected for them. 'We didn't have any choice about it,' said Edgar. 'It was down to Packer's advertising and marketing people. The colours left a bit of a legacy, though, with the Beige Brigade our equivalent of the Barmy Army. But it wasn't a flattering kit. It was so damn tight and it showed all the rolls if the guys were carrying a couple of pies, so you knew who hadn't done much training.'

Australia's six Tests were again interspersed with the expanded one-day schedule, which for Greg Chappell's team meant a potential of 45 days of international cricket in a period of 81 days from the end of November to the middle of February. A further 14 days would be required for travel between the host cities. When there were a few days without a game for Australia during that period, Chappell squeezed in two four-day Sheffield Shield games as captain of Queensland. That left him a maximum of 12 days for recuperation or practice ahead of 21 international matches across differing formats.

Australia would have more than two guaranteed days of preparation for only two of the six Tests. After the third Test against New Zealand, there were just two clear days before starting the series against India. The second India Test would begin after only one free day following a one-dayer against New Zealand, during which they needed to travel from Adelaide to Sydney. Significantly, if Australia were forced to play all five games in the World Series Cup finals they would face this schedule:

Thursday: first final in Sydney.
Friday: travel to Melbourne.
Saturday and Sunday: second and third finals in Melbourne.
Monday: travel to Sydney.
Tuesday: fourth final in Sydney.
Wednesday: practice/day off.
Thursday: fifth final in Sydney.
Friday: travel to Melbourne.
Saturday-Wednesday: Third Test against India in Melbourne.

Such madness had been created by recognition of the full commercial potential of limited-overs cricket, which the ACB had allowed Packer's company to exploit. It should not have surprised anyone when the exhausted Aussies collapsed to 83 all out in the fourth innings of that final Test to lose by 59 runs, with Chappell bowled first ball.

'When I saw the 1980-81 programme I felt that World Series Cricket had got us nowhere,' said Chappell. 'It was absolutely mad. Travel days, when you might have to make two connecting flights from one side of Australia to the other, were seen as days off for us. It was ridiculous, verging on a form of punishment.'

Edgar remembered the summer as a mix of the exhausting and the exciting. 'I'd never played in day-night matches so it took some getting used to the transition from day to night. It felt quite unreal and like a different game altogether. It really did feel like a circus, a travelling roadshow. Glamorous, I suppose. But it upsets your body clock and you had to manage all that. You are so wired up after the game and you would have a few beers back at the hotel and still be wired up at two in the morning. It was great to be part of, but the amount of travel was phenomenal. We must have had between 20 and 30 plane flights on that trip. If you went to England you had one flight in and one out.'

Chappell felt that the proliferation of one-day games threatened the primacy of Test cricket and was also aware of the strain it would place on him as captain. 'Five one-day internationals were many times more taxing than five days of a Test match,' he explained. 'For captaincy stress, two ODIs equalled one Test match. Things moved so fast, you had to keep so much on your mind.'

Chappell won the toss ahead of the third leg of the final series against New Zealand and, on a baking hot day when temperatures inside the MCG reached several degrees above the city's recorded high of 31.5 degrees centigrade, elected to bat. It might have been the last clear-headed decision he made that day. 'I wasn't fit to captain a rowboat, let alone the Australian cricket team,' was his self-diagnosis.

Brother Ian had stood down in 1975 after four years as Australian captain because he was 'buggered mentally – I was shot'. And for all the financial battles he had fought with the ACB, he had not had to deal with the frazzling effects of the modern schedule. As his country's new captain, with no coach or media manager to support him, Greg Chappell would start receiving phone calls at six in the morning and would hope that they ceased by midnight. All of that while trying to prepare his side physically and mentally for an ever-rotating format of cricket while jumping on and off planes. Midway through the summer he asked the ACB for some support in the shape of a manager or coach who could take over some off-field duties and was, in effect, told that if he wanted to be paid as a professional he had to work like one.

All this while being his team's most important performer. 'That was a challenging task to bat, to captain, to bowl 10 overs. I know I was struggling mentally and physically. I was struggling to sleep, struggling to eat and it was really starting to affect my ability to perform,' he admitted. 'I kept pushing myself and pushing myself and pretending that it wasn't an issue. Obviously it was an issue because it all bubbled up at the MCG.'

His batting was relatively unencumbered, the imperative of finding ways to score runs on a worn track and a pock-marked outfield keeping unwanted distractions from his thoughts. New Zealand seamer McKechnie conjured up a couple of unwanted memories when he said, 'That beige uniform was an awful clingy sort of clothing. It was tremendously hot and there was not a breath of air at ground level in the MCG. Greg took to me in the first couple of overs and smacked me for about five fours through the covers in the first two overs, so I had to come off and come back later.'

Having scored a half-century to see his team home 24 hours earlier, Chappell had moved to 58 when he hoisted a short ball from Lance Cairns high towards the deep midwicket boundary. Alert to the possibility of such an event, New Zealand seamer Martin Snedden was quick off the mark, running and appearing to catch the ball cleanly with both hands as he dived forward. Chappell, however, stood his ground, unconvinced that the catch had been taken cleanly. 'From where I was, he hadn't got there,' said Chappell, content to let the umpires decide – without the benefit of TV pictures that supported Snedden's appeal. 'There is no question in my mind that was a great catch,' said Richie Benaud on commentary.

Umpire Peter Cronin told Kiwi skipper Geoff Howarth he had not seen the catch because he was watching the batsmen grounding their bats while running, causing Snedden to recall his team's view that the umpires were 'competent but not to be trusted when the pressure was on'. Edgar recalled, 'It looked like a catch to me from where I was and I was over 100 metres away. He was just standing there and not going off and we thought. "What do you have to do? We know he is never going to be given out lbw and now they don't give catches either."'

Chappell went on to score 90 before giving an identical catch to Edgar. 'If he had got out,' McKechnie suggested, 'I don't think anyone else would have got as many runs so the score we were chasing could have been lower.' With opener Graeme Wood having scored 72 and sharing a partnership of 145 with his captain, Australia closed on 235 for 4. Chappell felt that on a decent surface 300 would have been an achievable score on the wide open spaces of the MCG.

McKechnie recalled how difficult conditions were for both batting and fielding teams. 'That wicket was very slow and low, and the slower you bowled the harder it was to hit you. There were no ropes then; the fence was the boundary in those days and that was almost 100 metres. If it went to the midwicket fence and you didn't have a decent arm you were embarrassed because someone had to come out and get it and throw it the last 20 or 30 metres. You could run fours with no problem. We always felt 235 wasn't out of the equation. If someone got 260 that was a stretch in those days, because even the West Indies weren't racking up 300 back then.'

Left-handers John Wright and Edgar got New Zealand off to a solid start, putting on 85 before Wright became the first of Greg Chappell's three victims. Edgar would go on to reach three figures while crossing the boundary only seven times, manoeuvring the ball into gaps and wringing every run out of his effort. 'It was best to be opening against a new ball that was hard and came on a bit,' he recalled. 'It got tougher as the innings wore on and the ball got softer. The boundaries weren't coming and we were running our butts off. At least with the size of the boundary you could hit it through gaps and get twos. I felt like it was going to be my day and we were going along OK but then we lost a couple of key wickets.'

Chappell, meanwhile, was becoming frustrated with his team's lacklustre fielding performance, sensing that they were going through the motions. His effort in bowling his 10 overs added to his already exhausted state. He'd suggested to the ACB before the game that the game should be reduced to 40 overs because of the heat; now he floated with Marsh that he should leave the field. 'You can't, mate,' Marsh told him. 'This is going to go on to the wire. You have got to be here.' Chappell compromised by spending a few overs on the boundary 'to give myself a bit of breathing space'.

In what became a bone of contention later, Chappell was happy to let Lillee complete his spell by bowling the penultimate over. And when Trevor Chappell held a fine catch to dismiss John Parker on the last ball of it, ending a partnership of 49 with Edgar, it seemed a reasonable enough decision with 15 needed to win off six balls.

The younger Chappell took the ball and, for the first time when hearing his name being chanted, realised it was intended for him rather than an older brother. Richard Hadlee drove the first delivery down the ground for four, but was then given out lbw by umpire Weser, despite a suspicion that the ball was skidding past leg stump. Stranded at the non-striker's end, Edgar noted, 'That was a shocker. Richard was the guy who was probably going to hit boundaries, but the finger was up in the middle of the appeal.' The new batsman, wicketkeeper Ian Smith, ran a couple of twos after swipes to the leg side, but then hit across the line again and was bowled by one that kept low.

New Zealand now needed six runs off the final ball to tie, an event that would guarantee the series going the full five-match distance, regardless of the result of game four two days later. As he sat with his head on his knees, waiting for the next man at the crease, Greg Chappell was well aware of that fact. 'I don't know that I was necessarily thinking about much at all,' he would tell the makers of the documentary, *Underarm*.

In his autobiography, however, he elaborated. 'I was sick of the MCG, sick of the constant travelling and being away from home and, probably for the first time in my life, sick of cricket,' he said. 'I was fed up with a thousand little things that all came to a head in that moment. I was beyond caring … After the great gamble of World Series, we were back to where we were in 1977. Or worse. The men who ran the game didn't care, weren't listening. I remember thinking as I walked up to Trevor from deep mid-on, "This is what I think of it all – cop this!"'

With that, and remembering West Indian paceman Wayne Daniel hitting a last-ball six to beat Australia in a Packer game, he issued his instructions to his brother. 'I wouldn't have asked anyone else to do it,' he would admit.

Unaware of what was about to transpire, McKechnie had walked to the crease calculating his best chance of scoring the necessary runs. 'It's a long walk out there and the shortest hit is straight,' he explained. 'I'm thinking that Trevor is a similar bowler to me: if I was bowling, where would I bowl to stop someone hitting the ball for six? I thought he is probably going to bowl it full and straight or similar to what he bowled to Smith, which was shorter in length and didn't bounce much. I'm thinking that I've got to advance to try to get it on the half-volley and hit it back over his head. That all got turned on its head when I got out there.

'I went to take guard and the umpire at the bowlers' end was walking over to the square leg umpire. I thought he was probably just checking that it's the final ball of the game. Then he came over to me and said the bowler was going to bowl underarm. You are stunned. You never thought that would happen. I remember I sort of walked up and down the wicket a couple of times trying to figure out what I do now.'

McKechnie remains too much of a gentleman to want to share what he said as he reached the bowler's end, but he added, 'In the end, the only thing I could think of was that I can't hit a six if the balls rolls along the ground and I'm not going to have a swing and get bowled by it and look like an idiot, so I have to just block it.'

Looking back, Greg Chappell wished someone had stopped him going through with his plan, but it was certainly not going to be Trevor, who concerned himself with following orders rather than asking any moral questions. McKechnie, meanwhile, still wonders what would have happened had Lillee been the bowler. 'On that day, Dennis might have been easier to hit for six because of the bounce on the wicket. When Ian Smith was bowled it was because he was trying to hit the ball through midwicket and it was only about eight inches off the ground. Dennis would probably have just told Greg to go and get stuffed – or something in more direct terms. It's poor Trevor I feel sorry for to this day.'

Lillee, who wrote in 2003 that 'Greg still regrets his decision', confirmed, 'If it had been me, I would have said no way. My attitude would have been if you don't think I am good enough to bowl a ball and not be hit for six, then don't ask me to bowl. I would have flatly refused … but Greg would not have asked me because he would have known what the answer would be.'

Edgar, in fact, remains convinced that Lillee deliberately stood inside the fielding circle for the final ball in the hope that a no ball would be called, although he has never found video or photographic evidence to prove that and his email to Lillee asking him about it went unanswered.

Chappell junior duly executed his task perfectly, rolling the ball directly towards the stumps without a hint of bounce. McKechnie blocked it disdainfully and tossed his bat away. 'It was a sad way to end what was a fine game of cricket,' he said. Booing broke out around the MCG as Chappell collected his cap from the umpire and turned to leave the field; any sense of victory replaced by an apparent desire to exit the scene of the crime as quickly as possible.

Passing the players on their way back to the dressing rooms was Howarth, intent on arguing with the umpires that what had happened was illegal. In England, Howarth played for Surrey under playing conditions that outlawed underarm bowling, but Chappell had been fully aware that no such law existed in Australia. Nobody had thought it was required.[4]

Marsh offered Howarth an apology and arrived back in a dressing room where 'you could have heard a pin drop'. It was Australian selector Sam Loxton, a member of the 1948 'Invincibles' team, who broke the silence, coming close to tears as he told the players, 'You may have won the game but you lost a lot of friends.'

McKechnie described the scene waiting for him in the New Zealand camp. 'Someone had smashed glass around the room and lights had been smashed. But by the time we were leaving an hour and a half later we were just trying to laugh about it, not knowing how much it would blow up.'

The reaction reached the highest governmental levels, with Australian Prime Minister Malcolm Fraser saying it was 'a great pity that it occurred', and his furious New Zealand counterpart Robert Muldoon describing the incident as 'an act of cowardice'. Muldoon added, 'I thought it was most appropriate that the Australian team was dressed in yellow,' while New Zealand Cricket Council chairman Bob Vance called it the 'worst sporting action I have seen in my life'.

The *Melbourne Age* was preparing an editorial in which it said, 'Australian cricket is in disgrace today and the country's reputation as a sporting nation severely damaged ... while we appreciate the pressures under which Greg Chappell acted we must also realise that he is an experienced and cool-headed cricketer. In this sense his decision was shameful.'

Benaud had told his Channel 9 viewers that this was 'one of the worst things I have ever seen done on a cricket field'. He put Greg Chappell's 'disgraceful performance' down to the fact that he mismanaged his bowlers, failing to ensure that Lillee had the final over. Chappell always disputed that, but even if it was true then it simply lent weight to his mitigation that 'I wasn't even aware until that moment of just how strung out I was and just how unfit to captain Australia I was'.

---

4 As well as banning underarm bowling, England had recently outlawed declarations in limited-overs games, a measure taken after Brian Rose closed Somerset's innings against Worcestershire after one over in a Benson and Hedges Cup group game in 1979. Rose's action preserved his team's overall run rate and guaranteed qualification for the quarter-finals

In modern, more enlightened times, the mental health challenges faced publicly by many high-profile cricketers mean that Chappell's actions would have been scrutinised more closely for a deeper underlying cause than mere gamesmanship or, as some said, 'cheating'.

Chappell's ghostwriter, Malcolm Knox, called his actions 'a public dramatisation of his private mental breakdown' and noted that the 'stigma would have been less if we had all known that the underarm ball was not a cynical ploy but an inarticulate cry for help'. Back then, though, no one would have thought to accuse Richie Benaud of lack of empathy when he said, 'We keep reading and hearing that the players are under a lot of pressure, and they are tired and jaded and perhaps their judgement and skill is blunted. Well, perhaps they might advance that as an excuse for what happened out there today. Not with me they don't.'

Chappell felt that Benaud 'ignored the fact that he and every other Australian captain has made mistakes under less pressure'. And while he would explain that his mental state informed his snap decision to rail against 'everything that was wrong about this new format', he has never attempted to argue that the exact nature of his protest was justified or excusable. He did make a knee jerk post-match comment that 'in my opinion it was fair play', but he would come to see that as a further indication of his poor mental state. A day later, he was persuaded by the ACB to issue a further statement:

> I have always played cricket within the rules of the game. I took a decision yesterday which, whilst within the laws of cricket, in the cold light of day I recognise as not being within the spirt of the game. The decision was made whilst I was under pressure and in the heat of the moment. I regret the decision. It is something I would not do again.

As well as persuading him to condemn his own actions, the ACB announced that it 'deplored Greg Chappell's decision' and regretted not 'foreseeing the need to include in the playing conditions a rule to prevent such an occurrence'. A rule to that effect was implemented immediately. Legal advisers told the ACB it could run into trouble if it chose to sack its captain for doing something that was legal at the time, although Chappell – who had already decided to miss the tour of England later in the year – looked back and said, 'They wouldn't have got any argument from me, I can promise you that.'

It was Chappell, then, who continued to lead Australia in the fourth final two days later, by which time Edgar had come to realise how insignificant his unbeaten century at Melbourne would be in the history of his sport. 'The Aussies had been training and we were walking into the training area,' he explained. 'Rod Marsh opened the gate for me and said, "Hi, Bruce. How you going, mate? Did you play in that game down in Melbourne? Because you would never have read about it." New Zealand was too busy declaring war on Australia to worry about my hundred.'

At the toss, Chappell said unconvincingly, 'I don't feel any more pressure than for any other game.' The hostility of the Sydney Cricket Ground crowd when he went out to bat showed what the public felt, prompting Howarth to tell him, 'You don't seem to be too popular out here,' as he gave him a pat and wished him good luck. Chappell remembered Howarth's actions as 'probably the greatest act of sportsmanship I ever was on the receiving end of'. And the standing ovation he received after a match-winning innings of 87 showed that the fickle public were quick to offer their own forgiveness.

Even when he next played in New Zealand the following season, redemption went with him. Someone in the Eden Park crowd welcomed him to the crease by sending a lawn bowls wood rolling out towards the middle, but by the time he was dismissed for 108 it was mostly cheers being delivered in his direction. 'It was quite a moving experience because it was the last thing I expected to happen,' he said.

Also unexpected to the New Zealand players had been the elevated place in their country's affections that they now seemed to occupy. 'We were superstars when we got back home,' said Edgar. 'The grounds were full and people were standing up and cheering us. In a way, the whole thing had been good for the game because it put bums on seats.'

It says much for Chappell's stature as a cricketer that events at the MCG, while an important part of his life story, have not defined him or tarnished his legacy as one of the most elegant batsmen to have graced the game. Sadly, for Trevor Chappell – a journeyman all-rounder without a similar resumé of great feats to fall back on – it is the one thing for which the sport remembers him. That is the biggest regret Greg has about the episode, calling his sibling 'an innocent bystander'.

Trevor Chappell acknowledges the incident as 'a piece of baggage you keep leaving and then somebody says, "Here you are, mate. This belongs to you."' Yet he insists he holds no animosity towards Greg. Nor, when he spoke to the *Underarm* documentary crew, did he claim it had 'messed up my life in any way'.

However, when Australia suffered its next great embarrassment, the 2018 sandpaper scandal in South Africa, it was Trevor Chappell who was sought out to give some insight on what a lifetime of shame might do to Steve Smith, David Warner and Cameron Bancroft. 'I was vilified for years and people will still ask about it,' he told the *Sydney Daily Telegraph*. And when he said that 'the quiet life certainly chose me after that – my marriage broke down and I never remarried or had kids' it was easy to infer that he was putting the blame for that on the infamy that he achieved on that fateful day.

'That was total bollocks,' said Ian Chappell in 2019. 'He is not affected by the bloody thing. Like a lot of other people, he is sick to death of hearing about the damn thing. He copped it on the chin and that is the way he is. I disagreed with Greg doing it in the first place – I don't have to defend Greg … he will handle it in his own way.'

Whether or not one considers Greg Chappell a villain or victim, the events of Melbourne can be considered a result and reflection of the development of limited-overs cricket and its expanding importance to the sport's wellbeing. Or, as reader William Penrose said in a letter to the *Melbourne Age*, 'Blame the takeover of the game by big business and big money and the resulting mania to win at all costs. It was not cricket, but it was Packer-ball.'

AUSTRALIA v NEW ZEALAND, Benson and Hedges World Series (3rd final)

1 February 1981, Melbourne Cricket Ground

Australia			Balls	4s	6s
AR Border	c Parker b Hadlee	5	8		
GM Wood	b McEwan	72	114	4	
*GS Chappell	c Edgar b Snedden	90	122	7	
MF Kent	c Edgar b Snedden	33	38	2	
†RW Marsh	not out	18	13	1	
KD Walters	not out	6	5		
Extras	(b 8, lb 3)	11			
Total	(4 wickets, 50 overs)	235			

Fall: 8, 153, 199, 215
Did Not Bat: KJ Hughes, GR Beard, TM Chappell, DK Lillee, MHN Walker
Bowling: Hadlee 10-0-41-1; Snedden 10-0-52-2; Cairns 10-0-34-0;
McKechnie 10-0-54-0; McEwan 7-1-31-1; Howarth 3-0-12-0

New Zealand			Balls	4s	6s
JG Wright	c Kent b GS Chappell	42	81	4	
BA Edgar	not out	102	141	7	
*GP Howarth	c Marsh b GS Chappell	18	24	2	
BL Cairns	b Beard	12	10	2	
MG Burgess	c TM Chappell b GS Chappell	2	5		
PE McEwan	c Wood b Beard	11	18		
JM Parker	c TM Chappell b Lillee	24	19	1	
RJ Hadlee	lbw b TM Chappell	4	2	1	
†IDS Smith	b TM Chappell	4	3		
BJ McKechnie	not out	0	1		
Extras	(lb 10)	10			
Total	(8 wickets, 50 overs)	229			

Fall: 85, 117, 136, 139, 172, 221, 225, 229
Did Not Bat: MC Snedden
Bowling: Lillee 10-1-34-1; Walker 10-0-35-0; Beard 10-0-50-2; GS Chappell 10-0-43-3;
TM Chappell 10-0-57-2.

Australia won by 6 runs. Toss: Australia **Umpires:** PM Cronin, DG Weser.
Man of the Match: No award.

7

'IF WE CAN DO IT ONCE, WHY NOT AGAIN?'

India v West Indies, 2nd One-Day International, 1983, Albion

If the story of India's unlikely, game-changing triumph in the 1983 World Cup has an identifiable starting point then it is appropriate that it should be in the Caribbean territory of Guyana, among the Indian-descended people who form the largest section of that country's diverse population. The narrative developed further among the colourful blooms in England's garden county of Kent, before climaxing amid the commotion and carnival of north-west London, but it was a breakthrough victory on the northern mainland of South America that provided the first significant chapter.

India would go into the 1983 tournament having only won one of their six previous World Cup games, against East Africa in 1975. A competition structure that now saw teams meet twice in the group stages seemed only to increase their opportunities to be found wanting in a format of cricket in which they were still disregarded, even though they had scheduled 27 ODIs between the second and third global tournaments, as opposed to only five in the four years leading up to the 1979 event. They won only ten of those games, though, and writer Scyld Berry had observed a year earlier that the Indian limited-overs game 'does not have the importance to lure cricketers away from the traditional virtues. They remain three- and five-day players'.

Yet seam bowler Madan Lal had seen some progress since being part of India's first Word Cup campaign. 'Most of the players were experienced players and we played a lot of one-day cricket,' he recalled. 'It was not like we were going to win the World Cup, but there was a seriousness there. In 1975 there was no seriousness.' It was events in Guyana's country region of Berbice in March 1983, less than three months before the World Cup, that imbued that more serious approach with a genuine sense of hope, even some belief.

One down after the first two Tests of their West Indies tour and losers of the first one-day international, India were expected to be routinely beaten again when they, along with their opponents and various members of the media, boarded military aircraft in Georgetown to be flown south-east down the coast to the little town of Albion, originally a major sugar plantation. Venue for two previous one-day internationals, the Albion Sports Complex put on its finery for the visit of a touring team sure to attract large local support. Indian workers had arrived in Guyana to work the plantations in large numbers in the mid-1800s and many locals still spoke Hindi. Traditional religious festivals were observed as part of their preserved ancestral culture. Meanwhile, the Indo-Caribbean population had produced many fine West Indies players; men such as World Cup winners Rohan Kanhai and Alvin Kallicharran.

It meant that the temporary stands constructed amid the greenery in order to house a crowd of 15,000 were divided in their loyalties. The fact that the match coincided with the Indian festival of Holi – celebrating the victory of good over evil – added to the carnival nature of the occasion.

Appropriately, and poignantly, the key figures for India on this day would be Sunil Gavaskar, deposed as captain after a 3-0 Test series defeat against Pakistan, and Kapil Dev, the dashing 24-year-old all-rounder who had replaced him as leader. According to author Ashis Ray in his study of India's history in the shorter game, the transition of leadership was significant. 'India's reticence in one-day cricket stemmed from the fact that Sunil Gavaskar had either been their pre-eminent batsman or captain during the evolution of the limited-overs game onto the international stage. At a time when Test cricket held centre-stage his percentage batting was crafted to India's needs. It was not because he lacked flair, but because he hated to lose.'

But now came Kapil, who 'was of a different mould'. Handsome, lithe and athletic, he uncoiled into his fast-medium bowling action like a cobra and struck the ball with power, purpose and lack of inhibition. Where India's team had previously been characterised by Gavaskar's doggedness and a group of spinners who could barely hit or field a ball between them, the presence – and ultimate promotion – of Kapil was a modernising influence.

In the field, he drove his team to reach the levels that were becoming the standard for any team hoping for limited-overs success.

To the point where he would eventually write, 'The subsequent transformation can be put down to one specific branch in which India learned to excel – fielding. It would have been impossible in the era of the great spinners for India to be any kind of force in one-day cricket.' An example, he felt, was the bespectacled slow left-armer Dilip Doshi, who played the last of his 15 ODIs under Gavaskar during the Pakistan tour. 'It must be said he was one of the worst fielders in the team,' Kapil said. 'His work on the field was pathetic.'

India's prowess in the field could wait on this occasion, with West Indies captain Clive Lloyd winning the toss and choosing to unleash his four fast bowlers. Accompanied by a makeshift opener in Ravi Shastri, Gavaskar was quickly on the offensive, cutting and driving to force Michael Holding and Andy Roberts out of the attack. The man who had batted 60 overs for 36 runs in the inaugural World Cup match eight years earlier reached a half-century off only 52 balls as the opening bowlers and debutant Winston Davis went for more than five an over. Only Malcom Marshall applied any semblance of control, which made it strange that he bowled only seven overs in the innings.

The score had reached 93 when Shastri, who would hit sixes in an over in a first-class game two years later, was dismissed by Marshall for a relatively circumspect 30. Mohinder Amarnath, a key figure in the coming weeks, helped add a further 59 runs before Gavaskar was run out ten short of his first century in one-day internationals. His innings, which included eight fours, had taken only 117 balls, an uncommonly high strike-rate for an opening batsman in the era.

With Lloyd having to combine the part-time spin of Larry Gomes and Viv Richards as his fifth bowler, Kapil was determined to keep West Indies under pressure, promoting himself to number four and launching into all-out attack. So disconcerted did Lloyd appear by Kapil's assault, which brought him 72 from 38 deliveries, that he allowed Gomes and Richards to bowl 16 overs between them, at the cost of 108 runs. Three sixes and seven fours flew from Kapil's bat and by the time Amarnath was bowled by Richards he had scored only 30 of the 131 runs scored while he was at the crease, happily ceding strike to his free-scoring partners.

After Kapil fell at 246, Yashpal Sharma and Dilip Vengsarkar hustled India through to 282 for 5 off the 47 overs that were allowed in the allotted time. Despite the loss of three overs, West Indies had never conceded more runs in an ODI. Suddenly, they didn't seem so invincible, especially when they slipped to 22 for 2 after Balwinder Sandhu trapped Desmond Haynes lbw and Kapil took a return catch to remove Gordon Greenidge.

Richards, of course, could make any team he played for appear unbeatable. While he was thrashing 64 off only 51 balls, with 11 fours and a six, India's total didn't seem so mighty after all, even with Lloyd having been caught by Amarnath off Madan Lal in the meantime. Yet when Richards lost his stumps to Madan Lal with the score on 98, the target retreated back into the distance.

Faoud Bacchus and Gomes were left to rebuild, settling for taking advantage of anything loose while prioritising the preservation of their wickets, an approach that allowed Gomes to score at almost a run a ball until he fell to Shastri for 26. As tension between the Afro-Caribbean and Indo-Caribbean sections of the crowd grew to the point of scuffles, Bacchus took the score to 181 before Shastri persuaded him to deliver a catch to Yashpal for 52. Then Marshall became the slow left-armer's third victim and, at 192 for 7, India were almost home. Jeffrey Dujon's unbeaten half-century was not enough to get them anywhere near and Kapi and Sandhu bowled tidily in the final stages to restrict the home team to 255 for 9. Other than when their team had been weakened by the non-selection of Kerry Packer's players, it was West Indies' first home defeat in a one-day international and India's first limited-overs win against them anywhere.

Quite simply, it was a result that no one had foreseen. And, according to Ray, 'I don't think many people realised the enormity of the win straightaway.' That was even truer when India lost the deciding ODI and went on to complete a 2-0 defeat in the five-Test series. But Kapil sensed that things were changing within the Indian team. For a start, he had seen their fielding hold up under pressure. 'We had one or two men who were not exactly hares on the field, but the general improvement in the fielding effort made the victory in that one-day international epochal,' was his verdict a few years later. More importantly were the indications of a new character in the side. 'It was this particular win which helped convince many of us that we could pull our weight together as a team in one-day cricket.'

Kris Srikkanth, who would open with Gavaskar in the World Cup, recalled, 'I can vividly recall the talk Kapil Dev had with the team before [it] started. He made us believe that the West Indies were beatable.'

The skipper's simple message before the opening game against West Indies at Old Trafford was, 'If we can do it once, why not another time?' No reason whatsoever – as proved by a comfortable victory in which Yashpal made a decisive 89. 'The first win gave us confidence and we were charged,' Madan Lal recalled.

But after beating Zimbabwe, India then lost to Australia and West Indies by wide margins before heading to Kent's rhododendron-bordered Nevill Ground in Tunbridge Wells to face Zimbabwe again. Yet to earn Test status, the World Cup newcomers had proved they were doing more than making up the numbers by beating Australia on the opening day of the tournament behind an exceptional all-round performance by Duncan Fletcher. The future head coach of England and India made an unbeaten 69 before taking the first four Australian wickets.

Kapil won the toss and elected to bat, something of a surprise to teammates with whom the skipper, unusually, had not shared his intention on the eve of the game. 'He informed Sunil as we were warming up,' wicketkeeper Syed Kirmani explained. 'If you are informed at the last moment it becomes very difficult, particularly for those players who started building up for the game from the previous night. Sunny was so furious hearing that we would bat first. All of a sudden he was told to pad up. He rushed into the dressing room and psychologically he wasn't prepared.' The out-of-form Gavaskar, who had been left out of the previous two matches, was hardly bosom buddies with his captain in the first place.

Kapil went off for a shower in anticipation of going in much later in the day at number six. Before long he was summoned urgently by a teammate. 'Skipper, we are two down.' After a scramble to get ready, he was walking out to bat at 9 for 4. 'It was cold and the ball was moving,' recalled Gavaskar, who'd been dismissed second ball. 'It looked like we would be bowled out for 70 or 80.' Even more so when the fifth wicket went at 17, at which point tailenders like Kirmani, who been enjoying a leisurely breakfast, frantically started pulling on kit and equipment.

Without knowing what would happen to Australia against West Indies on the same day, the Indian supporters feared another early end to a World Cup campaign. All-rounder Roger Binny stuck around to help his skipper take the score to 77 but India were still limping along at 110 for 7 at lunch, Kapil having not long reached a half-century. Fletcher was criticised for not having allowed opening bowlers Peter Rawson and Kevin Curran bowl their full allocation of 12 overs when India were struggling, while Zimbabwe wicketkeeper Dave Houghton recalled, 'The wicket took that little bit of extra time to dry itself out and it played quite nicely after lunch. Kapil changed gear.'

Gavaskar added, 'Kapil did not play any lofted drives till he reached 80. It was amazing to see him hit those sixes.' He would end with six of them, along with 16 fours. According to Houghton, 'He didn't miscue one ball. Everything that he went for he hit like a tracer bullet on the ground or like a missile out the ground.'

When Kapil clipped a Fletcher full toss towards mid-on he passed New Zealander Glenn Turner's World Cup-record score of 171, and when the innings closed at 266 for 8 from 60 overs, he was 175 not out off 138 balls. He had seen Madan Lal stick around to help him add 62 for the eighth wicket, before Kirmani contributed 24 to an unbroken partnership of 126.

India went on to win by 31 runs and the game went down in the mythology of limited-overs cricket, partly because there is no footage of Kapil's historic innings. Not only was it not one of the day's two games selected for live television coverage, an industrial dispute at the BBC meant that there was not even a single news camera there to capture events. The only visual record of the day exists through the archives of a couple of photographic agencies and their striking images of Kapil in full flight against a vivid floral backdrop.

As it happened, as far as the points table was concerned, the result was irrelevant. Whether they'd won or lost against Zimbabwe, India's progress to the semi-finals would be determined two days later against Australia, who had been beaten by West Indies in their penultimate group game. But it is reasonable to assume that without the reviving nature of Kapil Dev's innings, they would have found it more difficult to meet the next challenge at Chelmsford, where they shot out Australia cheaply to win by 118 runs. 'That innings gave the team the reassurance that, yes, we have the ability and we can win against any circumstances,' said Kapil.

The two medium-pacers who had dug in with Kapil at Tunbridge Wells – Binny and Madan Lal – each took four wickets against Australia, underscoring the importance of journeymen players being able to perform above themselves and ensuring that the Indian team was becoming greater than the sum of its parts. Even so, few people watching India's semi-final against England at Old Trafford expected it to result in anything other than determining one half a rematch of the 1979 final.

Not that England had reached the last four on the back of any great preparation and focus. 'This is what England thought of it,' said Graeme Fowler. 'All the teams assembled at Lord's for a massive tournament photograph taken by Patrick Eagar. He went on the balcony and got the teams to stand in lines. Everybody had a tour uniform except England. We were told to buy a suit. Then we all went to Buckingham Palace. I was introduced to the Queen and she actually said to me, "Why don't you have a uniform?" How embarrassing is that? That is what they thought of one-day cricket at that time.'

Fowler's opening partnership of 69 with Chris Tavaré, halted in the 17th over, was typical of England's standard approach to constructing an ODI innings. Four years earlier, they'd never threatened to chase down the West Indies' total of 286 in the final after Geoffrey Boycott and Mike Brearley had spent more than 38 overs compiling a 129-run opening partnership. Now Tavaré maintained a strike rate below 50 runs per 100 balls through the tournament, although on this occasion he and Fowler were not helped by a slow wicket that seam-bowling teammate Paul Allott described as 'more Mumbai than Manchester'. A regular procession of wickets thereafter saw the host team bowled out for 213, a total India passed with more than five overs remaining for the loss of only four wickets. Amarnath was Man of the Match after adding 46 to his bowling figures of 2 for 27, while Yashpal Sharma and Sandeep Patil both made half-centuries. The winning runs were scored with all of England's fielders hovering close to the pavilion to prevent being engulfed by an invasion of jubilant Indian supporters.

The disappointment of English fans was probably shared by most neutrals, who gave India little chance of making it much of a spectacle at Lord's. They might have beaten West Indies in an apparently meaningless game in Guyana and again early in the competition, but that latter defeat was the champions' only reverse in 16 World Cup games and didn't appear to matter. Look at the West Indies top four: Gordon Greenidge and Desmond Haynes, establishing themselves as one of the greatest opening pairings in the history of the sport, followed by Viv Richards and Clive Lloyd, both scorers of centuries in World Cup finals. And then there was probably the finest fast bowling quartet ever to take the field: Andy Roberts, Michael Holding, Malcolm Marshall and Joel Garner. As John Woodcock put it in *The Times*, 'No one in his right mind will confidently expect [India] to win.'

The Indian players, however, would cash in whatever the result. Srikkanth recalled them being told on the eve of the game that they were to receive a bonus of 25,000 rupees, win or lose. 'At that time our total tour fee was only five or ten thousand. We never ever thought about that kind of money. That probably gave us a lot of encouragement.'

With many Indian fans arriving on flights from home on the morning of the match, most of the Indian players – who knew they had already overachieved – were more worried about getting enough tickets for family members and friends than living up to any expectations in the final. Meanwhile, the half-dozen or so Indian journalists who had followed the entire tournament had their own issues of access to worry about. 'Since India were expected to be wooden-spooners, the Indian press corps' accreditation did not include a seat in the press box for the final,' explained Ayaz Memon. 'But we were not to be denied accreditation for the match, and we duly got it after some haggling.'

Kapil chose not to attempt any elaborate pre-match rhetoric in the dressing room. 'When you start winning you don't have to say much to the team. The team starts motivating itself,' he explained. Besides, his own performances – the feats that had seen him bracketed alongside Ian Botham and Imran Khan as the great swashbuckling all-rounders of the era – were sufficient inspiration for many. Zimbabwe's Fletcher had seen enough to remark, 'He was a tremendous player and he influenced that side just by his all-round ability. Like a lot of players like that he led from the front. If he had to bowl the overs he would do it; if he had to score runs quickly he would do it.'

Kapil, who had started as a slow bowler, always felt he had a licence to take risks and play naturally as a batsman because it was the second string to his bow. As a captain – perhaps aware of the failure of Botham as England's skipper, and maybe even the struggles of the greatest of all-rounders, Garry Sobers, in leading West Indies – he was keen to be seen as a more thoughtful figure. 'I want to be a captain who inspires through tactics as well as performance,' he said before the final.

Despite winning two previous finals after being inserted, Lloyd chose to let India bat first on what had been among the quickest and liveliest surfaces used in the tournament. When Kapil had seen how seen how much grass was on the wicket, he'd thought, 'What the hell is happening? This is not a one-day pitch, this is something unfair.' And his worst fears were realised when Gavaskar, who had an outstanding Test record against West Indies, edged Roberts to wicketkeeper Jeffrey Dujon for 2. He was replaced by Amarnath, whose two hundreds and an average of 66.44 in the recent Test series in the Caribbean proved that he made up in courage for any technical deficiencies he might have had against fast bowling – by which he had a habit of being struck frequently throughout his career. While Amarnath, who carried a lucky red handkerchief in his pocket, knuckled down to grinding out 26 off 80 balls, Srikkanth adopted an approach that changed little, whatever the surface or the opposition.

Writing in *The Observer*, Scyld Berry described the flashy, right-handed Srikkanth as 'part-Rajput, part cheeky Cockney lad with a tuppeny whistle'. And teammate Binny recalled of the man they called Cheeka, 'If [he] hadn't been a cricketer he could have been a comedian or an actor. We needed a person like Srikkanth in the team. When we were nervous he would fall over a kit bag or throw a cigarette in a kit bag and cause havoc in the dressing room. We needed someone to break that tension and pressure in those big games of ours.'

Having done well to glove a rising ball from Garner to safety, Srikkanth slashed him over the slips, hooked Roberts for four and six and then square drove Garner while down on one knee. 'It has to be one of my most gratifying knocks, considering it was a World Cup final and the team needed to get off to a good start,' he said. 'I just played my natural game and was a bit lucky that some of the shots came off.' Not long after slamming Holding down the ground, he played across the line to Marshall and was walking back to the pavilion before Dickie Bird even had the chance to raise his finger; out for 38 from a total of 59 for 2.

The remainder of India's innings became a battle to score runs against part-time off-spinner Gomes and ensuring they used up as many of their 60 overs as possible. A stubborn 10th-wicket partnership between Kirmani and Balwinder Sandhu got them into the 55th, Sandhu having been struck a fierce blow on the helmet by a Marshall bouncer. 'I can't think that is the right way to play the game of cricket,' offered former England batsman Tom Graveney in the TV commentary box. An all-out total of 183 seemed far from the kind of score to challenge a mighty batting order.

Kapil's message to his team was, 'Don't give it up easily. Let's make them work for it.' His logic was, 'It is only a small number, but if you count it, it is a hell of a long time to make 183 – so let's give the opponent a tough time.' And he offered his men a final reminder that 'these three hours could be the only time we have in our life' to go out and make history.

The West Indian openers took guard in their caps; no helmets needed against an attack that, Kapil apart, bore the look of a group of English county dibbly-dobbly seamers. But Hampshire's Greenidge should have played enough John Player League games to be on his guard against the effectiveness of such attacks. Instead, having scored one run and played with circumspection against the Indian captain, he watched the scarlet-turbaned Sandhu tiptoe his way to the crease and stood without playing a shot as the ball cut back up the Lord's slope and removed his bails.

'The Greenidge wicket gave us hope,' Sandhu recalled. 'None of us could contain our excitement. Srikkanth was the most excited, of course. He never needed a reason to be excited. Kapil Dev told us all to calm down.'

Just as in Berbice, Richards appeared to be in a hurry. He pulled Sandhu for four and scored boundaries off Kapil with a push through mid-off and a whip through the leg side. Memories of his 138 in the final four years earlier – and two Lord's centuries for Somerset in county finals – were looming large when he drove and thrashed Madan Lal for three rapid boundaries. West Indies passed 50 in the 12th over, but Madan Lal, anxious not to be taken off, had gone to Kapil and said, 'He is after me. There is a chance of getting him out.' And after having Haynes caught at cover, he saw Richards swing a shortish delivery high into the leg side. 'Good shot,' remarked commentator Richie Benaud, not noticing Kapil racing back towards the boundary from midwicket. 'Not so good,' Benaud added. 'Beautifully caught. He's hit that away to within 15 yards of the boundary and the Indian skipper has done a tremendous job to get back there.'

Richards was gone for 33 off 28 balls and Kapil claimed in the post-game interview that 'he was playing for 30 overs, not 60 overs'. Sandhu remembered, 'My ball to get Greenidge out gave us a foot in the door, but it was Kapil's catch which opened the door for us.'

Madan Lal struck again, Gomes jabbing to Gavaskar at slip. And then Lloyd went; another loose drive into the covers off Binny. Umpire Barrie Meyer couldn't believe what he was seeing, describing the West Indies as 'rather over-eager'. He was 'convinced that had India got a larger total, say 220 or 230, the result might have been very different'. The confused state of the champions saw Bacchus almost run out before he snicked Sandhu's innocuous wide delivery into Kirmani's gloves.

As in previous finals, fans ran excitedly to the field to greet each wicket. Yet this time it was Indian followers celebrating at the expense of the now subdued West Indians. They had plunged to 76 for 6, all the wickets having fallen to India's unsung medium pacers. 'Everybody knew how to swing the ball and it was an advantage because if it was a flat pitch they would have murdered us,' said Kapil. 'The ball was seaming, and it was more difficult for them to handle the swing than [for] our batsmen to handle the pace.'

Lloyd admitted, 'We got complacent. If we had to make 283 our attitude might have been different, but 183 you think, well, you are going to knock this off.' As Holding pointed out, 'No one took it upon themselves to say, "I am going to be responsible for getting these runs."'

Instead it was left to Dujon and the fast bowlers. Binny sensed a tension and observed, 'They were not playing their normal shots – even Dujon who never plays the shot he got out to.' The wicketkeeper took 73 balls to get to 25 before playing on as he tried to withdraw his bat against Amarnath with the score on 119.

Amarnath, the most harmless-looking of all the Indian bowlers, got Marshall to fence at a wide delivery and it carried comfortably to Gavaskar. Then Kapil trapped Roberts lbw, reducing the West Indies to 126 for 9. In the radio commentary box, former Indian wicketkeeper Farokh Engineer was alongside Brian Johnston, who asked whether Indian Prime Minister Indira Gandhi would declare a national holiday if their team held on to win. 'If she is listening, I am sure she will,' Engineer replied. Within minutes, the BBC received a call saying that Mrs Gandhi had heard the comments and was doing just that. 'Next time I met Mrs Gandhi,' Engineer would recall, 'she said, "Thank you, Farokh. You helped me get a few more votes."'

After the score had nudged up to 140 in the 52nd over, the hitherto patient Holding swung towards leg against Amarnath. He was struck on the pad and saw Bird lift his finger. BBC Radio's Christopher Martin-Jenkins hailed 'the greatest upset in the history of all sport' and described the Indian players grabbing stumps and charging back to the pavilion through a stampede of fans. Sandhu, stationed at long-off at the Nursery End, had the most ground to cover. 'I picked up one stump when I reached the pitch but saw that the crowd had already reached me,' he explained. 'They tried to take the stump away from me, but I fought and fought and fought to hold on to it.'

So unprepared were India for their victory that Kapil visited the West Indian dressing room and, indicating a supply of champagne bottles, suggested to Lloyd, 'Skipper, I don't think you'll need so many now – we'll need a few.'

For his three wickets and his vigil of almost two hours at the crease, Amarnath was named Man of the Match for the second time in four days. But it was the photo of the Prudential Cup held aloft by the handsome, smiling Kapil – the recipient of plenty of criticism on his team's tour of the West Indies – that was wired round the world. That the sport had a new global superstar was indisputable. What no one could have foretold was the paradigm shift that the moment would come to signify.

According to Sunil Valson, a member of the 1983 squad, 'The board started getting commercial benefits only after the World Cup win and for us it was a game-changer ... it changed the passion, the trend. Money came into the sport much later, but certainly it was a great victory that came against any expectations.'

But it went way beyond that.

No Indian cricket fan would ever forget it, however much they might achieve in the game themselves. In Bombay, a 10-year-old Sachin Tendulkar was among those enjoying 'a landmark event in my life'. He said, 'I still recall my friends and I celebrating all the wickets, right from Sandhu's epic delivery to Greenidge to Kapil's catch. We jumped and celebrated the fall of each wicket. What an evening it was.' And Rahul Dravid echoed such recollections. 'I remember watching that final against the West Indies at home on TV in Bangalore as a 10-year-old. After 1983, people really believed we could be good at cricket, especially the one-day game. The victory did a lot to inspire young kids in India to take to the game.'

Youngsters unfamiliar with their nation's exploits in Olympic hockey – where their gold medal in 1980 had been their eighth overall but first since 1964 – were enjoying an unfamiliar experience. Victory was 'a sign that they could compete with the best in the world', said author Mihir Bose. 'Apart from their triumphs in hockey, now fading fast from the memory, this was the first major world championship India had won in sport and the emotional satisfaction it provided was immense.'

And, having discovered something at which they could rule the world, they wanted more of it. Amarnath, whose father Lala had been the nation's first Test centurion, noted, 'It's not that we didn't play good cricket earlier, but somehow we didn't have any achievement to show. Before this, it was only hockey that we were masters at, but after the 1983 World Cup victory all parents wanted their kids to play cricket, represent India and become a world champion.'

Srikkanth recalled, 'The end result that came out was a revolution; this victory changed the shorter format cricket. It also turned the tide for us, it shaped all the budding cricketers in India when Kapil Dev collected the trophy at Lord's. It was a monumental victory; it changed the landscape of Indian cricket.' So deeply would the moment resonate that almost four decades later Bollywood dramatised the events in a movie entitled simply *1983*.

India had not staged a single one-day international until 1982, but Bose recorded, 'Now suddenly one-day cricket became the rage and the subsequent history of Indian cricket is the story of one-day cricket challenging the traditional game and quickly, and devastatingly, taking over… Indians at all levels were increasingly excited and enthusiastic for the one-day game, but increasingly cool about Test cricket.'

By the time they played the first match in defence of their crown in 1987, India had played a further 73 ODIs. They wasted little time in including a full five-game ODI series in the West Indies' tour later in 1983, part of the total of 34 matches they hosted in that four-year period, along with playing 15 in the United Arab Emirates at Sharjah. The one-day games against Pakistan that followed quickly after the World Cup victory were much better attended than the three drawn Test matches.

The increase in volume and interest in the shorter version of the game prefaced expansion of the Indian television landscape, leaving the country's cricket authorities well placed to take advantage. National broadcasts had been introduced in 1982 – the same year as the first colour transmissions – but when the Indian economy opened up in the early 1990s private broadcasters entered the market to rival the public service Doordarshan network.

An Indian team that had proved it could take on the world was the prized broadcast property. 'Cricket in India was tamasha – entertainment – and it was time for Indians to move from one form of entertainment to another,' Bose concluded.

And it was time for the sport's global sands to shift irrevocably.

WEST INDIES v INDIA, 2nd One-Day International
29 March 1983, Albion Sports Complex, Berbice, Guyana

India			Balls	4s	6s
SM Gavaskar	run out	90	117	8	
RJ Shastri	c Dujon b Marshall	30	56	1	
M Amarnath	b Richards	30	34	2	
*N Kapil Dev	b Roberts	32	78	7	3
Yashpal Sharma	c Greenidge b Davis	23	26	3	
DB Vengsarkar	not out	18	19	1	1
AO Malhotra	not out	1	3		
Extras	(b 1, lb 9, w 4, nb 4)	18			
Total	(5 wickets, 47 overs)	282			

Fall: 93, 152, 224, 246, 277.
Did Not Bat: S Madan Lal, †SMH Kirmani, BS Sandhu, S. Venkataraghavan
Bowling: Holding 7-0-49-0; Roberts 9-0-44-1; Davis 8-0-40-1; Marshall 7-0-23-1; Gomes 10-0-64-0; Richards 6-0-44-1.

West Indies			Balls	4s	6s
CG Greenidge	c & b Kapil Dev	16	28	1	
DL Haynes	lbw Sandhu	2	7		
IVA Richards	b Madan Lal	64	51	11	1
CH Lloyd	c Amarnath b Madan Lal	8	4		1
SFAF Bacchus	c Yashpal Sharma b Shastri	52	65	3	1
HA Gomes	c Kapil Dev b Shastri	26	28	1	
†PJL Dujon	not out	53	64	3	1
MD Marshall	c Sandhu b Shastri	5	6		
AME Roberts	b Kapil Dev	12	10	1	1
MA Holding	c Malhotra b Sandhu	2	8		
WW Davis	not out	7	12		
Extras	(lb 6, w 1, nb 1)	8			
Total	(9 wickets, 47 overs)	255			

Fall: 5, 50, 57. 66, 66, 76, 119, 124. 126, 140.
Bowling: Kapil Dev 10-0-33-2; Sandhu 10-0-38-2; Madan Lal 9-0-65-2; Venkataraghavan 10-0-63-0; Shastri 8-0-48-3.

India won by 27 runs. **Toss:** West Indies. **Umpires:** DM Archer, MN Baksh.
Man of the Match: N Kapil Dev.

'RICHARDS SPOILT THE GAME'
England v West Indies, Texaco
Trophy 1984, Old Trafford

It was described at the time as the best one-day innings ever played. In 1984, there was no disputing that statement. Nor in 2002, when *Wisden* attempted to apply a scientific formula to ranking the game's greatest performances. Another two decades on, many batsmen have scored more runs in a single knock, but still the feats of Viv Richards at Old Trafford command a place of their own in the history of limited-overs cricket.

As usual for the period, the three-game Texaco Trophy series, beginning on the final day of May, was viewed as little more than warm-up for the real business of the England-West Indies Test series to follow; albeit with the additional interest aroused by David Gower taking over as captain of the home side from Bob Willis after the team's unhappy 1983-84 winter. Along with Test series defeats in New Zealand and Pakistan, there had been lurid headlines in the tabloids and the labelling of the first leg of the itinerary as the 'sex and drugs and rock 'n' roll tour'. 'I recognise that we have lost some of the goodwill of the man in the street,' Gower confessed. But after reducing West Indies to 102 for 7 on the first morning of the international summer – during which the gates were closed on a full house – England's rehabilitation was well underway. The only fly in the ointment was that Richards was still in.

Asked to bat first by Clive Lloyd, England were gifted a dream start after only five runs had been scored when Desmond Haynes tried to steal a quick leg bye against Ian Botham and was thrown out by the bowler even after he had slipped while fielding the ball. Botham grabbed a more orthodox success when Gordon Greenidge edged a delivery that moved away into the gloves of David Bairstow:11 for 2.

Richards, who had come in at number three, signalled his intentions by flicking Botham to the midwicket boundary, prompting a rueful smile from his close friend and Somerset teammate as if to encourage him to continue to take such chances. When the ball was pitched a little wider, Richards hit it on the up over extra cover for four more, taking 16 off the eighth over of the innings.

Here we were again. Richards had been exerting his brand of brutality on English bowlers for a decade. A sporting all-rounder who represented Antigua at both football and cricket as a teenager, he quickly became an icon to sports fans on his home island. The generous funding of the Antigua Volunteers Cricket Committee sent him and fellow-countryman Andy Roberts to play English club cricket in Taunton and Southampton respectively in 1973. While the skilful and fearsome Roberts quickly became the spearhead of Hampshire's bowling attack, the potential of Richards would be recognised by Somerset.

England's bowlers first encountered him on their 1973-74 tour of the Caribbean. Richards made runs in both innings for the Leeward Islands, a match for which off-spinner Pat Pocock was grateful to have been left out. 'This big bloke came in with broad shoulders like a barn door and a hook nose,' he explained. 'Next to the ground in Antigua was this big wooden church and Viv was blasting sixes off Jack Birkenshaw, knocking the shit out of him. It started raining and they came off for a couple of hours, so when it stopped the umpires went out to inspect the pitch. As they get halfway out, Birky goes to the balcony, claps his hand and yells, "Hey umpires! Don't worry about inspecting t'wicket, go and check the ground in the churchyard."'

Even before his Somerset debut, Richards won selection for the West Indies tour of India in 1974-75, scoring a century in his second Test match. After making his mark in the first World Cup final with his brilliance in the field, he dominated the 1976 tour of England with his bat. And his attitude. Included in his trio of three-figure Test scores was a pair of double-hundreds – including 291 at The Oval – that had England skipper Tony Greig choking on his threat to make the West Indies 'grovel'.

Richards was very different in character to the man whose mantle he had inherited as the superstar of West Indian cricket, Garry Sobers. Richards's heart beat to the politics of his people's long history of struggle. Sobers was the greatest all-rounder the game had seen but was driven by other factors. He saw no barrier to taking part in an exhibition tournament in Rhodesia at a time when that country's white government was under sanctions imposed by the United Nations. While Sobers and others said that sport and politics should never mix, Richards described playing cricket as 'in itself a political action'.

And while Sobers approached the crease with the air of a man intent on having a good time, Richards strode slowly, a gunslinger sauntering out into the main street of a western town at high noon. As he arrived in the middle at Old Trafford, the slap of his palm into the top of the handle of his Duncan Fearnley bat looked like he was arming it ready for destruction. Even the way he chewed his gum carried an air of intent. His very nonchalance oozed menace.

He seemed to save many of his best performances for an opponent who represented the white colonials who had once ruled his homeland. Having scored his first ODI century against England at Scarborough in 1976, his 138 against the host country decided the final of the second World Cup in 1979 and would be named in that *Wisden* survey of 2002 as the second-greatest ODI innings in history – behind his Old Trafford effort. By the start of the summer of 1984 he'd made three more Test centuries against England and would eventually reach eight in a career total of 24, including one off only 56 balls in Antigua in 1986.[5]

'The whole issue [of race and apartheid] is quite central to me,' Richards once wrote. 'I believe very strongly in the black man asserting himself in this world and over the years I have leaned towards many movements that followed this basic cause.' Michael Holding, meanwhile, described Richards as being 'fiercely conscious of what success meant for the West Indies and West Indian people'.

On a practical rather political level, it became even clearer how much responsibility rested upon him at Old Trafford when Richie Richardson pushed a gentle return catch to Bob Willis. And after Richards took a couple of boundaries off Neil Foster – an edged slash and a flick between two men deep on the leg side – he saw

---

[5]   The innings stood alone as the fastest in Test history for almost three decades until equalled by Pakistan's Misbah ul-Haq and then beaten by the 54-ball effort of New Zealand's Brendon McCullum against Australia in 2016.

Larry Gomes bowled by a ball that off-spinner Geoff Miller turned past the left-hander's push: 63 for 4.

The two runs that Richards nudged through midwicket off Foster took him to 51 off 59 balls from a total of 83, but six runs later Lloyd, who had entered to a standing ovation from his adoring Lancashire crowd, swept Miller to Derek Pringle on the deep square-leg boundary. When Jeffrey Dujon eventually got on strike for the first time he proceeded to sweep the first ball he faced and top-edged to Mike Gatting. West Indies could do without any further self-inflicted damage, but when Richards under-edged the ball as he tried to force Foster into the off side Malcolm Marshall went careering down the track and was unable to return in time to beat a direct throw by Bairstow. West Indies were now 102 for 7 and looking for the respite that lunch would bring.

At last the batting team appeared to be making progress as the afternoon began. Richards again steered Foster to the boundary and dabbed Pringle to leg to take the total past 150 in the 36th over. Eldine Baptiste, the least celebrated of the West Indies pace quartet, had reached a solid 26 when Botham cut one away off the seam and took his edge. And then Joel Garner pushed the ball into the hands of the bowler, Foster, and the West Indies' innings appeared close to termination at 166 for 9.

With his own score on 98, Richards swung Foster untidily for a single to long-on. He pushed Botham lazily to leg for what appeared to be the run he needed to reach three figures, but timed it so well that it went to the boundary. Taking off his cap, he raised both arms to the crowd; the red, gold and green band on his left wrist dominating the image on TV screens. His seventh ODI century had taken 112 balls, which might not appear that eye-catching in the 21st century – but even the big hitters of the IPL era would have appreciated the all-out assault he now launched.

Stepping back outside his leg stump, he cracked the ball past Foster for four and then executed the merest flick over midwicket to dump Botham into the pavilion for the first six of his innings. His mate's reaction was considerably less jovial than a few hours earlier. Again, Richards backed away against Foster and clubbed him straight for six. This was not typical of the man they called 'Master Blaster', whose signature was whipping balls in a blur through midwicket from outside the off stump. So much so that Pringle recalled a team dinner before a Test match where 'the plan was if you don't get Viv Richards out before he gets to 10 you have got to bowl the ball eight inches outside off stump. I bowled a ball that was probably 10 inches outside off stump and he whipped it over square leg.' When Gower told his bowler to 'remember the plan', Pringle told him to ask the wicketkeeper where he had bowled the ball. 'He could make a mockery of anybody.'

And now he was doing exactly that to Gower's guarding of the leg side by reversing his usual method. Foster's response was to pitch shorter, which meant that he saw a pull shot send the ball to the boundary behind square.

It was Pringle's turn back in the firing line, immediately being muscled over long-on for six. And Richards showed his contempt for the placing of two men on the deep straight boundary rope by repeating the shot over long-off to reach 150. It had taken only 35 more deliveries since reaching his century. Holding could not resist laughing as he shook his partner's hand in the middle. This was what John Woodcock meant when he wrote of Richards in *The Times*, 'His demeanour was captivating.'

Willis had got away relatively unscathed, conceding only 22 in 10 overs, but he was not immune. Richards stepped to leg, waited for Willis's slower delivery and forced it through extra cover for four. 'There can never have been a batting genius with greater strength than Richards,' Woodcock's account continued. 'His forearms are like a brace of 6lb trout, in the pink of condition.'

To a fuller ball, Richards anchored his back foot, cleared his front foot and swung ferociously into the rain-covers that sat beyond the long-off rope. 'I bowled at some pretty good players, including Sobers, Kanhai and Barry Richards,' Willis recalled. 'But in terms of batting ability Viv was head and shoulders above any of them. I can only imagine how good Bradman was, but if you look at Bradman batting, the field never changed – apart from the Bodyline series. Even with everybody on the boundary, Viv would still be scoring fours and sixes. For my money, he was the best batsman there has ever been. We are all guilty of thinking that people from our generation are the best players, but I can't imagine anybody ever being able to better him. He seemed to see the ball a whole second before anybody else.'

A hack at Pringle's full toss crossed the boundary on the first bounce, and Botham was dispatched on the off side and then wide of the long-on fielder as the 10th-wicket partnership passed 100. The last ball of the innings saw Richards again stationed outside leg stump to thump Botham back down the ground for his 21st four. Along with his five sixes, it took his final score to 189 not out. No man had ever scored more in a one-day international. It had taken him 170 balls and come from a final 55-over total of 272 for 9. He had scored 93 from 57 balls in his partnership of 106 with Holding, who rarely looked troubled in surviving 27 balls and contributing 12 runs.

Shortly after the turn of the century, *Wisden* devised its system to objectively rate the greatest individual performances in one-day cricket. As well as accounting for the individual scores, additional factors such as strength of opposition, pitch conditions and the impact of the performance on the eventual result were included in an algorithm that rated each innings out of 300. The Manchester innings played by Richards was rated at 257.59, almost 12 points ahead of his match-winning century in the 1979 World Cup final. A further four points behind in fourth place was the Kapil Dev World Cup masterpiece against Zimbabwe.[6]

The numbers might have offered a sketch of Richards's innings, but offered little of the vividness of his brilliance. The boundary count spoke of his power but could not capture the sharpness of his eye, the conviction that he was above the mayhem being perpetrated around him. 'Just as Bradman used to do, Richards spoilt the game,' Woodcock concluded after England could muster only 168 in reply. 'He turned what might otherwise have been a close match into a runaway victory.'

England did win the second game of the series, but Richards smashed another unbeaten 84 off 65 balls to settle the decider at Lord's, establishing a pattern for the summer that would see West Indies achieve their famous 5-0 'blackwash' in the Test series.

---

6 Rated as the best bowling performance at that time was Gary Gilmour's 6 for 14 for Australia against England in the 1975 World Cup semi-final.

ENGLAND v WEST INDIES, Texaco Trophy, First One-Day International

31 May 1984, Old Trafford

West Indies		Runs	Balls	4s	6s
CG Greenidge	c Bairstow b Botham	9	11	1	
DL Haynes	run out	1	5		
RB Richardson	c and b Willis	6	24		
IVA Richards	not out	189	170	21	5
HA Gomes	b Miller	4	17	1	
*CH Lloyd	c Pringle b Miller	8	21	1	
†PJL Dujon	c Gatting b Miller	0	1		
MD Marshall	run out	4	3		
EAE Baptiste	c Bairstow b Botham	26	49	2	
J Garner	c and b Foster	3	5		
MA Holding	not out	12	27	2	
Extras	(b 4, lb 2, w 1, nb 3)	10			
Total	(9 wickets, 55 overs)	272			

Fall: 5, 11, 43, 63, 89. 98, 102, 161, 166
Bowling: Willis 11-2-38-1; Botham 11-0-67-2; Foster 11-0-61-1; Miller 11-1-32-3; Pringle 11-0-64-0

England		Runs	Balls	4s	6s
G Fowler	c Lloyd b Garner	1	5		
TA Lloyd	c Dujon b Holding	15	42	2	
MW Gatting	lbw b Garner	0	5		
*D Gower	c Greenidge b Marshall	15	38		
AJ Lamb	c Richardson b Gomes	75	89	8	
IT Botham	c Richardson b Baptiste	2	6		
†DL Bairstow	c Garner b Richards	13	34	2	
G Miller	b Richards	7	24		
DR Pringle	c Garner b Holding	6	21		
NA Foster	b Garner	24	38	2	
RGD Willis	not out	1	2		
Extras	(lb 3, nb 3)	9			
Total	(50 overs)	168			

Fall: 7, 8, 33, 48, 51, 80, 100, 115, 162, 168.
Bowling: Garner 8-1-18-3; Holding 11-2-23-2; Baptiste 11-0-38-1; Marshall 6-1-20-1; Richards 11-1-45-2; Gomes 3-0-15-1

West Indies won by 104 runs. **Toss:** West Indies. **Umpires:** DJ Constant, DJ Shepherd.
Man of the Match: IVA Richards.

9

'CAN YOU EVER HAVE A GREATER FINISH THAN THIS?'

India v Pakistan, Austral-Asia Cup Final, 1986, Sharjah

The crowd, colourful and chaotic, had been arriving since dawn. The Pakistani and Indian fans squeezed themselves into the bleacher seats and unfurled their flags and banners, while the cream of Sharjah society rubbed shoulders with visiting film stars and celebrities, more intent with being seen at this most special of occasions than concerning themselves with who would win the final of the Austral-Asia Cup. The richer Indians, cynical observers noted, could be recognised by their lavish vehicles, exotic food and equally striking female companions.

Yet whether hardcore or hanger-on, none of the estimated 20,000 at the Sharjah Cricket Stadium could have imagined that the events of a holiday Friday in spring 1986 would become the stuff of bedtime stories and historical documentaries. 'The game began at 9.30,' recalled Pakistan batsman Ramiz Raja. 'From 9.35 we were behind in the game until almost five o'clock.' Until, in fact, Javed Miandad fired what might still be the most famous single shot in the history of limited-overs cricket.

That the international game had found a home in Sharjah, the third largest city in the United Arab Emirates, was a result of the boom years of oil production in the Gulf states throughout the 1970s. Investment from the subcontinent and the migration of labour from both Pakistan and India meant the tripling of the ex-patriot workforce in the UAE by the end of the decade. And, of course, cricket followed.

Significantly, Abdul Rahman Bukhatir, the son of a judge, had lived in Karachi and returned to Sharjah as a cricket fan. An entrepreneurial free spirit, he set up local tournaments and leagues, forming the Sharjah Cricket Association and extending invitations to Pakistani teams to come and play. Pakistan opener Mudassar Nazar recalled representing a Pakistan International Airlines team, along with Imran Khan and Majid Khan, in 1977. 'I remember that myself and Majid both scored hundreds. I remember that well, because we got paid for scoring hundreds.'

In 1981, Bakhatir staged a benefit for his hero Hanif Mohammad at the newly built Sharjah Cricket Stadium, with Javed Miandad's XI playing Sunil Gavaskar's XI in what was Pakistan versus India in all but name. The emergence of Sharjah as a viable international venue coincided with India consummating its new marriage to limited-overs cricket at the 1983 World Cup, and when Sharjah duly hosted the first Asia Cup one-day tournament in 1984 it established its place in the sport's calendar. In his history of Pakistan cricket, *The Unquiet Ones*, Osman Samiuddin describes 'a cultural blast' in which 'thousands upon thousands of Indians and Pakistanis converged on tournaments once, sometimes twice, a year.'

It was, he states, 'a place each could call home among their people', adding, 'Here they could pretend to have undone years of demonisation, and fraternise, or at least assume cricket to be a greater shared experience than politics, diplomacy or conflict.' For many years, especially in the 1990s, Sharjah would become the principal home of India-Pakistan cricket when governmental and military relationships between the two countries made sporting visits to each other's countries impossible.

To fully chronicle the history of conflict between the nations since the Partition of India had created two separate dominions in 1947 would take several volumes and still never be complete. And, as much as opposing players might find camaraderie within the no man's land inside the boundary ropes, any cricket match between India and Pakistan was imbued with the blood of the battlefield. 'For many Pakistanis, India is anathema: if it weren't, what was the point in separating from it at Partition?' wrote former United Nations Under-Secretary General Shashi Tharoor in *Shadows Across the Playing Field*. 'For most Indians, Pakistan is equally so, a state founded on religious intolerance. Such visceral mutual antipathy, even if it does not always bubble up to the surface, underlies much of the tension in the India-Pakistan cricketing relationship.'

According to Ramiz, 'Games against India challenge you temperamentally. There is a lot of stress. Every shot is magnified and discussed; every team selection, every team plan. Then you have the passion of the crowd, especially in Sharjah where there was a large ex-pat population and therefore huge pressure to do well.'

Mudassar recalled, 'It was very, very daunting playing in front of those crowds because the Indians and Pakistanis were mixed in together. None of us wanted to lose. Those who did not have the right temperament did not survive. I never felt under that kind of pressure anywhere else in the world.'

If anything, the strain felt by the players in a limited-overs game was greater than in a Test match, the last seven of which between the two nations had ended in draws; no loss of face or diminished national pride. Either side of a 17-year break in competition between the nations, from 1961 to 1978, there had been a sequence of 12 draws. In the shorter format there was no safe option, no hiding place – only the joy of victory or the national humiliation of defeat.

By 1986, Pakistan had been the poor relations for some time, despite being considered the more adept team during the 1970s because of their players' exposure to English county cricket. India's global triumph in 1983 had changed all that. Victory in their most recent clash – also at Sharjah five months earlier – was only Pakistan's second win in the previous eight games against India, a sequence beginning immediately after the World Cup. 'We were getting beaten most of the time by India, so there was a psychological barrier and this was a very significant game,' said Ramiz. 'We were also coming off a tour of Sri Lanka where our major batsmen had not scored runs.'

Pakistan, who had never won a multi-nation tournament of any kind, had, however, reached the final of this Austral-Asia Cup with comfort, dispatching Australia and New Zealand – all out for 64 – by eight and 10 wickets respectively. India had been tested a little more in low-scoring three-wicket wins against New Zealand and Sri Lanka.

Imran Khan and Kapil Dev, the great all-rounders, went out for the toss. The whitest of wickets was surrounded by an outfield bleached in places to only the merest hint of green. Beyond the outfield, the stands hummed and rocked. Imran had little hesitation in asking India to bat on a strip that looked likely to play well throughout the 100 overs. 'In India-Pakistan matches there are always butterflies, no matter how many Tests, how many one-dayers, how many years of cricket you have played,' he admitted.

The Indian openers had batting styles as distinct and different as their headgear. Kris Srikkanth favoured the grill-less helmet popular with most batsmen of the time, while the veteran Sunil Gavaskar's compromise to safety was to wear a plastic skull cap with temple protection underneath his white sun hat. But while Gavaskar's headwear might have tended more towards flamboyance than his partner's, it was Srikkanth who possessed the ability, and the mentality, to go on the attack from the start. 'I always felt it was better that you went after the bowling,' he explained. 'You might get out first ball, you might get 50, you might get 70 but you keep putting pressure on the opposition. That is what I tried to do and sometimes I did it quite convincingly.'

The first run of the match was a leg bye off an Imran inswinger. Gavaskar timed an on-drive back past bowler Wasim Akram for the first four, the ball rolling gently to a boundary marked by a rope and punctuated with red flags that stood proud in the breeze. The lean-looking left-armer's response was a bouncer that passed over Gavaskar's head, followed by a short no-ball that had the batsman hopping and another short one that was allowed to pass on the rise outside off stump.

'Gavaskar was always the batsman who gave us the most problems,' Imran admitted. 'There were times others also batted well, but our problem with Sunil was that he played the most calculated innings. His mind management was the best. He managed his innings better than anyone else and he read the game very well.'

Srikkanth, meanwhile, posed a more visceral threat, opening his shoulders to heave Manzoor Elahi over mid-off and slashing Wasim over point off the back foot, lifting himself off his feet with sheer effort. Another ball by Wasim was pulled to the rope in front of square. Gavaskar, meanwhile, took the score past 50 by hooking Elahi uppishly just out of reach of long leg, before Srikkanth, bare-headed now, top-edged Wasim wide of third man. It was the start that Imran had feared when he made his decision at the toss. 'It was an absolute paradise for batting,' he said. 'It was a wicket that totally favoured the batsmen and, of course, both Srikkanth and Gavaskar took full advantage of those conditions and batted superbly.'

Having flayed Mudassar to the vacant deep cover boundary and executed a front-foot cut for another four, Srikkanth had helped

India to 82 in the 18th over. When he pushed the next delivery for a single to long-off it brought up his half-century off 59 balls. Still it was Gavaskar who gave Imran greater concern. 'Because he was holding up one end, Srikkanth was able to do all the strokeplay and it was a devastating partnership for us,' he remembered.

According to Srikkanth, 'Sunny and I had built up a good cricketing relationship, creating a partnership. We knew each other very well. In the earlier match we had a hundred partnership against Sri Lanka, so this particular match both of us were in good form. There is nothing like opening with Sunil Gavaskar. When my grandchildren grow up I can tell them I opened with [him]. Sunny had also changed his attitude towards the one-day kind of batting. He was not just going to stick around and stay out there. He also started playing shots. He made matters pretty easy for me.'

Abdul Qadir, the leg-spinner who had been casting spells on batsmen around the world in the four years since becoming a regular in the Pakistan team, bounced in on his exaggeratedly diagonal run and, for a while, slowed the run rate. He conceded only three off his first two overs, allowing him to persist with a slip. But then Srikkanth advanced to hit him straight for six and achieved the same result with a cross-batted swipe that sailed over long-off. A square cut for three made it 15 off the over and took the score to 114.

Yet three runs later, Srikkanth was not quite at the pitch of the ball and could only lift Qadir to Wasim. 'It was an arrogant dismissal,' recalled Srikkanth, who had made 75 off 80 balls. 'I hit him for two sixes and was going for a third six, but I am a person who believes that somebody has to keep taking chances.'

Gavaskar, having been joined by Dillip Vengsarkar, reached his half-century by pushing Tauseef Ahmed to midwicket for a single and his partner raised the 150 in the 33rd over by cutting Qadir for two. Vengsarkar lifted Tauseef over the leg-side boundary for six, but when he tried to do the same to Qadir the ball landed in the hands of Miandad – and spilled out. Imran was driven into the covers by Vengsarkar to take the score past 200 and then it was his turn to drop the ball, after Gavaskar drove Wasim to mid-off. Vengsarkar's quick single on to the leg side saw him reach 50 off 62 balls and India stood at 207 for 1 with eight overs remaining.

Gavaskar played an uncharacteristic slog to take Imran for another boundary, but Wasim removed Vengsarkar's leg stump with a yorker and repeated the trick to remove Kirti Azad without scoring. 'They batted so well and made the bowling look so easy that it sent the wrong message in the Indian dressing room and the rest of the batsmen tried to play as though they had also been batting quite a while,' said Imran. 'Wasim bowled superbly and we were able to reverse swing the ball and get back in the match.'

Ramiz continued, 'We always felt we could control the last 10 overs. We had leg-spinners and we could bowl 90mph yorkers, so we felt we had a clear advantage. Teams did not understand that. Our plan for the last 10 overs was to attack the opposition.'

Imran, from wide on the crease, bowled Kapil Dev with a ball that moved away from him. And, in his final over, he dismissed Gavaskar for 92 when he aimed a swing towards midwicket and the ball ricocheted on to the stumps off his pad. It matched his highest score in one-day internationals – although he would eventually score his only ODI century against New Zealand in the 1987 World Cup. In the final over, Wasim bowled Ravi Shastri and a run-out left India on 245 for 7.

Offered some width by Kapil, Mudassar drove the first ball of Pakistan's reply on the up to the cover boundary, but was soon trapped lbw by Chetan Sharma, promoting an eruption from the Indian fans. 'The idea was to build a solid foundation and have a good start, keep our wickets in hand and then go for the runs at the end,' Imran recalled. But after Mohsin Khan had taken Sharma for a pair of fours, Maninder Singh, wearing a pink patka and bowling his slow left-armers from round the wicket, hurried one through and bowled Ramiz as he played back.

At 39 for 2, Singh recalled, 'Now we thought we are in with a chance. Ramiz was the kind of player who, if you are chasing a target of 247 in those days, was somebody who could be there for 50 overs, get his hundred and the other players could revolve around him. Once we got his wicket we knew the only hurdle now is Javed Miandad.'

The sun-hatted Miandad, required to bat for the first time in the tournament, strode purposefully to the middle, arms circling and shoulders flexing. Singh wasn't expecting the new batsman to take any liberties with him, having been warned by him earlier in the day, 'Listen, Singh, we are going to get 30 runs off your 10 overs. We are not going to give you any wickets and we will accumulate the runs off the other bowlers.' Sure enough, Singh would go for only 36 runs in his allotted overs and would take no further wickets.

Off the mark with a nudge to fine leg for three, Miandad was soon changing his headwear to a cap and then bidding farewell to Mohsin, who was bowled off the bottom edge for 36 by Madan Lal. Salim Malik helped take Pakistan into three figures in the 28th over but was run out for 21 after being sent back by Miandad, who had played the ball to Srikkanth at short third man: 110 for 4.

Pakistan's required run rate was now above six an over. 'Our batting was never as strong as India's,' admitted Ramiz. 'Against India everyone felt there was a chance to become a hero, but this felt like a case of "accidents will happen". We didn't have the collective confidence at that stage.'

They did have the bloody-mindedness of Miandad, aged 28 and already a veteran of three World Cups. The youngest player to score 200 in a Test match, he had recently scored the third of an eventual six Test double centuries, while the two ODI hundreds he had made by that stage were both against India. His stubborn, combative nature had brought him into conflict with umpires, opposing fans and players and had placed him at the centre of what *Wisden* called 'one of the most undignified incidents in Test history' when he ended up brandishing his bat at Dennis Lillee during an on-field skirmish in Perth four years earlier. It was that quality that was to prove so valuable to Pakistan on this occasion. 'He kept his cool, he played absolutely true to his character as a street fighter,' Maninder Singh recalled, describing Miandad as 'a great character and one of the strongest players mentally in world cricket that I have ever seen.'

Ramiz added, 'Javed was a real pro and a good team player and he had a good record against India. He would never give up. He had that bull-headedness. He was a tremendous, shrewd batsman.'

Due in at number six, Imran was about to spring a surprise. 'We got ourselves in a mess because of the pressure,' he said. 'And then, with Javed trying to play a sheet-anchor role, the scoring rate fell.' Conscious of the need to accelerate, but wary of the potentially devastating impact of losing another frontline batsman, Imran promoted Qadir. 'We knew we had to take a chance somewhere, otherwise the scoring rate would be beyond our reach. Once the scoring rate goes above seven or eight an over it is very difficult to get back into the game. So, the idea of sending in Abdul Qadir at that stage was that he was a very good player of spin bowling. There were spinners operating and the idea was that he would put the pressure on and we could take a little gamble.'

With more than 130 needed off the final 19 overs, Qadir got to work by swinging a Madan Lal full toss to the long-on boundary. By the time he skied Kapil to substitute fielder Raman Lamba running back from midwicket, he had scored 34 off 39 balls, including one six, and had shared a partnership of 71. Pakistan stood at 181 for 5 in the 43rd over.

When Imran joined Miandad in the middle it was not exactly the renewal of a bromance. Miandad had given up the captaincy of the side after the home Test series against Sri Lanka in 1985 because 'Imran didn't give me his full cooperation in that series, and it was a great disappointment for me'. Miandad felt Imran had been reluctant to follow guidance on how he wanted him to bowl and decided that he no longer wanted to captain a team with him in it, preferring to go back to the rank and file. Having previously played under Imran's leadership, he claimed in his autobiography, 'I gave my best for Imran. I was hurt that Imran didn't return the gesture.'

That was all far from his mind, though, as he celebrated two hours at the crease by stepping down the track and clubbing a good length ball on off stump over cow corner and out of the ground, commentator Iftikhar Ahmed's description barely heard by viewers of Pakistan television above the din of the crowd. Wicketkeeper Chandrakant Pandit came up to the stumps to pin Miandad in the crease. The batsman's response was to swing the ball to the same area for four without moving his feet. Then he cut to the square boundary. At 209, Madan Lal bowled Imran when he stepped to leg to force through the off side. 'I was disappointed,' Imran said, 'I'd had an injury, so I wasn't really batting well at all. I was trying to play a steadying role because all I wanted was that we should have a partnership before we could launch ourselves against the Indian bowling.'

Elahi followed six runs later when he lofted Sharma to Shastri at long-off on the first ball of the 48th over. But at 215 for 7 – with

31 needed off 17 balls – Miandad still exhibited no hint of panic. 'Gradually I started taking chances,' he remembered. 'I'd hit a boundary and then stop for a few overs, before trying it again.' Having initially hoped to bat through the overs and save face, he now believed that victory was possible, so in tune with his task did he feel. 'I started working it out in my head what we needed every over, where to get it, who to work with.' He had, he said, become 'a computer'.

'He didn't play a very flashy knock,' recalled Srikkanth. 'He was hanging on there, getting his ones and twos.' And when Wasim joined him in the middle, Miandad's message was, 'I just need one person to stay with me and I will do it.'

Srikkanth overheard the conversation. 'I thought, "What is this guy talking [about]? Is he talking through his hat or something?" Because by the time the run rate has climbed up, they are losing wickets. He must be dreaming.' If he was, it was that which most sporty children have of being a national hero on the playing field. To prove that dreams might well come true, he promptly thumped an off-stump delivery high over long on for six.

A cut behind square, a trademark shot, brought up Miandad's hundred and with two overs remaining 18 were needed. Kapil had one over to bowl, while Sharma had bowled eight for 38 runs. The Indian skipper, reasoning that he could keep things tight in the penultimate over and give Sharma a cushion, took the ball and kept his end of the bargain by conceding only seven. Sharma would deliver the final over with 11 still required.

'I was the junior in the team and we had very senior guys playing in that game, who I thought will definitely come and bowl the last over with their experience,' Sharma recalled. 'But Kapil had a lot of confidence in me. He called me for the last over and just told me, "Try your best."' Hardly the most ringing endorsement.

'We were a little surprised Kapil didn't bowl the last over and instead gave it to Sharma,' said Ramiz, who also recalled. 'Javed had chosen a bigger bat about five overs earlier, using Wasim Akram's.' Not that Ramiz and his colleagues were hanging on every delivery from the players' balcony. 'We were very nervous, so none of us were watching. We were just huddled in the dressing room and we could keep hearing that thumping of feet as another batsman came back.'

Even Miandad's own mother had deserted her television set, unable to bear the tension. Later, Miandad would express his distress at stories – albeit potentially apocryphal – that people had died during the game because of heart conditions. In Islamabad, a session of the Federal Cabinet had been suspended and its members were watching the conclusion of the game, joining what historian Omar Noman estimated to be a global audience of a billion people. Indian team manager Raj Singh Dungarpur ensured viewers would not be able to see his reaction to the closing stages by leaving his seat in the stands for a more private location.

Miandad's objective going into the final six balls was to hit a couple of early boundaries and nudge a few more runs to win the match. So much for that cunning plan. He could only drag the first ball to long-on, Wasim sacrificing himself attempting to achieve a second run. But then another big wind-up from Miandad produced a boundary in front of midwicket.

Next ball, Miandad went down on one knee and the cameraman panned to the boundary in search of the ball. Yet Roger Binny had sprung from backward square leg to pull off an acrobatic stop, limiting the damage to one run. In the dressing room, Ramiz had assured Imran that he had seen Zulqarnain hit plenty of sixes in club matches in Lahore. Not today, though, the wicketkeeper being bowled first ball as he slogged wildly. Miandad, who had been halfway down the track by time the bails went flying, was stuck at the wrong end with five needed from the final two balls.

There are different accounts of what happened when Miandad met last man Tauseef Ahmed in the middle. 'I had to be at the other end for the last ball, otherwise we would have no real chance,' remembered Miandad, who insists he told Tauseef, 'Just touch the ball and run.' Tauseef's version is that it was he who told an uncertain Miandad to 'take a single, no matter what.'

The upshot was that Tauseef dabbed the ball into the off side and set off running. Mohammad Azharuddin, a brilliant fielder, messed up his throw to the bowler's end with both batsmen short of their ground. 'I really cursed him,' Sharma admitted. 'Both the players were standing in the middle and he just has to throw the ball in my hands and that was the end of the story for Pakistan.' Instead, Miandad could now win the game with a last-ball boundary.

Kapil approached his bowler and, perhaps for want of something to say, warned him not to bowl a no-ball. The Sharjah Cricket Ground was in a state of bedlam, but even the most frazzled brain knew what to expect. These were the days before the death-bowling 'variations' that have earned millions for their most skilled exponents. There can't have been a soul in the stadium who didn't believe Sharma would aim for the blockhole. Maninder Singh remembered, 'I was fielding at deep midwicket and I was very sure Chetan is going to bowl a yorker and the ball is not going to come to me in any case. An inside edge will go towards fine leg, an outside edge will go towards third man.' That, of course, depended on Sharma getting the ball in exactly the right place.

'My plan was to lean back, make room for myself and give it everything I had,' Miandad recalled. 'It was going to be a slog.' With 110 to his name from 113 balls, he was confident that he would pick up the flight of the ball quickly and equally sure that 'if the ball came on to the bat it would reach the boundary'.

'Can you ever, ever have a greater finish than this?' Iftikhar asked the television audience as Miandad counted the fielders, even though the position of each was already burned into his mind's eye. He said a quiet prayer.

Sharma ran in and bowled. A full toss on leg stump. Miandad's swing crashed down into the ball's flightpath and, instantly, the batsman raised both arms to the sky. 'When I saw Javed convert it into a full toss and hit it over midwicket, it just went over my head and I was numb for a second,' said Singh, one of the boundary fielders who could do nothing but stand disbelievingly with hands on hips.

In the commentary box, former Pakistan captain Mushtaq Mohammad could be heard screeching, incredulous and ecstatic. 'It's a six and Pakistan have won!' announced the more composed Iftikhar. 'Unbelievable victory by Pakistan!'

'That innings was like a gift to me,' Miandad would recall. 'That match was like a film. To describe it is impossible. This was a gift from God.'

Delirious fans began their race towards the middle and the batsmen sprinted past the distraught Sharma, both brandishing their bats. A handful of policemen, mirroring with their batons the victorious Pakistani pair's poses, tried to disperse the invaders. Miandad managed to swerve smartly to avoid the stampede, but Tauseef ran into the oncoming wave and was inadvertently upended by a policeman. It was almost as chaotic in the Pakistan dressing room, with younger players, including reserve seamer Mohsin Kamal, crying and even those with years of experience unable to comprehend what they had witnessed. The Indian headquarters offered a stark contrast, although there were tears in there, too. For 10 minutes there was barely a sound beyond the mournful sniffs of a tearful Sharma. Police and their dogs patrolled the corridor outside to prevent unwanted intrusion into the losers' grief.

When the teams were summoned for the prize-giving, Imran graciously asked Miandad to receive the trophy for the team. 'We went and picked Javed up,' said Ramiz. 'It was one of the greatest one-day knocks ever. He paced it to perfection.'

Miandad, who received a congratulatory telephone call from Pakistan president Muhammad Zia-ul-Haq, would come to recognise his innings as 'the single most important achievement in my professional career'. In the short term it certainly made him Pakistan's most valuable sporting property. Once the team had received the welcome of thousands of fans in Lahore and Karachi on their return home, Miandad received gifts ranging from small trinkets to a Mercedes car. 'We were instant heroes,' said Ramiz. 'We were given gold chains and all kinds. Javed made a killing. He was a guest in about 30 different events after that.' Refuting claims that one hit made him a millionaire, Miandad did say 'that innings transformed the way I was seen and respected as a cricketer and a batsman, and it ultimately transformed the way I saw myself'.

According to Shashi Tharoor, there were 36 songs composed and released in Pakistan celebrating the victory. Of greater relevance for the Pakistan team, who won 18 of their next 24 games against India in Sharjah, the Miandad miracle was recognised years later as the moment in which they began their march towards winning the World Cup in 1992. 'We never looked back,' said Ramiz, 'We gained a lot of self-belief. Having won from that situation you feel you can win from any situation.'

As well as belief, Pakistan's winning formula owed much to the addition of Waqar Younis to their pace attack and a policy of picking players for specific roles. 'We had the bowling to bowl out teams,' Ramiz explained. 'Imran's view was that if you can bowl out teams you had a greater chance of winning. That was the best way to limit the opposition score. And we picked the side looking at the one-day tempo. Saeed Anwar was included because of his ability as a one-day batsman. We had a leg-spinner to attack and we had players who could reverse swing the ball, like Wasim and Waqar. Other teams did not understand that back then.'

As for Sharjah, Miandad put it on the map as an international venue. It became the primary stage for India-Pakistan games throughout the 1990s, when regular cricketing relations between the nations were again suspended, and staged a variety of bi-lateral, triangular and multi-nation tournaments. But after Pakistan beat Zimbabwe there in 2003, in cricket's 2,000th ODI and Sharjah's 198th, it was another seven years before international cricket returned.

The spectre of match-fixing that had loomed over the sport since 2000[7] was a particularly virulent threat in what were considered non-traditional venues; places such as Singapore and Toronto – both of which had hosted ODIs between India and Pakistan – and, for all its history, Sharjah. Various contests there were subject to official investigation, and at least one alleged illegal bookmaker was seen flaunting himself in the VIP sections. The Indian government instructed its team not to visit and all major international cricket there was eventually suspended. BBC cricket correspondent Jonathan Agnew stated, 'I would swear under oath that two of the dozen or so matches I have witnessed on that desert ground over the years were fixed.'

Ironically, Miandad told the ICC's investigation that he had resigned as Pakistan coach in 1999 because he believed some of his players deliberately underperformed against England in a match played in Sharjah.

Yet others argued that the venue was irrelevant, a red herring. 'It has nothing to do with Sharjah,' said Mudassar. 'It is a global thing. Instead of targeting cricket grounds they should be targeting the players. They should answer for their actions and come clean.' And former teammate Asif Iqbal, who played a 20-year role in the staging

---

7 More in Chapter 14

of games in the emirate, insisted, 'To my mind all the matches in Sharjah were fair and honest cricketing encounters.'

No report has ever proved otherwise. In fact, Lord Condon, who led the investigation and set up the ICC's Anti-Corruption Unit, said in 2002, 'It is a misapprehension that the focus was on Sharjah. It was really Sharjah who knocked on our door, asking us for help in installing security and vigilance systems.'

It needed the granting of ODI status to more of the ICC's associate members, along with Pakistan's need to find new home venues in the wake of the terrorist attack on the Sri Lankan team bus in Lahore in 2009, to see Sharjah's eventual return to the international circuit. At the time of writing no venue has hosted more one-day internationals, the 200-mark having been reached as long ago as 2010 in a game between Afghanistan and Canada.

Yet, despite the volume of matches and the whiff of controversy, the mention of Sharjah to many cricket followers still means only one thing: four to win, one ball remaining, one wicket in hand, and Javed Miandad at the crease.

INDIA V PAKISTAN, Austral-Asia Cup Final

18 April 1986, Sharjah Cricket Stadium

India			Balls	4s	6s
K Srikkanth	c Wasim b Qadir	75	80	8	2
SM Gavaskar	b Imran	92	134	6	
DB Vengsarkar	b Wasim	50	64		1
K Azad	b Wasim	0	3		
*Kapil Dev	b Imran	8	8	1	
C Sharma	run out	10	10	1	
RJ Shastri	b Wasim	1	2		
†CS Pandit	not out	0	2		
Extras	(lb 6, w 2, nb 1)	9			
Total	(7 wickets, 50 overs)	245			

Fall: 117, 216, 216, 229, 242, 245, 245
Did Not Bat: M Azharuddin, S Madan Lal, M Singh
Bowling: Imran 10-2-40-2; Wasim 10-1-42-3; Elahi 5-0-33-0; Mudassar 5-0-32-0; Qadir 10-2-49-1; Tauseef 10-1-43-0

Pakistan		Balls	4s	6s
Mudassar Nazar	lbw b Sharma	5	22	
Mohsin Khan	b Madan Lal	36	53	4	
Ramiz Raja	b Singh	10	15	
Javed Miandad	not out	116	114	3	3
Salim Malik	run out	21	37	
Abdul Qadir	c sub b Kapil Dev	34	39	1	1
*Imran Khan	b Madan Lal	7	10	
Manzoor Elahi	c Shastri b Sharma	4	5	
Wasim Akram	run out	3	4	
†Zulqarnairn	b Sharma	0	1	
Tauseef Ahmed	not out	1	1	
Extras	(lb 11)	11		
Total	(9 wickets, 50 overs)	248		

Fall: 9, 39, 61, 110, 181, 209, 215, 236, 241
Bowling: Kapil Dev 10-1-45-1; Sharma 9-0-51-3; Madan Lal 10-0-53-2; Singh 10-0-36-1; Shastri 9-0-38-0; Azharuddin 2-0-14-0.

Pakistan won by 1 wicket. **Toss:** Pakistan. **Umpires:** D Archer, A Gaynor.
Man of the Match: Javed Miandad.

10

'NOT BAD FOR CLUB CRICKETERS'

Australia v Pakistan, World Cup semi-final, 1987, Lahore

If legend is to be believed, it was overbearing MCC officials who helped loosen the English grip on the hosting of cricket's World Cup. Having staged the first three tournaments, the Test and County Cricket Board (TCCB) watched India's joyous acceptance of the trophy at Lord's and began looking forward to hosting again four years hence.

Yet Narendra Kumar 'NKP' Salve, president of the Board of Control for Cricket in India (BCCI), was formulating a different idea; partly inspired by the home of cricket's refusal to increase his allocation of two tickets when his own nation unexpectedly reached the final. 'This incident had far more adverse impact on my mind than mere denial of four passes for a cricket match,' he recalled. Feeling slighted, he rather fancied the idea of being the one making those decisions next time. So, when West Bengal politician Rajesh Khaitan suggested to him that India make a bid to host the tournament, it was all the encouragement he needed.

Salve was aware of the obstacles. No sport clung more tightly to tradition than cricket, and it had taken less than a decade to establish the apparently unshakeable convention of the World Cup being won at the headquarters of MCC. He knew there would be concerns over the sport's infrastructure and facilities in India, which remained primitive in spite of the population's fanaticism about cricket. And there was little chance of getting significant money out of the Indian government to bankroll the costs involved.

Yet Salve had seen his team play World Cup games in England at the modest surroundings of Chelmsford and Tunbridge Wells and knew he could put together a more imposing and profitable collection of stadia. He just needed some help from a neighbour. Hoping that the notion of subcontinental solidarity against the old English masters would prove more powerful than local squabbles, Salve approached Nur Khan, the retired air marshal who was head of the Pakistan Cricket Board. Via

Khan, Pakistani President Muhammad Zia-ul-Haq was recruited to take the idea of a joint bid to Indian Prime Minister Rajiv Gandhi. And with the two governments in accord, the bid now had enough grounds and sufficient seed funding to take on the English. And, of course, it was going to be hard to deny the nation that had the World Cup in its possession. As journalist Ayaz Memon noted, 'What India [in 1983] did was turn the game completely on its head in the power matrix.'

Jagmohan Dalmiya, then treasurer of the BCCI, was the author of the India-Pakistan proposal to be put before the ICC in July 1984, enabling Salve to promise, 'We have addressed every issue.' On a financial level, it was so far ahead of England's bid that they could have enforced the follow-on. The seven full-member nations of the ICC would each be guaranteed £200,000 if the tournament found a new home, as opposed to £53,900 plus any pre-payday inflation for staying in England. The qualifying associate member would receive £175,000 instead of £30,200, and the other associates would get £20,000 for watching the action in India and Pakistan, as opposed to England's offer of £11,666. Tournament prizemoney would be £99,500 versus £53,000. The loss of Prudential as sponsors after its patronage of the first three World Cups was more than made up by Salve securing the support of Reliance, the Bombay-based petrochemical and textile company.

Without the numbers on their side, England tried to lean on the regulations, specifically the ICC's Rule 4 (C), which stated, 'Recommendations to member countries are to be made by a majority of Full Members present and voting and one of which in such a majority should be a Foundation member.' In other words, as the TCCB was quick to point out, any bid should automatically fail if it lacked the support of either England or Australia, the two Foundation members. BCCI president Raj Singh Dungarpur pointed out, 'The concept was well beyond the Western world's imagination that India and Pakistan could jointly hold the World Cup.' It was decided that a simple majority vote would suffice, and a 16-12 result sent the 1987 World Cup outside of England for the first time. 'The organisation of the 1987 tournament was the first indication that the subcontinent was no longer content playing second fiddle to either England or Australia,' author Boria Majumdar stated in *Eleven Gods and a Billion Indians*.

Salve, who could be excused a little gloating, said that the decision threatened more than a century of English 'supremacy in the administration of international cricket' and noted with gleeful sarcasm, 'The Mecca of cricket all these long years had been Lord's. If the finals of the World Cup, the most coveted international cricket event, were played at any other place it would shake the very foundation on which the super edifice of international cricket administration was built.' Salve was quick to note that the voting had not been along strict lines of colour, with Holland and Canada among those voting for the more lucrative package. 'India and Pakistan and her friends had shown that England and her allies that they were no longer supreme in the matters of cricket administration,' he wrote.

MCC President Colin Cowdrey stated, 'As much as we love to host the World Cup in England, we recognise it is for the wider benefit of cricket that the venue should be allowed to circulate' – which was a good deal more gracious than the earlier attempt to invoke the small print of the rulebook.

The risk of bad light meant that the World Cup would be played over 50 overs instead of 60, while the introduction of the fielding circle would further bring the event in line with the modern nature of one-day cricket. But the scepticism that remained about the subcontinent's ability to manage the logistics of the event was magnified by incidents such as that at India's ODI against Australia in Jamshedpur in October 1984. With the local airfield unable to accommodate a plane big enough to carry players and kit, the teams' uniforms had to be sent from the previous game in Calcutta by road – only for a delayed start to that 175-kilometere journey leaving the players waiting for the kit to arrive at the start time of 9.30 a.m. It was another three hours before the game began, and only 31 balls before rain washed it out. Confidence in India and Pakistan remained high enough, however, for them to mount another joint bid to stage the next tournament in 1991-92 – although, with the 1987 event yet to take place, it was Australia that was awarded the right to host for the first time.

As it turned out, players were generally impressed by what greeted them, even the Australians, who on one occasion had to load their own suitcases from the airport tarmac to the roof-rack of their bus. Batsman Mike Veletta recalled, 'About 11 or 12 of us had been to

India on the 1986 tour, so for us it was nothing new. But it was amazing when we got there that the facilities were so much better than one year later. There was grass on the outfield in Madras,[8] where a year earlier had been impacted mud.'

Fast bowler Craig McDermott felt Australia's recent tour meant they were 'well-versed in the conditions' and argued, 'Where a lot of other teams like England and New Zealand were shitting themselves about getting sick in the conditions and had doctors with them, we had already been through all that. We were pretty relaxed.'

On the field, the new world order looked likely to be confirmed when the Reliance Cup – as the 1987 tournament was officially labelled but rarely referred to – progressed to the semi-final stage. Pakistan would face Australia in Lahore, while holders India faced a repeat of their 1983 last-four battle against England in Bombay. The dream final was only a couple of days' cricket away.

When Richie Benaud introduced highlights of the first semi-final to Australian viewers on Channel 9, he reminded them of the shifting sands of power in the sport by observing that the previous three finals had been played at Lord's – 'which used to be the home of cricket, but I see they are talking of moving it to the subcontinent now.'

Pakistan's status as favourites to reach the final was beyond debate. They had topped Group B by winning five of their six games, their only defeat coming in a meaningless last match against a West Indies side heading for an early exit. 'In subcontinental conditions, we had the best team, we had the best combination,' captain Imran Khan recalled. They also had fanatical home support.

According to fast bowler Wasim Akram, 'It was a dream come true, playing in a World Cup in Pakistan in front of my own people. I remember coming out of the hotel, I was only 21, and there were thousands of people just waiting to meet us.' Veletta's overriding memory of the 40,000 crowd inside the Gaddafi Stadium is, 'There was a ladies' stand and there were thousands of screaming ladies there making a whole host of noise. We were up against it. It was exciting.'

Australia had surprised many observers by securing their first semi-final berth since 1975; winning five of six games and being denied top place in Group A on run rate by India, the only team

---

8   Name changed to Chennai in 1996

to beat them. Allan Border's team had arrived at the tournament with low expectations after enduring a miserable middle of the decade. As well as suffering Ashes defeats in England in 1985 and at home in 1986-87, Australia had won only one of their previous four home summer tri-series ODI tournaments. And there had been the defection of many leading players to an unofficial Australian team taking part in tours of South Africa in successive southern hemisphere summers in defiance of that nation's banishment from official cricket. It robbed the side of names such as former skipper Kim Hughes, Terry Alderman, Rodney Hogg and Carl Rackemann.

Tom Moody, one of the junior members of the squad, admitted that 'nobody even thought twice about us going into the last four' and called it a 'watershed time for Australian cricket, where a lot of the team were new.' He added, 'It was really only Allan Border that stood out like a lighthouse,' calling him 'the iconic figure in Australian cricket at that time'.

But there were advantages of having a new, unscarred group of players. 'I don't think anyone in our group felt we were in any kind of disarray,' Veletta argued. 'We were a little naïve and we shut ourselves off from a lot of that stuff. That truly worked in our favour, along with winning our first game against India, which was a significant momentum push for us.'

The Australians had also seen signs of encouragement in the way they were beginning to respond to Bob Simpson, the former Test captain who had been appointed as the team's coach in 1985. Border described him as 'a stickler for doing the simple things well', something that had often appeared beyond the Aussie players. 'The theory was you work hard, you keep working hard on all the basics,' Border explained. 'It sounds ridiculous, but it was like an under-eights team when you are just going through all the basic drills. We started getting a little bit fitter, watching what we ate and drank a little bit more. We had a no-drinking policy before a big game, which was unheard of in those days.'

Veletta continued, 'Bob had filtered through a number of players and the squad looked so different to a year before. He was starting to mould a group of people that he could trust and work with. We had an uncomplicated gameplan. We never knew if it was true, but Bob said 80 per cent of sides who score the most singles in one-day cricket win. For us, that was a key sticking point; turning the strike over. There are simple things that you do. And we spent so much time on our fielding. We beat New Zealand in a rain-affected game in Indore and the next day Simmo had us up practising on the grass in front of the hotel. The New Zealanders, who'd had had a big night out, were on their balconies saying, "Look at these idiot Australians." It typifies what was important to us.'

The young Australian team welcomed the opportunity to work hard. 'We were training in 40-degree heat,' said all-rounder Steve Waugh. 'We were training while other sides were watching. They thought we were crazy, but we wanted to put those hard yards in so we were ready for the tough moments in the game.'

Meanwhile, captain Border – three years on from Hughes's tearful resignation during a series against West Indies – was growing into the role he never much fancied. Waugh said, 'There was a lot of pressure on Allan Border in those early years because we were a losing side. He was a really good leader by actions, not so much his words, but in that World Cup he really stepped up to the plate and grew as a leader and brought a lot of young players on and gave a lot of players responsibility.' Waugh, a mere medium-pacer, found himself bowling the death overs, and relishing the challenge. 'That took a lot of courage,' he said of Border's trust in him. 'It was his way of leading the team, by putting you on the line.'

Australia's players approached their semi-final as, Border said, 'a nothing-to-lose type scenario'. With Pakistan bearing the pressure of being home favourites, the approach was, 'Let's give it to them, boys.' The task of motivating his players had been rendered unnecessary not only by the occasion but by a newspaper article in which the great Pakistan batsman Zaheer Abbas had called the Australian team 'not much better than a bunch of club cricketers'. Border shared the article with his men and watched them simmer.

'It was white noise in the background,' said Veletta. 'The only way to prove these guys wrong was to deliver on the field. If nothing else, it gave us stronger resolve. The group had come together well by then. Craig McDermott was having a second coming in world cricket and he and Bruce Reid were a fantastic opening combination. Steve made his reputation as a one-day bowler and he and Simon O'Donnell were probably the first true exponents of the slower ball.'

Veletta's mid-tournament displacement of Moody was the team's most notable personnel move. 'Tom was the better bowler than me, but we didn't need another bowling option because our bowlers had delivered so much. That gave me an opportunity.'

Border won the toss against Pakistan and saw his openers reach 73 in the 18th over before Geoff Marsh was run out by a direct hit by Salim Malik from square leg after being sent back by David Boon. Dean Jones, whose emergence as a world-class batsman had been one of the happier tales of Australian cricket in the mid-80s, arrived at the crease on the back of three half-centuries in the group games. Jones had come to global prominence when he battled sickness and dehydration to score 210 against India in Madras in 1986 in cricket's second tied Test and his belief was that 'ODI cricket was harder to play than Test cricket'. He explained, 'One-day cricket will show up your weakness quicker than Test cricket. If you can't throw over 50 metres, you will be sorted out. If you can't bowl a ball in the block-hole under pressure, you are going to be sorted out. If you can't swing the ball in the first 15 overs, you are going to be sorted out. If you don't have the power to hit over the top … you are going to get sorted out.'

In the group matches, a six hit by Jones off Maninder Singh had been the key to Australia's one-run win against India in Madras. Initially ruled as a four, Jones and the Australians persuaded umpire Dickie Bird to change his call to a six in the break between innings, with the agreement of opposition skipper Kapil Dev. The additional runs proved the difference between victory and defeat when Waugh bowled Singh on the penultimate ball of the innings with two needed for victory.

Now, Jones survived an early lbw shout by Abdul Qadir, and when the leg-spinner got one to turn and bounce between bat and pad it was Pakistani wicketkeeper Saleem Yousuf who was the victim. Struck in the face, Yousuf departed with blood coming from his mouth, leaving Javed Miandad to take the gloves. Miandad quickly made his mark by flattening all three stumps in attempting to run out Boon, prompting commentator Jack Bannister to note wryly, 'There was never any danger of Javed not taking off the bails.'

Boon had reached 65 when he missed a delivery from Salim Malik that went past leg stump. Miandad, taking a half-step back in the typical manner of a non-specialist keeper, managed to grab the ball and reach back to the stumps to execute the stumping. With the score still on 155, Jones was bowled attempting to flay spinner Tauseef Ahmed through the off side. Veletta's timely 48 from 50 balls helped redirect the Australian innings. 'I ran out Allan Border,' he laughed, 'which wasn't deliberate, but got Steve Waugh in.'

Imran was determined to take centre stage on what was intended to be his final international on home soil. He removed Veletta's leg stump; left Greg Dyer's off peg leaning drunkenly towards the ground; and then completed the set by sending McDermott's middle stump cartwheeling. Yet Waugh was determined that Australia would not be denied a final flourish. He swung the first ball of the last over beyond the long-on boundary and struck two more fours as 18 came from Saleem Jaffar's final six balls, giving his team a final total of 267 for 8. 'Not bad for club cricketers,' Border assured his players in the dressing room.

Pakistan's reply could hardly have made a worst start. Mansoor Akhtar pushed the third ball of McDermott's opening over into the off side and Border picked it up cleanly in his left hand. At the bowler's end, Ramiz Raja had gone too far down the wicket and had no chance of beating Border's throw to McDermott. 'We didn't play well against Australia,' Ramiz admitted. 'There were a couple of bad umpiring decisions also, and then the Australians were very good – they bowled well, they caught well.'

The bowling of 22-year-old McDermott had been a threat throughout the tournament, including ripping out India's middle order with a four-wicket burst in that narrow group victory. He would finish with 18 wickets, tying the then-World Cup record set by India's Roger Binny four years earlier. Working on his run-up with the great Ray Lindwall had, he felt, given him greater control of his craft. In the build-up to the event 'I spent a lot of time executing my yorkers and slower balls and things like that'.

Having been a little too close to leg stump with his early deliveries, McDermott saw Mansoor play across a straight one and lose his middle stump. Miandad entered at 37 for 2 and betrayed his nerves by almost triggering a mix-up with Malik on his first ball. Waugh came into the attack and Malik, on 25, played too early at his first delivery, lobbing a catch to McDermott at mid-off and reducing Pakistan to 38 for 3.

But now came a partnership that threatened to decide the game. Imran, whose day this was perhaps destined to be, made 58 from 84 balls, with four fours, sharing a stand of 112 in 26 overs with Miandad. Imran was happy to come down the wicket to the seamers and quick to rock back when the ball was dropped short. Waiting on a delightful on-drive to take the score past 100, Imran had taken his side to 150 when – to the naked eye – he appeared to have missed a swipe at Border's left-arm spin. Greg Dyer whipped off the bails, but it was Dickie Bird at the bowler's end who gave Imran out caught behind. A stare at Bird, an emphatic tuck of the bat under his arm and the tearing off of batting gloves made clear what Imran thought of the decision. 'Everything went wrong that day,' he recalled. 'Umpiring decisions went against us. I was given out when we were just getting into a winning position. It was a nightmare.'

Border remembered, 'There were moments when the game was drifting away from us. Particularly with Imran Khan and Javed Miandad at the crease, the game was still in the balance, but we just bowled and fielded like terriers.'

Wasim Akram marked his entrance by clubbing McDermott and Border for sixes. McDermott doused his fireworks, though, by bowling him with the kind of yorker that was becoming his trademark. Ijaz Ahmed was caught in the deep to make the score 192 for 6. Pakistan's hopes rested on Miandad's ability go on in the manner of his heroics at Sharjah a year and a half earlier, but this time he was unable to accelerate beyond the steady pace he and Imran had been setting earlier in the innings. When he was bowled swinging across the line against left-armer Reid, his 70 runs had come from 103 balls and he had found the boundary only four times.

The patched-up Saleem Yousuf and Qadir scored at better than a run a ball to keep Pakistan in the contest, needing 32 off the final 20 balls. But McDermott was ruthless, getting Yousuf, Jaffer and Tauseef Ahmed to nick balls to Dyer in quick succession and sealing Australia's 28-run victory. On commentary, former England captain Tony Lewis observed, 'That is a moment of tremendous jubilation and achievement' as the final wicket was celebrated and souvenir stumps were grabbed. 'Absolutely ecstatic,' was how Border described his team to the broadcast crew at the ground. 'Not too many gave us a chance to get this far.'

According to Alan Lee, writing in *The Times*, 'There were players with head in hands, supporters and even journalists in tears. They simply had not prepared themselves for failing before the final.' Imran remembered seeing fans crying as he drove away from the stadium. 'I think 1987 was one of the more painful experiences in my cricketing career because were the best team,' he said. 'At the time I was thinking it was my last international match anyway, so that was a really sad moment.'

* * *

The following day, the second half of the Asian dream died when England beat India, largely on the back of a brilliant innings of 115 by Graham Gooch, who swept the Indian spinners into submission and shared a partnership of 117 with captain Mike Gatting. Gooch, whose involvement in England's rebel tour of South Africa in 1982 meant he was only given a visa to enter India when he publicly renounced apartheid, had spent the days before the game practising a range of sweep shots against local bowlers. It got to the point where one left-armer asked Gatting, 'Why is Mr Gooch sweeping every ball? Are we going to bowl at him that badly?'

Teammate Bill Athey said, 'Goochie's hundred was an innings that I don't think anyone else on our side was capable of.' In reply, India were bowled out 35 runs short, despite beginning the final 10 overs needing only 50 to win with five wickets in hand.

At the end of a four-week tournament that had signalled the trend for ever-longer World Cups, Australia could put their place in the final down to hard work, team spirit and well-executed plans, while England could congratulate themselves on having travelled with a tropical disease specialist and a microwave oven. On the field things had been a little more haphazard, with Athey recalling, 'There wasn't any out-and-out preparation. It was just a question of switching into one-day mode. You were one of the best players, so you played one-day and five-day cricket.'

In Calcutta, it was the Aussies who found themselves as the fans' favourites. 'Having beaten Pakistan, and India having lost to England in the other semi-final, we went into Eden Gardens and had 95,000 on our side, which was a big advantage,' Waugh recalled. After a solid start, built around Boon's 75, Australia needed another understated gem of an innings by Veletta – who hit six boundaries in scoring 45 off 31 balls – to set England a target of 254.

England looked well placed at 135 for 3 after 31 overs, with Gatting unbeaten on 41. 'He had the game by the short and curlies,' according to Veletta. Border opted to bring himself on because 'something had to happen'. It happened immediately. Gatting had been reverse-sweeping successfully throughout the competition and opted to do so against Border's first ball. Yet as it drifted towards – or even outside – leg stump, the England skipper could only edge the ball onto his shoulder and into the grateful gloves of Dyer. *Wisden* would record it as 'a moment too crass to contemplate'.

'Had I left it, it would have been a big wide,' Gatting would admit ruefully. 'But you have got yourself into a rhythm and you knew where it was going to be bowled. If it hadn't been bowled so far down the leg side and had it not hit my shoulder, it would have been three.'

Athey, who made 58 and attempted to rebuild with Gooch, admitted, 'We should have won the final. We blew it. We didn't bowl particularly well and then there was Gatt's dismissal. It certainly wasn't the reason we lost, but it turned the game. In one ball, the whole psychology of the game had changed. In those days the reverse sweep was considered very risqué.' Fans back home in Australia would have relished the sight of Gatting coming unstuck had they been able to see it. Channel 9's decision to show the first innings live and a condensed two-hour version of the second innings on a delayed basis left the nation's hardcore cricket fans listening to the BBC radio commentary instead. They heard England, having required 46 off the final five overs, beginning the last needing 17 – thanks to the heavy bat of Phillip DeFreitas. The task proved beyond Neil Foster and Gladstone Small, leaving Australia the winners by seven runs. Veletta fielded the final delivery and 'stupidly gave the ball back instead of putting it in my pocket'.

Australian cricket was heading back to where it felt it belonged. 'I think the 1989 Ashes series was the main turning point,' Veletta suggested. 'Mark Taylor, Waugh and Jones had a cracking series and our plans and strategy were really strong. I think following that series was when we felt Australian cricket was back up there.'

But was it the 1987 World Cup that laid the foundation? 'Absolutely. People could see that Border and Simpson's work was instrumental because they complemented each other so well. All Allan wanted to do was play cricket, while Bobby was so good at organising and brought great international experience. He had captained all over the world and that was something we didn't have. Under them, we managed to generate some belief.'

While that lay in the future, the realisation on the night of what his team had achieved was, according to Waugh, driven home by the scenes around Eden Gardens. 'All the fireworks were going off above us,' he explained. 'I honestly felt I was in a Hollywood movie. It was like *The Natural*, where Robert Redford's hit the ball into the lights and everything is going off.'

As the smoke cleared, the 1987 World Cup had earned its place in the history of the sport, proving that the security blanket of Lord's was not necessary to stage a successful tournament. One of the founding fathers of international cricket had won its first World Cup and would, before long, be dominating tournament after tournament. The other would have to endure a further three decades of hurt.

PAKISTAN v AUSTRALIA, World Cup Semi-Final

4 November 1987, Lahore

Australia

		Runs	Balls	4s	6s
GR Marsh	run out	31	57	2	
DC Boon	st Miandad b Malik	65	91	4	
DM Jones	b Tauseef Ahmed	14	8	2	
*AR Border	run out	18	22	2	
MRJ Veletta	b Imran	48	50	2	
SR Waugh	not out	32	28	4	1
SP O'Donnell	run out	0	2		
†GC Dyer	b Imran	0	1		
CJ McDermott	b Imran	1	3		
TBA May	not out	0	2		
Extras	(b 1, lb 19, w 13, nb 1)	34			
Total	(8 wickets, 50 overs)	267			

Fall: 73, 155, 155, 215, 236, 236, 241, 249
Did Not Bat: BA Reid
Bowling: Imran Khan 10-1-36-3; Saleem Jaffar 6-0-57-0; Wasim Akram 10-0-54-0; Abdul Qadir 10-0-39-0; Tauseef Ahmed 10-1-39-1; Salim Malik 4-0-22-1.

Pakistan

		Runs	Balls	4s	6s
Ramiz Raja	run out	1	1		
Mansoor Akhtar	b McDermott	9	19		
Salim Malik	c McDermott b Waugh	25	31	3	
Javed Miandad	b Reid	70	103	4	
*Imran Khan	c Dyer b Border	58	84	4	
Wasim Akram	b McDermott	20	13		2
Ijaz Ahmed	c Jones b Reid	8	7	1	
†Saleem Yousuf	c Dyer b McDermott	21	15	3	
Abdul Qadir	not out	20	16	2	
Saleem Jaffar	c Dyer b McDermott	0	2		
Tauseef Ahmed	c Dyer b McDermott	1	3		
Extras	(lb 6, w 10)	16			
Total	(49 overs)	249			

Fall: 2, 37, 38, 150, 177, 192, 212, 236, 247, 249
Bowling: McDermott 10-0-44-5; Reid 10-2-41-2; Waugh 9-1-51-1; O'Donnell 10-1-45-0; May 6-0-36-0; Border 4-0-26-1.

Australia won by 18 runs. **Toss:** Australia. **Umpires:** HD Bird, DR Shepherd.
Man of the Match: CJ McDermott.

11

'I'VE NEVER SEEN A 22 BEFORE'

England v South Africa, World Cup semi-final, 1992, Sydney

The dominance and vibrancy of advertisements for Coca-Cola, Foster's Lager and Gio Australia created a confusion of colour around the Sydney Cricket Ground scoreboard, yet there was no missing the stark message conveyed at its centre. Picked out in giant white letters on a green background was 'SOUTH AFRICA TO WIN' and below, in yellow and white on black:

NEED 22 RUNS

OFF 1 BALL

Only 12 minutes earlier, the same scoreboard had signalled that the team playing in their first World Cup required 22 runs off 13 balls to beat England and advance to the final. They had four wickets remaining, with big-hitting all-rounder Brian McMillan and wicketkeeper Dave Richardson well set. They had a chance, even if only a small one.

And then it rained. And the flaw in Richie Benaud's thinking was exposed.

South Africa's arrival on the sport's biggest stage – two years after Nelson Mandela's long walk to freedom and four months after they marked their readmission to world cricket with a highly symbolic one-day international series in India – had been one of the talking points of the 1992 tournament. The decision to add South Africa to the eight-team field had been taken as late as three months before the competition began, causing a reshuffle of the fixtures but representing a public relations triumph. In the republic itself, the inclusion of their team was seen as much more than commercial opportunism.

Batsman Peter Kirsten, who'd had to content himself with playing in all the 'rebel' Test matches of the 1980s, recalled, 'The release of Nelson Mandela opened up everything. Suddenly we were going to India, a week after we had been playing club cricket. India played a very important part with the Friendship Tour and the reception we got from the Indian public was just goose-pimple stuff. There was such a feeling of pride. It was the first time we had felt like we were representing our country. The rebel tour matches were not recognised by people of colour in our country – quite rightly so.'

The African National Congress (ANC), Mandela's party, had been among the strongest voices lobbying for South African inclusion in the World Cup. The ICC was reluctant to give approval before the result of the country's referendum asking the white population if they would support the abolition of apartheid. But with the voting scheduled for a few days before the semi-finals, the ICC accepted the assurance of ANC's sports head, Steve Tshwete, that the result would be the desired one.

'The incredible thing about playing in 1992,' said batsman and fielding phenomenon Jonty Rhodes, was that 'even though there wasn't yet a democracy there was so much support from the entire country. The reception from everybody across all cultures and races was incredible.'

Kirsten continued, 'The South African public were engrossed in the tournament, even though games in Australia were early hours of the morning in South Africa. It was a very emotive and significant time for the country with a referendum coming up. Nelson Mandela was very supportive of the team and we felt like we playing for him and Steve Tshwete.'

The original South African squad had excluded 36-year-old Kirsten, along with veteran batsman Jimmy Cook and all-rounder Clive Rice, because 'they thought we were over the hill'. The support of Wessels saw Kirsten added to the squad. 'I thought the ship had sailed on my playing in an event like that,' he said. 'But I was playing really good cricket and sense prevailed. I played well in the World Cup.'[9]

In an era before it took a four-year 'reset' for a country to get themselves ready for a World Cup, South Africa's late inclusion did not mean they were unprepared for what lay ahead. 'We might have been unprepared mentally,' said Kirsten, 'but physically we were very prepared because we were in a middle of a domestic season and they chose the people who were in form. We had two weeks of build-up, so we were fit and we were ready. We had some new guys like Jonty Rhodes and Hansie Cronje, but we also had experienced

---

9 410 runs at an average of 68.33

players. We had some good warm-up games and then beat Australia in our opening game, which was like, "Crikey, Moses!"'

Staged in Australia for the first time – with 13 games in New Zealand – and featuring the nine teams playing in a round-robin format to determine the semi-finalists, the event had Kerry Packer's fingerprints all over it. The defining features of limited-overs cricket in Australia since the arrival of World Series Cricket – coloured kits and a white ball – would at last be used in the World Cup. Even the timing of February and March 1992, rather than retaining the traditional four-year cycle, was a result of the Australian Cricket Board being unwilling to disrupt its season, in particular the profitable Packer-inspired triangular World Series Cup that had become a fixture of its summers.

The increase of matches from the previous 27 to 39 spread across 33 days enabled the organisers to squeeze maximum value out of the sale of TV rights, especially when they adopted an approach of selling to the bidders with the most money – the world's burgeoning satellite sports stations – rather than those offering broadest exposure. According to author Edward Griffiths, in his book on the first 40 years of one-day cricket, traditionalists felt 'the 1992 World Cup was the occasion when the ICC crossed the Rubicon by allowing business, marketing and other commercial considerations to take precedence over pure sport. They felt that, in terms of its size, policy and tone, the tournament was irreversibly spoiled.'

Yet for cricket fans of a certain age, the tournament retains a magical presence in the consciousness – partly for its vividness, and probably thanks to the easy access to matches on YouTube and via frequent re-runs on sports stations needing to fill air time. One could argue, though, that the tournament was a triumph of style as much as substance. Pakistan's victory is rightly fêted in that country, but for all the colour and carnival, the overriding image of the competition for many is that scoreboard in Sydney; and its legacy is the names Duckworth and Lewis.

For many years, games curtailed by rain had been decided by the teams' average run rate, an obviously flawed system that made no allowance for wickets lost or the match situation when weather intervened. Australia sought to contrive a more efficient system and the authoritative figure of Benaud helped to come up with a mechanism that was introduced in 1991 and would be used in the World Cup: the Most Productive Overs formula. Under the new rules, if the second innings was reduced by the weather to, say, 40 overs, then the target would be however many the team batting scored in its most productive 40 overs. Or, put another way, if the team batting second lost two overs, then the team batting first could just eliminate its worst two overs – perhaps a couple of maidens – from the target it had set the opposition.

An apparent improvement on simple average run-rate, Most Productive Overs only worked at maximum efficiency if rain fell conveniently between innings and the number of overs lost was not further impacted during the course of the second innings. For that reason, it was obvious that the rule strongly favoured the team batting first.

So when South African South African captain Kepler Wessels announced, 'We'll have a bowl,' when the coin came down his way before the semi-final against England, commentator Ian Chappell, who was hosting proceedings for the broadcasters, was quick to pounce.

'Kepler, not too worried about the rain?' he asked, knowing that the forecast for the day predicted a downpour at some point.

'Yes, it's a calculated risk,' Wessels admitted. 'If it rains while we are bowling it's not too bad. The problem comes if we're batting tonight and it rains. That is a risk we are prepared to take.' Wessels, who had played for Australia in Sydney many times before South Africa's readmission,[10] had consulted local weather experts and been told of the likelihood of rain, but that it was impossible to predict when it might arrive. 'I won the toss and decided to bowl first under helpful conditions, which was a good decision,' he insisted. 'But we just weren't as good with the ball as we were at different times in that tournament.'

Kirsten argued, 'If anyone knew Australian conditions well it was Kepler. He would have consulted others about the decision, but he was quite an independent sort of captain. Generally speaking, we backed our fast bowlers to take early wickets.'

---

10 Hailing from Bloemfontein, Wessels played for the Australian XI in World Series Cricket before representing the official Australia team in 24 Test matches and 54 one-day internationals between 1982 and 1986.

After their opening-game win against Australia, South Africa had been beaten by New Zealand and Sri Lanka before getting their tournament back on track by overcoming West Indies to begin a streak of three victories. 'It was pulsating, mind-blowing stuff playing for your country,' said Kirsten of his first World Cup. 'This was the real thing. This was what it should have been like, and what we had missed out on while we were isolated.'

South Africa's first game against England had seen their opponents reach their target with one ball to spare in a match that, ironically, had been subjected to the accursed rain rule. On that occasion, England's target had been reduced by only 10 runs when nine overs of their innings were lost. 'You were penalised for being good at bowling,' was how it felt to England batsman Alec Stewart. 'It didn't make sense. It was silly.'

The rules were not all stacked in favour of the team batting first, however. The strict three-and-a-half hours allocated to each half of the match in order to fit within television schedules meant that the first innings was simply cut short if time was reached before 50 overs were completed, with equal overs allotted to the second innings. It meant that – despite the threat of a financial penalty – a team going around the park was encouraged to waste time and burn overs, limiting the damage and giving itself a shortened run chase. Which is what happened when Graeme Hick began to find his groove after England's openers, Graham Gooch and the pinch-hitting Ian Botham, had fallen early on.

Hick, surprisingly, survived an early lbw appeal against Meyrick Pringle and then edged the same bowler to Wessels at slip off a no-ball – 'a mistake that cost us dearly' according to the skipper – before capitalising with some crisp shots off the back foot. He and Stewart shared a stand of 71 before the arrival of the left-handed Neil Fairbrother meant that constant field changes, along with delays as the ball was dried to combat the drizzle, reduced the over rate to a snail's pace. 'Did they use that as a tactic because they were going to be up against it and therefore our closing overs were not bowled?' pondered Stewart. 'The common consensus was that, yes, they did.'

Hick reached his 50 from 55 balls, punishing Adrian Kuiper when he dropped short with his medium pacers to drive England towards the 150 mark in the 30th over. He cut and drove Allan Donald as

South Africa's spearhead gave up 14 in an over, sharing a partnership of 73 before Fairbrother departed for 28. Hick fell for 83 off 90 balls when he cut Richard Snell to Rhodes at backward point.

Allan Lamb and all-rounders Chris Lewis and Dermot Reeve, knowing that the innings was approaching a premature end, were forced to swing hard and run fast, with Reeve making effective contact to contribute an unbeaten 25 off 14 to England's final total of 252 for 6. With Donald walking slowly back to his mark after going for 17 runs in the first five balls of the 45th and final over, the scoreboard clock had ticked over to the finishing time of 6.10pm. In the commentary box, David Gower noted it was 'a tactic that has worked very well', adding, 'The last thing they would have wanted to see is another 17, 18 runs coming from the next over.' When the umpires removed the bails after a single was scored off the last ball, fellow commentator Bill Lawry could only lament, 'That's a disappointing aspect.'

Injured England all-rounder Derek Pringle recalled, 'They cynically bowled their overs slowly to stop us taking advantage of the death that we had planned for. We kept wickets in hand and then they didn't bowl the last five overs.'

Gooch said of his team's total, 'We thought we could protect that. We were confident.' Even more so when Wessels was dismissed, although he remained on the field to act as runner for Kirsten, who had injured his hamstring in the field. When Kirsten, scorer of four half-centuries in the tournament, lost his off stump to Phillip DeFreitas, the game was well poised with the score 61 for 2 in the 12th over. Andrew Hudson advanced to 46 off only 52 balls, but then misread Richard Illingworth's arm ball and was given out lbw, before Kuiper clubbed a couple of straight fours off England's spinner. He and Hansie Cronje had added 41 to the total when he tried one big hit too many against Illingworth and was bowled for 36.

When Cronje was caught by Hick at deep square leg, South Africa were 176 for 5, with the drizzle falling and the required run rate rising. Rhodes contributed a typically urgent 43 off 38 balls before being caught by Lewis at point: the fielder having been moved to where the batsman had just slashed a boundary. 'I got a little carried away,' Rhodes admitted.

McMillan and Richardson found themselves needing 47 off 32 balls. They ran some twos, managed one boundary between them, and became increasingly wet as the rain intensified. At 231 for 6, there were 22 needed off 13 balls. 'We were definitely in with a shot. We still had others to come who could bat a bit,' according to Kirsten, while Wessels recalled, 'The game could have gone either way, and then the rain came.'

Umpires Brian Aldridge and Steve Randell spoke to each other and then to Gooch as he attempted to dry the ball on a towel. 'While they are doing all this talking they could be doing a lot of playing,' Chappell told TV viewers. Eventually, with the time now showing 9.52pm, the players left the field. According to co-commentator Lawry the rain was 'getting heavier by the second'.

The umpires remained on the field, joined by England coach Micky Stewart and South African coach Mike Procter and manager Alan Jordaan. Wessels watched from the pavilion, 'I knew we were in trouble because I knew how the calculations were going to go. Once we had been off the field for 10 or 12 minutes we were going to struggle.'

Derek Pringle added, 'We knew that there was no leeway because of the TV schedule and once it rained for five or 10 minutes we knew that was going to be it. My feeling from the sidelines was that it was going to be a tight finish, but there is no way I thought South Africa were definitely going to win that game, even before the rain.'

According to Stewart, 'We were winning the game. Nowadays you would do 22 off 13 with your eyes closed, but back then it was like chasing 40 now because that was the way the game was played. You look at what their scoring rate had been. Why would it suddenly accelerate three- or four-fold against the bowlers we still had available? So, sympathies? No, none at all.'

The covers came on and, quickly, came off again. Play had been halted for 11 minutes when it was announced that the game would resume with the loss of one over. England, in effect, had one maiden over removed from their innings, meaning that the target was still shown on the scoreboard as 22, but with only seven balls remaining. By the time the players were ready to take the field at 10.08pm another over had been lost; another maiden discounted from England's innings. The scoreboard displayed its unforgettable message that 22 were needed from one ball.

'Somehow I don't think that's possible,' said the typically laconic Gower in the commentary box, while the 28,000 crowd booed their disapproval at being deprived of the exciting finish they'd waited for all day. Lamb found himself walking back out alongside McMillan, the batsman who was on strike. 'You make sure it's a bloody big hit because you've got to get that off one ball and I've never seen a 22 before,' Lamb told him.

As it turned out, the scoreboard had got it wrong. The rules stated that South Africa only had to meet their new target rather than surpass it, so it was 21 to win. When McMillan pushed a disinterested single off DeFreitas's gentle delivery, England had officially won by 19 runs under the MPO system. 'It was a bit stupid making us go out for that one ball,' suggested Stewart.

Wessels called the anticlimax 'devastating'. Outside the South Africans' dressing room, Meyrick Pringle stood on the stairs and cried. 'It was a phenomenal day and tour for us, but it was sad to go out of the tournament the way we did,' he would recall. Other tears were shed away from anyone's gaze. The South Africans, whose popularity had grown with the historic result of the referendum five days earlier, undertook a lap of honour. A similar reception would await them back home, with thousands greeting their arrival in Johannesburg.

'Things were happening too quickly,' a philosophical Kirsten said. 'There is no way we could suddenly come in and get to the final. It was somebody upstairs saying, "No, you need to wait a while." I think it was divine intervention. It would have been too surreal for us to get to the final.'

Writing in the *Melbourne Age*, Englishman Peter Roebuck was more unforgiving. 'Seldom can so much harm have been done to any game by application of finicky rules by authorities who plainly knew no better,' he wrote. The fault, however, had been less in the way the regulations were applied on the night than in their misguided conception. The ACB's Graham Halbish argued, 'I don't think this World Cup semi-final is a complete farce,' choosing to blame 'an act of God' rather than shortsighted planning. But, as Roebuck's colleague, Patrick Smithers, pointed out, 'Last night's chaos has irreparably damaged the credibility of the 1992 World Cup.'

'It was a very unfair way to do it,' Lamb recalled in 2009, although Gooch, like Stewart, retained little sympathy South Africa's manipulation of England's innings. 'People said was a ridiculous rain delay, but people also forget what happened earlier in the game. When they were under pressure they slowed it down.'

But given that two wrongs don't make a right, even in the often quirky mathematics of cricket, it was clear to anyone with an interest in the game that a further method of deciding rain-interrupted contests was required. As England seamer turned cricket writer and broadcaster Mike Selvey commented, 'It was an appalling rain rule. We all admire Richie Benaud enormously, but that was a *faux pas*.'

Commentators had always been quicker to highlight the obvious failings in systems such as average run-rate and MPO than to offer any realistic alternatives. But when Christopher Martin-Jenkins had told radio listeners a couple of years earlier that 'surely someone, somewhere could come up with something better' than simple run rate the ears of English mathematician and cricket fan Frank Duckworth had pricked up.

'My love of cricket came first,' Duckworth explained, 'but I have always been interested in applying statistics to outside topics.' He had even sent Football League secretary Alan Hardaker a study of attendance figures in the early 1970s, only to receive an instant reply that dismissed Duckworth's analysis and conclusions, despite it being a time when the sport was fighting to arrest the decline in crowd numbers. 'Obviously he just never read the thing. He thought, "Who the hell do these people think they are telling me what my own data has to say?" He knew it all.'

That experience meant that when Duckworth, more than a decade later, began playing around with data from his favourite sport, there was no thought of his work ever going before officialdom. A member of the Royal Statistical Society, he wondered how a system might work that took into account wickets lost, rather than focusing solely on runs and overs. He realised that 'a fair correction needed to take account of not just how many overs were lost but the state of the match'. His view was, 'This required a mathematical relationship to be established, giving the number of runs that could be scored from all combinations of overs remaining and wickets in hand.' He named the formula he devised to make such calculations

CODA (Cricket: One-Day Analysis). 'From my experience with Alan Hardaker I didn't expect it to ever see the light of day,' he admitted. 'It was really prompted by Christopher Martin-Jenkins.'

When he heard about the Most Productive Overs system to be used in the 1992 World Cup, Duckworth had scoffed. 'It was obviously quite useless because it made no allowance whatsoever for the time when the interruption occurred. It would have been not too bad if the overs lost were all at the start of the innings. But if an interruption occurred late on obviously it was going to not be appropriate. In the classic case in the semi-final it occurred right at the end of the game and it was the last overs that were lost.'

The debacle spurred Duckworth to make a presentation of his new formula at a statistical conference later in the year. 'I suggested that putting numbers into it would be a good statistical exercise and the message got back to Tony Lewis[11], who was a mathematics lecturer at the University of the West of England. He wrote to me and asked for my permission to use my paper for a research project, and we started discussing it together. We only lived five miles apart, which was really quite remarkable.

'The fact that it was a university project was very useful because it came to the attention of the TCCB. I had already been in contact with [chief executive] Tim Lamb and when Tony wrote to him to say we were now putting in numbers based on real cricket matches rather than my guesswork he invited us to make a presentation.'

As well as inserting real matches into their algorithms, the duo had continued to refine the basic principles of a system that calculated revised targets based on how many run-scoring resources – i.e. wickets and overs – a team had lost and had left. 'One of the first things we did was to improve the formula and make it more logical,' Duckworth explained. 'I worked on a formula on a flight to Hawaii and sent a fax to Tony from my hotel in Waikiki and from then on we called it the Waikiki Formula.' It formed the basis of the Duckworth-Lewis Method that they presented to the TCCB in October 1995 and to the ICC the following year. 'It was favourably received by the ICC and we were only in there about 10 minutes. It was quite an ordeal because there we were face to face with a panel that was like a who's

11 Not to be confused with the former England captain and BBC commentator

who of the cricket world. The chair was the great Clyde Walcott, who we both remembered taking our bowlers apart.'

The outcome was that the system was used for the first time in international cricket at Zimbabwe's game against England in January 1997 and formally adopted by the ICC in 1999. The authors, however, had to settle for the deep satisfaction of what they had achieved rather than financial gain. According to Duckworth, 'We couldn't sell it because you've got to prove a thing before it had any value and you can't prove it without it being used. We just had to give it to them. We did negotiate a consultancy for maintaining it and making the computer program that was distributed around the world. But we had to give the intellectual property rights to the ICC as a condition of our consultancy agreement. It was about 2004 before we negotiated that so they had used it for five years before we got a penny from it – apart from our travel expenses. We didn't even get those on our first visit to London, but we didn't like to ask.'

There have been compensations, though, not least the MBEs that Duckworth and the now deceased Lewis earned for their work. 'It is very rewarding to see the method still in use,' Duckworth continued. 'I remember sitting in a bar with my wife in Australia and watching a match and the score went up on the television with "DL" on it. The fact that the D is me, that is quite something.'

Despite criticism, which persists even now, that the system is not easily understood and its implementation requires an in-depth chart of scenarios that change from over to over, no one has yet come up with a better system. Besides, informative scoreboards and TV graphics – even phone apps for club cricketers – mean technology has more than caught up with the complicated mathematics. 'I think our system is fundamentally right and it will be just a matter of refining it as time goes on,' Duckworth concluded. 'People always ask how you allow for the fact that they might have kept Brian Lara back to number 11. You can't. You have to assume that the number 11 is the worst batsman. You can't take account who is actually in and out without asking the captain to rank his team before every match and that would be absolutely impractical. There has to be a compromise between getting it absolutely right and being practical.'

Since Duckworth and Lewis's retirement in 2014, the task of getting it as right as possible has fallen to Australian professor Steven Stern.

To keep Duckworth-Lewis-Stern, as it is now known, reflective of trends in the game, it is overhauled every two years after studies of scores in 50- and 20-over cricket.

So what about the 1992 semi-final? Under Duckworth-Lewis, South Africa would have needed four to tie off that final ball against England, five to win. Would Brian McMillan have been able to muscle Phillip DeFreitas to, or over, the SCG fence? Not even Duckworth or Lewis can tell us that.

* * *

Events in Sydney meant that, for the second straight World Cup, a neutral crowd for the final was united in its opposition to England, with the 87,000 mostly-Aussies at the Melbourne Cricket Ground cheering for a Pakistan side again led by Imran Khan. Having decided not to retire after all following the 1987 World Cup, Imran had been persuaded to continue beyond another planned retirement in 1990 because of his involvement in raising funds for a new cancer hospital in Lahore.

'The board of governors of the hospital, who were my friends, advised me if I did not play cricket I would not be able to raise the money to build the hospital, so the last two and a half years I only played for the cancer hospital,' he explained. 'The amounts involved to build the hospital were phenomenal and I knew it would have to be something like winning the World Cup that would give us the boost to collect that amount of money.'

Imran said he played the tournament with a strong sense of destiny, even after Pakistan won only one of their first five matches. When he tossed up with Australian captain Allan Border before their next game in Perth, he wore a T-shirt with a tiger on it. 'It's what I have been telling Allan,' he told Ian Chappell. 'I want my team to play like a cornered tiger. You know, when it's at its most dangerous.' The words might have been forgotten had Pakistan not proceeded to win their final three group games to sneak into the top four and then knock out league leaders New Zealand at Auckland's Eden Park, ending a run of three consecutive semi-final defeats.

New Zealand had won seven of their eight matches after settling on a plan that would take advantage of the slower tracks in their home country, opening the bowling with off-spinner Dipak Patel and supporting him a motley collection of medium pacers who would frustrate the hell out of big-hitting opponents desperate for pace on the ball. In elegant skipper Martin Crowe they also possessed the man whose 456 runs at an average of 114 and a strike rate of 90 would see him named the player of the tournament. Had he not suffered a hamstring injury at the crease in the semi-final he would not have seen his runner get himself run out when he was nine short of a century, and New Zealand might have made more than the 262 that Pakistan were able to overtake with an over remaining.

One of Imran's mid-tournament decisions had been to push himself up to number three in the batting order, from where he top-scored in the final with 72 as Pakistan, having won the toss, made 249 for 6 in their 50 overs. As England headed into the 35th over on 138 for four, with Fairbrother and Lamb having added 69, Imran decided to give the ball to Wasim Akram.

'We took wickets to win the World Cup, rather than containing runs,' Imran explained. 'Wasim Akram was a wicket-taker. I did not want him to bowl as a run stopping bowler... I wanted to use his overs to take wickets and so even if he bowled wide balls or no-balls I wanted him to bowl fast so he got us breakthroughs.'

Fairbrother squeezed out three runs in the first four balls, before Wasim, switching to round the wicket, sent down a delivery that went outside Lamb's defensive push to strike the off stump. Lewis then thought the first ball he faced was so far outside off stump that he thrust out his leg and offered no shot, only for it to loop around his pad and bowl him. The match had turned in the space of two deliveries and Pakistan went on to bowl out England for 227 to win their first World Cup by 22 runs. Across their nation, the people of Pakistan raced into the street to begin an evening of celebrating the country's greatest sporting achievement; and less than three years later, the Shaukat-Khanum Memorial Hospital opened in Lahore.

Meanwhile, the phrase 'cornered tigers' would enter the sport's lexicon; just as assuredly as Duckworth-Lewis.

ENGLAND v SOUTH AFRICA, World Cup Semi-Final
22 March 1992, Sydney Cricket Ground

England			Balls	4s	6s
*GA Gooch	c Richardson b Donald	2	8		
IT Botham	b Pringle	21	27	3	
†AJ Stewart	c Richardson b McMillan	33	58	4	
GA Hick	c Rhodes b Snell	83	90	9	
NH Fairbrother	b Pringle	28	50	1	
AJ Lamb	c Richardson b Donald	19	22	1	
CC Lewis	not out	18	17	2	
DA Reeve	not out	25	14	4	
Extras	(b 1, lb 7, w 9, nb 6)	23			
Total	(6 wickets, 45 overs)	252			

Fall: 20, 39, 110, 183, 187, 221
Did Not Bat: PAJ DeFreitas, RK Illingworth, GC Small
Bowling: Donald 10-0-69-2; Pringle 9-2-36-2; Snell 8-0-52-1; McMillan 9-0-47-1; Kuiper 5-0-26-0; Cronje 4-0-14-0.

South Africa			Balls	4s	6s
*KC Wessels	c Lewis b Botham	17	23	1	
AC Hudson	lbw b Illingworth	46	53	6	
PN Kirsten	b DeFreitas	11	26		
AP Kuiper	b Illingworth	36	44	5	
WJ Cronje	c Hick b Small	24	46	1	
JN Rhodes	c Lewis b Small	43	39	3	
BM McMillan	not out	21	21		
†DJ Richardson	not out	13	19	1	
Extras	(lb 17, w 4)	21			
Total	(6 wickets; 43 overs)	232			

Fall: 26, 61, 90, 131, 176, 206
Did Not Bat: RP Snell, MW Pringle, AA Donald
Bowling: Botham 10-0-52-1; Lewis 5-0-38-0; DeFreitas 8-1-28-1; Illingworth 10-1-46-2; Small 10-1-51-2.

England won by 19 runs (MPO). **Toss:** South Africa. **Umpires:** BL Aldridge, SG Randell. **Man of the Match:** GA Hick.

12

'WHAT A LITTLE GEM OF AN INNINGS'

Australia v Sri Lanka, Benson and Hedges
World Series, 1996, Melbourne

It wasn't a bad ball. Australian seamer Paul Reiffel, bowling the second over of the innings, followed protocol by aiming for the top of middle and off. The kind of delivery that, even in a limited-overs contest, most openers would be happy to play with a defensive bat so soon after arriving at the crease. Romesh Kaluwitharana had other ideas. Before Reiffel, the Aussie fielders and the crowd at the Melbourne Cricket Ground could register what had just happened, the ball was banging second bounce into the fence at midwicket, whipped there with a contemptuous flourish by the Sri Lanka batsman.

When Kaluwitharana, having almost holed out to cover point, thumped Reiffel over mid-on and took advantage of the vast MCG outfield to run four it was clear that his first boundary had been no aberration. It was part of a planned assault. Craig McDermott delivered the fifth over of the innings and Sri Lanka's diminutive wicketkeeper sent him to the third-man boundary with a flat-footed prod, before swivelling as though on castors to pull through midwicket for another all-run four. Sri Lanka's total at the end of the over was 27 for 1, which might not sound remarkable to modern ears, but compared favourably with Australia's 9 for 1 at the same stage of their innings. The host nation in the 1995-96 Benson and Hedges World Series tournament had recovered from 54 for 4 to score 213 for 5 in their 50 overs, Ricky Ponting making 123, his first ODI century, before being run out on the final ball of the innings.

Having lost three of their four games in the tournament, Sri Lanka had decided that a change in approach was needed. Perhaps not only for their current engagement, but if they were to make an impact at the World Cup, for which they had been awarded status as joint-hosts with India and Pakistan. 'We had to create something, we were not a brilliant side,' captain Arjuna Ranatunga admitted. 'We had Aravinda de Silva, one of the best batsmen in the world for me, [but] we needed to rally round him, support him and look after the middle order.'

Sanath Jayasuriya, who had found his way into the national team as a left-arm spinner, had been promoted to open the batting over the previous year, but the identity of his partner was still a matter of debate. Roshan Mahanama had failed three times in Australia, including a first-baller in Sri Lanka's sole win, against West Indies, and had been replaced at the top of the order by Chandika Hathurusingha, who was promptly dismissed for nought by Curtly Ambrose.

Kaluwitharana, a right-hander of no great consistency, had opened when he first batted in an ODI, before settling into the sixth or seventh slot. His form in the World Series had done little to suggest that he might be the answer up top: scores of 8, 0, 8, 0 for a total of 16 runs off 40 balls. It was a surprise, then, when Ranatunga asked him, 'Why don't you open? Let's see in these four games if you can open. If you fail you can go back to your normal position.' To a man who had been dropped after scoring a century on his Test debut in 1992, such an assurance was important. 'I will protect you,' his skipper promised. 'I will give you that guarantee.'

The instructions were clear: go for his shots from the start and take advantage of only two men being allowed outside the fielding circle in the first 15 overs. To hell with preserving wickets. In the sixth over, he aimed a big swing at a Reiffel half-volley on off stump, slamming it for four past short cover. Reiffel brought up fine leg to drop a man back to the off-side boundary, only to see Kaluwitharana lean across and help the ball past the short fine left leg off the front foot for another boundary. Soon afterwards, he whipped a delivery wide of mid-on to bring up the 50 with a dashing shot that reflected the flash of green on his blue shirt. Shane Warne allowed another boundary by misfielding after Kaluwitharana forced Shane Lee behind point and Warne himself was slashed over extra cover. Kaluwitharana reached his half-century off 45 balls, laying back when he picked up Warne's shorter length and cutting through the off side for an all-run four. He proceeded to sweep Warne to the boundary from middle and off; then repeated the shot with enough pace to beat the fielder who had been placed squarer on the leg-side boundary. After 23 overs, he had made 76 off 74 balls out of a score of 126 for 2.

Going down on one knee, Kaluwitharana played Michael Bevan behind square. McDermott's fumble close to the boundary tempted him to come back for a second and he just failed to beat the throw to wicketkeeper Ian Healy. Run out for 77. 'What a little gem of an innings it was,' said commentator Tony Greig, who was particularly captivated by the man he christened 'Little Kalu'. He was named Man of the Match after Sri Lanka got home by three wickets in the 48th over.

'When we talked about the defeat straight after the game,' said Ponting, 'we thought his effort was a fluke – it was only his second innings as an opener in ODI cricket and most people in those days still thought it was a top-order batsman's job to build a platform and help ensure there were wickets in hand for a late assault.'

But there was more to come as the tournament moved to Perth, then the fastest wicket in the world. After a heavy defeat by Australia, Sri Lanka faced the West Indies' fast bowlers once more. 'When [Curtly] Ambrose lets go of the ball it comes from about nine or ten feet; the bounce was steep as well,' Kaluwitharana explained. 'When Sanath faced the first ball the wicketkeeper was on the 30-yard circle. Seeing that did put some fear in me.'

He did a good job of hiding it, hooking Courtney Walsh for four. Even being hit in the ribcage by Ambrose couldn't slow him down, pulling him over the rope at square leg and then whipping a good-length ball to the cover-point boundary. He clipped Walsh through midwicket and drove him in classic style for yet another four, before pulling Ian Bishop in front of square. 'This little fella is really exciting,' chuckled Greig. 'This is as exciting an opening partnership as you could wish to see,' he continued as the score moved towards 80 without loss.

'From nowhere Sanath and I became the hot topic with our belligerent batting,' Kaluwitharana recalled. 'The transformation was dramatic. In size, we both were small. We were playing against mighty West Indies and Australia and taking on Craig McDermott and Curtly Ambrose. Tony Greig saw that change and that's the time he started backing Sri Lanka. And "Little Kalu" was born. It was almost like he loved saying it, and it did have a good ring to it. Many have tried to say it like him but failed.'

Kaluwitharana fell for 50 off 54 balls, including five fours and a six, and was again named man of the match as his team successfully defended what ended up being a modest total of 202. In the final round-robin match, he launched himself into attack again as his side chased 243 to win against Australia. Glenn McGrath got the punishment this time; a gloved pull, a slap over the covers with minimal back-lift, similar punishment to a slower delivery, and a hook behind square. Four every time. His half-century arrived on his 31st ball and it needed a brilliant catch by Mark Waugh after he pulled Warne off the front foot to end his innings at 74 off 68 balls, including eight fours. Another Sri Lanka victory, another man-of-the-match award.

Sri Lanka's Australian coach, Dav Whatmore recalled that the establishment of the Jayasuriya-Kaluwitharana combination 'became the real turning point in the ability to put the pressure back on the opposition in the first 15 overs'. He explained, 'These boys were very talented on both sides of the wicket, front and back foot, and they were encouraged to play their natural game rather than just go out and pinch hit.'

Ranatunga reflected, 'We knew that we had got the two openers. This is the plan we should go to the World Cup with; with two openers who might get about 120 runs, then the middle order can control because we never had any so-called match-winning bowlers.' They did, of course, have Muttiah Muralitharan, but quite what the future held for him was uncertain after he'd been no-balled for throwing by Australian umpire Tony McQuillan against West Indies. He missed Sri Lanka's last five matches of the Benson and Hedges tournament and faced various ICC tests so that he could return to action. Ranatunga continued, 'We decided, OK, we will try to put a side in. Even if they get 300 we are comfortable chasing 300. That's the plan we had and it worked.'

The notion of a pinch-hitting opening batsman was not new in itself. Ian Botham had fulfilled the role for England in Australia as long ago as 1982-83 and had batted in that position throughout the 1992 World Cup. 'Botham was a fine striker of the ball,' recalled teammate Alec Stewart. 'The more balls he could face the better it was. He played strong shots and put the pressure on the bowling attack as soon as he could, and obviously the new ball flies off the bat. But it was a calculated tactic with Botham playing in an attacking but responsible role.'

Yet Botham achieved a strike rate of only 58.35 in the 1992 tournament – even Alastair Cook would end his ODI career with a

77.13 strike rate – and when Botham fell, England reverted to caution in the early overs, keeping wickets in hand for the second half of the innings. 'That was how the format was for everyone around the world,' said Stewart. 'Back then 50-over cricket was a diluted version of four-day cricket; nowadays it is an extension of 20-over cricket in mindset and approach. Botham was a fine ball-striker, but Kalu and Jayasuriya took Sri Lanka to another level. When Sri Lanka came along in 1996 with a different approach, things changed.'

Where Botham – and others such as New Zealand's Mark Greatbatch – had represented a one-man tactic, Kaluwitharana was the embodiment of an overall team strategy. He told the *Indian Express* in 2017, 'We used to see boring starts in ODIs, with teams happy with 30 or 35 on the board [in 15 overs]. Then Sanath and I came on board and changed the game. The initial reaction was, "What the hell is this?" and we were criticised. Now it has changed because everyone is doing it, scoring 300 for fun. Sanath and I were exceptions then, nowadays they are all freaks.'

The duo's approach, he said, was, 'To play the natural cricket we knew, which was to dominate the bowler. Our defence was to attack.' Explaining that 'we both saw the ball early and we played all round the wicket', he added, 'Unless one of us was doing something stupid, we never said anything. We only said, "Going is good. Let's keep going like this."'

There are those who point out that the story of Kaluwitharana at the top of the order for Sri Lanka is more about myth than numbers that stand up to scrutiny. He would make only a small individual contribution to Sri Lanka's stunning success in the 1996 World Cup, with 73 runs in six innings. Those runs came off a mere 59 balls, but he returned only two double-figure scores in the tournament and made 8, 0 and 6 in the knockout matches. He would end his 189-match ODI career with a batting average of just 22.22, saving many of his best performances for Australian soil, including four half-centuries when he returned for the 1998-99 tri-series against the hosts and England. The last of those, 68 against Australia at the MCG, was eclipsed by someone batting in his own image, wicketkeeper-opener Adam Gilchrist blasting 154 off 129 balls.

Kaluwitharana's greatest contribution was those three innings in Australia in early 1996 that persuaded Sri Lanka to settle on an all-guns-blazing approach, thereby freeing Jayasuriya to become one of the most destructive forces in limited-overs cricket. By the end of 1995, Jayasuriya had played in 91 ODIs – at the top of the order more often than not – and had made one century. He was averaging just under 28 as an opener and had a strike rate below 80. In 1996 and 1997, batting mostly with Kalu, he made five hundreds and 13 fifties in the course 56 ODIs, scoring well over 2,000 runs at nearly 42, with a strike rate of 113.

'That series was a big factor in us going on to win the World Cup,' Kaluwitharana argued. 'Sanath and I continued to get us off to good starts often, which helped us win many games.' Which might be stretching the truth somewhat, but they did share partnerships of 53 and 83 in Sri Lanka's victories over India and Kenya in their second and third group games. The platform they set in the latter of those games allowed their team to reach 398 for 5, then the highest score in ODI history.

Three on-field victories were enough for Sri Lanka to finish top of Group A, having also been awarded victories over Australia and West Indies. Those nations had chosen to forfeit rather than play in Sri Lanka after a terrorist bombing at the Colombo Central Bank less than a month before the tournament. The incident, which would leave 91 dead and approximately 1,400 injured, was said to be the work of the Tamil Tigers as part of the separatist civil war that had been ongoing for well over a decade. While Australian coach Bobby Simpson said that "nobody wants to play cricket while bombs are going off", the tournament organisers refused to reschedule games and pointed out that terrorists in the country had never targeted sporting events.

Top spot in the group meant Sri Lanka travelled to Faisalabad for a last-eight game against England, whose progress – if such it could be called – had been down to wins against the United Arab Emirates and the Netherlands. The biggest criticism of the competition had been that it had taken 32 group games to eliminate the four minor nations, while teams like England could lose all three matches against more renowned opponents and still reach the knockout stage.

England soon discovered that they were playing a different game to Sri Lanka. They needed the hitting of Phillip DeFreitas, who made 67 off 64 balls after being promoted to number five, to post 235 for 8, but it offered an insignificant target to the scorched-earth approach of their opponents. When England captain Mike Atherton asked slow left-armer Richard Illingworth to bowl the second over, Kaluwitharana cover-drove the first ball he faced for four, clipped the second through mid-on for another boundary and was bowled behind his legs trying to sweep the third.

'Myself and Kalu were not afraid to get out,' said Jayasuriya. 'We just played our natural game. If we got out that was bad luck because we had lots of batting in the middle with experience.' Jayasuriya's approach on this occasion resulted in one of the most explosive of all World Cup innings as he blazed 82 off 44 balls. He warmed up by skipping down the pitch to put Illingworth over midwicket and over the bowler's head, before flicking the ball to the on-side boundary from deep in the crease. Seamers Peter Martin and Darren Gough were just as vulnerable. After reaching his fifty by forcing DeFreitas through the covers, Jayasuriya celebrated by clubbing him straight for six before muscling the ball with a cross bat over long-on for another maximum. His third six landed on the roof behind the same victimised bowler. One delivery after Dermot Reeve took out his leg stump off a no-ball, Jayasuriya was dismissed by Jack Russell's slick leg-side stumping. There were 113 on the board in only the 13th over, allowing Sri Lanka to cruise to victory with more than nine overs in hand.

'At the start we never thought we would win the World Cup,' Kaluwitharana confessed. 'So we had no pressure. When we came to the semis, we were nervous. That was the time we started thinking, "If we can do this it can put Sri Lanka on the map."'

Sri Lanka batted first against India, in front of a crowd approaching 100,000 in Calcutta's Eden Gardens. 'We had ten people waving our Sri Lankan flag,' Kaluwitharana observed. 'We had only each other.' It was so noisy that the openers realised they would have to communicate through eye contact and sign language. It never came to that. With only one on the board, Kaluwitharana slashed his first delivery to third man and Sanjay Manjrekar took the chance. Then Jayasuriya flayed Javagal Srinath to exactly the same fielding position, where Venkatesh Prasad was waiting: 1 for 2 off four balls.

After de Silva's 66 helped Sri Lanka recover to a competitive 251 for 8, it was Kaluwitharana's glovework to Jayasuriya's bowling that made the vital contribution. Sachin Tendulkar, whose 65 had carried his side to 98 for 1, was struck on the pad as he tried to turn the ball to leg and, driven by instinct, set off on a run, unable to believe he'd failed to make contact. Kaluwitharana scooped up the ball and, before Tendulkar could ground his bat, took off the bails. 'It's a stumping that changed cricket in Sri Lanka,' is Kaluwitharana's not unreasonable assessment. 'The way he battled that day, if he hung around for longer we would have lost.'

India crumbled to 120 for 8, at which point some spectators began lighting fires in the stands and tossing debris on to the field, causing match referee Clive Lloyd to stride out and award the abandoned match to Sri Lanka. They would now contest the final at Lahore's Gaddafi Stadium against Australia, who won an exciting semi-final by defending 207 against West Indies.

Set 242 to win in the final, Sri Lanka again had to do without a contribution from their top two. Jayasuriya was run out and Kaluwitharana flubbed an attempted pull off Damian Fleming to Bevan at midwicket to leave them 23 for 2. But then de Silva, the man skipper Ranatunga had hoped would be given most freedom by the tactics of the opening batsmen, won them the game. Having already taken three wickets with his modest off-spin, he guided his team home with a beautiful unbeaten 107 off 124 balls, his 5ft 3in figure a picture of poise, balance and timing as he found the boundary 13 times. On a turning track, de Silva made light of the threat of Warne, who finished with 0 for 58 from his 10 overs. He shared a third-wicket partnership of 125 with Asanka Gurusinha, before he and skipper Ranatunga added an unbeaten 97 to reach the target in the 47th over. For the fourth time in the tournament, de Silva was named Man of the Match.

It had been a remarkable triumph for a country that had lived through years of murderous internal conflict and, on the cricket field, had become accustomed to making up the numbers. Not any more. Not only did the World Cup heroes earn a duty-free certificate allowing them to bring in luxury goods tax-free, the elevated status of cricket in Sri Lanka allowed more players to give up their day jobs, while the new global champions were suddenly in demand. Invitations to lucrative events in places such as Singapore, Sharjah and Nairobi followed. 'The cricket board would have to fight tooth and nail to secure tours,' said Whatmore, 'but now the offers and invitations were always going to arrive after that, so you played more games.' Which, of course, meant more revenue and the establishment of a virtuous circle.

On a broader sporting canvas, even if the approach that Sri Lanka had pioneered had not exactly carried them all the way through to the triumph that made all of this possible, it had awoken other teams to the possibilities of batting in a 50-over innings. Outside of some notable pockets of resistance, the ODI game would never be the same again.

AUSTRALIA v SRI LANKA, Benson and Hedges World Series

9 January 1996, Melbourne Cricket Ground

Australia			Balls	4s	6s
MJ Slater	c Kaluwitharna b Munasinghe	2	17		
*MA Taylor	c Kaluwitharna b Munasinghe	9	38		
MEWaugh	b Munasinghe	0	4		
RT Ponting	run out	123	137	7	1
SG Law	c Tillakaratne b Wickramasinghe	8	15		
MG Bevan	not out	65	87	5	
Extras	(lb 2, w 2, nb 2)	6			
Total	(5 wickets, 50 overs)	213			

Fall: 8, 10, 33, 54, 213
Did Not Bat: S. Lee, †IA Healey, PR Reiffel, SK Warne, CJ McDermott
Bowling: Vaas 10-3-41-0; Munasinghe 10-1-30-3; Wickremasinghe 6-0-29-1;
Dharmasena 10-0-31-0; Jayasuriya 10-0-56-0; Kalpage 4-0-24-0

Sri Lanka			Balls	4s	6s
ST Jayasuriya	c Lee b Reiffel	17	14	2	
†RS Kaluwitharana	run out	77	75	12	
AP Gurusinha	run out	0	1		
PA de Silva	lbw b McDermott	35	53	1	
RS Mahanama	lbw b Bevan	51	71	4	
HP Tillakaratne	lbw b McDermott	0	1		
RA Kalpage	b Warne	1	6		
HDPK Dharmasena	not out	28	57	1	
WPUJC Vaas	not out	0	5		
Extras	(lb 7, w 5, nb 2)	14			
Total	(7 wickets; 47.3 overs)	214			

Fall: 17, 39, 127, 144, 144, 147, 209
Did Not Bat: AMN Munasinghe, GP Wickramasinghe
Bowling: McDermott 10-0-42-2; Reiffel 10-0-47-1; Lee 6-2-26-0; Warne 10-1-37-1;
Waugh 6-0-31-0; Bevan 5.3-0-24-1

Sri Lanka won by 3 wickets. **Toss:** Australia. **Umpires:** DJ Harper, AJ McQuillan.
Man of the Match: RS Kaluwitharana.

13

'WE ALL FAILED IN THE SEARCH FOR ANOTHER RUN'

Australia v South Africa, World Cup semi-final, 1999, Edgbaston

Over the years, Daryl Cullinan has become symbolic of the rivalry between Australia and South Africa at the end of the 20th century; unfortunately for him because of the much-publicised problems against Shane Warne that undermined an otherwise outstanding batting record in Tests and one-day internationals. Yet there are no South Africans who played against Australia in the semi-final of the 1999 World Cup who do not carry scars; marked for life by a match that is never spoken of between them. 'To this day nothing has been said,' according to Cullinan. 'We all failed in the search for another run.'

Steve Elworthy, whose career took him from bowling for South Africa in that game to organising the 2019 tournament in England, confirmed, 'I have not spoken about it outside of interviews and people wanting to talk about it in my role running the World Cup. I can't remember having this conversation with any of those guys. We have never spoken about it. People just put it to the back of their minds. There are too many "what ifs". We know we could be World Cup winners.'

South Africa's first decade back in world cricket had begun with rain-soaked frustration in Sydney in 1992. But by the time the World Cup returned to its original home in 1999, the leadership of former England batsman Bob Woolmer had turned them into tournament favourites. The scorer of centuries in three consecutive Ashes Tests – spread over two series – Woolmer had first represented England as a specialist one-day all-rounder in 1972. And after coaching Warwickshire to various trophies before taking over the South African team in 1994, it was in one-day cricket in particular where Woolmer's innovative approach to coaching was most obvious, despite the six-game losing streak with which he began his new role. He introduced thoughtful and targeted training techniques – for example, including basing the training of wicketkeepers on what he observed about the movement of football goalkeepers – and actively encouraging batsmen to make use of the reverse sweep as a way of innovating at the crease. How Mike Gatting must have wished he'd coached his England side.

Batsman Gary Kirsten, who would go on to be an international coach, recalled, 'We had been playing an old-style of cricket, which was outdated. Bob was the first coach who got us to look at playing one-day cricket differently. He changed the team significantly and asked, "Who are the kind of individuals we need to allow us to play differently to how we have in the past?" In Hansie Cronje, he had a young captain who was willing to try things. We were all quite young and keen to change and try something different.

'Bob was always dabbling with things. He had a creative mind, a bit of a scientist angle to him. He taught me to be open-minded to different things. The modern game now is very different to what it was in the '90s and Bob was a trailblazer. As a modern coach you have to be open-minded to work out where your competitive advantage is as a team. Every coach is in that space now, with the use of analysts to help build match strategies and evaluate players.'

Woolmer, who clearly would have loved the forensic approach to achieving success in Twenty20 cricket, was one of the earliest adopters of computerised scrutiny of the game, even though there were those who initially told him to 'stick to the basics of coaching' rather than seeking technological help. He explained, 'My enthusiasm had been fired by discovery of the fact that match analysis could be made easier by a day's play being condensed into just 55 minutes. Each player's game profile could be extracted with the click of a mouse.' His dream, he said, was to have every player's dismissals available 'at the touch of a button to be able to tell the bowlers where the best area to bowl would be and what types of pitches these batsmen liked to bat on'.

When South Africa arrived in England for the first World Cup there in 16 years their winning percentage in ODIs under Woolmer since those early defeats was more than 75. Yet when they had played in Australia's annual tri-series in the summer of 1997-98, they beat their hosts four times in the group games and took a 1-0 lead in the best-of-three final, only to be beaten on consecutive days in Sydney. It had been a similar narrative in the pre-Woolmer days of

1993-94. It was why Steve Waugh spoke of South Africa's 'tendency to choke under pressure'.

'It was always one of the biggest rivalries,' said Elworthy. "You think about the Springboks against the Wallabies in rugby, too. It was a huge thing. You were brought up with that rivalry. And that Australian team was arguably one of the best international teams ever assembled in terms of their depth and quality. Warne, McGrath, the Waugh brothers, Gilchrist, Ponting… world beaters in their own right.'

Peter Hanlon, in the *Melbourne Age*, described the South African team as 'a military outfit, far too clinical to garner affection,' adding, 'For [captain Steve] Waugh, beating them these days is even better than knocking off the Poms.'

South Africa had beaten Australia to pick up the gold medal on the only occasion men's cricket had been included in the Commonwealth Games, in Kuala Lumpur in September 1998. The competition was given List A status, rather than full ODI, but Woolmer felt that his team's four-wicket victory, achieved with four overs to spare, broke any inferiority complex his team might have been labouring under. A month later, they won the first edition of the ICC Champions Trophy in Bangladesh; a simple knockout competition in which they chased down West Indies' 245 in the final with three overs remaining.

According to Kirsten, however, they were still developing. 'We had kind of proven our worth as one-day team, but Australia were probably slightly ahead of us in skill, even though we had some individuals who could win games out of nowhere. We were still a work in progress, not the complete article. We were mentally immature as a group, even though we had made great strides in our ability to win games.'

A new format for the 1999 World Cup saw the teams split into two groups. The top three in each progressed to the Super Six, facing the qualifiers they'd not yet played and carrying forward the points gained against the teams who had advanced with them. Woolmer, who would be departing as South Africa's coach after the tournament, was in a heightened state of anticipation. 'After the ups and down of five years with the national side, this would be the culmination of all my efforts,' he recalled.

South Africa's status as 11-4 favourites to lift the cup was justified by four victories in their ive Group A matches, opening with a win over India during which Woolmer's desire to push the boundaries of innovation fell foul of the ICC. Fielding first, Cronje and Allan Donald emerged from the Hove pavilion with earpieces held in place by sticking plaster, enabling the coach to pass instructions and suggestions to his captain and fast bowler. The devices had been tried in benefit matches and in South Africa's warm-up games in England without attracting attention. Woolmer had found nothing in the regulations to prevent their use. Television cameras were quick to bring South Africa's methods to viewers' attention, while Indian opener Sourav Ganguly challenged umpire David Shepherd about them shortly before a drinks break. 'Bob's view was that you send messages out via the third man or during the drinks break and you can chat then,' said Elworthy, 'so why couldn't he just talk to you from the side of the field by having someone pop in an earpiece?'

Cronje made no attempt to hide what was going on and Shepherd called on the advice of match referee Talat Ali, who in turn consulted the ICC. He was told that the earpieces were unfair, even though they were not prevented by any regulation. While the players were taking their refreshments he took the field and ordered them to be removed.

'All I was trying to do was give help and advice,' Woolmer explained, offering a hypothetical example of Donald needing some words to address 'technical faults'. 'I'm sorry if I've upset anyone. I've tried to be innovative. The idea was to take the game forward.' Citing the example of American football, he added, 'I felt it was a really good idea. Hopefully it will make life easier for the cricketer.' More than two decades later, the cricketer is still having to manage without such assistance in his ear.

South Africa's one defeat in the first phase was against surprise package Zimbabwe, who edged out hosts England for third place on net run rate as a result. England's three victories had all been comfortable run chases, but they ended up being criticised for cruising home rather than going after rate-boosting quick wins. It meant they were eliminated before the official song of the tournament – 'All Over The World' by ex-Eurythmic Dave Stewart – was released as a single.

The final game of the Super Six stage offered South Africa the chance to get rid of Australia, too. Already assured of a place in the top four and a semi-final berth, Woolmer's side knew that victory over their great rivals at Headingley would leave the Aussies stuck in fifth place and on the plane home. Having lost their second and third games of the competition to New Zealand and Pakistan, Australia had been playing must-win games for several weeks. 'I think perhaps we put too much emphasis on winning the World Cup and forgot the process needed to get there,' captain Waugh said in explaining his team's slow start. 'We'd gone straight from the West Indies to England so we'd been on the road for a couple of months already. Shane Warne had just been dropped in the Test series, which probably was a little bit disruptive to the team. There was a lot of commotion around that.' The decision of Waugh and coach Geoff Marsh to loosen their rules about bedtime and alcohol intake coincided with an upturn in fortunes. 'Once we decided to pull back and relax,' Waugh recalled, 'we started to do better.'

It was Waugh, one of the sport's great fighters, who ensured that they advanced to the last four by scoring a brilliant unbeaten 120 off 110 balls, cancelling out a century by South Africa's Herschelle Gibbs and seeing his team reach their target of 272 with two balls remaining. When they'd still needed 120 off the final 20 overs, Waugh, on 58, had clipped Lance Klusener to midwicket, where Gibbs allowed the ball to slip from his hand as he began tossing it up in celebration. Commentator David Gower had already exclaimed, 'That's out'. Legend has it that Waugh told Gibbs, 'You just dropped the World Cup,' although players close enough to eavesdrop all insist that he actually said, 'You've just cost your team the game.' After years of media embellishment, Waugh smiles, 'People like that line, so let's leave it as it is.' Warne, meanwhile, was able to bask in the fact that he'd cautioned teammates the night before not to be too quick to depart the crease if caught by Gibbs because he had seen him lose control of the ball before. There were also suggestions that if the fielder had merely continued his celebrations after the ball hit the ground – rather than pulling up in shock and desperation – the umpires would have allowed the catch.

Australia's win meant they faced South Africa at Edgbaston four days later for the right to play in the final against Pakistan, who had overwhelmed New Zealand in the other semi-final the previous day. Importantly, as it turned out, the Headingley victory also meant they had jumped above South Africa on net run-rate for second place in the Super Six table, the deciding factor in the unlikely event of the semi-final ending in a tie.[12]

'The semi-final, for me, is almost less relevant than the round-robin game against Australia,' said Kirsten. 'That game was a little bit scary for me because we had a great opportunity to win and we blew that. That took its toll mentally on us, and now we were up against Australia again and they had the capacity and experience to manage themselves through that kind of situation.'

The focus of the media in the days before the game was South Africa's reputation for being unable to win when it counted. 'I never said South Africa were chokers, I said they couldn't play well under pressure,' Waugh said, before digging his knife in a little further. 'But if remarks like that upset them, then they have problems.'

Woolmer, who had just ruled himself out of contention to succeed David Lloyd as England coach, did indeed sound upset when he told reporters, 'When you call us chokers, you have to go back to pre-1997. This is 1999, the choking thing is all played out.'

Elworthy recalled, 'Clearly there is a little apprehension because it is a semi-final, but there was also the view that if we had got through it we felt we would win the World Cup because of the quality of side Australia were. We really had them on the rack in the first game before they came back, and when you started listing the names in that South African team we felt we could go toe to toe with them. So there was an incredibly positive mood in the camp.'

When Cronje won the toss and elected to bowl, he told his players before they took the field, 'We know we can beat these guys. Let's not let ourselves down.' And for much of the day, they didn't. In the first over, Mark Waugh was unable to prevent Shaun Pollock's lifting delivery brushing his glove on way to wicketkeeper Mark Boucher. For a while Ricky Ponting threatened to dominate, pulling successive deliveries from Elworthy for six and four. He was just as punishing outside off stump, slashing Elworthy past third man and

---

[12] Even with their loss to Australia, South Africa would have topped the Super Six table had they won that first-round match against Zimbabwe. It would have meant them carrying forward an additional two points from a victory against England – who would have qualified for the Super Sixes – instead of being burdened with a defeat against Zimbabwe.

cutting Pollock square. But with the score on 54 in the 14th over, he drove loosely at Donald and found Kirsten at short cover. The final ball of the over – Donald's first – bounced and moved as it went across left-hander Darren Lehman and Boucher took another catch, justifying the tactic of holding Donald back until the first bowling changes were made.

Adam Gilchrist fell to the last ball of the 17th over, caught by Donald at third man after throwing the bat at Jacques Kallis, leaving Australia 68 for 4 and needing another big innings from Steve Waugh, who had been a fraction of an inch away from being run out when Kirsten's diving underarm throw slid past the stumps. So determined were he and Michael Bevan not to lose another wicket that when Waugh edged Lance Klusener for four it had been nine overs since the last boundary. Bevan, who scored eight runs from his first 40 balls, pulled to the rope in the same over to take the score into three figures after 30 overs.

The landmark appeared to free Waugh's shackles. In the space of two overs he took Elworthy for four on either side of the wicket and twice swung Klusener down the ground, the first effort bouncing just short of the rope and the second going the extra few yards for six. He reached his half-century with a cover-drive against Pollock, but in the 40th over he tried to feather the same bowler behind square and was caught by Boucher. Pollock wasted little time in swinging one back in to trap Tom Moody lbw on the back foot.

After that, Warne managed to bash a few, wickets fell frequently and Bevan was last out for 65 in the final over, nicking to Boucher to give Pollock his fifth wicket to set alongside Donald's four. A total of 213 was hardly one to send shivers down the spine of the South Africans, who were reminded by Cronje, 'It's not done yet. Keep concentrating and finish the job.'

Gibbs seemed intent to do so in quick time, punishing the Australian bowlers when given any width outside off stump – batting 'like a man on a mission to redeem his soul', Warne would write. With the wicket showing little of its early-morning menace, Kirsten profited when Glenn McGrath strayed towards leg and Gibbs sent Paul Reiffel to the long-on boundary with barely a defensive push. He then forced McGrath off the back foot for another four and punched Reiffel straight.

Waugh turned to Warne, who had endured a difficult few months. Still recovering from shoulder reconstruction, he had been dropped in the West Indies and, although taking 12 wickets in Australia's eight World Cup games, had looked far from being the match-winner of earlier in his career. Warne even feared that defeat at Edgbaston might mean the end of his ODI career.

But the second ball of his second over changed all that. Bowling to the right-handed Gibbs, his delivery dipped and pitched outside leg stump before jack-knifing across the batsman and brushing the top of his off stump. The comparisons with the 'Ball of the Century', with which he had dismissed Mike Gatting in an Ashes Test match six years earlier, were obvious and immediate; Gibbs's disbelief no less real than the England man's had been. He had not heard the ball hitting the bails and was initially confused by Gilchrist's excitement behind the stumps. The significance of the moment was apparent to all, not least the bowler himself, who raced around screaming, 'Come on! Come on!'

Rejuvenated, Warne struck again in his next over. Kirsten attempted to sweep from outside off and found the ball spinning from the foot marks to his off peg. Warne windmilled his arms in celebration and his teammates found belief flooding back into their bodies. Waugh recalled 'the pent-up force that [Warne] had suppressed in his system' and added, 'His drive and will were literally scary, but he sparked life into others who were tensing up under the South African onslaught.'

Cronje lasted only two balls against Warne, given out caught at slip even though the ball appeared to have struck his toe rather than his bat. Even umpire David Shepherd seemed to have been swept up by the tornado of energy and sheer will that was Warne. With three wickets in eight balls without conceding a run, the great leg-spinner had put his team back on top.

Another golden arm made it 61 for 4, Bevan's direct hit from short extra cover running out Cullinan, slow to respond to Kallis's call. As had been the case when Australia batted, the fifth-wicket pair had no choice but to rebuild. Boundaries were scarce as the watchful Kallis and the busy Jonty Rhodes nudged the score along, until Rhodes swung Mark Waugh over the deep midwicket rope and South Africa reached 144 for 4 from 40 overs. 'We had the game in the bag,'

Woolmer recalled. 'Or so I thought'. With seven per over needed from the final 10, they could have done without Rhodes holing out for 43, especially with Warne still having two overs to bowl.

Warne's final over was the 45th, which began with 53 needed from 36 balls. Kallis took three after Reiffel fluffed a chance at mid-off, and Pollock bashed the next two balls for six over long-on and four through the covers. After the batsmen changed ends with a single, Warne's penultimate delivery removed Kallis, who appeared to be deceived in the flight and lobbed a tame catch to Steve Waugh at cover.

Even the players were having trouble keeping up with the drunken manner in which the game was swaying back and forth. 'Neither team was at their best in that game,' Kirsten recalled. 'Steve Waugh made the comment that towards the end of the game both teams were making a lot of mistakes; it was just that one team made one more mistake than the other.'

Bevan, who was giving what journalist Peter Roebuck called 'the greatest exhibition of fielding' he had seen, recalled, 'I remember thinking, "We're going to win this. No, we're going to lose this. No, we're going to win this." Every over.' According to Ponting, 'It was one of those days in the field when you dared not lose focus for even an instant in case the game found you out.' Off the field, squabbles broke out between the wives and girlfriends of the two teams, while the South African players sought ways to deal with the excruciating drama – which, in Donald's case, meant removing himself from the dressing room and watching with fourth umpire Roy Palmer. In came Klusener, the man of the tournament. The brutal lower-order hitting of the player nicknamed Zulu – he hailed from Natal Province and was a fluent Zulu speaker – had been a feature of the previous few weeks; the kind of specialism that, added to useful seam bowling, would make millions for the likes of West Indian Andre Russell in the franchise Twenty20 leagues that lay years ahead. So rich was his vein of form that he would conclude the calendar year of 1999 with 824 runs in 24 innings at an average of 94.89 and a strike rate of 102. On this day, he brought to the crease a World Cup batting record that read: 12*, 52*, 48*, DNB, 52*, 46*, 4, 36 – a total of 250 runs off 213 balls. It was a surprise to most that South Africa had waited so long before sending him out to bat. 'There was this belief in the team,'

Elworthy explained, 'particularly because of the way Lance had been playing. He had pulled games out of the fire.'

On this occasion, he wasted little time before flaying Damien Fleming through the leg side but quickly lost Pollock at the other end when he edged into his stumps. Tight bowling from McGrath and Fleming starved Klusener of the strike and made the target 24 off 14, although South Africa's hitman reduced it by six runs off the next two balls by finding the boundary wide of third man and running two more to deep midwicket. But just when South Africa appeared to have the momentum, the course of this remarkable match changed again.

McGrath took out Boucher's middle stump as he hit over a yorker and two balls later Elworthy failed to beat Reiffel's throw to the bowler as he tried to secure Klusener a second run. Replays confirmed that the stumps had been broken by the ball rather than McGrath's hand and Donald made the walk of a condemned man to the middle, an experience he likened to 'flying with one wheel off, waiting for the crash landing'.

Another 16 were needed from eight balls, with one wicket remaining. Australia's game, surely – especially when Klusener picked up McGrath's full toss and hit it straight at Reiffel, five yards in from the boundary at long-on. The fielder's arms went up, but the ball bounced off his hands, and plopped beyond the rope for six runs. A single kept Klusener on strike for the final over. Nine to win.

'I still had pads on and I was sitting in a room at the back,' Elworthy explained. 'Edgbaston was still like a football changing room, all pokey and not much viewing anywhere. Most of the guys had got seats up the front and I was in the back, where there was a TV on top of one of the lockers. There were one or two people in there, including Herschelle, and I watched things unfold between there and popping my head out the front to see what was happening, not quite believing what was going on in front of my eyes.'

Bowling round the wicket, Fleming delivered the first ball of the final over to Klusener. 'The plan was simple: fire those yorkers in and give him a single,' Waugh recalled. The ball was full and wide but the burly South African jammed his bat down to squeeze the ball square for four. Donald reckoned he had never seen a ball hit harder – until the next one. With commentator Bill Lawry matched in his state of excitement by the crowds standing and screaming in the stands, Klusener remained expressionless; evidently untouched by the tension and turmoil around him. 'I'm still in awe at his calmness as I think of the bedlam out in the middle,' Donald said later. Klusener stepped back and muscled the ball through the off side, all along the ground for four more. Scores level with four balls left. In the dressing room, Cronje's head went into his hands. At least his team were now on the right side of the equation.

Two slips and a ring of fielders was the Australian shape as Fleming announced his intention to bowl over the wicket. 'We were shitting ourselves,' was Waugh's admission of how the Aussies were feeling at this point. Meanwhile, Woolmer tried to calm the players who were getting ready to break into the pile of beer and bubbly in the dressing room. 'We were out of our chairs,' Pollock admitted. 'We thought that was game over.'

The next ball was short and Klusener, one clean connection away from the final, banged it straight to Lehmann at mid-on. Donald, who according to the *Melbourne Age* had 'set off like a greyhound from a vet', was almost run out as he scrambled back. 'That's it – our last chance gone. We'll need a miracle now,' Waugh admitted to himself. But perhaps the close call influenced what happened next because when Klusener scuffed a full ball back past the bowler and charged off running, Donald remained in his crease. He was still there as his partner was arriving at his end. Inexplicably, there had been no conversation between the two batsmen, no agreement on strategy. Presumably Klusener had expected his bat to do the talking.

Without knowing what was or wasn't said in the middle, or referring specifically to the final over, Kirsten felt, 'We lacked a bit of maturity in those pressure moments. Some individuals did not always handle themselves well in the big moments. If we were ever going to get exposed in games it was going to be around that. We did not always make good decisions when it was absolutely required.'

Elworthy recalled, 'It was a case study of high-performance athletes not communicating in a high-pressure situation. After almost being run out at point-blank range they didn't walk down the wicket and have a conversation. One had thought he was going to be run out and shouldn't have run and the other thought he should have run but didn't. So then they ended up doing the reverse.'

170

Fleming observed, 'I know if I was batting with Steve Waugh or Michael Bevan we would have just said, "Just bat the next two balls. If we can't hit it through the infield we'll run off the last ball."' In fact, neither side had attempted to take deep breaths and clear their heads. In his excellent 20-year retrospective of the game for *Cricket Monthly*, Rob Smyth pointed out that while there had been 91 seconds between the delivery of the second and third balls of the over, only 36 seconds elapsed between third and fourth. Waugh confessed, 'I can't criticise [the batsmen] too much because we didn't have much of a plan either.'

With Klusener's momentum carrying him on towards the exit, Donald had no choice but to run, even though by now he had managed to drop his bat, and his legs 'felt like jelly'. Mark Waugh's toss at the bowler's end missed the stumps, but Fleming calmly picked up the ball and rolled it along the ground towards Gilchrist. The last time an Australian bowler had propelled the ball down the wicket underarm it had caused an outcry in world cricket; this time it broke the hearts of the South African nation as the wicketkeeper removed the bails with Donald yards from safety. 'I heard [Klusener] say "yes" straightaway and knew Donald had gone back,' said Fleming. He also attributed his instinctive action of underarming the ball down the wicket to team's ten-pin bowling outing a couple of days earlier.

Yellow Australian uniforms flew in all directions, creating a spectacular photographic record of the decisive moment. 'We ran around like prison escapees,' said Waugh, while Bevan recalled, 'I just ran to the bloke nearest me and screamed in delight'.

The game was tied. Australia were in the final because of their higher placing in the Super Six table, although Waugh and other players confessed that they had merely been celebrating the avoidance of defeat without realising what the tournament rules stated. Meanwhile, South Africa, in the eyes of the world, were confirmed as 'chokers'. When it came to the vital moment, they had needed one run from four balls with the most destructive batsman of the tournament at the crease. Klusener observed that it should have been a recognised batsman out there with him rather than Donald – but, after all the twists and turns of the day, South Africa could hardly have chosen a more favourable scenario for the game's climax.

In 1992, their semi-final dressing room had been dominated by anger and frustration; this time it was inconsolable and incredulous, with players crying under the towels with which they were covering their heads. 'It was absolutely devastating,' Elworthy remembered.

'The scene resembled that of a refuge in the midst of a natural disaster,' observed Woolmer, who signed to return to coach Warwickshire within hours of the game's conclusion. 'I felt sick to my stomach. It hurt not because I wanted to win the World Cup more than anything else but because we were comfortably the best-equipped team in the competition.' He concluded, 'I could never blame Lance or Allan, only empathise with them for something that will live in their minds forever.'

Cronje emerged to face interrogation by Ian Chappell at the presentation ceremony. 'Jonty and Jacques gave us a real chance and unfortunately things didn't run our way towards the end,' he said. 'It's as close as you can get, I suppose,' he shrugged, his eyes darker than ever, as though they'd shrunk back into his head in refusal to accept what they had witnessed.

Steve Waugh had gone around the South African players offering handshakes and 'hard luck'. According to Kirsten, 'The Australians handled themselves very well. They knew what it meant for us as a cricket nation and I thought they were led very well by Steve Waugh in their approach and assisting us through the disappointment.' Waugh looked hardly less frazzled than his opposite number when he told Chappell, 'That was best game of cricket I've ever played. In that situation you've just got to hold your nerve.'

The second World Cup semi-final of 1999 cannot be said to have had far-reaching repercussions, or symbolised seismic events that were changing the sport. It was, pure and simple, a great game of cricket, tension stretched to breaking point across several thrilling, draining hours; a day that will live forever in the history of the shortened form of the sport. 'It was one of my career highlights,' said Kirsten. 'To play in one of the greatest one-day games ever played with so much at stake.'

But there were some footnotes. When Australia bowled out Pakistan for 132 to win the final by eight wickets it was the first of three consecutive World Cup triumphs. By the time they were lifting the third of those trophies in the West Indies in 2007, the two men who had plotted to beat them throughout the latter half of the 1990s, Hansie Cronje and Bob Woolmer, were both dead. And in the case of Cronje, his reputation had gone as well.

AUSTRALIA v SOUTH AFRICA, World Cup Semi-Final
17 June 1999, Edgbaston

Australia			Balls	4s	6s
†AC Gilchrist	c Donald by Kallis	20	39	1	1
ME Waugh	c Boucher b Pollock	0	3		
RT Ponting	c Kirsten b Donald	37	49	3	1
DS Lehmann	c Boucher b Donald	1	4		
*SR Waugh	c Boucher b Pollock	56	76	6	1
MG Bevan	c Boucher b Pollock	65	101	6	
TM Moody	lbw b Pollock	0	3		
SK Warne	c Cronje b Pollock	18	24	1	
PR Reiffel	b Donald	0	1		
DW Fleming	b Donald	0	2		
GD McGrath	not out	0	1		
Extras	(b 1, lb 6, w 3, nb 6)	16			
Total	(49.2 overs)	213			

Fall: 3, 54, 58, 68, 158, 158, 207, 207, 207, 213
Bowling: Pollock 9.2-1-36-5; Elworthy 10-0-59-0; Kallis 10-2-27-1; Donald 10-1-32-4; Klusener 9-1-50-0; Cronje 1-0-2-0.

South Africa			Balls	4s	6s
G Kirsten	b Warne	18	42	1	
HH Gibbs	b Warne	30	36	6	
DJ Cullinan	run out	6	30		
*WJ Cronje	c ME Waugh b Warne	0	2		
JH Kallis	c SR Waugh b Warne	53	92	3	
JN Rhodes	c Bevan b Reiffel	43	55	2	1
SM Pollock	b Fleming	20	14	1	1
L Klusener	not out	31	16	4	1
†MV Boucher	b McGrath	5	10		
S Elworthy	run out	1	1		
AA Donald	run out	1	1		
Extras	(lb 1, w 6)	6			
Total	(49.4 overs)	213			

Fall: 48, 53, 53, 61, 145, 175, 183, 196, 198, 213.
Bowling: McGrath 10-0-51-1; Fleming 8.4-1-40-1; Reiffel 8-0-28-1; Warne 10-4-29-4; ME Waugh 8-0-37-0; Moody 5-0-27-0.

Match Tied. **Toss:** South Africa. **Umpires:** DR Shepherd, S. Venkataraghavan.
Man of the Match: SK Warne.

14

'THE TRUTH WILL SET YOU FREE'

India v South Africa, 5th One-Day International, 2000, Nagpur

It was 6.30 a.m. when Herschelle Gibbs answered a knock at the door of his Nagpur hotel room and found South African captain Hansie Cronje outside in the corridor. This was early for the skipper to come calling, even on the day of the team's fifth and final one-day international against India. Cronje entered and sat on the bed. Gibbs's roommate, fast bowler Henry Williams, was in the shower.

'I've got a man here in India and you can make some good money if you do what he's asking,' were the words that slipped effortlessly, and explosively, from Cronje's lips. 'He's offering $15,000 if you go out for less than 20 in today's game.'

A thought flashed instantly through the mind of Gibbs, who would be opening the batting for his team. 'My mum's house needs to be paid off. I might as well try to make some money.' He gave Cronje his answer. 'OK. Cool.'

Gibbs would describe it as a 'spur-of-the-moment decision' that he came to regret, and admitted – remarkably, given the huge step it represented – that 'I genuinely didn't give it too much thought'. As well as what this says about Gibbs's state of mind at the time, it is an indication of the trust that Cronje engendered among his players; a sense of security that everything would be all right. Emerging from the bathroom, Williams was offered money for ensuring that his 10 overs went for more than 50 runs. 'If Hershy says yes, I'll go along with it too,' he replied.

A few hours later, Gibbs was heading out into the middle of the Vidarbha Cricket Association Stadium after India, leading 3-1, had won the toss for the first time in the series and chosen to field. The first wicket fell in the second over, when the left-handed Gary Kirsten pushed Venkatesh Prasad towards mid-off and failed to beat a direct underarm hit by Sachin Tendulkar.

Gibbs faced the experienced Javagal Srinath in the third over, nonchalantly flipping a ball from off stump behind square leg for four. 'He's not taking any prisoners today,' Tony Greig observed from the commentary box, adding 'Gibbs is on fire' when, in Srinath's next over, the batsman drove him on the up to the extra-cover boundary.

Sixth over, Prasad bowling, and Gibbs 19 not out. Far from looking for a way to get back to pavilion, Gibbs again seized upon what looked like a decent off-stump delivery and whipped it to the rope backward of square leg. 'They don't quite know what to do to Gibbs today,' Greig chuckled. 'He is taking them on the off and the on side. He is smashing them to every corner of the ground.'

It was not what had been scripted in the dawn hours. But by now, Gibbs's head was in a different place to that which it had occupied while Cronje had been sitting on his bed. Throwing away his wicket for less than 20 might not irrevocably impact the outcome of the match, but it was, he realised, a huge risk. The consequences of being found out could deprive him of his career. Before the game even began, he'd told Cronje he couldn't go through with it. Far from appearing disturbed, the captain casually responded, 'Don't worry about it, Hersh. Let's just forget about the whole thing.' So calm had Cronje appeared, Gibbs wondered if it had been a joke all along.

It meant he suffered no pause as he left the 20 mark behind him, coming down the track to smack Prasad wide of mid-off for his sixth boundary in a score of 27 off 12 balls. Anil Kumble was pulled for four when his first delivery to Gibbs dropped short and the leg-spinner then missed an easy-looking return catch. That left Gibbs free to slam Prasad back over his head for another four.

At 66 for 3, Gibbs was joined by Cronje and together they added 60, the skipper making 38 off 31 balls before falling with the score on 126 in only the 15th over. Gibbs in the meantime advanced to a half-century. He flicked Srinath past fine leg; rocked onto the back foot to lift the same bowler to the cover boundary; and advanced to hit off-spinner Nikhil Chopra straight to reach his milestone on the 30th ball he faced. Having been dropped again, by Tendulkar at short extra cover, Gibbs's quick feet enabled him to send Sridharam Sriram inside-out to the boundary on the off side; then he was on the march again to deposit Chopra over the sightscreen and down on one knee to sweep him fine for four. 'What a day he's having,' gasped Greig. Certainly not the one he'd been planning at 6.30.

'It wasn't like I was just slogging,' Gibbs recalled. 'I was playing proper cricket shots.'

It needed a swift pick-up and pinpoint throw by Sriram in the covers to dismiss him for 74 off 53 balls after he responded to Mark Boucher's call for a quick single. He departed wiping the sweat from his shaven head. South Africa's innings eventually reached 320 for 7, Lance Klusener showing his form of the World Cup by scoring an unbeaten 75. For India to win they needed to achieve what at the time would have been the highest successful run chase in ODI history.

With Gibbs having failed to truncate his innings as originally planned, it was now the turn of Williams to come nowhere close to the performance that had been proposed earlier in the day. Far from giving up 50 runs off 10 overs, he completed only 1.5 overs before succumbing to an injured right shoulder. The commentators were warning against him continuing as he ran up to bowl his final delivery, a short ball outside leg stump that Ganguly helped round the corner into the grasp of Steve Elworthy.

Williams took no further part in what proved to be a thrilling contest. Tendulkar, who hit four sixes in his 93, and Dravid put on 180 in less than 24 overs before both fell on 193. Despite losing wickets steadily, India were still in the game when they reached the final 18 balls needing 18, only for Klusener to take his third wicket to remove Robin Singh and for the final two men to be dismissed by run-outs on 310 in the penultimate over. 'And that, I thought, was that,' said Gibbs, after what he called a 'small brush with a nasty part of cricket'.

* * *

In the first days of April, rumours began circulating that Indian police had a recording of a telephone conversation between Cronje and a representative of a betting syndicate, a man named Sanjay Chawla. Police in Delhi then released a transcript in which the South African captain offered information about his team and tactics. He revealed that off-spinner Derek Crookes would open the bowling – the kind of knowledge that gamblers craved in order to take advantage of the various bets being offered – and there was also an agreement reached about the runs to be scored by Gibbs. So serious were the repercussions that Aziz Pahad, South Africa's Deputy Minister of Foreign Affairs, quickly contacted the Indian government, while further conversations took place between the High Commissioners to each country.

'These allegations are completely without substance,' was Cronje's immediate response, telling a press conference, 'I want to make it 100 per cent clear that I deny ever receiving any sum of money during the one-day international series in India. I want to also make it absolutely clear that I have never spoken to any member of the team about throwing a game.'

At the distance of more than two decades and with Cronje's name now so inextricably linked by history to the darker side of the game, it is easy to overlook the seismic nature of these allegations in South Africa. In his book '...And Nothing But The Truth'?, author Deon Gouws noted that this episode concerned 'arguably the cleanest character in the world of cricket'. He continued, 'Respected the world over as a great captain, a high-quality all-rounder and a fierce competitor, very few people would believe that he would ever be guilty of unethical behaviour.' Cronje was also a committed Christian, about which he was very public. 'It simply seemed unthinkable,' wrote Gouws, 'that he of all people would ever contemplate involvement in shady dealings.'

Along with World Cup-winning rugby captain, Francois Pienaar, Cronje was seen as a key figure in post-apartheid South Africa, the mutual respect between him and the new president, Nelson Mandela, setting an example of the tolerance and cross-community support needed to take the nation forward into its new era. The South African team's former strength and conditioning coach, Paddy Upton, told Netflix's *Bad Sport* series, 'Next to Mandela, Hansie was probably the next highest regarded citizen.' Even an outsider, the BBC's Jonathan Agnew, was able to observe, 'He was on a pedestal the like of which I don't think I had ever come across before.'

Seam bowler Elworthy was so unaware of anything untoward at Nagpur that two decades later he had to look up the scorecard online to remind himself of what happened in the match before talking about it. 'Honestly, I knew absolutely nothing about it. It was a normal tour match. But I was never really what I would call a permanent member of that team at any point. I came in and out over the course of five years. Compared with the core team, I was a bit of an outsider. I was always made to feel very welcome, but I was outside of the inner circle. It was a devastating shock to me when I heard about it.'

Cronje addressed his teammates in their hotel in Durban, prior to an ODI series against Australia, and assured them that the story was untrue. His men believed him without question and felt comfortable in telling him so. Elworthy was live on South African television when the story broke, appearing on the *Extra Cover* show hosted by Mike Haysman. 'I said there is absolutely no way in the world that is true,' he remembered. 'Rod McCurdy[13] was also on the show and he said, "I wouldn't be surprised. Where there is smoke there is fire."'

There were personal reasons for Elworthy's scepticism about allegations that appeared out of character. 'I'd had a benefit year in 1999 and Hansie was going to be a speaker at one of the functions right after the World Cup. As devastated as we were, he sat with me on the flight home and spent hours working through his speech and my speech and giving me pointers on what to do. Then he stayed in Pretoria to do the benefit stuff with me rather than flying home first to Bloemfontein. That is how he was. That he wanted to support me after such a monumental occasion spoke absolute volumes for the guy. He truly was an inspirational guy, just awesome.'

According to Boucher, 'I always had a good strong relationship with Hansie... Just about everyone who played under him will say the same.' Even Woolmer, who admitted 'there were times when I thought I could not trust him', concluded, 'Always his beliefs led me to reckon that he would not let me down.'

The public's disbelief in what they were hearing heightened when some South African media members picked up on an Indian broadcast interpretation of the transcript, in which voiceover artists – both Indian – were used to re-enact the discussion. Apparently not realising this was a dramatisation, it was reported that the tape was clearly a fake and sounded nothing like the Proteas skipper.

---

13 Former Australian cricketer who settled in South Africa after taking part in his country's rebel tours there in the mid-1980s

Yet several days after the original story broke, a guilt-ridden Cronje confided in Ali Bacher. The managing director of the United Cricket Board of South Africa (UCBSA) had already stated publicly, 'The allegations are outrageous. Hansie Cronje is a man of unquestionable honesty and integrity.' But now he found Cronje telling him that he had not been 'entirely honest', confessing to forecasting results for an Asian bookmaker in return for $15,000. He had never, he stated, been involved in match fixing. The UCBSA had little choice but to sack him as captain and order a full inquiry. 'We in South African cricket are shattered,' Bacher told another press conference.

The King Commission, to be led by Judge Edwin King, was scheduled for two months later. 'Complete and utter shock,' was what Elworthy felt as he realised that the accusations against a man who had grown up wanting nothing more than to captain South Africa in international cricket, and had done so for six years, might well be true.

Shaun Pollock was named as South African skipper to face Australia, telling the players to stick together and reminding them of the responsibility they now had towards themselves and their country. But Boucher recalled in his autobiography that 'it honestly felt like everyone was in mourning' and were left wondering if they had unwittingly played a part in dishonest matches. For his own part, he began wondering about the moment in the Nagpur game when Cronje, unusually, had asked him as wicketkeeper to stand up to the stumps while he was bowling and then uncharacteristically fired four byes down the leg side.

Cronje, meanwhile, had approached Gibbs and instructed him to deny everything. In the same trusting manner in which he'd originally gone along with a captain of whom he was 'in awe', Gibbs agreed. When he spoke to Bacher he was advised to save his version of events for the official inquiry in Cape Town. As the hearing grew near, Gibbs was 'shitting myself'. The pressure of maintaining his silence led to a stress-related migraine during a round of golf in Cape Town and many sleepless nights. He and Cronje had maintained to each other that they would continue their denials. Yet a week before proceedings began Gibbs unburdened himself to Boucher over a few drinks. 'If you lie you could go to jail,' Boucher counselled.

Gibbs decided to tell the truth, beginning with sharing his story with his manager, Donné Commins, and lawyer Peter Whelan.

Boucher was surprised at Gibbs's jovial mood at the beginning of that meeting but revealed, 'There were plenty of times in Hershy's life when I could see that he wanted to cry rather than smile, but crying didn't fit into who Herschelle Gibbs was, so he forced himself to laugh instead.'

Then Gibbs called Cronje and told him what he intended to do. He also committed to share with the commission a previous incident in 1996, when Cronje had got the team together before a game in India and told them, 'I know a guy.' On that occasion the offer had been $250,000 to the team if they lost, which Gibbs described as 'tempting' because they were without many leading players because of illness and injury.

'You never really knew exactly where you stood with Hansie,' Boucher suggested. 'You never knew whether it was serious or whether he was kidding.' On this occasion Boucher felt that 'the offer was very lighthearted', recalling, 'We didn't take him seriously. As always, if in doubt with Hansie just laugh.' In the end, the suggestion was rejected because there was no unanimous acceptance, but 'it hadn't been an immediate and strong reaction to an activity totally abhorrent to the notion of sport', Gibbs remembered.

Kirsten's memory of the incident is somewhat different, recalling a more serious and sinister tone. 'I swear you could have heard a pin drop onto a carpet at that moment,' he said of Cronje's proposal. 'Nobody moved a muscle. In retrospect I think I'd gone into instant shock.' He remembered 'a cold, cold feeling in the room and deathly silence' before senior players spoke for the rest of the team by saying they would be 'crazy' to consider the offer.

But Kirsten also explained that by the time South Africa were back in India in early 2000, there had been so much global discussion of match-fixing that it had become part of the daily banter and discussion among the squad. Cronje used to joke about becoming involved, with comments such as, 'If you make nought today, somebody will get very rich,' making it hard for players to know if he was ever being serious. Kirsten believed that any number of players could have stated they had been the subject of an approach, depending on their interpretation of comments made by the skipper. 'All his life he'd been a practical joker and it was perfectly possible to believe he was messing around again.'

Gibbs recalled Cronje reacting to his declaration of intent about his testimony with such calm acceptance that he immediately suspected that his captain had also decided to come clean in front of the commission. There were several days of evidence – including Gibbs, of course – before Cronje was due to give his version of events. Spin bowler Pat Symcox related the story of the 1996 offer in India and told of Cronje approaching him with a proposal to throw a Mandela Trophy game against Pakistan in Cape Town in 1995. Crookes said he had been approached during a flight to the 1996 game and thought other players had been spoken to individually before the team meeting. He also explained that he had opened the bowling in the controversial ODI in Nagpur after being told following the first game that he would not be asked to fulfil that role again. He expressed surprise that he was allowed to bowl a full complement of 10 overs, which cost 69 runs, after being 'taken to the cleaners' by the batsmen in his first five overs.

In the testimony of batsman Peter Strydom, focus was turned on the Test match against England at Centurion in January 2000, when Cronje had suggested to English counterpart Nasser Hussain that each side should forfeit an innings of a rain-wrecked match in order to manufacture a run chase on the final day. Set 249, England won by two wickets and Cronje was hailed for the way he had saved a dead game. The 'spirit of cricket' was invoked in many of the tributes to his sportsmanship. Strydom said Cronje had been interested in the odds on the game before and after the declarations and forfeits and had asked him to place a bet. The bet never went on because Strydom couldn't get the odds. He also testified that Cronje had offered R70,000 if South Africa scored less than 250 in a Test in Mumbai. Strydom, whose Test career consisted of only those Centurion and Mumbai matches, said he would have considered the offer had he been at the end of a long career rather than trying to establish one.

The highlight of Bacher's appearance was when he declared, 'I would sum up my feelings as follows, that if the bookmakers can get to Hansie Cronje they can get to anybody in world cricket.' Next in the order was Klusener, who said Cronje asked him, Boucher and Kallis before the Second Test in India if they were interested in an offer. They declined.

On the sixth day, it was Cronje's turn in the hot seat, with a live television audience hanging on every word. As he took his seat, he was told to volunteer all possible information by King, who even reminded him that the Gospel of St John promised, 'The truth will set you free.'

Cronje's truth included the information that he had been approached by a man calling himself 'John' before the Mandela Trophy game, offering money for the South Africans to throw the match. He also revealed that, having taken money from Sanjay Chawla, he had 'got into something from which it was very difficult to get out'. He accepted a mobile phone from Sanjay that would be used to phone him for information, and he talked about the pressure that was now being put on him. He said he'd pretended to play along with an arrangement to lose the first one-day international in Cochin earlier in the year but did nothing about it. For the next three ODIs he did some forecasting free of charge, and then gave in over the game in Nagpur. He said that was the end of his contact with Chawla.

Cronje also spoke about someone he knew as Sunil, who approached him about match fixing during the 1996 tour. Around the same time he was introduced to Mukesh 'MK' Gupta, who made the Mumbai offer that the South African team ended up discussing. Cronje said the introduction had been made by Mohammad Azharuddin, India's captain at the previous three World Cups, who denied the allegation. For a few months after the tour, Cronje supplied Gupta with information for $50,000. Investigation of Cronje's bank account revealed another deposit of $30,000, which he said he was unsure about but assumed it could also have come from Gupta.

Then there was Marlon Aronstam, a professional bookmaker, who approached Cronje and offered a gift and donation to charity if the declaration and forfeitures took place in Centurion. Cronje received payment and a leather jacket, with the money said to be in respect of future information. Finally, he said he declined another offer of $200,000 in Sharjah after the conclusion of the India tour. He left the hall after 40 minutes and the Commission adjourned for six days before Cronje's cross-examination. During that procedure it emerged that he had negotiated a payment of $25,000 for Gibbs and Williams in Nagpur, not the $15,000 he told them about. 'Maybe I was trying to cut something for myself,' he said. He also revealed that when the story broke in the media he was scared enough that he hid money in different places in his house. His testimony ended in a shower of tears.

Gibbs said of Cronje, 'getting easy money was his weakness. He wanted to do his utmost to get it.' Cronje, whose public profile had brought him a wide range of endorsement deals, had made no attempt in his testimony to deny his enjoyment of money. But what made Cronje's deeds even more troubling to many observers was the uncomfortable perception that the captain of South Africa had used his position to put pressure on two young non-white players.

After a tearful Aronstam gave his own testimony, the Commission heard from Hamid 'Banjo' Cassim, a go-between for Cronje and Chawla, who testified that Azharuddin, who would be dropped from the Indian team two months later while under investigation for corruption, would ring Cronje multiple times per day.

The first punishments handed out by the UCBSA's disciplinary committee as a result of the revelations were the banning of Gibbs and Williams from international cricket until the end of 2000, with fines of R60,000 for Gibbs and R10,000 for Williams, who has since denied receiving a financial offer from Cronje. Strydom was acquitted of the charge of trying to place a bet during the Centurion Test.

In October, with the King Commission still not concluded, came the UCBSA verdict on Cronje: banned for life from playing any role in cricket. President Percy Sonn said, 'Cronje won't play any further part in South Africa as a player or administrator. We made a decision after considering Cronje's evidence to the King Commission and a few other factors. There was no need to wait for the commission to run its course. The available evidence provided sufficient grounds for a life ban.'

As reporters and investigators continued digging, it would emerge that Cronje had possessed more than 70 bank accounts in the Cayman Islands. It was a number that suggested that the match-fixing problem brought vividly to life by events in Nagpur and their aftermath was more widespread than had so far been revealed.

Even while the Cronje affair was playing out in painful public view, a commission led by Justice Malik Qayyam in Pakistan was finding former Test captain Salim Malik and bowler Ata-ur-Rehman guilty of match-fixing. Life bans were imposed on both men, although the former's was overturned by a Pakistani court in 2008 and the latter's lifted by the ICC in 2006.

In November 2000, Azharuddin was banned for life by Board of Control for Cricket in India, which concluded that he 'contributed substantially' towards the increased connectivity between players and bookmakers and said that evidence 'clearly establishes that he took money' to fix matches. Teammates Ajay Jadeja, Manoj Prabhakar and Ajay Sharma and team physiotherapist Ali Irani were found guilty of having links to bookmakers, with the ban imposed on Jadeja overturned by the Delhi High Court in 2003 for lack of proof.

Azharuddin, too, continued to maintain his innocence and in 2012 a High Court ruling in Andhra Pradesh set aside his ban. 'I feel really happy at the judgement, though the legal process took quite a long time,' he said. 'It is a pity that the life ban was imposed without proper evidence against me.' Apparently his name had not been entirely cleared, however, and he was reportedly denied tickets to the 2017 ICC Champions Trophy in England.

Meanwhile, Cronje's life ban – his life, in fact – had proved to be tragically short. In June 2002, as the 32-year-old was attempting to build a new career as a businessman after a failed appeal against his ban, he and two pilots were killed in a mountainside plane crash in the Western Cape, not far from his home. No suspicious circumstances were reported at the time, but it did not take long for speculation to develop about foul play; rumours over unpaid debts or as-yet unspoken revelations. It was the final macabre twist to a story that had offered the first real proof that the glossy veneer of one-day cricket's big hits and dramatic finishes hid a murky sub-culture.

INDIA v SOUTH AFRICA, 5th One-Day International
19 March 2000, Vidarbha Cricket Association Stadium, Nagpur

South Africa			Balls	4s	6s
G Kirsten	run out	1	7		
HH Gibbs	run out	4	53	13	1
ND McKenzie	c Karim b Kumble	13	18	2	
DN Crookes	b Kumble	14	7	3	
*WJ Cronje	c Dravid b Chopra	38	31	3	2
†MV Boucher	c Kumble b Prasad	62	93	3	1
DM Benkenstein	b Tendulkar	24	44	1	
L Klusener	not out	75	58	8	3
PC Strydom	not out	0	0		
Extras	(lb 1, w 2, nb 10)	13			
Total	(7 wickets, 50 overs)	320			

Fall: 9, 42, 66, 1126, 161, 205, 319
Did Not Bat: S Elworthy, HS Williams
Bowling: Srinath 6-0-65-0; Prasad 6-1-46-1; Kumble 10-0-61-2; Chopra 10-0-57-1; Sriram 6-0-36-0; Singh 1-0-6-0; Tendulkar 10-0-31-1; Ganguly 1-0-17-0.

India			Balls	4s	6s
*SC Ganguly	c Elworthy b Williams	6	11	1	
SR Tendulkar	c Elworthy b Crookes	83	89	7	4
R Dravid	run out	79	70	11	
A Jadeja	b Elworthy	10	28		
S Sriram	c Boucher b Elworthy	12	15	1	
J Srinath	c Strydom b Klusener	20	18	2	
RR Singh	c Cronje b Klusener	29	35	2	
†S Karim	c & b Klusener	22	17	4	
N Chopra	run out	3	8		
A Kumble	run ou	5	4	1	
BKV Prasad	not out	0	2		
Extras	(b 4, lb 8, w 14, nb 5)	31			
Total	(48.5 overs)	310			

Fall: 13, 193, 193, 214, 221, 259, 290, 304, 310, 310.
Bowling: Williams 1.5-0-11-1; Crookes 10-1-69-1; McKenzie 0.1-0-0-0; Elworthy 8-0-50-2; Cronje 9.5-0-62-0; Klusener 9-0-59-3; Strydom 10-0-47-0.

South Africa won by 10 runs. **Toss:** India. **Umpires:** F Gomes, SK Bansal.
Man of the Match: L Klusener.

15

'THE DEATH OF DEMOCRACY'

Zimbabwe v Namibia, World Cup, Harare Sports Club, 2003

The rain fell. With Pakistan 73 for 3 from 14 overs, the rain fell. Like divine intervention, perhaps a blessing on the course of action he had taken three weeks earlier, the rain fell and fell. And it might just have saved Henry Olonga's life.

The resulting wash-out in Bulawayo gave Zimbabwe a share of the points in their Group A match in the first stages of the 2003 World Cup, ensuring they qualified for the Super Sixes round of the tournament. The journey the team would now make to South Africa for those matches was a flight to freedom for the 26-year-old fast bowler, the first black man to play Test cricket for his country. No longer would he have to keep a gun close to his side; no more would his father receive messages from police contacts warning him, 'Tell your son to get out of the country'. No more would he be looking over his shoulder or wondering who was bugging his phone.

Such events had become the frightening reality of Olonga's life since he and teammate Andy Flower had chosen Zimbabwe's opening World Cup game against Namibia in Harare to tell the world what they thought of the way in which their country was being ripped apart under the regime of President Robert Mugabe.

Leader of the Zimbabwe African National Union – Patriotic Front, Mugabe had been his country's leader since 1980, being elevated from prime minister to president seven years later. In 2000, he began a plan of land reforms that included the redistribution of thousands of farms; a campaign that saw government-backed invasions of white-owned properties by armed gangs. Within two years it was estimated that around 3,500 farms had been forcibly seized.

Flower visited his friend Nigel Huff's farm, which had been thriving until becoming a victim of Mugabe's reforms. 'Nigel said we had a moral obligation not to go about business as usual during the World Cup,' Flower told BBC Radio several years later. Huff insisted that the tournament was an opportunity to inform the world about events in Zimbabwe. 'It changed the way I viewed the country and our participation in that World Cup,' Flower said.

Olonga was not an obvious person for Flower to select as an ally. The fact that one was black and the other white – a powerful image to present to the world – was, on the face of it, the only thing that made them a natural pairing. While Olonga had been battling to establish himself in the team and had not always seeing eye to eye with coaches and management, Flower had single-mindedly turned himself into one of the finest batsmen in the world. They had usually found themselves on the opposite sides of the typical dressing-room politics. 'I had never engaged in too much friendly banter with Andy,' Olonga explained. 'That's just the way it was and the just the way we related.'

Not that Flower was viewed in any way as an establishment figure. His second spell as national captain had ended in 2000 after he threatened to lead his team out on strike before a Test match against England at Lord's because of poor pay, an event he felt was a 'pivotal moment' in the development of Zimbabwe cricket and the treatment of its players. 'They didn't want someone with that sort of power in charge of the national side,' he concluded.

Olonga was surprised, and confused about his teammate's intentions, when Flower suggested after a net session before the World Cup that they meet at a shopping mall. 'I thought Henry might grab the concept and have the courage of his convictions to take a stand,' Flower explained.

The concept in question had been suggested by Huff: that the Zimbabwe team should boycott the World Cup as a way of taking a stance against the way the country was being torn apart. 'I was being asked to come on board because they thought I could persuade the black players to refuse to play,' said Olonga. 'It was a hell of a thing to ask anybody to do.'

While agreeing with the principle of protest, Olonga looked at his young teammates' excitement at playing in the world's premier tournament and knew he could not, and should not, ask them to pull out. There was also a concern that the interpretation of outsiders would be that the white majority in the team had exerted an undesired influence over their black colleagues. The players agreed that whatever they did should be just the two of them and should deliver the message: 'We are together, we are Zimbabweans, we are proud of it, and we disagree with what's going on in his country.'

Even Grant Flower, who was keen to stand alongside his brother and teammate, was discouraged from becoming involved. 'I did ask Andrew if I could join in, but they thought it would be a stronger position with one black guy and one white guy,' he explained.

Olonga suggested seeking the advice of David Coltart, a lawyer, civil rights campaigner and, since 2000, an elected member of Zimbabwe's House of Assembly as a representative of the Movement for Democratic Change. He was no stranger to harassment by Mugabe's henchmen. At Coltart's suggestion, it was decided that the protest would take the form of a written statement and the wearing of a black armband to symbolise that they were mourning the death of their nation's democracy. Tactics decided, the next issue to be settled was how and when to distribute the players' words.

British journalist Geoffrey Dean was in Harare to cover what appeared likely to be a low-key game against Nambia for *The Daily Telegraph*. 'I was sent to do all the Zimbabwe matches,' he remembered. 'I had covered a lot of their matches since they got Test status in 1992 so I was very much the Zimbabwe specialist and had got to know a lot of the players very well. Some were close friends, Andy Flower being one. The day before the match I was chatting to Andy after nets and he said, "Can you help me with something tomorrow? It's very important. I can't tell you what, but I need you to be outside the back of the pavilion when play starts at 9:30. You will meet somebody you will know and they will give you something." I had no idea what I was going along for.'

The time had been chosen because by then the teams would have been named, the toss staged, and play would be about to begin – too late for the Zimbabwe Cricket Union to withdraw anyone from the match.

Olonga spent the evening before the game sharing his intentions with his flatmates. He had not told his father what was planned but had eased his conscience somewhat by having a conversation in which they agreed that it was time for 'someone' to make a stand against the government. He neglected to mention it was to be him.

On the morning of 10 February, Flower called his teammates to gather round him in the dressing room. 'Henry and I have done something,' he said, indicating a cricket kit bag in the corner. 'If anybody wants to have a look and read what is in there, please feel free.' Olonga and Flower watched their colleagues' reaction as they read. 'It told us everything we wanted to know,' said Olonga. Now there was the practical problem of fashioning a black armband. The duo had run out of time to acquire formal cloth armbands so were reduced to improvising with black sticky tape.

Meanwhile, Dean arrived at the designated meeting place and was greeted by Flower's father, Bill, who handed him a pile of statements and instructions to deliver them to the written and broadcast media immediately. 'I reckon there would have been about 50,' Dean recalled, 'all individually signed by Andy and Henry. I read it before I gave it to them and I knew it was going to be dynamite.' These are the words that Dean shared with the press box and the broadcast booths:

> It is a great honour for us to take the field today to play
> for Zimbabwe in the World Cup. We feel privileged
> and proud to have been able to represent our country.
> We are however deeply distressed about what is taking
> place in Zimbabwe in the midst of the World Cup and
> do not feel that we can take the field without indicating
> our feelings in a dignified manner and in keeping with
> the spirit of cricket.
>
> We cannot in good conscience take to the field and
> ignore the fact that millions of our compatriots are
> starving, unemployed and oppressed. We are aware
> that hundreds of thousands of Zimbabweans may even
> die in the coming months through a combination of
> starvation, poverty and Aids. We are aware that many
> people have been unjustly imprisoned and tortured
> simply for expressing their opinions about what is
> happening in the country. We have heard a torrent of
> racist hate speech directed at minority groups. We are
> aware that thousands of Zimbabweans are routinely
> denied their right to freedom of expression. We are

aware that people have been murdered, raped, beaten and had their homes destroyed because of their beliefs and that many of those responsible have not been prosecuted. We are also aware that many patriotic Zimbabweans oppose us even playing in the World Cup because of what is happening.

It is impossible to ignore what is happening in Zimbabwe. Although we are just professional cricketers, we do have a conscience and feelings. We believe that if we remain silent that will be taken as a sign that either we do not care or we condone what is happening in Zimbabwe. We believe that it is important to stand up for what is right.

We have struggled to think of an action that would be appropriate and that would not demean the game we love so much. We have decided that we should act alone without other members of the team being involved because our decision is deeply personal and we did not want to use our senior status to unfairly influence more junior members of the squad. We would like to stress that we greatly respect the ICC and are grateful for all the hard work it has done in bringing the World Cup to Zimbabwe.

In all the circumstances we have decided that we will each wear a black armband for the duration of the World Cup. In doing so we are mourning the death of democracy in our beloved Zimbabwe. In doing so we are making a silent plea to those responsible to stop the abuse of human rights in Zimbabwe. In doing so we pray that our small action may help to restore sanity and dignity to our Nation.

'They are familiar words,' said Flower years later. 'I have a copy framed in my house and just occasionally if I come across it I read the entire statement again. I love the way it was written; the meaning in some of those sentences is very sad because it is a reminder of what was happening in that country at that time and some of the people who went through agony and lost their lives.'

Here was cricket's equivalent of the moment at the 1968 Olympics in Mexico when American sprinters Tommie Smith and John Carlos donned a black glove each and gave the clenched fist salute on the medal podium after the 200 metres final. Cricket had been the subject and backdrop of previous protests – the D'Oliveira affair and the efforts to stop various South African tours during apartheid to name the most obvious – but this was the highest profile on-field demonstration by its participants against outside political forces.

As the match progressed, with a distracted Flower contributing 39 to a winning Zimbabwe total of 340, word of the players' actions spread throughout the crowd – even though the armbands were tough to make out on anything other than a close-up TV shot or photograph. Some in the 4,000 crowd found a way to create their own armbands; others displayed hastily-made signs of support. By the time Olonga had bowled three overs in a rain-shortened Namibia reply and the game had finished in a resounding Zimbabwe victory, the story had gone around the world. The local media, of course, made little of it, but elsewhere it was front- and back-page news.

In England, the courage of Flower and Olonga was juxtaposed with the ongoing uncertainty of the English cricket authorities over whether they were sending their team to trouble-torn Zimbabwe to fulfil their World Cup fixture. Typical were the words of Dean's *Daily Telegraph* colleague Martin Johnson. 'While England continued to dither and dawdle,' he wrote, '(if they'd stopped shaving at the start of the great debate, they'd all look like WG Grace this morning), two senior Zimbabwean cricketers were, by contrast, issuing a statement of unparalleled political forcefulness, not to mention bravery.'

Dean recalled his fears about the possible consequences now facing Flower and Olonga. 'They weren't close friends, but they both felt strongly enough to do what they did together. I was concerned for them knowing how things work in Zimbabwe, with the government and secret police. Because the World Cup was on and so many media people were there, I didn't think anything would happen to them immediately.'

He was less worried about the repercussions of his own involvement but did start receiving voiceless telephone calls to

Sussex celebrate their success in the inaugural Gillette Cup in 1963, when skipper Ted
Dexter (centre) was quick to adapt to the tactical requirements of the competition.
(Evening Standard/Hulton Archive/Getty Images)

Lancashire were the masters of English one-day cricket for many years, with influential captain Jack Bond at the helm.

(Hulton Archive/Getty Images)

England's Brian Close captained England as they clinched the Prudential Trophy,
cricket's first full one-day international series, by beating Australia 2-1 in 1972.

(Hulton Archive/Getty Images)

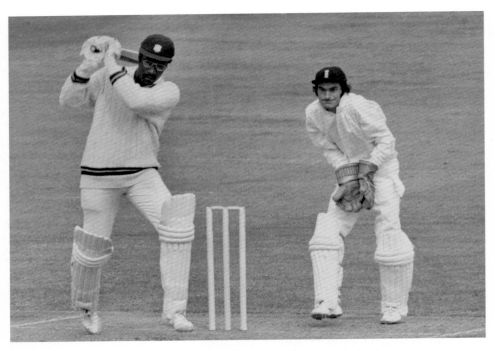

West Indies captain Clive Lloyd, here playing against England, was
the star in the first World Cup final at Lord's in 1975.
(Leonard Burt/Hulton Archive/Getty Images)

Kerry Packer's World Series Cricket changed the sport in November 1978 when it turned on the lights
at Sydney Cricket Ground and saw 50,000 cram inside for a match between Australia and West Indies.
(Adrian Murrell/Getty Images)

Australian all-rounder Trevor Chappell, who was ordered by brother Greg to bowl underarm to batsman Brian McKechnie in order to ensure victory in the 1980-81 World Series Cup. *(Adrian Murrell/Getty Images Sport) caption*

Kapil Dev and Mohinder Amarnath with the World Cup after India's shock 1983 victory over holders West Indies, a result that had its roots a few months earlier and would help to re-draw cricket's global map. *(Hulton Archive/Getty Images)*

The unbeaten 189 by Viv Richards against England at Old Trafford
in 1984 is considered one of the greatest ODI innings.
(Patrick Eagar/Popperfoto/Getty Images)

Pakistan's Javed Miandad became synonymous with the desert venue Sharjah when he hit a last-ball six to beat India in a dramatic final in 1986.
(Aamir Qureshi/AFP)

Australia, led by Allan Border, beat England in the final of the 1987 World
Cup, the first time the tournament had been staged outside England,
after Mike Veletta's heroics in the semi-final against Pakistan.
(Hulton Archive/Getty Images)

The decision of South African captain Kepler Wessels to bowl first exposed his team to
the quirk of the rain rule in their 1992 World Cup semi-final against England, a match
which led to Duckworth-Lewis becoming an integral part of limited-overs cricket.
(Ben Radford/Hulton Archive//Getty Images)

The performance of opening batsman Romesh Kaluwitharana in Sri
Lanka's one-day contests in Australia cemented the revolutionary approach
that would carry them to triumph in the 1996 World Cup.
(Clive Mason/Allsport/Getty Images)

Shane Warne dismisses South Africa's Gary Kirsten in the epic 1999 World Cup semi-final at Edgbaston, where the scores ended up tied, leaving the Aussies heading to the final because of earlier results.
(Clive Mason/Getty Images Sport)

Sacked South Africa captain Hansie Cronje shows the strain as he admits his role in match-fixing to the King Commission of Inquiry in June 2000. Much of what was revealed centred on a match in Nagpur earlier in the year.
(Anna Zieminski/AFP/Getty Images)

Zimbabwe's Henry Olonga wears a black armband at the 2003 World Cup game against Namibia to denote the 'death of democracy' in his country. The protest by him and Andy Flower forced them out of their homeland.
(Alexander Joe/AFP/Getty Images)

Professional 20-over cricket was launched in England in 2003 as a way of attracting new crowds. The novelties presented to the public included pop acts such as Atomic Kitten, who performed at Trent Bridge as Surrey dominated the first Twenty20 Cup Finals Day.
(Tom Shaw/Getty Images)

Makhaya Ntini and Herschelle Gibbs celebrate South Africa's remarkable last-over victory over Australia in Johannesburg in March 2006. Having become the first team to concede 400 runs in an ODI, the Proteas were propelled to victory by a brilliant 178 by a hungover Gibbs.
(Hamish Blair/Getty Images)

St Patrick's Day, 2007, and Ireland's cricketers get the party started after an historic World Cup victory over Pakistan in Jamaica. A few hours later came the tragic news that Pakistan coach Bob Woolmer had been found dead.
(Jewel Samad/AFP/Getty Images)

The triumph of a young India team over Pakistan in the final of the inaugural World Twenty20 in South Africa in 2007, an event the BCCI were reluctant to take part in, catapulted cricket into a new era.
(Tom Shaw/Getty Images)

Bollywood star Shah Rukh Khan, owner of the Kolkata Knight Riders, arrives at – and adds to – the frenzy of the Indian Premier League's first player auction in Mumbai
(Pal Pillai/AFP/Getty Images)

Chris Gayle played one of his most destructive innings when he blasted an unbeaten 175
for the Royal Challengers Bangalore against Pune Warriors in the 2013 IPL season.
Here he hits out against the same opponents a year earlier.
(Manjunath Kiran/AFP/Getty Images)

Sachin Tendulkar picks up more runs against South Africa at Gwalior on his way
to becoming the first player to reach 200 in a one-day international.
(Manan Vatsyayana/AFP/Getty Images)

Carlos Brathwaite (right) has just launched his fourth successive final-over six
off England's Ben Stokes to win the World T20 final in Kolkata in 2016.
He and colleague Marlon Samuels were part of a West Indies team
that benefitted from the growth of franchise cricket.
(Dibyangshu Sarkar/AFP/Getty Images)

Sarah Taylor and captain Heather Knight rush to share the moment of victory
with Anya Shrubsole after her sixth wicket secures England's dramatic
win in the 2017 Women's World Cup final at a packed Lord's.
(Adrian Dennis/AFP/Getty Images)

It's coming home! More than four decades after hosting the first World Cup, English cricket watches
captain Eoin Morgan lift the trophy after the drama of a super-over victory over New Zealand at Lord's
(Clive Mason/Getty Images)

his hotel room in the middle of the night once he had moved on to Bulawayo for the next game. 'I was told it was a classic tactic of the Central Intelligence Organisation, trying to rattle me. I moved out of the hotel and stayed with a friend so I could get some sleep. I had written some fairly critical stuff about the Zimbabwean government, so I don't think I was very popular with them, but I didn't get hassled at the ground and they knew I was leaving and wouldn't be a problem for them once the World Cup was over.'

For Flower and Olonga the stakes in the long term could not have been higher, even though Olonga admitted, 'I hadn't thought that far ahead. In fact, I hadn't a clue. Yes, I had been warned of the dangers of the actions we were about to take but in my optimism I naively still expected to live out the rest of my life in Zimbabwe.'

Flower would relate to Sky Sports, 'There was an element of fear about the repercussions of standing up against a regime like Mugabe. Everyone is well aware of what happens to people that cause trouble in the country. That was why we were making the statement in the first place. There was widescale rape and torture and murder of anyone that became too powerful in leadership terms in the country … but there was also an element of this obligation that we had to try and do something.

'Henry was not only very being very brave physically, but he was being very brave given that he had just started his international cricket career and he was effectively ending it at the age of 26… For him to sacrifice his cricketing future to make that one-off statement was an incredible example of sacrifice and bravery.'

Olonga was dropped from the team and was eventually barred from entering the field to fulfil 12th-man duties. He was confronted at the games by members of Mugabe's youth militia and received threatening emails and telephone messages. There was talk of the players being charged with treason and Olonga feared he 'could be carted away at any minute and never be seen again'.

Indirectly, the England team came to Olonga's aid. One group determined not to see England offer support to the Mugabe regime by turning up to play had sent them a letter saying, 'Come to Zimbabwe and you will go back to Britain in wooden coffins.' Amid accusations of being frightened of financial implications and the loss of World Cup points, the ECB eventually confirmed they were not sending their players to Zimbabwe, citing safety concerns rather than being seen to have passed judgement on the political situation.

Olonga, who has always chosen to believe that Nasser Hussain's team acted morally more than pragmatically – even if no one would come out and say it – now had a possible passage out of Zimbabwe. While England's forfeit ended up costing them a place in the Super Sixes, the points Zimbabwe were awarded, along with wins against Namibia and the Netherlands, meant avoiding defeat against Pakistan in Bulawayo would put them on a flight to South Africa to continue their participation in the tournament. In his hotel room on the eve of the game, Olonga – who held strong religious beliefs – prayed for help.

And it arrived. In torrents. 'Wave after wave after wave of this rain kept coming,' Olonga remembered. 'As the rain continued and continued my sense of fear and trepidation lessened and lessened.' The match was abandoned; his prayers answered. He boarded his team's flight to South Africa and bade farewell to his homeland.

He was not safe yet, however. Once Zimbabwe had lost their three further matches and his teammates had returned home – or, in Flower's case, packed up his home, tied up business affairs and headed to England to continue his career with Essex – Olonga was stuck in South Africa. He was virtually broke and condemned to hiding away from Zimbabwean authorities and secret police at a friend's home while he figured out his next step. 'Henry was saying that he wasn't going back,' Dean explained. 'He was looking to get to England. He said to contact him every day, and if he didn't answer the phone or send me a text to say he was OK I should raise the alarm. I did that and fortunately he always responded, and sure enough he got flown out by a benefactor.'

That man was David Folb, owner of the fund-raising all-star team, Lashings World XI, for whom Olonga played and attended events over the course of 12 years in England. Meanwhile, he was forging a new career as a classical singer, which saw him release albums and appear in various TV talent contests. He also composed the lyrics for 'Our Zimbabwe', a song that was banned on Zimbabwean radio and television until Mugabe was removed from power by his own party in 2017. Having met and married an Australian, Tara Read, he and his family moved to Adelaide in 2016.

Neither player regretted their actions. Flower wishes he had been media-savvy enough at the time to have found a way to achieve even greater amplification of their message. And he regrets that he got on with earning a living in cricket – a career path that eventually led him to coaching the England team – without continuing a political campaign. 'I had a young family,' he told Neil Manthorp in his *Following On* podcast. 'I didn't feel like I had the energy or the time or the focus away from playing to devote to campaigning. So there's a regret, and a slight guilt actually, that there are so many genuinely brave people that remain in Zimbabwe; that work every day for correcting or bringing attention to human rights problems in the country; that fight for the opposition party; that fight to make things better in the country; that work for charity organisations and that do so much good in our country. Ours was a very small gesture to try and highlight some of that. Theirs is the real work.'

ZIMBABWE v NAMBIA, World Cup, Pool A

10 February 2003, Harare Sports Club

Zimbabwe		Balls	4s	6s
CB Wishart	not out	172	151	18	3
MA Vermuelen	c and b Louw	39	66	7	
A Flower	c Karg b Louw	39	29	3	1
GW Flower	not out	78	55	4	2
Extras	(lb 17,w 4, nb 1)	12			
Total	(2 wickets, 50 overs)	340			

Fall: 107, 174
Did Not Bat: DD Ebrahim, GJ Whittall, †T. Taibu, HH Streak, BA Murphy, DT Hondo, HK Olonga
Bowling: Synman 10-0-49-0; Burger 10-1-70-0; BL Kotze 10-1-75-0; Louw 10-0-60-1; DB Kotze 7-0-56-0; Burger 3-0-23-0.

Namibia		Balls	4s	6s
R Walters	c Taibu b Streak	0	1		
S Swanepoel	c Streak b Whittall	23	47	2	
AJ Burger	c Flower b Streak	26	18	3	1
D Keulder	c Ebrahim b Whittall	27	46	3	
BG Murgatroyd	c Wishart b Flower	10	26	1	
LJ Burger	not out	4	10		
*DB Kotze	not out	5	3		
Extras	(lb 1, w 8)	9			
Total	(5 wickets, 25.1 overs)	104			

Fall: 1, 40, 80, 94, 98.
Did Not Bat: †M Karg, G Synman, JL Louw, BL Kotze
Bowling: Streak 5-0-35-2; Hondo 6-1-20-0; Olonga 3-1-8-0; Murphy 1-0-7-0; GW Flower 5.1-1-13-1; Whittall 5-0-20-2

Zimbabwe won by 86 runs (D/L). **Toss:** Namibia. **Umpires:** DL LOrchard, SJA Tauffel. **Man of the Match:** CB Wishart.

16

'WELCOME TO A REVOLUTION'

Twenty20 Cup Finals Day, Trent Bridge, 2003

It had been roughly four decades since English cricket decided that the limited-overs version of the game was its gateway to financial salvation. Now, similar conversations were taking place in county committee rooms and the offices of power at Lord's. Test cricket remained well-supported and the County Championship meandered its way through the summer, looking for ways to become more productive for the England team and more compelling for fans and sponsors. Insurance company Frizzell needed to pay only £1 million for four years of naming rights to the competition. The one-day tournaments – two cups and a league – had lost much of their lustre and money-spinning capacity. Lancashire, for example, attracted only 700-odd non-members for three home games in the final season of the Benson and Hedges Cup

John Carr, the former Middlesex batsman who was director of cricket operations at the ECB, had set about convincing the counties that a shorter form of the game offered the same promise of salvation as the 60-over (originally 65) Gillette Cup had done. Approval for a pilot competition was given in 1999, and Glamorgan and Worcestershire even played a friendly 25-over match in front of a few hundred fans. There was still much work to do, however, in finalising playing conditions, devising a tournament format, and figuring out how to sell it to the county membership and a wider public.

That task fell to Stuart Robertson, head of marketing at the ECB, who recalled, 'There seemed to be no real appetite to bring together short-form cricket and no weight of argument behind it.' Considering himself 'the voice of the consumer' and adopting an attention to detail that future Twenty20 team analysts would appreciate, Robertson realised that data – in the form of customer research – was the bedrock of such an argument. If he was to arrest the 17 per cent fall in attendance at county cricket over the second half of the 1990s, he needed to know what was keeping people away from the grounds. As well as analysing every piece of fan information that the ECB already possessed, he commissioned a series of focus groups and a questionnaire to be distributed to 4,500 households. Women, inner-city residents and minority communities were among the sectors invited to offer their opinions of a sport that traditionally and historically was not exactly known for embracing them.

'Inaccessible' was the word that Robertson saw repeatedly on the reports in front of him; either because of the inhospitable, elitist aura around the game, the cost of playing it, or the fact that matches were generally staged when only the rich or retired could attend. Respondents were asked specifically if they would attend shorter matches staged in the evening. Unsurprisingly, 'it was the groups who were totally underrepresented in existing attendance who were massively over-represented in their expression of interest in attending if it was played as a shorter form,' according to Robertson.

Like an opening bowler clutching a new Dukes ball, he had his most potent weapon; sufficient to get the Professional Cricketers' Association and the county's marketing men to buy into his idea. There was still some stubborn middle-order resistance from the county chairmen, but after late-night lobbying from ECB chairman Lord Ian MacLaurin their defences were broken to the point where the vote in favour of introducing a new competition passed 11-7.

Hampshire chairman Rod Bransgrove recalled, 'Stuart did well to get any resource to research non-members, because the normal way to find out if a change was acceptable in cricket was to ask the 100,000 people or so who had a stranglehold over the game through the county chairmen, who really saw their role as representing their members. They hadn't considered that by representing their members, they were necessarily limiting the scope of the game.'

Twenty-over cricket was far from an alien concept, of course. 'We'd all played 20-over cricket at clubs and schools,' said former Leicestershire seam bowler Charles Dagnall. 'Six o'clock 20-over cricket was what you played at the under-13 to under-18 level.' And there had even been a professional version during the 1990s in New Zealand, where Martin Crowe had helped to devise Cricket Max, although that actually comprised four 10-over innings. Another unique part of that format was the 'Max Zone' behind the bowlers' arm, where boundaries had double value, enabling Craig McMillan to reach a century for Canterbury off 20 balls, including four eights and a 12. To prevent bowlers aiming too far outside the stumps to avoid the straight hit, wides carried a two-run penalty.

New Zealand staged the first international Cricket Max series against England in 1997, although Lancashire seamer Ian Austin said, 'I can't see it taking off around the world.' It didn't, fading out early in the new century. Even Crowe was forced to admit that 'it was too contrived to some people'. Such comments highlight one of the biggest issues facing the organisers of the Twenty20 Cup: the perception of authenticity. 'If the cricket had been rubbish, and the players took it as a complete joke, it would have died very quickly,' said Robertson.

According to Dagnall, 'We, as players, were crying out for something like this. We knew what it could be. We were hitting a different time, getting the after-work crowd and families. We knew the possibilities of making cricket cheaper and more accessible.' That might have been less true, however, at a bigger club such as Surrey, whose players were used to appearing in Test matches and major county finals. Their former England batsman, Ian Ward, remembered the reception among players at The Oval being 'lukewarm'. He added, 'You could cut and paste most of the criticism of The Hundred[14] from what was said about T20 at the time. It was taking players out of their comfort zones; it was not played at international level etcetera. I remember saying to the members, "Do you want this?" and they said "no" to a man.'

Trial games between Gloucestershire and the Lashings World XI and friendlies between Hampshire and Middlesex were staged to iron out the laws of the format, while Paula Warren, a former ICC employee, had the idea of a finals day featuring two semi-finals and a final. A mid-summer fixture list was constructed to take advantage of long, light evenings – not every county having yet installed floodlights – and the Benson and Hedges Cup was sacrificed. Robertson's research, identifying a need for off-field entertainment as well as high-impact action, was warmly received by those responsible for selling the game at the counties, who eagerly set about hiring cheerleaders and musicians, purchasing fireworks and

---

14 The even shorter version of cricket outlined by the ECB in 2019 and launched on the field in 2021

bouncy castles and, in the case of Worcestershire, installing a jacuzzi by the boundary.

'Welcome to a revolution in cricket,' boomed the voice over the public address system at Southampton's Rose Bowl as the tournament began on 13 June 2003 – a Friday evening – with Hampshire hosting Sussex. On this occasion, the revolution was televised, with the head of Sky Sports, Barney Francis, determined to offer a broadcast that reflected the innovative nature of the tournament. A quarter of a century earlier, Kerry Packer's World Series Cricket had pioneered the concept of interviewing players on the boundary edge immediately after their dismissals. Among the 'big demands' Francis made to the ECB was that they supported his desire to speak to players while they were on the field. 'I had an idea to try to create some new things and some of them got through and some of the didn't,' he explained.

The intention was to bring the personalities of the players into the living room rather than subject the viewer to a bowler's back and the facelessness of a helmeted batsman. For that to be truly effective, not only were players introduced with graphics that focused on favourite music and films as much as their averages, but it required a commentary team in tune with the required dynamics of the presentation. While the likes of Ian Botham and Michael Holding opted out because they felt the cricket was not serious enough, one man in the booth appeared born for the format.

Former England batsman and coach David Lloyd had what Francis called the 'infectious enthusiasm and wonderful turn of phrase that I suppose is a great bonus to Twenty20', a game that was 'the perfect vehicle for him'. Already a fixture on the Sky team, it was the short game that allowed him to take a step forward and turned 'Bumble' into a national figure, although he claims there was no strategic plan behind it. 'With me, commentary just happens,' Lloyd said. 'I saw T20 immediately as great entertainment. I liked the idea that it was quick. It has all changed now and is sometimes like a game of bloody draughts. It is not the same game as it was in 2003, when it was first invented and was just great fun.'

Dagnall, who would before long be commentating on those same T20 games for BBC Radio and Sky, said, 'T20 was the marriage between television and the spectator experience, and the commentators had to try to get over what was going on in the crowd rather than it feeling staid. The person who did that the most was Bumble. He transformed cricket so that personality among the players was not to be shunned or looked down upon. He was the conduit to personality coming out and mixing it with highly-skilled cricket.'

Back to opening night, and in *The Daily Telegraph* Derek Pringle called the game 'bewildering' because of the pace of batsmen coming and going. His point was that a match that at times appeared to be a mere backdrop to the beer, barbecue and fairground attractions actually required more concentration than longer forms of the game. 'The game's subtleties have been supplanted by brute force as fodder for the masses,' he observed.

Twenty years on, the force would have become even more brutish, and new subtleties would have come to be recognised. For now, though, the fact that the PA announcer mistook Wasim Akram for Simon Katich, and the 8,500 crowd was 30 per cent female was more notable than the nuances of Hampshire's five-run win. The first evening's five games attracted 30,000 – almost five times the amount who attended the zonal games in the previous year's Benson and Hedges Cup.

It was Surrey's second match, played at the Metropolitan Police ground in suburban East Molesey, that helped make Ward a convert to the competition. 'Once we played the game, we knew we were onto something,' he explained. 'One of our first matches was at Imber Court and there would have been about 4,500 people there. There were kids playing cricket everywhere while it was going on, both teams bowled about 18 overs an hour because there were penalty runs if you didn't, and I remember walking off at the end and my wife and was there and I was back in the village at 9.30 and the sun was still out. I thought, "Actually, that was bloody good." It was a different kind of event.'

Simon Hughes had seen enough on the first evening of the Twenty20 Cup to predict correctly in his *Daily Telegraph* column that Twenty20 cricket would 'ultimately raise the standard and breadth of shot-making, of fielding and of bowling strategy'.

Ward continued, 'In terms of how the cricket was going to be played there was definitely reticence from a lot of players. I spent a career trying to bat all day, not trying to smack boundaries and sixes inside the first six overs. It took a lot of people's games forward. I remember talking to John Emburey about Andrew Strauss and he was convinced that Strauss's participation in T20 allowed him to find extra scoring shots once he played Test cricket. It had benefits going into the longest form of the game and you saw that with Ben Stokes at Headingley.[15] Some of that was straight out of T20.'

A summer heatwave helped maintain high attendance throughout the inaugural tournament. And Finals Day, staged at Trent Bridge, would provide a fitting climax: contested by Surrey, the powerhouse county of the time; Gloucestershire, the turn of the century's strongest limited-overs unit; a star-studded Warwickshire team; and the overachieving Leicestershire, on their way to becoming England first's T20 specialists. The importance that teams had come to attach to the competition was evidenced by Leicestershire leaving star Indian batsman Virender Sehwag out of their County Championship game against Sussex to rest his aching back for their semi-final against Warwickshire; an unremarkable piece of selection when viewed through a present-day lens but significant enough to make headlines in 2003. At Surrey, Ward remembered the county's ambition being 'driven very much by the players' competitiveness'. He said, 'We went into it with quite a relaxed attitude, but after that year it was, "Bloody hell, this is a tournament that everybody wants to win."'

In the first semi-final, Australian Brad Hodge hit 66 to help Leicestershire to a competitive 162 for 7 against Warwickshire, but fast bowler Jamie Grove was about to experience the downside of the high stakes and the high pressure of county cricket's new day in the sunshine. The former England Under-19 international, who had reached the age of 24 without establishing himself as a first-teamer, was brought on by Leicestershire skipper Nixon to bowl the fourth over. Twelve deliveries later, including three wides and three no-balls, Grove had conceded 20 runs. It could have been worse had the free hits been more severely punished.

'I hadn't played for about three-and-a-half weeks and had three epidurals in my back,' he explained. 'I'd not even been allowed to leave my home. They let me bowl three balls the day before the finals and when we turned up it had been really dewy overnight. You

---

15 In his match-winning innings of 135 not out in the third Test against Australia in 2019.

couldn't use the run-ups, so we were bowling off about three paces before play. I declared myself fit and I had an absolute nightmare.' More shocking to Grove than his figures were the comments that appeared on fan forums on the club's website, threatening both him and his wife.

'I know I completely screwed up. There were 20,000 people telling me that. But I'd helped get us to the bloody finals day.' Disappointed by what he thought was lack of support from his county – a situation unlikely to be repeated in the modern era of greater awareness of the damage caused by online abuse – Grove was unsurprised when he was released by his club and saw his professional career come to an end. The story is an illustration, albeit an ugly one, of the immediate profile and importance the Twenty20 Cup had achieved.

In the second semi-final, Ward's 49 and Azhar Mahmood's three wickets saw Surrey to a five-run win. 'I remember Bumble criticising me on Sky, calling me a pinch blocker,' said Ward. 'I was just trying to find a way to get something competitive because we had a fantastic bowling attack and the pitch was a bit tricky.'

But finals day was intended to be about more than mere cricket. The sideshow elements of the earlier rounds were cranked up to the max, with an obstacle race between county mascots and a performance by Atomic Kitten, the pop trio from Liverpool who were one of that year's big things. Andrew Miller wrote for Cricinfo:

> 'Hello, you're lovely,' announced a beery Brummie
> from behind a makeshift barrier, but for the most part
> the onlookers gawped like a herd of cricket fans. The
> only murmur of disquiet came from a Gloucestershire
> man with a rapidly dissolving cardboard tray of lager,
> whose patience came close to snapping … 'Is this a
> ****ing cricket match or what?' he asked. Well, quite.

Warwickshire won the toss in the final and quickly regretted their decision to bat as Surrey seamers Azhar and Jimmy Ormond enjoyed early-evening assistance from the conditions. Former Leicestershire man Ormond, discarded by England after two Test matches – partly because of perceived lack of fitness – extracted movement and bounce from the wicket, forcing Neil Carter to play on and getting one past the bat of Nick Knight. Azhar then got Ian Bell to pop one up to backward point and Ormond induced Jim Troughton and Dougie Brown to edge to slip and wicketkeeper respectively, leaving Warwickshire on 33 for 5 in the seventh over. 'I talked about a procession,' said Lloyd on Sky's commentary. 'It's a stampede is this.'

'The way Ormond bowled tonight is the way he has bowled all year,' Surrey captain Adam Hollioake would explain. 'He used to try to swing the ball away a bit more, now he runs in Australian-style and hits the wicket hard, which has made him more consistent. We signed him because we thought he was the best young bowler in the country. Thankfully no one else seem to rate him highly.'

Ward remembered, 'Jimmy was a terrific bowler, particularly on that pitch. It was a little bit up and down and a bit two-paced. He was tall, strong, quick and just slammed it into the pitch.'

Much has been made by T20 statisticians in modern times of the truism that teams losing three wickets in the six-over powerplay are beaten in around 80 per cent of their matches. That much was evident even after these early skirmishes. Writing in *The Daily Telegraph* after Finals Day, Simon Briggs said, 'This early period is increasingly being seen as the key to Twenty20 success, even more so than the first 15 overs in a standard one-day match.'

Trevor Penney and Tony Frost both fought their way into the 30s as Warwickshire tried to rebuild, but their efforts barely got their team into the 19th over. Facing a target of only 116, Surrey were clear winners from the moment the first ball of their reply went for four byes. Ward, hardly known as a trailblazer at the top of the innings, piled into Carter for four boundaries before the end of the opening over – a square carve, a drive through the off side, a back-foot push and a swing wide of mid-on. 'I found a bit of rhythm in the final,' Ward explained. 'By that time, it was a bit dewy and the ball skidded on a little. The pitch changed quite dramatically from earlier on.'

Alistair Brown, who had once hit a double-hundred in a 40-over game, steered Waqar Younis for a pair of fours before blasting a six over long-on and bringing up the 50 in the sixth over with a bottom edge. Dougie Brown found his namesake advancing down the wicket to lift him over long-off and saw Ward pull him to the rope, a shot he repeated off Waqar's final ball to make the score 77 without loss after eight overs.

Ward progressed towards his fifty by forcing Collins Oboya over the midwicket boundary and reached the landmark with a classic on-drive against Graham Wagg. As well as wearing a camera on his helmet, Ward was wired up for communication with the commentary box and he had David Fulton in his ear telling him, 'You just carry on.'

'I'll try,' was the batsman's reply, at which point he top-edged a pull shot high into the air and was caught.

'I am not sure Wardy is going to thank us too much,' said co-commentator Mark Butcher, but such was the challenge of batting in the viewer-friendly world of Twenty20. Besides, Ward welcomed it. 'I remember it being a very busy day because I was working for Sky, commentating on the first semi-final and then I was mic'd up and wearing the helmet camera in the semi-final and final. I was involved right from coming on air to the last ball. I had done a little bit of commentary for Sky on county cricket and took a general interest in the industry. I was fascinated by how it was broadcast. It was in my interests to do what Sky wanted me to do because I was building relationships there.'

The game was almost won when Ward got out and Surrey confirmed themselves as the new format's first champions after Brown reached his own half-century and Mark Ramprakash slapped a slow long hop from Knight through extra cover for the winning boundary. 'I remember it being a fantastic day,' Ward concluded. 'It wasn't exactly a football crowd, but it was rowdier and a different sort of atmosphere to when I played in a Lord's final.'

* * *

Nervous about attendance, many of the matches in the inaugural season of Twenty20 had been staged on the counties' smaller out-grounds. The biggest advance in 2004 was the inclusion of Lord's, where 21,000 advance tickets were sold for Middlesex's derby against Surrey. Touts swarmed around St John's Wood underground station as though it was the first day of a Test match. Inside the ground, an environmental team monitored sound levels in order to prevent upsetting the locals who, during an England one-day international against West Indies four years earlier, had complained about Jools Holland's performance – on the basis of volume rather than an objection to his boogie-woogie piano stylings. 'It is a learning experience,' said MCC chairman Roger Knight. 'We could not get the license we needed to stage the final last year because of concerns about the noise and we want to show we can keep the volume at a reasonable level.' The night's attendance ended up beating the 24,450 who had seen the second day of the same teams' County Championship contest in 1953.

The second season saw players becoming more aware of the opportunities offered by the combination of the new on-field format, a different style of television coverage and big crowds in the stadium. 'I loved it when the TV cameras came,' said Dagnall, who would be at the centre of one of more remarkable games of the Twenty20 Cup's second season. 'I was in my brother's band, I like to perform and show off. It was easy to do in T20 because you weren't put down for it. Personality made for better TV. And by that stage I had started working at Radio Leicester, doing the odd bit of sport in the winter.'

When Nottinghamshire visited Leicestershire, Dagnall 'had a night out'. He continued, 'It was a local derby and Grace Road was heaving. It was on television and Kevin Pietersen was playing and he was the big story in county cricket because he would qualify for England that winter. Everything was going on. We had guys who had won "the best seats in the house" in the local paper and were sitting on sofas on the boundary in front of the scoreboard and the pizza delivery guy drove on the pitch to give them pizzas. If you took a catch in the crowd you won a year's supply of beer. You couldn't get from the dressing room to the pitch without pushing through this enormous crowd.'

Leicester ended up defending a total of 150 and, with Nottinghamshire on 24 for 1, Dagnall had Bilal Shafayat caught by Jeremy Snape at backward point. Pietersen entered the arena and was immediately given out lbw. 'I have gone crazy,' Dagnall remembered. 'I have got the big draw out first ball. I wasn't an England star, but this was a chance for no-names to have a day out. It was the celebration of the unheralded cricketer.'

There was more celebration on the way, this time when Notts batsman Russell Warren smote Dagnall over square leg for six and one of the lads in the sofa seats leapt to his feet to grab his beer for a year. 'He takes a brilliant catch after being obstructed by Darren Maddy leaping for it, and Bumble has gone nuts,' recalled Dagnall, who took out Warren's leg stump next delivery. Off he charged off another victory run before his blond highlights disappeared under the arms of his teammates. 'The place has gone ballistic,' he added, 'and I've got tears in my eyes. The sequence of events in that game showed the changing landscape in cricket; showed what it could be.'

Notts were eventually bowled out for 110 and Dagnall, named Man of the Match, had entered the sport's consciousness. 'I had taken four wickets on telly, got Pietersen out first ball, plus I was a character with the way I carried on like a chump. The following year I had an operation on my shins and Sky needed a commentator two days later. They got me a taxi from the hospital to Old Trafford. They obviously knew I had done a bit of commentary on local radio and knew I was a character and might be good value.'

Leicestershire's unheralded team would go on to beat champions Surrey in the 2004 final, before reaching Finals Day for the next two seasons, winning their second title in 2006. 'At Leicestershire were convinced from the start that we were going to take it seriously,' said Dagnall, 'because we knew others wouldn't and because we weren't very good at the other games. We also had forward-thinking cricketers within that dressing room, people like Brad Hodge, Jeremy Snape, Darren Maddy and Daffy [Phil DeFreitas]. There were a lot of bits-and- pieces cricketers who could actually win you a game and it only took one player to win a game.

'Some of the practice sessions were hysterical. We were trying all sorts: people running up and stopping and then running up again; bowling while looking over at third man; bowling from 26 yards. Seeing if anything worked. A lot of sides thought spinners were going to be fodder, but we had three and put the boundaries out as far as they could and let people try to smash them. There was also this theory that sixes and fours is what was going to happen, so all of those ring fielders were right back on the circle, happy to give away one. But we had our backward point and extra cover on the one rather than letting them have singles. We had specific fielders for specific roles. Maddy and Stevens were our best fielders and they were the boundary riders. The taller fielders, like me, were long-on and long-off. If somebody went for the sweep Paul Nixon was already down at fine leg as soon as he saw it – he was one of the first wicketkeepers to do that.

'We had the idea of winning games in the penultimate over; that was something that we were very hot on. I go back to the 2004 final when it was up in the air and Jeremy Snape went big in that penultimate over.' Snape's straight drive for six against Surrey captain Hollioake helped reduce their target from 20 needed in two overs to four off the final six balls, inflicting upon Surrey their first defeat in the competition. 'It was little tactical things like that which we were genuinely at the forefront of,' Dagnall added. 'We didn't have the best players. Surrey had the best players, but we worked out a formula in those first few years.'

According to Ward, 'That was a feature of Leicester's cricket back then in all formats,' but Surrey, with their all-star squad, had a somewhat different approach. 'I remember a conversation with Mark Ramprakash prior to T20 starting. We were talking about what would be important: good fielding, running between the wickets, little margins. Adam Hollioake said, "I disagree. It is about hitting sixes and taking wickets." And that was before a ball was bowled. Once we were emboldened to do that and it took some of the pressure off.'

Big hitting versus the science of minor tactical tweaks that could have a major impact. That balancing act would become the essence of Twenty20 cricket; a challenge that would engage some of the sport's brightest minds over the next couple of decades and create a spin-off industry of on-field analytics. Not at all what was envisaged when the first bouncy castles were being inflated on the boundary.

SURREY v WARWICKSHIRE, Twenty20 Cup Final

19 July 2003, Trent Bridge

Warwickshire			Balls	4s	6s
NM Carter	b Ormond	8	12		1
*NV Knight	b Ormond	8	6	1	
IR Bell	c Clarke b Azhar	5	11		
JO Troughton	c Brown b Ormond	1	3		
TL Penney	b Hollioake	33	21	2	2
DR Brown	c Batty b Ormond	0	3		
†T Frost	c Ormond by Saqlain	31	35	1	
GG Wagg	b Hollioake	5	6		
CO Obuya	c Ward b Saqlain	17	11	1	1
NMK Smith	run out	1	2		
Waqar Younis	not out	0	1		
Extras	(w 4, nb 4)		6		
Total	(18.1 overs)	115			

Fall: 16, 20, 22, 32, 33, 63, 83, 112, 115, 115
Bowling: Ormond 4-0-11-4; Azhar Mahmood 3-0-22-1; Saqlain Mushtaq 4-0-35-2; Clarke 4-0-20-0; Hollioake 3.1-0-27-2

Surrey			Balls	4s	6s
IJ Ward	c Waqar b Wagg	50	28	8	1
A Brown	not out	55	34	6	3
M Ramprakash	not out	4	5	1	
Extras	(lb 4, w 2, nb 4)	10			
Total	(1 wickets, 10.5 overs)	119			

Fall: 100.
Did Not Bat: R Clarke, *AJ Hollioake, Azhar Mahmood, GP Thorpe, †JN Batty, IDK Salisbury, Saqlain Mushtaq, J Ormond.
Bowling: Carter 2-0-20-0; Waqar 4-0-29-0; Brown 2-0-24-0; Obuya 1-0-18-0; Wagg 1-0-20-0; Knight 0.5-0-4-0.

Surrey won by 9 wickets. **Toss:** Warwickshire. **Umpires:** B Dudleston, JW Holder. **Man of the Match:** J Ormond.

17

'IT'S A 450 WICKET. THEY ARE 15 SHORT'

South Africa v Australia, 5th One-Day International, Johannesburg, 2006

Mickey Arthur and Graeme Smith, coach and captain of the South African team, had a decision to make. As their colleagues and Australian opponents went through warm-ups at The Wanderers ground in Johannesburg, Arthur had shared with Smith the news that batsman Herschelle Gibbs had spent the whole night before this decisive game of the five-match ODI series drinking – and heaven knows what else – and was still the worse for wear. Only they and assistant coach Vincent Barnes knew why Gibbs had seemed so subdued at breakfast that morning. 'This is unacceptable behaviour,' Arthur stressed. 'But do we pull him out of today's game in the warm-ups or do we talk to him after the game?'

Arthur remembered, 'This was a five-match series that was tied at 2-2. It wasn't just some arbitrary ODI, this was the final and South Africa hadn't beaten Australia in many ODI tournaments at that point. There was a massive upswell of support in South Africa and the games had grown to massive proportions in terms of it almost being a cup final. We both decided that Hersh was too much of an asset to risk leaving out in a final game, and because nobody knew we could make it an internal disciplinary matter.'

The coach made his way over to Gibbs. 'Look, Hersh, you're playing,' he said. 'But at the end of the game we need to have a serious chat with you.'

Within a couple of hours, it was events on the field that had Gibbs's head spinning rather than the effects of his night-time antics. No team had ever conceded 400 runs in a one-day international. Yet with every ball that Ricky Ponting and Michael Hussey crashed to the boundary history drew closer. Australia had 301 runs on the board after 40 overs when Gibbs passed wicketkeeper Mark Boucher between overs and remarked, 'Bouch, they could get 400 here.'

'Try again, Hersh,' was the reply. 'Do the math. We're going to do bloody well to keep them to 400.'

With only two wickets down, Boucher could be excused his fatalism. From the moment Australia won the toss and chose to bat, the bowlers had done nothing but serve up the ingredients of a run feast. Adam Gilchrist, who by now was renowned for his ability to brutalise opening bowlers, and Simon Katich, who wasn't, reached a 50 partnership in the eighth over – the former racing along with pulls, cuts and audacious flicks, while the latter punished the bad balls with a more orthodox ruthlessness. It was Katich, though, who struck the first six of the innings when he lifted Johan van der Wath into the crowd beyond midwicket and Gilchrist who was first out, caught at mid-on for 55 with the score on 97 in the 16th over.

Katich reached his half-century off 60 balls, while Ricky Ponting's 16 off his first 22 balls faced gave little hint of what was to come. In the 22nd over things took a turn as Ponting edged, pulled and clipped Roger Telemachus for three boundaries. By the half-way mark of the innings, at 164 for 1, his 37 runs scored had overtaken balls faced.

'The Wanderers always does give runs,' explained Arthur. 'We looked at the wicket the day before and we knew it was very good wicket. The ball travels a lot further in the Highveld than at normal grounds because of the altitude and the field is fairly small so it is always conducive to high scoring.' All the more reason for bowlers to be at the top of their game.

'We bowled poorly,' said Arthur. 'I remember us bowling a lot of no-balls [10], and the ball just kept disappearing all over the place. Ponting played unbelievably well. He hit cover drives and the ball would ricochet off the boundary before you could even blink. When they hit it in the air you thought "out" but it just carried into about the tenth row.'

Twice in successive deliveries Ponting put Jacques Kallis in the crowd on the leg side, before giving van der Wath the same treatment. In the 31st over it was Makhaya Ntini's turn to watch Ponting's shot sail over midwicket, but two balls later he ended Katich's innings at 79 when his uppercut only reached Telemachus at third man. Ponting moved into the 90s by pulling Kallis for six off the front foot, and Michael Hussey scored 4, 6, 4 off successive balls by Kallis.

Ponting reached his century off Smith and a series of off-side fours from both batsmen saw them charge into the final 10 overs. Telemachus tried bowling wider of off stump, only to see both men sweep him through the on side, and Hussey found the extra yards to take Andrew Hall over square leg. The sixes were flying now: two drives by Ponting off Ntini and another against Kallis; Hussey against van der Wath.

Hussey eventually fell for 81 trying to smash Hall over long-on, but Ponting reached 150 two balls later with his ninth maximum. The 48th over saw the disintegration of Telemachus, back in the side after four years. His first four attempts were all no-balls, with Ponting and new batsman Andrew Symonds scoring an additional 15 runs off them. The sixth legal deliveries at least brought the downfall of Ponting, caught for 164 with the score 407 after what he described as one of his finest innings. Brett Lee and Symonds swung and sprinted to post a final total of 434 for 4 and Telemachus surveyed the carnage of his two final overs, which had cost 40. 'It was a terrible feeling to be the first team to concede 400 runs, on our own turf,' recalled Gibbs. 'We were among the top cricket teams in the world. It was downright humiliating.'

South Africa headed back to the dressing room, where they had to suffer the sounds of celebration coming from their opponents. The only natural response was the kind of gallows humour usually reserved for hapless village teams.

'That is a 450 wicket,' Kallis dead-panned. 'They are 15 runs short.'

According to Boucher, 'Suddenly there was a lot of laughter and plenty of swearing, but at least it wasn't bottled up inside. We had nothing to lose. What the hell. Let's give it a go. Before that moment, I don't believe anybody would have even talked about trying to win. It seemed too ridiculous.'

Arthur remembered, 'It was properly daunting and I thought we had absolutely no chance. I didn't know what to say or what to do. The sponsors, Standard Bank, had a mascot, this branded duck, who spend the day mingling with the crowd. I remember that the duck was sitting with his head in its hands. I thought, "Even the mascot doesn't give us any chance." And then Kallis came in he changed the mood. I remember I was always setting targets and I said, "Right, this is where we want to be," and I think it was 160 for 1 after 20 overs. That's the target we put up on the board. With that I looked at Herschelle and he just burst out laughing and I said, "Right, let's forget the target. Let's just go and play."'

The empty seats in the stands as the second innings approached suggested that few were expecting history to be made. After all, it had taken 2,349 ODIs for a team to score as many runs as Australia had managed, so what were the odds of that record lasting only half a match? Australian skipper Ponting warned his men, 'Let's pretend we're defending 200. Don't think you'll coast through.' The very fact he needed to deliver such a message spoke of the apparently impregnable position in which his team found themselves.

In the second over of the innings, Boeta Dippenaar was bowled by Australian left-armer Nathan Bracken, bringing Gibbs to the crease. 'Boeta was a very good player, but he wasn't massively explosive,' said Arthur. 'Boeta still reckons he was he was man of the match because if he had used up five overs instead of allowing Herschelle to come in we wouldn't have won.'

Yet the sight of the approaching Gibbs held little fear for the Aussies, based on what they had witnessed the previous evening. With both teams staying in the Sandton Sun Hotel, Bracken and Hussey had passed Gibbs in the bar as they headed out for a quiet dinner. The South African batsman appeared to have a different kind of night planned. He already seemed drunk to the Australian duo, who returned later in the evening to find him still going strong. Hussey recalled, 'Just before I went to bed an hour later I looked over the railing outside my hotel room and there he was, still in that spot. At least he was a free wicket.'

Arthur continued, 'Hersh is a wonderful character and I love him. He's a lovable rogue. He used to get really nervous and was virtually an insomniac. And he always does things out of proportion. So if he decides to go to the gym, he goes to the gym for 24 hours every day for a week. He doesn't do things in moderation. He went down to the bar and I think that one bottle of wine led to another. It is a very upmarket hotel and where the bar is situated there are all these ballrooms. I think there was a masked ball and Hersh had decided to sit there and tell the ladies what he thought of their outfits. The hotel manager said we had to get him out of there. The Aussie boys had gone to dinner and come back and, seeing Hersh still sitting at the same place, thought he would be an easy wicket.'

Gibbs had arrived at the breakfast table not long after leaving a female companion and returning to his own room. Yet he believed that the cocktail of Red Bull and painkillers were disguising the state in which he found himself and didn't realise that Arthur knew of his antics. Players remained unaware of the situation, with Boucher admitting, 'I would have been pretty annoyed if I'd known that he'd been half drunk at breakfast.'

It had been a relief to Gibbs that South Africa fielded first and that he was involved in no significant moments during Australia's innings. 'I should not even have been on the field for the start,' he would admit. Feeling somewhat revived by the time he put on his pads, he still might have hoped for a longer rest before having to go out to bat first wicket down. 'Memories of my big night had not receded quite as far back as I would have liked,' he said. The Aussies were not going to miss this opportunity. 'Obviously they'd spread the word that I had been as pissed as a fart the night before.'

'Are you still happy?' chirped Hussey. 'You don't look so happy.'

The comments came from all angles. 'Give Hersh another glass of wine.' 'Come on, Hersh, just one more.'

Having eased himself in with nine runs from 13 balls, Gibbs came down the wicket to force Bracken over the covers for four and produced the same result next ball while remaining in the crease. Neither was the shot of a man fighting a hangover. Then he was in position quickly to pull Brett Lee flat for six. 'Herschelle was a happy-go-lucky guy,' said Arthur, 'but when he had the bat in his hand he had this dogged determination. He was a fighter; he was a winner. He was very competitive and that came out in his cricket.'

Suddenly there was a hum of anticipation around the ground, reflected in the voice of commentator Tony Greig when he said, 'Right, now we need the South African captain to come to the party' – before Smith obliged by using quick feet to produce a couple of leg-side boundaries.

When Gibbs steered a single to third man it took him to 50 off 46 balls, but Smith was travelling even faster, going to his fifty off 33 balls with a swipe through mid-on. South Africa, ahead of Australia at the same point in the innings, reached 150 in the 19th over as Smith motored on, lofting Symonds over midwicket and hitting Michael Clarke straighter over long-on. 'The scary thing was,' Hussey wrote, 'the comparisons kept going up on the board, and they were always 15 or 20 runs ahead of us. Batting without any hope of winning was such a dangerous thing. They had complete freedom. I thought, "Far out, they're going to win easily."'

According to Arthur, 'Because the expectation of the win had been taken away, the guys could just go and bat. The amazing thing in that chase was that the required rate was above eight an over and it never got above 10 until about over 42, and that just shows how calculated the chase was. The only reason it went up was because we suddenly realised, "Shit, we can win this, we'd better play properly."'

Smith holed out to Hussey for 90, scored from only 55 balls. For all the brilliance of the innings so far, the chase would soon flounder unless Gibbs could maintain the momentum while a new man played himself in. His response was to flick-sweep the next ball over square leg for six. When he stepped down the wicket and flat-batted Clarke over mid-on for four he had reached 97 off 78 balls. The next delivery brought an upright cover drive that pierced the field and took him to his century.

'That's a home run over third base,' exclaimed the greatest of all South African batsmen, Barry Richards, when Gibbs's front-foot pull sent Mick Lewis over the ropes at cow corner. And with the commentators urging Gilchrist to stand up to the stumps, Gibbs anchored himself outside the crease to thump a half-volley over extra cover.

He recorded in his autobiography, 'I was seeing the ball as if it were a football. I couldn't miss a shot. If I look back on the footage of the match I can see my eyes look deep-set in my skull – always a sure sign that I've had a big night. No doubt I was tired, but in a way that helped. I didn't run a hell of a lot that day. I just stood there and teed off.'

Gary Kirsten, who had not long retired after many hours at the crease with Gibbs, recalled, 'Hersh's level of skill meant he could be very dangerous on any day, and the fact that no one expected us to win that game just freed him up mentally. He could go and take it on and express himself to his fullest. The game doesn't always work like that and there are times when you need a different style, but that innings was all systems go from the beginning. Play it as aggressively as you can and, because he plays good cricket shots up front anything was possible. That innings was probably a good indication of who he is as a person; the way he was freed up to play.'

South Africa were more than halfway towards their target at the 25-over mark and when Gibbs hit a Lewis full toss straight to Bracken at mid-off and saw the ball fall to the ground, Greig could not resist harking back to 1999 by asking, 'Has he dropped the cup?' There were 182 needed from 22 overs as the batting powerplay ended. Staying on leg stump and opening up the off side, Gibbs bounced Lewis over extra cover again, before planting his foot down the track and swinging the ball over long-on. Greig, never one to need much invitation to get overexcited on commentary, yelled, 'Who would believe what is happening here?'

Having passed 150, even the good balls were fodder to Gibbs, who managed to get underneath a Bracken yorker from round the wicket and sent it over the off-side boundary for six. The loss of AB De Villiers, caught inside the long-on rope, barely made Gibbs blink, leaning back to hoist Symonds over long-on and sending the next ball, a full toss, even further in the same direction.

'A sense of stress came over me as captain that I'd never felt before,' said Ponting. 'I had nowhere to turn and having grown more and more exasperated with all the mistakes that we had committed, I dreaded the idea of making one myself.'

As the prospect of victory became less of a crazy dream, Boucher, the next man in, began to worry about the carefree Gibbs, predicting that 'as soon as he realised we had a chance he would get out'. Addressing those yet to bat, he said, 'Look, Hersh will get out now, but he's given us a chance. Let's not panic. The tail is going to have to wag big-time, but we've done it before and we can do it again. This time it'll be the biggest day of our lives.'

Sure enough, Gibbs finally misjudged one, apparently caught in two minds as he lifted Symonds into the hands of Lee, three-quarters of the way back at extra cover. 'One of the great innings of all time' – Greig's description – had ended at 175 off 111 balls, including 21 fours and seven sixes. The last 125 runs had been scored off 64 deliveries. Boucher's memory of Gibbs's innings was that 'he was the only person in the country who could have played it'.

Gibbs raised both arms to the cheering crowd and headed towards the South African changing room. 'I'm sitting right on the end and he has got to come past me as he goes into the dressing room,' Arthur recalled. 'He walked past me, taking his gloves off with his bat under his arm, and he looked at me and gave me a wink and said, "Right, coach. What are we gonna do about this now?" I said, "Nothing, No one's going to find out." He said, "Yes, that's right." and we have had a laugh about it ever since.'

It was a sign of the magnitude of South Africa's task that a score of 299 for 4 at the departure of Gibbs still left them still needing 135 with 18.1 overs left. Kallis squeezed Symonds through cover point, prompting Richards to tell viewers, 'Every time we look up the ball's disappearing.' But then there was a hiatus, with three overs passing without a boundary and Symonds then holding a diving return catch to dismiss the man then ranked the best ODI batsman in the world. Boucher had originally told Kallis to bat through the innings while he and others chanced their arms, but now he took heed of what Arthur had told him before he went to the crease. 'Bat until the end, Bouch, and we win the game.'

By the time Boucher pounced on Lee's wide half-volley, more than eight overs had elapsed since the last boundary. But the dismissal of Justin Kemp followed, and with seven overs left 77 runs were needed.

Two thumping straight sixes by van der Wath off Lewis helped the equation, and the all-rounder immediately set upon Bracken, with a four to cow corner and another long six off successive balls. 'It got us back to within striking distance,' said Arthur. 'It was a match-winning contribution.' Van der Wath fell for 35 when he slapped a full toss to Ponting at extra cover, but Telemachus quickly paddled another boundary and poor old Lewis went for three more fours in his next over, giving him match figures of 0 for 113.

Now only 13 were needed from the final two overs. A diving Hussey in the outfield gave Bracken his fifth wicket to remove Telemachus, but Boucher – who had moved relatively quietly into the 40s at a little over a run a ball – and Andrew Hall knocked the ball into gaps and the last over began with seven required and two wickets in hand. Hall had arrived at the crease with the same message as his previous two teammates. 'You must stay here,' Boucher was instructed. 'We will take the chances.'

By now, the noise from the crowd sounded like the screaming of a jet engine. 'About a quarter of the way through our reply, people who had left started coming back in again,' said Arthur. 'At the end of the game the atmosphere in the ground was … well, I get goosebumps talking about it now. It was the same day as the Cape Argus, which is a massive bicycle race in Cape Town, and it virtually stopped. People were running into the tent at the finishing line to watch the climax of this game.'

Boucher drove the first ball of the 50th over into the boot of the bowler, Lee, and ran a single. Then Hall found a gap to force the ball to the long-on boundary, leaving two to win off four balls. Boucher had visions of the 1999 World Cup semi-final playing in front of him as he walked down the pitch to tell Hall not to think only of singles. 'If it's in your area, then don't second guess yourself, have a go,' he told him, adding, 'Just please keep it on the ground.' Boucher ended up blaming himself for Hall being caught at mid-on when he tried to repeat his previous shot without the same conviction.

When last man Makhaya Ntini left the safety of the players' balcony 'his eyes were as big as saucers', according to Arthur, who added, 'I can't believe we are chasing 434 and we are going to be 433 all out because Brett Lee is going to give him a yorker and we will lose by one run.'

Ntini arrived at the crease, spinning his bat nervously. 'I walked over to meet him and his eyes were all over the place,' remembered Boucher, who warned his partner to expect a yorker, to get his bat on the ball and to look at him to see if they were running. 'I was terrified for him. I couldn't bear the thought that this historic game had come down to him. He didn't deserve this.'

Lee let fly and even over the din from the stands a high-pitched cry of joy could be heard from Ntini as he steered the ball down to third man for a game-tying single. Arthur repeatedly punched the air on the balcony, knowing his men could not lose this remarkable match. 'Makhaya backed away and somehow managed to get bat on it,' he recalled. 'That was the best shot I've ever seen him play. He's gone running down the wicket like we have won the World Cup and he's dancing and jigging like he's just got 150.'

Now Boucher told himself to be bold – just as his team had been throughout the innings – and he punched a full delivery from Lee over mid-on for the winning runs.

Arthur and his players clambered over the balcony balustrade to the seats below – 'I nearly tore my hamstring doing that' – and began celebrations that belonged more to a World Cup final than a bi-lateral series. 'There was always the traditional Australia-South African rivalry and they'd had one or two over us, so for us it was massive,' Arthur explained. Boucher said that things became 'a blur' but remembered 'shaking like a leaf' as he did a television interview. Shaun Pollock, who missed the game injured, was clearly emotional as he congratulated the man who hit the winning runs.

And the fans who had stayed in their seats in the middle of the day or found their way back later had an experience they would be able to brag about for decades to come. 'There are tears,' said Greig over television shots of emotional fans embracing. 'They are crying out there.' And, for once, no one was accusing him of exaggeration when he concluded, 'The South Africans at the Bullring today have seen the best one-day international ever played.'

According to Arthur, 'We forgot all about our bowling performance straightaway because we had the best fines meeting ever in the dressing room. By the time we woke up the next morning it was clear the whole country had come to a standstill, so there was absolutely no analysis whatsoever of that game.'

And for Gibbs, an episode that could have had serious repercussions ended up becoming the stuff of after-dinner speeches and chapters in books, adding to the legend of one of limited-overs cricket's most celebrated figures. Arthur explained, 'It almost became the tradition when we went to the Wanderers. "Hersh, how many are you gonna have tonight?" We played the West Indies in an ODI game there and had a team dinner the night before. Hersh sat next to me and he had steak and chips and a bottle of wine, and all the boys are watching him. Hersh being the guy that binges, he ordered another steak and chips and another bottle of wine. Everyone said, "Hersch will get a hundred tomorrow," and he went out and got 102 to win us the game.'

SOUTH AFRICA v AUSTRALIA,
5th One-Day International
12 March 2006, The Wanderers, Johannesburg

Australia		Balls	4s	6s
†AC Gilchrist	c Hall b Telemachus	55	44	9	
SM Katich	c Telemachus b Ntini	79	90	9	1
*RT Ponting	c Dippenaar b Telemachus	164	105	13	9
MEK Hussey	c Ntini b Hall	81	51	9	3
A Symonds	not out	27	13	3	1
B Lee	not out	9	7		
Extras	(lb 4, w 5, nb 10)	19		
Total	(4 wickets, 50 overs)	434		

Fall: 97, 216, 374, 407
Did Not Bat: DR Martyn, MJ Clarke, NW Bracken, SR Clark, ML Lewis
Bowling: Ntini 9-0-80-1; Hall 10-0-80-1; van der Wath 10-0-76-0;
Telemachus 10-1-87-2; Smith 4-0-29-0; Kallis 6-0-70-0; Kemp 1-0-8-0.

South Africa		Balls	4s	6s
*GC Smith	c Hussey b Clarke	90	55	13	2
HH Dippenaar	b Bracken	1	7		
HH Gibbs	c Lee b Symonds	175	111	21	7
AB de Villiers	c Clarke b Bracken	14	20	1	
JH Kallis	c and b Symonds	20	21	1	
†MV Boucher	not out	50	43	4	
JM Kemp	c Martin b Bracken	13	17	1	
JJ van der Wath	c Ponting b Bracken	35	18	1	3
R Telemachus	c Hussey b Bracken	12	6	2	
AJ Hall	c Clarke b Lee	7	4	1	
M Ntini	not out	1	1		
Extras	(b 4, lb 8, w 4, nb 4)	20		
Total	(9 wickets, 49.5 overs)	438		

Fall: 3, 190, 284, 299, 327, 355, 399, 423, 433
Bowling: Lee 7.5-0-68-1; Bracken 10-0-67-5; Clark 6-0-54-0; Lewis 10-0-113-0;
Symonds 9-0-75-2; Clarke 7-0-29-1.

South Africa won by 1 wicket. **Toss:** Australia. **Umpires:** Aleem Dar, BG Jerling.
Man of the Match: RT Ponting, HH Gibbs.

18

'FROM THE MOST AMAZING VICTORY, THE ATMOSPHERE CHANGED'

Ireland v Pakistan, World Cup, 2007, Kingston

Niall O'Brien gave up the futile quest for sleep and forced himself out of bed. Two hours of shut-eye would have to do. The same sense of resignation had led him to pass up the chance to bat in the nets the previous day as Ireland prepared to face Pakistan in the group stages of the 2007 World Cup. So out of form did he feel that scratching around against his teammates' bowling would only have depressed him further.

A little more than 24 hours later he found himself without meaningful rest once more, not exactly an uncommon occurrence for an Irishman on the morning after St Patrick's Day. But now he was a national hero. Meanwhile, the very structure of cricket's global showpiece had been called into question; and the sport was waking to tragic news of the sudden, mysterious death of one of its most recognisable figures.

The ICC had made two significant decisions in relation to the latest World Cup. Not only would the cricketing nation that had dominated its early years, the West Indies, be hosting the tournament for the first time, but the field had been expanded by two teams to 16. That meant four groups of four playing out preliminary matches for the purpose – so the organisers hoped – of giving the two leading nations in each section some competitive warm-up games before they got down to the real business of the Super Eights round-robin. The 51 matches would stretch out across more than six weeks, the longest tournament yet. It was also the first World Cup to have the 'powerplays' dotted throughout the innings rather than having a simple 15-over period of fielding restrictions up front.

The expanded entry pool meant that Ireland, whose match the previous summer against England had been their inaugural official one-day international, qualified via the 2005 ICC Trophy to participate for the first time. In the 1980s and '90s the Irish might have got used to Billy Bingham's Northern Ireland sides or the Republic teams of

Jack Charlton overachieving at football's World Cups, but few were expecting much of the teachers, farmers, salesmen and journeymen county players who made up the national cricket squad. After all, they had managed to win only one of nine games against the English counties after being invited to participate in the reorganised Cheltenham & Gloucester Trophy (successor to the old Gillette Cup and NatWest Trophy) during the 2006 English season.

'A lot of guys didn't see the value in playing in that tournament because they were coming up against pros on a Sunday, having been working 50 hours in the week,' said wicketkeeper O'Brien, who was about to join Northamptonshire after being warned that his path at Kent would be blocked by the return of Geraint Jones to county duty after losing his England place. He and young Middlesex batsman Eoin Morgan were the only full-time professionals in a team that felt they had more potential than results suggested. 'Ahead of the World Cup we played in Kenya in a 50-over tournament that was a qualification competition for the T20 World Cup in South Africa – which made no sense. We played terribly. I played horrifically and hardly got a run, so I went to the World Cup feeling so far removed from ideal personal preparation.

'But as a team we felt we had what it takes to get through our group. We were very experienced and had a very settled team. We worked our socks off and also had a really good time off the field and that helps the morale. No way were we there to make up the numbers.'

It was same kind of team spirit that had characterised the football teams of Bingham and Charlton. 'It would have been very easy to look around at the riches everybody else had and what we lacked,' said all-rounder Kyle McCallan. 'We were very, very tight as a team. We didn't have the analysts and fitness coaches and team doctors that other teams had, but we made the most of our limited resources.'

Documentary maker Paul Davey, who observed the mood of the Irish camp close up, confirmed, 'The only people who thought it was just going to be a lot of sunshine and fun were some of the journalists. There was one broadcaster in particular who was well pissed off when Ireland did well because he thought it was just going to be a jolly. The team 100 per cent thought they were going to do well. That belief came from Adrian Birrell.'

South African Birrell, a former national service soldier who had coached in the townships of his country before the end of apartheid and played as an all-rounder for Eastern Province, had been in charge of the Ireland team for five years by the time of the World Cup. A believer in the kind of analysis software that could assess players' performance and physiology, he also had a way of galvanising every member of the squad. Davey observed, 'He grew up on a game reserve in South Africa and talked about the lions; how if one was injured sometimes the pack would let it die and sometimes they would slow down and wait for it to get better. He said it was because they knew that animal's value to the pride. He got it into the team that if you were 12th man you have got to do everything you can to prove your value and help the team, whatever your role.'

Based in Kingston, Jamaica, and playing all their games at a refurbished Sabina Park, Ireland were rated 14th in the world at the start of the event, which they began against Zimbabwe, the lowest-ranked of the ten full ICC members. According to the long-serving Peter Gillespie, 'That first morning, going into a proper stadium and proper warm-up facilities, knowing the eyes of the world are on you, it was phenomenal.'

O'Brien admitted that 'we were very nervous in that game' and were indebted to Australian-born opener Jeremy Bray's unbeaten 115. 'Thankfully, [umpire] Ian Gould must have forgotten his glasses,' he added, 'because he was stone dead in front of all three. It hit him on the shin and would have been crashing into middle stump half-way up.' Ireland still appeared unlikely to avoid defeat after posting 221 for 9, especially when Zimbabwe needed only 15 to win off the final six overs with four wickets in hand. Ireland's scratchy fielding – which included dropped catches and boundary fumbles – had even prompted commentator Michael Holding to ask, 'What is going on out there?'

But then skipper Trent Johnston's right-arm seam went for one run in his ninth over; Andre Botha conceded only two singles; and Johnston completed his spell by giving up two more. 'There was just a gut feeling that we are not losing this game of cricket,' McCallan recalled. 'The crowd were going mad and you could see that the Zimbabweans were panicking.' According to Johnston, 'We had spoken the previous night and that morning about how these guys could crumble. I could see it in the Zimbabwean eyes that they were gone.'

Botha's final over of medium pace produced a wicket and a single run and Zimbabwe still needed nine off two overs. They immediately lost their eighth wicket when Kevin O'Brien removed Prosper Utseya via a catch by Morgan and, after four more dot balls, a run-out meant Zimbabwe entered the final over with only one wicket remaining, At least the short, powerful figure of Stuart Matsikenyeri, with 66 to his name, was on strike.

Five untidy slow balls by Andrew White later, the scores were level, although Ireland had almost snatched victory on the penultimate delivery when Johnston attempted a great diving effort that left him nursing a shoulder injury for the rest of the tournament. 'TJ had used all the bowlers,' said O'Brien. 'He'd had to roll the dice and bring people back a bit earlier than he would have liked. He had to bowl Andrew Wright, who literally bowled straight breaks. The last ball was right in the slot and all the bloke had to do was lay a bit of bat on it because all the field were very close for obvious reasons.' Instead, Matsikenyeri drove at an inviting-looking delivery and completely missed. A jubilant O'Brien took off the bails and then, with the batsman having remained in his crease, tossed the ball back to White to run out the non-striker. 'I had to remind myself not to throw it eight feet back in the air to the bowler,' he recalled.

Ireland, who had escaped with a tie, celebrated as though they had won. 'It was just euphoria,' was McCallan's description. Yet far from feeling that they'd achieved the result that justified their presence in the Caribbean, Ireland wanted more. Birrell, who had decided that this tournament would conclude his stint with the team, told the players in the dressing room after the game, 'That was a fantastic effort. There was a huge amount of belief there. If we beat Pakistan we go through. Come Saturday we are not the favourites, we are the underdogs. We can go in and express ourselves freely.'

With that, a chorus broke out of 'Ireland's Call', the nation's sporting anthem written before the 1995 Rugby World Cup by Phil Coulter, who had helped to pen the England 1970 football team's 'Back Home', as well as hits for the Bay City Rollers. 'Ireland, Ireland, together standing tall,' they bellowed. 'Shoulder to shoulder, we'll answer Ireland's call.'[16]

It was Johnston's call at the toss two days later that set up an historic day. 'I remember drawing the curtains back at 6 a.m. and it was really dark and drizzly,' O'Brien explained. 'It looked like I had woken up in my mum and dad's house in Dublin on a winter afternoon. When we got to the ground and pulled the covers off we couldn't believe it. I remember saying to Trent, "If there is one thing you do at this tournament you have got to win that toss." We had the seamers to unsettle Pakistan and we knew they could be vulnerable against the moving ball. There was a couple of thousand people in at the toss and there was a big cheer when Ireland won it.'

Birrell remembered, 'When I saw the pitch I was shocked because it was green and that played into our hands because Irish players play on green wickets and there are not too many green wickets in Pakistan. After winning the toss there was just an air about our whole camp that this was an opportunity here that we could exploit.'

Pakistan, beaten by West Indies in their opening match, had been coached since 2004 by Bob Woolmer, who had taken over from Javed Miandad. In *Wounded Tiger*, his history of Pakistan cricket, Peter Oborne explained, 'Woolmer won the trust of a disparate group of players, refused to allow dressing room coteries and privileges for senior players, and lifted the squad's physical, technical and mental performance. Woolmer himself absorbed and respected the culture of Pakistan and championed his players against prejudiced critics at home and abroad.'

Woolmer was confident that this group of players could deliver the global triumph his coaching résumé still lacked, although he acknowledged the nervousness around his team when interviewed on the field before the Ireland match. 'It's a real banana skin-type game,' he said. 'We know what we have to do.'

When some of the Pakistan fans suggested to the Irish players that they should be 'in the pub drinking Guinness' as they took the field, Johnston recalled that 'you could see the guys grow an extra

---

16 The Ireland fans' preferred song was 'C'mon Ireland', written by Martin Byrne in response to a public appeal for an anthem for the team. The line 'Win or lose, we're going to have the craic' summed up their approach to their time in the Caribbean.

half-inch'. They were soon standing even taller. As the end of the opening over approached, commentator Tony Cozier was discussing a 'shaky start' by the Irish, but then David Langford-Smith got one to bounce and nip way from just short of a length and O'Brien's catch removed Mohammad Hafeez.

Boyd Rankin, a farmer who would go on to play Ashes cricket for England, saw Imran Nazir edge one to the third-man boundary; then kick the ball away from his stumps after a bat-pad deflection; and survive a tough return catch. But then Younis Khan edged Rankin to Botha in the slips. By now, Cozier was saying, 'We are in danger of an Irish explosion here today.'

Pakistan recovered to pass 50 with only two wickets down, but after Mohammad Yousuf drove Johnston square for four he got under the ball when he tried to repeat the shot and was caught at backward point by Porterfield. Skipper Inzamam-ul-Haq nibbled at Botha and Nazir followed suit a few runs later: 66 for 5. From behind the stumps, O'Brien had the best view of proceedings. 'It was nipping around. Boyd bowled loads of wides, but Langford-Smith started well and Botha was remarkable. He bowled 75 miles an hour on a sixpence and the Pakistan batters just had no answers. Their feet weren't moving and they didn't know whether to attack or defend. Unlike the Zimbabwe game, everything they nicked or hit in the air was caught.'

O'Brien took a sharp catch standing up to his brother, Kevin, and it needed some slashes and slogs by Kamran Akmal to take Pakistan into three figures. The final four wickets all fell to catches in the deep and Ireland were left requiring only 133 to win. And then it hit them. The magnitude of the opportunity they had been presented with.

'It was quite tricky at half-time,' said Birrell, who was wound so tightly that he followed most matches on TV while pacing the dressing room. 'Suddenly the nerves kick in. We can win.' While Birrell advised his men to 'just chill', skipper Johnston took a more pro-active approach. 'We have got a massive fucking chance to go to the Super Eights and stay in the West Indies for an extra four weeks,' he exhorted. 'Do you want to be back in Dublin on Monday teaching or farming? I sure as hell don't want to be back there selling fabric.'

As Niall O'Brien summarised, 'Kenny Carroll was a postman. It was freezing back in Ireland, so why would you want to go back and deliver post and get chased by an Alsatian rather than stay in the Caribbean and play against the best players in the world?'

At 15 for 2 – after Bray and Morgan were offered no reprieve by the umpire against Mohammad Sami – O'Brien was next man up in the long order of Irish left-handers. He crashed a short ball square for four and then pushed tidily through mid-off for three, before finding the boundary again with the straightest of bats. 'I was buzzing,' he remembered. 'Without wishing your teammates to fail, I liked to get in the contest early. I tended to play better if I got out there quickly as opposed to walking out at 120. I got one out of the middle down the ground very early, which is something I don't do very often. The previous six weeks evaporated in one shot. That is how simple batting can be and that is why the game is played in the mind. Kyle McCallan called me a peacock and I was strutting around with my chest out as if I was coming off five hundreds on the bounce. I didn't feel I was in any trouble against pace or spin. I was in complete control; one of few occasions I felt like that in my career.'

A slash over the slips was less elegant than the drives and punches off the back foot that followed, each run being accompanied by a growing crescendo from the increasing number of 'Blarney Army' Irish fans, around 2,000 of whom were reckoned to have made the trip to the Caribbean, supplemented by ex-pats working in Jamaica and the Cayman Islands. 'There was a cracking atmosphere,' said O'Brien. 'More and more people came in as they heard there was an upset on the cards and by the end there was about 5,000 there. A lot of the locals got behind us after the Zimbabwe game and there are quite a lot of similarities in the people of the Caribbean and the Irish in their way of life, so I think they related to us.'

Davey, who had hit upon the idea of his documentary after a chance meeting with O'Brien in Australia, where he had been living and O'Brien coaching, said, 'I could really relate to the cricket fans in Ireland because I am a League of Ireland soccer fan. Irish cricket fans don't do it for the glamour, and they love it when people show an interest in their passion. The fans were a mixture of the hardcore; people in America who went down there for a bit of a jolly; and random people who just happened to be in the Caribbean. There was one couple who were on their honeymoon from Australia. He and his wife got married a few days before and when they went to the World Cup to support Ireland he became this Larry the Leprechaun figure.'

Another wicket fell on 62 when Hafeez made his arm ball hurry through to bowl Porterfield for a valuable 13, and Hafeez was ruled by umpire Brian Jerling to have caught Botha at short leg off Sami, even though the bat and ball had clearly not been in the same neighbourhood. O'Brien, who could not help a gesture of disbelief at the non-striker's end, got on with the business in hand, turning Sami to fine leg to reach a half-century out of a score of 74 for 4 and cutting Umar Gul between two fielders for his fifth boundary.

A brief adjournment for bad light saw Ireland's target revised by Duckworth-Lewis to 128 from 47 overs, which O'Brien reduced by four with a flashy shot in front of square. The cheers that greeted the 100 were repeated when O'Brien skipped out of his crease to land Shoaib Malik in the stands behind long-on. But then there were groans as he tried the same shot to the next ball and was stumped in a flurry of flailing limbs for 72.

'My own disappointment was the way I got out. leaving the team in the lurch,' he admitted. 'After the adrenaline of hitting a massive six I should have taken some deep breaths and started again. Instead, I had a rush of blood and before you know it you are face down in the muck. If there was one moment I could take back in my career it would be that. I would love to have finished 85 not out, walking off with my brother. That would have been amazing. I still thought when I sat down, "Well, it is only 20 to win, we should be fine." Before I had both my pads off there were two big roars.'

White, who had clipped his first ball behind square for four, offered an easy short-leg catch off Iftikhar Anjum and then McCallan edged the next delivery to slip. There were still 15 needed with three wickets remaining. 'I'm not going to lie,' added O'Brien. 'We were panicking. You are just hoping that the boys get the job done, especially when you should have done it yourself. If Ireland hadn't won that game it would have been my fault and I don't know how I would have coped with that.'

Kevin O'Brien, whose big-hitting would find fame against England four years later, was not for moving. His 16 runs took 52 balls and were worth far more as he and skipper Johnston pushed towards their target. O'Brien punched the air when a quick single put Ireland level with their reduced target and Johnston picked up Azhar's slower ball to launch a match-winning six into the crowd. As his team concluded their frenzied on-field celebrations with a lap of honour, Johnston raised four fingers towards Davey's camera and gave a joyous cry of, 'Four weeks!'

Writing in Ireland's *Sunday World*, Con Houlihan equated the magnitude of the upset to that of North Korea beating Italy in the 1966 football World Cup in England. 'In a way it was even more sensational,' he said. 'In soccer you can snatch a goal and hold on to it, as North Korea did; in cricket you are thoroughly assessed over a much longer period.'

Commentator Aamir Sohail had spoken of the 'historic pictures' viewers were witnessing, but the more poignant shot turned out to be that of Woolmer closing his silver laptop and, with an air of resignation, sliding it into his Pakistan team backpack. Under no illusions about the implications of defeat – although not yet aware that effigies of him and Inzaman were already being burned on streets in Pakistan – he told the BBC's Alison Mitchell, 'To fall out like this is very disappointing.' He continued, 'I'll sleep on my future. I have said that I'm reluctant to continue in international cricket, purely from travelling and so on, but I will stick to coaching at a different level. But I think a decision's probably been made for me.'

Woolmer had a couple of beers in the Polo Lounge at the Pegasus Hotel and headed to his room. During a restless night he emailed his wife, Gill, shortly after 3 a.m. and shared his fears with Ivo Tennant, the journalist with whom he was collaborating on a book. Admitting that 'I don't know what is going to happen', he signed off by recalling the setback of South Africa blowing the World Cup semi-final against Australia eight years earlier. 'What a miserable day it has been. Almost as bad as Edgbaston in 1999.'

Meanwhile, Ireland had achieved the greatest feat in their cricketing history. On St Patrick's Day. It was time for a party. Stopping briefly at the Pegasus to pick up a change of clothes, they drove north to the tourist town of Ocho Rios, where hundreds of Irish fans were staying at the Sunset Grande Hotel. 'The owners invited us all for two days and two nights to celebrate with the fans,' Niall O'Brien recalled. 'There were about 1,500 fans there and in the surrounding area. We had a cracking time and the place ran out of alcohol. I had to do a thing with Sky News at about 2 a.m. Caribbean time and I was there on air with my dad, very drunk.'

A few hours later, however, came the most sobering of news. Woolmer had been found dead when a chambermaid at the Pegasus made her mid-morning visit to his room. He was 58 years old.

'I got a room at the hotel in Ocho Rios,' said Davey, 'and this party went on until about 4 a.m.. The next morning I had to do an interview with a guy who dresses like a leprechaun and we were both hung over and I was kind of doing it out of courtesy because, having beaten Pakistan, the leprechaun wasn't really the story anymore. Then I met a journalist from the BBC and he said, "Have you heard? Bob Woolmer's dead." I got him to speak to my camera and suddenly, from the most amazing victory, the atmosphere changed.'

Police called the initial autopsy 'inconclusive' and said they were treating the death as suspicious. Days of confusion, rumour and innuendo followed; the chaos captured vividly by Davey on video and eventually shared with the world on his *Breaking Boundaries* documentary. Returning from their celebrations, the Ireland players found the atmosphere 'chilling', according to Johnston, who had been housed down the corridor from Woolmer. Still with a final group game to prepare for, the players spent the time locked in their rooms.

The hotel lobby became abuzz with police, government officials and media members, some of whom protested with news desks back home that they were not trained crime reporters. Ireland team manager Roy Torrens told Davey's camera, 'It's pure pandemonium here. I am not really sure anyone knows what's happened.'

Davey recalled, 'Kingston is a dangerous enough place and everybody huddled together out of safety. We knew the hotel backwards at this point but when we came back it just wasn't real. TV companies were broadcasting live from the lobby; the head of the police came in and all the journalists were running around after him. There was just strange stuff going on. The PR guy for the Pakistan team was in the bar one night shouting to the media, "It's murder, it's murder." It made us all feel really uneasy because we didn't know what was going on.'

The Ireland squad were unsettled further when news arrived that Bob Kerr, the former president of the Irish Cricket Union, had died in his bed at the Sunset Grande. Such was the dark mood of the week that police were required to state that there were no suspicious circumstances surrounding the 68-year-old's death.

Four days after the discovery of Woolmer's body, Jamaican Commissioner of Police Lucius Thomas led a press conference in which he announced, 'The pathologist's report states Mr Woolmer's death was due to asphyxiation as a result of manual strangulation... it is now being treated as a case of murder.'

Speculation went through the roof, with theories citing everyone from disgruntled fans and bookmakers to the players themselves. Police told Woolmer's wife Gill and sons Dale and Russell that their lives could be in danger and warned them not to travel to Jamaica. Pakistan team trainer Murray Stevenson, who had been particularly close to Woolmer and had been required to identify the body, was forced to ask himself, 'Are you next?'

Once they had arrived in Guyana after losing their final first-round match against the host nation, the Ireland players found the police knocking on their doors, looking for alibis and fingerprints. 'It was a bit ridiculous,' said O'Brien, whose teammates had not been in the hotel on the night of Woolmer's death. 'We had to do statements and fingerprints after we had flown to another country. It was an absolute shambles, not the most professionally run investigation of all time.'

Yet British-born Mark Shields, the deputy police commissioner in charge of the investigation, had never been convinced it was murder. Woolmer, a diabetic who acknowledged that he was overweight, had clearly been struggling for breath at the time of his death but Shields had seen nothing to suggest a struggle or forced entry into the room. He was as surprised as anyone when the pathologist reported that the hyoid bone in the coach's throat was broken, an indicator of strangulation. 'Where is the bone? Can we see the bone? Has it been X-rayed?' were the questions he asked, as he explained to Alison Mitchell a decade later.

Once the bone had been extracted and examined, Shields discovered that it had not been broken. At that point, the likelihood of murder began to recede, although the same pathologist who had suggested strangulation then declared that Woolmer's body presented levels of an insecticide chemical. That was later attributed to a fly spray used in the mortuary.

In November, an 11-strong jury ruled that the evidence presented during a month-long inquest left them unable to determine whether Woolmer had been murdered or died of natural causes. The open verdict was 'disappointing' to Shields, but he – and Woolmer's family – understood why it had been delivered and were satisfied that the idea of foul play had, effectively, been laid to rest.

* * *

In the aftermath of victory over Pakistan and with an apparent murder mystery swirling around him, Ireland manager Torrens had faced the kind of practical problems unappreciated by his peers, whose priority was checking their teams' hotel arrangements for the Super Eights. 'I am ringing employers in Ireland asking if they can give their guys time off for another month to play cricket,' he laughed, pointing out that it was good fortune that some of those very employers were themselves in the Caribbean.

The Irish spirit seemed to be everywhere, as Davey discovered. 'The mobile phone company Digicel was owned by Ireland's richest man, Denis O'Brien, and he heard what I was doing. He rang me in the lobby on the Digicel mobile I was given by the marketing manager and he said, "I am paying for all your flights and accommodation for the rest of the tournament." It was phenomenal. And when I got home and got the film finished he got me on a number of radio stations to talk about it.'

Of course, this was not the way the tournament organisers had scripted events. The violation of regulations for which they would eventually rap Davey's knuckles – such as getting physiotherapist Ian Knox to film for him inside the dressing room – were minor irritants for the ICC. Of far greater concern was the fact that Pakistan were supposed to have advanced, ensuring that plenty of television eyeballs were focused on their remaining games, including the guaranteed box-office contest against India. Yet India were gone, too. On the day of their great rivals' collapse against Ireland, they had been beaten by Bangladesh and had their fate sealed by a subsequent loss to Sri Lanka.

So it was Ireland versus Bangladesh in Barbados four weeks later, rather than the clash of the arch-enemies. Whatever ended up on the scoreboard would be less significant to the ICC than those lost audience numbers and the discontent of sponsors and broadcasters that would accompany them.

For Ireland, beaten comfortably in three previous games in the second stage of the competition, this was the game they felt could give them the win that would secure full ODI status. And so it turned out, Porterfield's 85 helping them to 243 for 7 and the bowlers sharing out the wickets as they dismissed their opponents for 169. 'In my five years that was our most complete match,' said Birrell.

McCallan, who stressed how important it was for Ireland not to be seen as 'one-hit wonders', recalled another tearful lap of honour and Birrell wondered what he would say before his team's final game, against Sri Lanka in Grenada, his last match in charge. In the end, he gave way to fears that emotion would get the better of him and, instead, wrote out his speech and handed each player a copy to read. 'That was pretty touching in itself,' said Johnston, whose emotionally drained team were bowled out for only 77.

It was an unhappy note to end what Birrell was not alone in describing as 'a journey of a lifetime', but the team returned home to discover how much their performances had meant in their homeland. Having received a call of congratulations from Irish president Mary McAleese while they were in the Caribbean, they now met with the Rev. Ian Paisley and Martin McGuinness, whose Democratic Unionist Party and Sinn Fein had, in the midst of the World Cup, reached an historic agreement of cooperation that allowed power to be restored to the Northern Ireland parliament at Stormont. McCallan commented, 'Let's hope our politicians can work together as well as we did in the World Cup.'

Fêted in the aftermath, the players also learned how many pubs and clubs had been home to cricket viewing parties while the tournament had been in full swing, creating a legacy that would see the country awarded Test-match status ten years later. 'It put cricket on the map in Ireland,' said O'Brien. 'It gave the board a bigger opportunity to secure sponsorship and invite the bigger teams, and it gave us a bit more standing in the world game. Lads like Paul Stirling and George Dockrell, who went on to play for Ireland, said they watched the games and there would have been thousands of others who took up cricket. The game as a whole started to thrive.'

But while Irish cricketers started rehearsing the stories that would be told for years to come about the time they took on the world, the world – in the form of the ICC – was determined to safeguard against future similar narratives. No longer could the risk be run of India and Pakistan playing less than a full complement of matches and not facing each other.

By the end of 2007, the decision had been taken to reduce the field for 2011 back down to 14, split into two groups. That guaranteed at least six matches per team. India and Pakistan eventually met in the semi-finals, but when the same format was agreed, belatedly, for 2015 in Australia and New Zealand, the big two were in the same group.

And when the tournament returned to England in 2019, the number of competitors would be slashed to ten teams, all playing each other in a round-robin format – nothing left to chance. 'There are lots of commercial implications to consider,' said ICC chief executive Dave Richardson after the 2015 event. 'We also need to have a look at the attendances at all the associate games, what were the viewing figures, and see where they really stand.'

Never mind that Ireland had won three matches in that tournament – more than England. They would be absent from the 2019 event after failing to qualify for one of those precious places.

But they would always have Jamaica.

IRELAND v PAKISTAN, World Cup Group D

17 March 2007, Sabina Park, Kingston

Pakistan			Balls	4s	6s
Imran Nazir	c Morgan b Botha	24	51	3	
Mohammed Hafeez	c NJ O'Brien b Langford-Smith	4	6	1	
Younis Khan	c Botha b Rankin	0	3		
Mohammad Yousuf	c Porterfield b Johnston	15	31	2	
*Inzamam-ul-Haq	c Morgan b Botha	1	3		
Shoaib Malik	c NJ O'Brien b KJ O'Brien	9	25	2	
†Kamran Akmal	c Johnston b Rankin	27	47	4	
Azhar Mahmood	c Johnston b Rankin	2	21		
Mohammad Sami	c Bray b McCallan	12	34	1	
Iftikhar Anjum	not out	8	43		
Umar Gul	c sub (JF Mooney) b McCallan	1	13		
Extras	(lb 3, w 23, nb 3)	29			
Total	(45.4 overs)	132			

Fall: 7, 15, 56, 58, 66, 72, 103, 105, 130, 132.
Bowling: Langford-Smith 10-1-31-1; Rankin 9-1-32-3; Botha 8-4-5-2; 7-1-20-1;
KJ O'Brien 6-0-29-1; McCallan 5-4-1-12-2.

Ireland			Balls	4s	6s
JP Bray	lbw b Sami	3	13		
WTS Porterfield	b Hafeez	13	50	1	
EJG Morgan	lbw b Sami	2	5		
†NJ O'Brien	st Akmal b Shoaib	72	107	6	1
AC Botha	c Hafeez b Sami	0	6		
KJ O'Brien	not out	16	52	2	
AR White	c Hafeez b Iftikhar	4	3	1	
WK McCallan	c Younis b Iftikhar	0	1		
*DT Johnston	not out	9	14	1	
Extras	(lb 2, w 11, nb 1)	14			
Total	(7 wickets, 41.4 overs)	133			

Fall: 7, 15, 62, 70, 108, 113, 113.
Did Not Bat: D Langford-Smith, WB Rankin
Bowling: Gul 9-0-24-0; Sami 10-0-29-3; Iftikhar 10-0-29-2; Azhar 7.4-1-25-0;
Hafeez 4-0-15-1; Shoaib 1-0-9-1.

Ireland won by 3 wickets. **Toss:** Ireland. **Umpires:** BF Bowden, BG Jerling.
Man of the Match: NJ O'Brien.

19

'IT OVERTURNED THE LANDSCAPE
OF THE SPORT'

*India v Pakistan, World T20
Final, Johannesburg, 2007*

It had been 24 years since the World Cup triumph that made India fall in love with the limited-overs game and changed the very nature of cricket. Four years of Twenty20 represented a further evolution. But as the format's first world championship approached in September 2007, there was little suggestion that the same nation was about to turn the story of 20-over cricket into one of revolution.

Only three days before the inaugural World T20 – as it was billed – began in South Africa, India's finest were in England, concluding a seven-match series in the version of the sport that still drove its global finances, 50-over internationals. With a lucrative ODI schedule to maintain along with the traditional Test programme, India had little interest in dabbling with the short game. They had only ever played one T20 international and an indication of the BCCI's priorities was that the big three of Sachin Tendulkar, Rahul Dravid and Sourav Ganguly would be sitting out the new global tournament in order to be well rested for another seven-game ODI marathon at home to Australia.

'There was no preparation at all,' recalled Dinesh Karthik, Man of the Match in India's one low-key T20 contest in South Africa almost a year earlier. 'We had won the Test series in England and lost an ODI series in the seventh game, and some people wanted to take a break because their bodies were tired. We had to go to South Africa right from England so there was an opportunity for a lot of the young boys to come through.'

Ironically, it had been India's desire to maximise the potential of the 50-over game that ensured they would be among the 12 teams competing in the 20-over competition in South Africa. Having not staged the World Cup since 1987, India's bid to host the 2011 tournament had appeared doomed when it landed on the ICC's desk three weeks late and with twice as many venues as suggested in the event guidelines. The BCCI might have been ambivalent towards Twenty20 but it did give them some leverage, threatening to withhold participation from the ICC's latest showpiece unless they were given the opportunity for a deadline-busting presentation of their 2011 plans. And, after the events of the 50-over World Cup earlier in the year, the ICC couldn't afford for India not to show up.

Although memorable for the likes of Ireland and Bangladesh, the tournament in the Caribbean was characterised by the death of Bob Woolmer; for being over-long and limited in the amount of compelling cricket it offered; for unrealistically high ticket prices; and for the unsatisfactory experience for many fans, forced to consume sponsors' products and seemingly denied the opportunity to enjoy themselves in the stands by party-pooping organisers.

Rather than concluding with a final to make people forget what had gone before, the Australia-Sri Lanka climax in Barbados was appropriately shambolic. Starting late because of rain and reduced to 36 overs, further bad weather reduced Sri Lanka's run chase by two more overs. When bad light forced the players from the field after 33 overs, Australia were so far ahead on Duckworth-Lewis that they began their celebrations in the belief that the game was over. The podium and sponsor boards were even being set up for the post-match ceremony. At that point umpires Aleem Dar and Steve Bucknor shooed away the stage hands and their presentation props and mistakenly instructed the teams that because they were off for bad light rather than rain they would have to play the final three overs, even if it meant returning the next day. Captains Mahela Jayawardene and Ricky Ponting agreed that was ludicrous, given that Sri Lanka needed 61 off three overs with three wickets remaining – not a concession any team would be so quick to grant a decade or so later. Sri Lanka agreed to bat on in complete darkness against Australia's spinners. Those spectators who bothered to remain at the Kensington Oval booed their way through the final deliveries as Sri Lanka added nine runs, before the umpires admitted their error, Fittingly, a sponsor's board collapsed during the tournament's last press conference.

The responsibility for proving that world cricket could indeed stage an event in keeping with its status fell to former South African seam bowler Steve Elworthy, the tournament director. Given 18 months to plan, pressure on Elworthy and his team to deliver successfully had grown immeasurably since the debacle in the Caribbean.

'This was the first event in the ICC's next cycle of rights after the 2007 World Cup,' Elworthy explained. 'That goes down as one of the toughest World Cups because India and Pakistan both got knocked out early and we were on the back of that. There was a continual reminder of this black cloud hanging over you, and without a doubt the need to get the ICC events back on track. With the new rights, the global partners' landscape changed and we had new broadcasters and new commercial partners and sponsors, some of whom weren't involved in cricket at all previously. We were told in 2006 we were going to host it so we had a very short period of time to put it together. It was incredibly complicated because a lot of the new partners weren't aware of their rights or what was expected on the ground. There was a lot of pressure.'

Elworthy could at least fall back on South Africa's track record of delivering a successful domestic 20-over tournament, the Standard Bank Pro20. 'We've been selling out matches and that's a bit of a factor,' he said when the tournament was announced. 'We've learned how to put these matches on and in our presentation to the ICC we could show we have escalated the game.'

According to Gerald Majola, the chief executive of Cricket South Africa, 'We have to ensure that every person is able to enjoy the event and that the stadia are full. We looked at the previous two ICC tournaments and in my opinion they were not successful. So we have looked at those pitfalls and will take care of those in South Africa. We understand what Pro20 has done for cricket in South Africa. We wanted to make it a truly national game accessible to all.'

All meritorious ambitions, but Elworthy also remembered, 'There was definitely a level of scepticism about the tournament because Twenty20 was still being seen as a bit of a gimmick. I am not sure Pakistan or India were even playing it at home. There was a conversation about whether T20 should even be an international competition at that time because around the world it was reinvigorating domestic cricket and bringing in capacity crowds. It was flying. I remember having debate after debate because the 50-over game was still a huge success in terms of the number of people coming to matches.'

Men's international Twenty20 cricket had begun as recently as February 2005 – although, as it had in staging the first limited-overs World Cup, the women's game had led the way when England faced New Zealand at Hove the previous year. The first men's match, between New Zealand and Australia in Auckland, was treated lightheartedly, with the home side resurrecting their beige uniforms of the early 1980s and several players wearing false facial hair and afro wigs. With New Zealand still needing 45 to win off the final ball, Glenn McGrath bowled a Trevor Chappell-style underarm delivery. Aussie skipper Ricky Ponting said of the format, 'It's difficult to play seriously,' – but not before he had applied himself enough to score an unbeaten 98.

By the time first World T20 was staged, Australia were the most experienced team with six matches in the format, ahead of New Zealand's five. Only 16 Twenty20 internationals had been played in all, mirroring closely the 18 one-day internationals contested before the first World Cup in 1975. Another obvious comparison to that first global tournament was that this new addition to the calendar would span only 13 days, with matches restricted to Durban, Cape Town and Johannesburg.

The sample size of previous T20 internationals was too small to establish meaningful rankings for the format, so the seedings for the event were based partly on form in ODIs. It was no surprise that the first-round groups thrown up by those rankings found India and Pakistan in the same pool, along with Scotland. The ICC was leaving nothing to chance this time, especially as neither of the Asian giants were certainties to make the latter stages of the tournament.

Not for the first time, Pakistan were creating their own problems, with fast bowler Shoaib Akhtar sent home prior to the tournament for attacking teammate Mohammad Asif. 'I hit Asif with a bat,' Akhtar admitted, claiming that his victim had accepted his apology but the incident had been escalated to team management by Shahid Afridi, with whom he had been arguing when Asif got involved. Asif, who ended up with a bruised thigh, said that Afridi had been urging Akhtar to see the responsibility he had to nurturing the younger players in the squad. 'He told Shoaib that juniors were wary of him,' Asif said.

Such pre-tournament turmoil was nothing new. A year earlier both Akhtar and Asif had been sent back to Pakistan before the

Champions Trophy in India after testing positive for the banned steroid nandrolone in an internally administered test. Both men appealed successfully against their respective two-year and one-year suspensions, meaning they were eligible to disrupt preparations again ahead of the World T20. Meanwhile, even India's own fans were nervous about their chances. 'When the T20 format of the game was first introduced in the global circuit, not many expected the Indian team to make waves,' said Tarkesh Jha, a writer for the Bharat Army website. 'This was going to be a format dominated by hard-hitting batsmen, something that we lacked in abundance at that point in time. Most of our legends have been "touch" players, as one may say, who banked more on timing the ball to perfection rather than butchering it to the stands using brute force.'

Since the 50-over World Cup earlier in the year, India had parted company with head coach Greg Chappell, whose two-year reign had been punctuated by reports of clashes with senior players – spats that would reverberate for many years. Most notable was his fall-out with former skipper Sourav Ganguly, of whom Chappell said, 'He didn't particularly want to work hard. He didn't want to improve his cricket. He just wanted to be in the team as captain, so that he could control things.'

Ganguly, speaking about Chappell in 2016, recalled that in 2005 he 'had an opportunity to select the coach. I thought I messed it up.' And Tendulkar told ghostwriter Boria Majumdar that he felt Chappell had 'pushed our cricket back by at least four years' and even suggested to the BCCI that he should not accompany the team to the World Cup in the Caribbean. 'This was based on a premonition it would all end badly for us with him around.' Lalchand Rajput, who had played a handful of internationals as a batsman, was the latest in a line of interim coach/managers ahead of Gary Kirsten's full-time appointment in 2008.

The tournament could not have been given a more robust push start, with the home nation beating West Indies in a game featuring more than 400 runs and two magnificent innings by the stars of limited-overs batting. First Chris Gayle bludgeoned 10 sixes on his way to scoring 117 off 57 balls, before Herschelle Gibbs responded with an unbeaten 90 from 55 deliveries as South Africa surpassed their opponents' 205 with more than two overs in hand.

Gibbs, the man accused of 'dropping the World Cup' eight years earlier, was clearly enjoying the big stage of global events a little more these days. A few months earlier, he had become the first player to hit six sixes in a single ODI over when he launched an assault on Netherlands off-spinner Daan van Bunge in a World Cup game on the Caribbean island of St Kitts. Four of his blows flew over long-off with the other two targeting the leg-side boundary, including the final-ball blast that ended up on the roof of the stand beyond midwicket. 'The last two balls landed in the right areas for me to have a go and luckily I didn't miscue either of them,' he explained, having determined after the first four blows to target a place in history.

India, meanwhile, reached a pivotal moment as early as the fourth day of the new T20 tournament when they faced Pakistan in Durban. With a washout against Scotland having left them in danger of elimination if they lost, the local Indian population filled the Kingsmead ground but were left fearing the worst after four early wickets fell against Asif's seaming deliveries. A half-century by Robin Uthappa and a watchful 33 by MS Dhoni, captaining the team for the first time, got them to 141 for 9. If Pakistan could reach that target in 14.4 overs, India would exit the tournament on net run rate. 'I just wanted to win,' recalled Pakistan captain Shoaib Malik. 'If we had a good start we might go for it.'

Instead, Pakistan still needed 39 to win off 14 balls, at which point Misbah-ul-Haq reduced the target with 10 runs from two deliveries, before a wayward sequence by Ajit Agarkar meant there were 12 required from the final over, bowled by seamer Sreesanth. Misbah stepped back to drive him to the off side and reach his fifty, and the scores were level with two balls remaining. Sreesanth didn't risk a full delivery and watched Misbah miss his attempted cut. One ball left. This time Misbah made contact but could only bunt it into the covers, from where Yuvraj flipped the ball back to the bowler to complete an easy run-out.

The commentators had warned of the consequences of a tie but neither team appeared aware that it meant a five-man bowl-out to determine the winner. There was a delay of several minutes while officials consulted rulebooks before the action continued. Sehwag, Harbhajan and Uthappa hit with their deliveries, while Pakistan had three misses. 'I am happy to win a cricket match three-nil,' said a sardonic Dhoni.

Just over a week later, on the afternoon of South Africa's Heritage Day holiday, the same two teams met in Johannesburg in what many commentators described as 'the dream final'. Both India and Pakistan had topped their second-stage groups before comfortably winning semi-finals against Australia and New Zealand respectively. 'It was my first experience of the rivalry between India and Pakistan,' said Elworthy. 'I had never really seen the significance of the match-up between those two, but the ticket sales were just unbelievable. We probably could have sold out the Bullring three or four times over.'

Sehwag's groin injury meant an international T20 debut for Yusuf Pathan but did not prevent Dhoni giving his batsmen first knock after winning the toss. His target, he said, was 180. Slow to respond to Gambhir's call, Yusuf was almost run out on the very first ball but survived to hit Asif down the ground for six as India scored 13 in the opening over. He'd made 15 when he fatally skied a pull shot. After Uthappa was caught trying to hit Sohail Tanvir over cover, India were 40 for 2 from the six powerplay overs, their progress stalling.

Gambhir decided that good placement on a fast outfield was a more effective approach than trying to hit over the top, while fellow left-hander Yuvraj Singh drove Shahid Afridi down the ground for his first boundary. Much was now expected of Yuvraj following India's earlier game against England in Durban, where he became the first man to hit six sixes in a T20 over in a blistering assault on Stuart Broad. The final shot sailed beyond the midwicket boundary to take him to 50 off 12 balls, still the fastest half-century in international cricket at the time of writing.[17]

But on this occasion, having seen his colleague skip down and flay Afridi for six and move the score into three figures with more well-directed boundaries, Yuvraj fell for only 14 when he top-edged a leg-side swish and bowler Gul gathered himself below the ball for a simple catch. Gul, as usual being used in the second half of the innings, startled Dhoni with an unintentional, but unsettling,

---

[17] Appropriately, in the commentary box at the time was Ravi Shastri, who in 1985 became the first Indian and only the second player after Garry Sobers to hit six sixes in a first-class over.

beamer and quickly cleaned him up off the inside edge. India went 25 balls without a boundary before Gambhir smashed Gul into the scoreboard. Once he had gone, caught paddle sweeping for 75, it was the creativity and force of Rohit Sharma that got them up to a final total of 157 for 5, well short of the skipper's target. 'Make no mistake,' said David Lloyd on commentary, '157 in Twenty20 cricket is a good total,' – not an argument many would make a few years later.

Mohammad Hafeez perished early in Pakistan's reply, offering a straightforward slip catch, but Imran Nazir unleashed a full-blown offensive against Sreesanth. By the time sixes had flown over midwicket and third man and fours hammered either side of the wicket, the second over of the innings had cost 21 runs. Yet Nazir was gone before the powerplay had concluded, run out for 33 after failing to respond quickly enough to Younis Khan, who'd come to the wicket when Kamran Akmal missed a big in-swinger to give left-armer RP Singh his second wicket.

With the pitch apparently becoming slower, Pakistan needed someone to hold the innings together as Gambhir had for India. Instead, the top order came and went. When Afridi holed out to the first legal delivery he faced, the Wanderers seemed to have been transformed into a corner of India, even down to the sight of Bollywood superstar Shah Rukh Khan celebrating on the big screen, which in turn created a greater state of frenzy among the fans. More of him later.

When Irfan took his third wicket to leave Pakistan struggling at 104 for 7 after 16 overs, it was again down to Misbah to carry Pakistan's hopes. His response was to swing Harbhajan for three leg-side sixes, inspiring Tanvir to do the same twice to Sreesanth, who then took out his opponent's off stump. Pakistan were 20 short of victory with two overs and two wickets remaining.

Three runs from four balls, then RP Singh removed the leg stump of an off-balance Gul. Just when it looked like India were closing out their victory, Asif edged for four and 13 were needed from the last over; Misbah on strike. Joginder Sharma began with a wide; then Misbah played and missed before smashing the next delivery far beyond the straight boundary. With six needed from four balls, Misbah chose clever over clobber and stepped across his stumps to flip the ball towards fine leg. But with too much elevation and not enough power, the ball fell into the hands of Sreesanth to secure a five-run victory for India, the team who had been given no more chance of becoming global champions than their 1983 predecessors. 'Unbelievable scenes here at the Bullring,' said commentator Ravi Shastri as the reserves and support staff raced to join their teammates, determined to make the most of a party they had almost opted to miss.

'It was my debut World Cup; I had just made my T20 debut in that tournament,' recalled Rohit Sharma, who was then 20 years old. 'Luckily that catch went into his hand; Sreesanth was there to take the catch. I remember everyone running on to the ground. It was helter-skelter.'

The champagne taste left in everyone's mouth by events in South Africa was a lot sweeter than the sour grapes of the 50-over World Cup earlier in the year. Karthik, who had played in India's early games in the tournament, said, 'You can't wax eloquently enough about how much that World Cup did for world cricket. Yuvraj Singh's six sixes, India and Pakistan playing a tie, the final almost going down to the last ball. I don't think you could have scripted it better. It was just fun to play in and fabulous for the sport.'

'It is one of those things I will treasure for the rest of my life,' said Dhoni, unaware of the triumphs of captaincy he would add to his résumé in the coming years, including further ICC triumphs in the 2011 World Cup and 2013 Champions Trophy. 'No one expected us to win.'

Nor did anyone fully expect the consequences of a success that India was craving after a decade that had witnessed the stain of match-fixing and the disappointments of World Cups. 'There was a chance that people would have drifted away from the sport,' Jha argued. Instead he would be able to reflect, 'It overturned the landscape of the sport in this country. It helped the T20 format attain interest beyond boundaries. Cricket was no more a sport of only [those] from the metropolitans. It spread across barriers, reached the unknown audience yet again on a daily basis, and all of it could happen because of one more reason; the advent of the Indian Premier League.'

* * *

244

The BCCI had agreed to the concept of the IPL shortly before the World T20. It could never have imagined the boost to those plans that Dhoni's team would drop in its laps, especially as the launch of the league was initially a defensive manoeuvre against the rival Indian Cricket League.

Tracing the exact birthplace of the IPL idea is a little like asking historians to pinpoint the first identifiable game of cricket; a maze of differing claims and theories. The man who would be the IPL's first commissioner, Lalit Modi, was undoubtedly the one who gave the idea form, but authors Alam Srinivas and TR Vivek catalogue various other origin stories in their study of the early years of the competition. 'While most BCCI functionaries readily credit IPL as the brainchild of Modi, there are other claimants to the provenance of IPL or similar ideas for a city-based cricket league in India,' they wrote in *IPL: An Inside Story*.

Madhav Rao Scindia, a former minister in the Indian National Congress and part of the royal family of Gwalior, had been thinking of a city-based league back in the 1990s – a competition that would attract the world's best players – and had created a blueprint around 1996.

Another thinking along the same lines was Modi, who had studied in the United States at Pace University in New York and Duke University in North Carolina. By now he had moved on from the family business, where he had served as president of the International Tobacco Company, and had established his own media distribution company. A disciple of the US system of franchise sports, he proposed a 50-over competition to the BCCI, assisted in his presentation by influential advertising executive Piyush Pandey and ex-India batsman Arun Lal. When BCCI chairman Jagmohan Dalmiya told Modi that such a proposal could only come via a state cricket association, not a private individual, Modi teamed up with Scindia, who was president of the Madhya Pradesh Cricket Association. This time the BCCI, nervous about private team ownership, also refused to entertain the notion of overseas star players, without which Modi knew the idea was doomed commercially.

Another party, the GMR group which would go on to own Delhi's IPL team, made fruitless presentations to the BCCI, while Shailendra Singh, of Mumbai-based advertising and promotion company

Percept, said his experience of putting on fundraising all-star games gave him the necessary experience to stage what he referred to as a 'glam cricket league'.

Dalmiya and the BCCI managed to keep such ideas at arm's length until their hand was forced by Subhash Chandra and his Zee TV network. Like Kerry Packer in Australia three decades earlier, Chandra was frustrated at being blocked from acquiring television rights for the sport, despite a history of generous offers. As Packer had, he decided to set up his own organisation, the 20-over Indian Cricket League; even getting Tony Greig on board as ambassador, recruiter and broadcaster. Scheduled to begin in November 2007, shortly after the first World T20, it quickly became clear that a competition unauthorised by officialdom would be staffed mostly by players at the tailend of their careers. But when the names of some current players started to emerge as candidates, the BBCI decided that it needed to respond with a 20-over tournament of its own.

Besides, Modi, who was now vice-president of the BCCI under new leader Sharad Pawar, could see that the environment was ready for what he envisaged. India's economy was growing at an annual rate of almost nine per cent; the percentage of people living in poverty had almost halved over the previous two decades; and the middle-class was expanding exponentially. Modi hatched a plan with Balu Nayar and Andrew Wildblood of IMG over tea at the Wimbledon tennis championships.

The resulting two-page proposal from IMG suggested overhauling Indian domestic cricket with a city-based 20-over league, with teams owned by rich individuals or corporations. In September, with the World T20 looming, the BCCI met in Singapore – consulting with the boards of Australia and South Africa – and agreed the formation of the Indian Premier League. While Modi would have preferred a 2009 launch, the spectre of the ICL made it imperative, he believed, to begin play early in 2008. There would also be a Champions League staged later in the year, pitting the top T20 teams from various domestic competitions against each other.[18]

---

18 The CLT20, as it was known, proved to be a shortlived enterprise. With its first season cancelled in the wake of the Mumbai terrorist attacks, it ran for only six seasons before being dropped after the 2014 season.

Sundar Raman, head of media planning agency Mindshare, was brought on board as the IPL's chief operating officer. 'Our common vision was to make the IPL the best sporting league in the world,' he said. But could that really be done in so little time? 'Speed was of greatest importance. With the timelines we were given I don't think anyone in our team slept for more than four hours a day.'

According to Nayar, 'We were briefing a few investment bankers and sports marketing agencies in New York and when we told them that a league of this scale and ambition was to be rolled out in three months they nearly fell off their seats. They thought we were out of our minds.'

Without the exploits of the Indian team in South Africa, it might have been an impossible task. But the final's Indian television audience of 400 million and the victory parade on the players' return home was evidence of a new-found passion for this version of the sport, which might just enable the IPL to pull it off. According to Elworthy, 'The 20-over game would definitely have grown organically as most countries had domestic leagues and were starting to play internationals. But the first World T20, especially the final, was a definite catalyst. It was just unbelievable. I didn't realise the power of those two nations.'

Karthik concluded, 'It set the tone for the rest of the world to look up and say, "Wow, that is a format we need to take seriously." And you see where it is today.'

INDIA v PAKISTAN, World T20 Final

24 March 2007, The Wanderers, Johannesburg

India			Balls	4s	6s
G Gambhir	c Asif b Gul	75	54	8	2
Yusuf Pathan	c Shoaib b Asif	15	8	1	1
RV Uthappa	c Afridi b Tanvir	8	11	1	
Yuvraj Singh	c and b Gul	14	19	1	
*†MS Dhoni	b Gul	6	10		
RG Sharma	not out	30	16	2	1
Irfan Pathan	not out	3	3		
Extras	(lb 1, w 4, nb 1)	6			
Total	(5 wickets, 20 overs)	157			

Fall: 25, 40, 103, 111, 130.
Did Not Bat: Harbhajan Singh, J Sharma, S Sreesanth, RP Singh
Bowling: Asif 3-0-25-1; Tanvir 4-0-29-1; Afridi 4-0-30-0; Hafeez 3-0-25-0; Gul 4-0-28-3; Arafat 2-0-19-0.

Pakistan			Balls	4s	6s
Mohammad Hafeez	c Uthappa b RP Singh	1	3		
Imran Zazir	run out	33	14	4	2
†Kamran Akmal	b RP Singh	0	3		
Younis Khan	c Y Pathan b J Sharma	24	24	4	
*Shoaib Malik	c RG Sharma b I Pathan	8	17		
Misbah-ul-Haq	c Sreesanth b J Sharma	43	38	4	
Shahid Afridi	c Sreesanth b I Pathan	0	1		
Yasir Arafat	b I Pathan	15	11	2	
Sohail Tanvir	b Sreesanth	12	4	2	
Umar Gul	b RP Singh	0	2		
Mohammad Asif	not out	4	1	1	
Extras	(b 1, lb 4, w 6, nb 1)		12		
Total	(19.3 overs)	152			

Fall: 2, 26, 53, 65, 76, 77, 104, 138, 141, 152.
Bowling: RP Singh 4-0-26-3; Sreesanth 4-1-44-1; J Sharma 3-3-0-20-2; Yusuf Pathan 1-0-5-0; Irfan Pathan 4-0-16-3; Harbhajan 3-0-36-0.

India won by 5 runs. **Toss:** India. **Umpires:** MR Benson, SJA Taufel.
Man of the Match: Irfan Pathan.

20

'YOUR LIFE IS CHANGED FOREVER'

*Royal Challengers Bangalore v Kolkata Knight
Riders, Indian Premier League, Bengaluru, 2008*

Ross Taylor had seen enough of Brendon McCullum in their six years
as New Zealand teammates to give his new colleagues a warning.
'He is going to come out pumped and come out swinging,' was the
gist of the message he delivered to the Royal Challengers Bangalore
as they held their final team meeting before the inaugural contest of
the Indian Premier League.

Challengers captain Rahul Dravid was happy to put Taylor's theory
to the test immediately, inviting McCullum's Kolkata Knight Riders
to bat first. But not before Bengaluru's M. Chinnaswamy Stadium
had been introduced to the personality of the new competition with
a spectacular opening ceremony featuring fireworks and lasers,
dancing by the cheerleaders of Washington's NFL team, and the
symbolic signing of a 'sprit of cricket pledge' by the captains of
the eight competing teams. The usual collection of Indian cricket
board big-wigs said their pieces before IPL Commissioner Lalit Modi
declared the tournament open.

And then it went flat. As the second over began, only three extras
were on the board and McCullum was scoreless from five balls. He
took a swing at the first ball from Zaheer Khan and hit nothing but
air. This was not what Taylor had predicted. And it was not part of
the grand plan that, via a mix of meticulousness and madness, had
brought the IPL to life in astonishingly quick time.

Once the intention to launch in 2008 had been stated publicly
and the celebration of India's World T20 triumph had calmed, the
IPL's first task had been to run a tender process to identify eight
team owners, who would then select a home stadium from the list
of potential options.

Some of those owners would become as much the face of
the league as those hitting the sixes and taking the wickets. The
$10,000 cost of acquiring the application document – designed to
scare away time-wasters and nosy parkers – could not deter 90

bidders from declaring their interest, although as the grand reveal at Mumbai's Wankhede Stadium on 24 January approached only ten proposals had been received that fulfilled all the technical and financial requirements. Some additional tenders did materialise, but when the BCCI suggested that the deadline be extended to allow them to be considered, the original bidders, not surprisingly, vetoed the idea.

The achievement of attracting as many confirmed candidates as they did in such a condensed timeframe should not be underestimated, however, especially amid a deepening global financial crisis and the plummeting of the stock markets. The business plan presented to prospective owners warned of potential losses for the first four or five years, but the opportunity to make big money once the second television deal kicked in. 'You could lose $20 to $30 million if the league fails,' recalled Peter Griffiths, one of the IMG executives tasked with building the franchise model for potential investors. 'But if it succeeds you are going to own one of eight franchises in a cricket-mad country,'.

Prospective owners had been invited to submit their bid to purchase a franchise in one of 15 possible IPL cities, with the minimum price set at $50 million. The two lowest bidders turned out to be a consortium led by Deutsche Bank and a group led by Anil Ambani, whose brother Mukesh, head of Reliance Industries Ltd and ranked by *Forbes* as Asia's richest individual, entered the highest offer at $111.9 million. For that he chose to acquire the Mumbai team and the rights to stage the first final. Close behind was the $111.6 million spent by Vijay Mallya's UB group, who opted for Bangalore, which would stage the opening ceremony and inaugural game. The *Deccan Chronicle* was the other applicant to more than double the floor price in grabbing Hyderabad for $107 million.

Indian Cements (Chennai, $91 million) and the GMR Group (Delhi, $84 million) offered further corporate power, but what the IPL and its commissioner Lalit Modi really wanted was some glamour. It was provided by Bollywood icon Shah Rukh Khan, whose entertainment company bagged Kolkata for a touch over $75 million, and actor and producer Preity Zinta, who led a group that paid $76 million for the rights to the Mohali team, which would become the Kings XI Punjab. Modi's view was that the Indian population was obsessed with cricket and Bollywood. 'If you fixed the two together it would be so powerful and dynamic.' He called it 'a reality show beyond comprehension'.

Griffiths remembered, 'In one of the early meetings Lalit said, "We are going to go primetime; we're going to play in the evenings when TV is usually showing soap operas." Most households only had one television, so IPL matches needed to appeal to the whole family. In that first season pretty much every team had some kind of Bollywood connection. It was absolutely key for Lalit because he wanted the whole family watching.'

The bargain hunter of the franchise bid process was London-based Manoj Badale, whose Emerging Media paid $67 million for the Jaipur franchise, to be named the Rajasthan Royals. The antithesis of Bollywood glamour, his group slipped away from the event unmolested by the media.

The windfall of more than $723 million from the new owners had been partly driven by news that the IPL had secured a ten-year television deal with Sony-World Sport worth $1 billion, the same price ESPN Star had paid the ICC for eight years of broadcast rights to its global tournaments. Sony had held those ICC rights until India's early exit from the 2007 World Cup and Rohit Gupta, president of Sony Entertainment Television, explained that 50-over ratings had been declining for four years because viewers, especially the younger ones hooked on Premier League football from England, 'didn't have the eight hours to watch an ODI'.

Quite apart from the money they were able to offer, Sony represented a good fit for the IPL; being a non-sports station used to presenting a broad range of entertainment to casual viewers. 'There had to be action of some sort all of the time,' was Gupta's approach, which chimed perfectly with the vision Modi had been selling to prospective franchise holders.

The IPL was determined that the action would begin even before the players took the field. To that effect, the teams' squads would be constructed via the league's first auction at Mumbai's Oberoi Hilton Tower Hotel on 20 February, two months before the scheduled start of the season.

Much thought had been given to the best way of allocating players; the priorities being to offer fair value, avoid the kind of frenzy that would push prices too high, and ensure an even spread of talent across the teams. One method examined was a Dutch flower auction, where the clock begins with the price high, and values drop as the clock it ticks down. In the end, a traditional open ascending bid auction was recommended.

The BCCI signed deals with 77 Indian and overseas players, who agreed to play for whichever franchise made the highest bid that met or exceeded their reserve price. In return, the BCCI guaranteed the players' three-year contracts if the whole enterprise flopped. It was a significant step to be taken by any cricket governing body; not organisations normally associated with bold gambles.

Five 'icons' were automatically allocated to their local sides – Sachin Tendulkar to Mumbai Indians, for example – and guaranteed to earn 15 per cent more than their highest-paid teammate. A sixth proposed icon, VVS Laxman, asked to be sold in the auction. The world's best players were available to the highest bidder, with teams given a $5 million budget for salaries and allowed a maximum of eight overseas players, only four of whom could play in any match. The players would be offered in auction in 'sets', based on specialism and international status, with the order within each set determined by the drawing out of small cricket balls bearing a specific player's auction number.

Sotheby's Richard Madley was recruited by IMG's Andrew Wildblood, a former cricketing teammate, to conduct the sale and to put a gloss of propriety on what seemed to many like a rather undignified procedure. 'I came in as a technical adviser,' he recalled. 'Then, having helped them write the rules, they said, "Get yourself a visa; you are coming out next week. You are conducting the inaugural IPL auction."' Unaware of quite what he was flying into, Madley walked from his hotel to the Wankhede Stadium to meet and brief the franchise owners on procedures on the eve of the auction. 'When I saw there were 100 journalists and 20 TV crews I thought, "This is going to attract a bit of attention."'

The scene inside the auction room the next day was chaotic. Every owner except Mukesh Ambani of Mumbai was keen to be seen among the laptops, scouting notes and coaching staffs at the tables of their respective teams. Mallya had pulled up in a red Bentley, while the unobtrusive Badale and his Rajasthan colleagues made a typically low-ley arrival in a Honda and were assumed by many observers to be fellow media members. According to Griffiths, 'Big Bollywood, big tycoons, big players; this was the day you realised that this is going to go absolutely crazy.'

Aware of the unusual and historic nature of auctioning professional sportsmen, Madley's unfamiliarity with the rich and famous of Indian society helped him treat it as calmly as he would any other auction. It took a little time before he presided over a blockbuster bidding contest. Even Shane Warne, the fifth name to emerge, was sold only for his base price of $450,000, which offered an indication of the measured manner in which Rajasthan, in particular, would apply themselves to their task.

Madley recalled, 'The auction actually started steadily, with Shoaib Akhtar selling to Kolkata and Shane Warne to Jaipur for his base price. And then out of the bag came a small cricket ball with the name MS Dhoni ... the IPL auction had taken off.' Chennai threw $1.5 million – almost a third of their budget – at India's T20 captain, the highest figure of the entire auction. Owner N. Srinivasan, chairman of Indian Cements, explained, 'We wanted him at any cost.'

'We originally put the top 12 players into one group,' Griffiths explained. 'As I was flying to India for the auction I had a nightmare that Dhoni was going to come out 12th and all these great players who preceded him would go unsold because everyone was waiting for Dhoni. Why spend any money before Dhoni goes? So we made a really last-minute change to a group of six and moved some of the other top players into a second group. And Dhoni did come out last!'

Hyderabad (Deccan Chargers) went on to make Australian all-rounder Andrew Symonds the second-richest player in the league at $1.35 million. They had already spent $700,000 on explosive Aussie wicketkeeper-batsman Adam Gilchrist, a sum that ensured few people had much sympathy when he said 'there was an element of feeling like a cow' in the bidding process.

The approach of most teams appeared somewhat scatter-gun, with some signing big names who would excite the fans and look good alongside the owner in photographs rather than putting together a well-rounded T20 team. The obvious exception was Rajasthan, who picked up overseas players such as Graeme Smith, Justin Langer and Younis Khan at bargain prices. In his book with Simon Hughes,

A New Innings, Badale explained that his staff had identified their top three options for each role in the team and a maximum spend on each. 'Commentators focus naturally on the value of a player but not sufficiently on the value of a player in a particular role, for a particular team,' he argued. 'I was keen on the use of data and analysis, having read Michael Lewis's brilliant *Moneyball*. Statistics that are typically used to gauge players are often misleading.'

The Royals saw little point in spending all their dollars on eight imports when only half could play. Even they, however, were not immune to the adrenaline rush. 'We couldn't resist and made mistakes,' admitted Badale, who would see Langer and Younis spend the season on the bench. 'I started to panic about our lack of international-class Indian players – so we went all out for Mohammad Kaif and overpaid.'

The policy of investing in the young Indian players who would form the nucleus of the team saw them pay $675,000 for Kaif and $475,000 for Yusuf Pathan. But they still ended up being fined for not reaching the minimum spend level of $3.3 million. 'They never got excited,' Madley told Indian spinner Ravichandran Ashwin's YouTube channel on the eve of the 2022 auction. 'Manoj Badale was just very, very cool. A pattern started to emerge about the teams, the franchise owners … Some were very excited and wanted the cameras and weren't sure what they were bidding on and others were quite reserved and businesslike.'

Most people would have put Bangalore in the first group, with the flamboyant Mallya wearing 'diamonds in his ears that almost blinded me', according to Madley, who remembered, 'There was a bit of rock and roll on the RCB table at times. I think there was perhaps a little bit of getting carried away slightly and paying more than they thought.'

As the surprisingly cheap bidding paddles – pieces of foam and card stuck together with glue – were raised to change lives and, ultimately, the structure of the sport, it wasn't just the established and recently retired players who were benefiting from the biggest contracts of their lives. A separate stage of the selection process was dedicated to uncapped Indian players who were members of their country's 2008 Under-19 World Cup squad. Prices were set at $50,000 and they were picked in an American-style draft. Among those who cashed in was an incredulous Virat Kohli, who would be joining the galaxy of stars in Bangalore. 'We were all in Malaysia for the Under-19 World Cup,' he recalled. 'That moment for us was so amazing. Because the amount that we got picked for when they announced it, we couldn't believe it because it was absolutely crazy.'

The scene was set. Now for the games. But as big a deal as the opening match would be, there was little opportunity for the organisers to devote too much time to it. 'Because of the way the calendar worked, there were two games the next day,' said Griffiths, 'so we flew out of Bengaluru the next morning and were constantly on the road for the next 44 days. We were trying to get a lot of stadiums event-ready. We were running around trying to sort out accreditation and logistical issues. The opening game was just the beginning of a long road.'

For 26-year-old McCullum, it was a life-changing journey. 'I was just a young kid back then, so I was in awe of Shah Rukh Khan,' he recalled. 'I was so out of my depth even just around the superstars in my cricket team, let alone the megastar who owned our team.'

The first few balls he faced on the opening night reinforced his insecurities. But he connected through midwicket and then gave the IPL the first six in its history; a top-edged swing that sailed over the third-man boundary. The next ball went where McCullum intended, clipped through square leg for four more. Once he had pulled Praveen Kumar from outside off stump, McCullum had reached 23 from 13 balls by the end of the third over, with Sourav Ganguly yet to score.

A flat six over square leg and a monstrous drive over extra cover was how McCullum greeted South African paceman Ashley Noffke, but with only one four in the next five overs it was the final ball of the ninth over before he reached 50. The introduction of left-arm spinner Sunil Joshi saw McCullum rediscover his range.

Meanwhile, remembering that many of his team had never played in front of such a big crowd, Dravid described some of them as 'rabbits in headlights'. He added, 'When I captained later on you kind of knew how to react to situations like that.' For now, Joshi watched a slog sweep soar over the square-leg boundary and, one ball after he almost bowled McCullum as he tried a repeat, the New Zealander plonked him over long-on with a shot played virtually one-handed.

A more subtle touch was employed against Jacques Kallis before McCullum greeted the wrist spin of Australian Cameron White by skipping down the track for a six and a four. A pull over midwicket for another maximum took him to 99 at the end of the 15th over. 'My game has been very similar all the way through,' he said years later. 'If it is short and wide, cut. If it is short and high, pull it. If it's full and on the stumps, whack it straight. Anything between you try to find a way. I tried to maintain that throughout my career and it was no different on that occasion.'

At the earliest opportunity he steered two runs against Noffke to reach his century from 53 balls, bringing images of a celebrating team owner to the screen; a jig of joy that became even more frenzied when he saw his investment paddle Zaheer Khan from off stump over fine leg for yet another six. Kallis twice disappeared into the crowd over long-on in the 19th over.

McCullum was not finished. Kumar began the last over with a full toss that flew over midwicket and the second ball was pulled for the batsman's 13th six. Four runs off the next three balls felt like victory for the bowler, but the innings ended, appropriately, with the ball landing in the stands yet again. The IPL had begun with T20's highest individual score, 158 not out from a score of 222 for 3. The match turned out to be a one-sided victory, but McCullum ensured that the new venture had its grand opening. His innings lives on in a way that no final-ball victory could possibly have done.

'Your life is changed forever,' were the words Ganguly offered to his somewhat dazed teammate once he returned to the dressing room.

'I didn't quite know what he meant at the time but I 100 per cent agree with him,' McCullum recalled, speaking in 2020 as head coach of the Knight Riders. Shah Rukh Khan had ended up promising him, 'You will always be part of this team' – even after his playing career in the IPL eventually took him elsewhere.

* * *

The on-field problem of dealing with McCullum had been the immediate preoccupation for Challengers skipper Dravid, but he would reveal the doubts he harboured about the long-term viability of the IPL. 'None of us knew what to expect,' he said. 'We knew it was big and obviously the number of requests I had for tickets proved it, but I thought, well, maybe people will come for one or two games or even one season, but how is the economics going to work out long term?'

Neither he, nor the league's investors, need have worried. As television audiences soared for this new nightly soap opera, the $4 million Sony had been predicted to lose on their TV rights during the first season became an estimated profit reported at $75 million. Bollywood studios delayed releases of new movies while households were content to spend every evening huddled in front of IPL action.

When the *Economic Times* reported a survey revealing that viewers remembered the Bollywood stars they had spotted on screen more than the players, it merely proved the success of the league in reaching a non-traditional cricket audience. Authors Alam Srinivas and TR Vivek observed, 'This was the new India. An India where the grotesque display of wealth by the IPL team owners and their army of celebrity friends was part of the entertainment package. Teeming thousands who watched the spectacle were also part of the new young and aspirational India, whose appetite for intimate knowledge about the lives of the rich and famous was insatiable.'

By the time the final came around, between the Chennai Super Kings and Rajasthan Royals, there was no doubt about the success of the league and no shortage of people basking in its success. The day before the season concluded at Mumbai's 60,000-capacity DY Patil Stadium, BCCI president Sharad Pawar, who was also then India's Food and Agriculture Minister, declared, 'I am extremely proud that whatever we have seen over the last 44 days is a product of India,' pointing out that the game would be seen in 122 countries. According to Modi, the IPL had quickly become 'a global representation of India and what the modern-day India stands for and its successes'.

For those who felt a little queasy at the sight of the excesses of the IPL, there was perhaps some satisfaction to be drawn from the on-field outcome of its first season: a triumph for the Royals. The team characterised by sound management and frugality – relatively speaking, of course – found that achieving lower overheads, imposing lower wages on itself and offering less flashy entertainment to its fans was no impediment to winning games.

While rumours circulated of teams offering lavish gifts as incentives to their players, the Royals' concession to treats for their men was getting sponsors, the Kingfisher beer company, to throw them a disco after each home victory.

With star signings and young talent calmly executing their assigned roles, the Royals won 11 of their 14 regular-season games. Their Australian all-rounder, Shane Watson, was named player of the tournament, but it was Warne's assured captaincy that appeared to give them the edge over their rivals. 'His cricketing acumen was extraordinary,' Badale told Simon Hughes, 'His captaincy was a combination of meticulous planning and gut instinct. He was also surprisingly strict off the field.'

After beating Delhi in the semi-final, the Royals got across the line against Chennai to be crowned the first champions. Having begun the last over of the season needing nine runs to reach their target of 164 with three wickets in hand, seam bowler Sohail Tanvir pulled the final ball for the winning single. Appropriately, Warne was at the crease with him. 'It was an incredible night, even in a country famed for its cricketing passion,' said Badale.

Such was the instant success of the IPL that even a relocation to South Africa in 2009 – because the Indian elections occupied the resources of the security services – could not halt its momentum. The crowds across the eight venues were enthusiastic hosts and the Indian television audience didn't mind where the games were played as long as they could see them.

Ironically, the man who lit the rocket under the IPL, McCullum, felt that he struggled to follow its path into the cricketing stratosphere. 'It set me back a couple of years if I am honest,' he told ESPN. 'It launched me in terms of people's expectations, and it took me a little while to try and deal with that. You set lofty goals for yourself in what is attainable, and it took me a few years to realise those days don't come around very often.'

But he ended reinforcing Ganguly's prediction. 'The 158 changed my life.' Just as it helped change his sport.

ROYAL CHALLENGERS BANGALORE v KOLKATA KNIGHT RIDERS, Indian Premier League

18 April 2008, M. Chinnaswamy Stadium, Bengaluru

Kolkata			Balls	4s	6s
*SC Ganguly	c Kallis b Khan	10	12	2	
†BB McCullum	not out	158	73	10	13
RT Ponting	c Kumar b Kallis	20	20	1	1
D Hussey	c White b Noffke	12	12	1	
Mohammad Hafeez	not out	5	3	1	
Extras	(b4, lb 4, w 9)	17			
Total	(3 wickets, 20 overs)	222			

Fall: 61, 112, 172.
Did Not Bat: LR Shukla, WP Saha, AB Agarkar, AB Dinda, M Karthik, I Sharma
Bowling: Kumar 4-0-38-0; Khan 4-0-38-1; Noffke 4-0-40-1; Kallis 4-0-48-1; Joshi 3-0-26-0; White 1-0-24-0.

Bangalore			Balls	4s	6s
*RS Dravid	b Sharma	2	3		
Wasim Jaffer	c Ponting b Dinda	6	16		
V Kohli	b Dinda	1	5		
JH Kallis	c Karthik b Agarkar	8	7	1	
CL White	c Saha b Agarkar	6	10		
†MV Boucher	c Karthik b Ganguly		7	9	1
B Akhil	c Ponting b Agarkar	0	2		
AA Noffke	run out	9	10	1	
Praveen Kumar	not out	18	15	1	2
Zaheer Khan	b Ganguly	3	8		
SB Joshi	c McCullum b Shulka	3	6		
Extras	(lb 8, w 11)		19		
Total	(15.1 overs)	82			

Fall: 4, 9, 24, 24, 38, 38, 43, 57, 70, 82.
Bowling: Dinda 3-0-9-2; Sharma 3-0-7-1; Agarkar 4-0-25-3; Ganguly 4-0-21-2; Lakla 1.1-0-12-1.

Kolkata won by 140 runs. **Toss:** Bangalore. **Umpires:** Asad Rauf, RE Koertzen. **Man of the Match:** BB McCullum.

21

'TAKE A BOW, MASTER'

*India v South Africa, 2nd One-Day
International, Gwalior, 2010*

The first one-day international hundred had been scored by England's Dennis Amiss in the format's third match. After 2,961 ODIs in the men's game, no one had yet gone on to reach a double century, although two men, Pakistan's Saeed Anwar in 1997 and Zimbabwe's Charles Coventry 12 years later, had come within six runs.[19]

By 2010, Sachin Tendulkar had been playing international cricket for more than two decades and had scored 92 hundreds for India, 45 in the one-day game. His own highest score in ODIs had been achieved only a few months earlier – an unbeaten 186 against New Zealand at Hyderabad – and he had just scored two centuries in the Test series against the South African tourists.

No one would have been bold enough to predict that an ODI double-ton was imminent, not least Tendulkar himself. With his 37th birthday approaching, he was feeling every one of those years as he paced the Indian team hotel in Gwalior, his nation's 'City of Kings', ahead of the second of three 50-over contests against the Proteas. 'I was starting to feel really tired,' he remembered. 'It had been a long season and my body was beginning to raise some objections. I had aches and pains everywhere.'

Teammate Dinesh Karthik explained, 'We played the first ODI in Jaipur, left the next day and had only one day of practice before the game in Gwalior, so it was a quick turnaround. If you keep doing that, then as you get older you are obviously going to feel it and feel tired. I'm sure that is what happened on that occasion.' At least the Indian team's headquarters offered an uncommon slice of tranquility. 'Gwalior was a very different place,' Karthik continued. 'We stayed in a beautiful palace-cum-hotel, which was one of the better places I have stayed while travelling for the sport. It was a very quiet and secluded place, a rarity in India.

---

19 Belinda Clark of Australia had achieved the feat in 1997 against Denmark

We were given privacy and we had a good get-together as a team after we travelled.'

On the morning of the game, Tendulkar spent 90 minutes on the treatment table with physiotherapist Ntin Patel, sharing with him his desire to win the game so that India would have an unassailable 2-0 lead in the series, allowing him to request to be left out of the third and final match three days later. Such a plan would not have sat well with the ticket-holders for that upcoming game in Ahmedabad, of course, but for the 30,000 at Gwalior's Captain Roop Singh Stadium Tendulkar's desire for some time off was to give them a day they would never forget.

Originally a hockey stadium and named after a former star of that sport, the venue had a history of being kind to batsmen. 'It is a pretty small ground with a very fast outfield,' said Karthik. 'A lovely wicket to bat on.'

The prospect of a favourable environment seemed to serve as a tonic to Tendulkar. 'When I got to the ground all the pains and aches had just disappeared,' he wrote in his autobiography. Skipper MS Dhoni's decision to bat – despite the relative coolness of the afternoon, the rain of a couple of days earlier and the threat of evening dew – saw Tendulkar at the crease as the match started. It would be 'one of those days when everything seemed to go my way'.

South African Gary Kirsten, who had been coaching the Indian team for the past two years, remembered, 'Sachin was in a very happy place as a player. He was back opening the batting, which is what he wanted, and on a good deck he was going to be able to express his ability.' While that didn't mean Kirsten could foresee what was about to unfold, he did know that 'with his consistency the potential was always there for a special innings'.

Having seen Virender Sehwag survive a difficult caught-and-bowled chance against Dale Steyn, Tendulkar took advantage of left-armer Wayne Parnell over-pitching in the second over, leaning into drives on either side of the wicket to score his first two boundaries. 'I pushed at a ball from Wayne Parnell in the second over and was amazed to see it racing to the boundary,' he said. 'After that the balls consistently hit the middle of my bat.' If that reads like an over-simplification of his genius, then it certainly reflects the visual impression of his innings. The flick of the wrists that dispatched

Steyn to the leg-side boundary from off stump could have offered no clearer image of effortlessness.

After Sehwag slashed Parnell into the hands third man, Karthik arrived to enjoy the view from the non-striker's end. 'Sachin Paaji[20] was a very good partner to bat with because he gave a good insight into what the bowler was doing and what was happening off the wicket,' he explained. 'He encouraged you to express yourself with your batting and he gave me the freedom. We always had a good understanding and we ran the quick singles.' Yet there was always an element of anxiety that went along with any partnership with India's hero. 'The biggest pressure I felt batting with Sachin was that you were gonna run him out one day,' Karthik laughed. 'That fear of having stones pelted at me; that was something in the back of my mind when I batted with him.'

While Karthik made his own intentions clear with successive boundaries off Parnell, Tendulkar peppered the off-side boundary, a pair of fours off each opening bowler taking the score to 74 for 1 off 10 overs, by which time he had scored 46 from 32 balls. 'The plan was to just keep it simple and to try and prevent him from scoring boundaries,' Parnell told firstpost.com in a retrospective on what would turn out to be an historic day. 'Someone with his skill level, he just kept piercing the field the whole time and kept scoring boundaries. And he was actually scoring quite quickly for someone who wasn't really known to score that quickly in one-day cricket. That day it just seemed like there was a magnet in his bat and the ball was just attracted to the centre of [it], and he just kept hitting everything past fielders and into the gaps.'

A leg glance against slow left-armer Roelof van der Merwe took Tendulkar past 50, and as the score mounted he continued to open up the off side to dispatch both spin and seam. One such lofted shot off van der Merwe ended a quiet four-over spell without a boundary and took India to 129 off 20 overs, the 'Little Master' now unbeaten on 79.

Content to help Tendulkar manoeuvre singles against the accurate seam bowling of Charl Langeveldt, Karthik clearly enjoyed the

---

20 Loosely translated as 'big brother' Paaji was term of endearment used by many of the Indian players in relation to Tendulkar introduction of Jacques Kallis, advancing to drive him for four and swinging him over deep midwicket for six in the next over. This day was all about Tendulkar, though, and he reached his 46th ODI century by playing the last ball of the 28th over to deep point for a single off JP Duminy. 'At no point did it look like we were ever going to get him out,' Duminy admitted. 'He dominated from ball one. It was quite a small field at Gwalior but anything we threw at him he had answers to.'

Karthik remembered, 'We both got going and it was an attacking partnership, even though Dale Steyn was bowling well. Sachin didn't have a very flamboyant style, but when he got going he just took off. There were some mind-boggling shots. He took Parnell apart, coming inside and flicking him, and he was going over the covers to Kallis and he belted JP Duminy a bit. It was a masterclass'

He also recalled that Tendulkar's physical challenges became apparent the longer they shared time at the crease. 'It was one of those innings where he didn't run for everything. He knew if he played a couple of dot balls he could get a boundary or two to make up for it. I recall a couple of shots where he said, "That's OK. Let's not run for this." He wasn't pushing himself. Even though the outfield was fast it wasn't an easy place to run singles because the ball was going to the fielders much quicker than you thought. But he made use of the boundaries. One thing that was beautiful about Sachin's batting was his ability to use angles. He was very flexible with his wrists and his ability to use his bat position to find the gaps was second to none. He used his bat like a sword in a soldier's arms. He could beat you behind the keeper, or he could put it back past the bowler. All these shots came very naturally to him and his biggest strength was that his grip allowed him to do that. It made his game even better on a day when he was tired.'

As if to celebrate his century, Tendulkar smashed a short ball from Kallis through the leg side and clubbed the bowler back over his head. Duminy was punished, too, a good length ball slammed into the stands behind long-on and another full ball sent whistling back past his upstretched hand. There had been no discussion in the middle of Tendulkar's intentions, however. 'I think he was just going to try and play his shots,' said Karthik. 'He teed off after getting to 100 but you tended to do that. He was playing cheeky shots and obviously he connected with almost everything that came to him that day. He certainly wasn't planning to score 200. It was unthinkable then.'

But with Tendulkar on 124 and 17 overs left, the buzz was spreading through the crowd and commentary boxes of the possibility of history being made. Karthik recalled the 'phenomenal' atmosphere, although he would not be around to see if his colleague could achieve the unthinkable. After Karthik toe-ended a pull off Parnell to midwicket, Tendulkar powered on. He squeezed a Steyn yorker behind square for four and, having missed two balls outside off, walked across his stumps to steer the next ball to the rope in front of square leg. Parnell was smashed through extra cover and another Steyn full ball on off stump somehow found its way to the mid-wicket boundary.

Parnell recalled, 'There was actually a shot he hit off Dale Steyn where he kept on walking onto the off side and hit it through the leg side. So what the captain then went and told Dale was to bowl full and wide. I was at deep square leg and came into the ring and was next to the square-leg umpire. And I remember like once or twice, he obviously knew it was going to be wide but he still managed to get the ball past square leg for four.'

Tendulkar's next landmark, 150, was reached by clipping Parnell to the leg-side boundary. By now his partner, Yusuf Pathan, having taken consecutive boundaries off Steyn, was warming up, swinging Parnell, from round the wicket, high over square leg to take his score to 24 from 13. 'Just back yourself,' Tendulkar told the all-rounder. 'Whatever shots you play, enjoy yourself. Keep watching the ball closely. You play your game and I will keep going.'

According to Pathan, 'When someone of the stature of Sachin Tendulkar is going like that, the confidence shoots up. It goes on a different level. That happened that day.'

As if to prove his ability to pace an innings to perfection, Tendulkar ended the 40th over on 160, exactly on course for the landmark score of 200. The act of clouting Langeveldt from short of a length over the midwicket boundary with the intent of a Sunday village slogger put him ahead of the clock. The loss of Pathan to a catch by AB de Villiers barely caused him to blink; his response being to plant his left foot well outside leg stump and smash the final two balls of van der Merwe's wicket-taking over down the ground for four and six: 179 not out; eight overs remaining.

Kallis gifted Tendulkar a full toss to equal his ODI best of 186 and a series of ones and twos put him on 193 in the 45th over.[21] A scampered two to fine leg off Parnell took him to the highest score recorded in a one-day international, but by now the crowd would not have been satisfied with such a meagre achievement. Nor would Tendulkar, who had been thinking of a double hundred once he had reached 175. 'I had lost a bit of strength by then and, unable to play big shots, switched to finding the gaps and running hard,' he said. 'I was still running even when I was in the 190s while Dhoni was pounding the bowling at the other end.'

Dhoni's fast hands and elastic wrists shot him to 28 off 16 balls, scoring 10 off Parnell's last two deliveries to leave the shellshocked bowler with figures of 2 for 95 from 10 overs. For Tendulkar, the equation was now four runs in four overs. Two singles either side of the wicket off Steyn and a push to long-on against a Langeveldt full toss took him to 199. Two overs left and Dhoni on strike. Four, six, four, single off the last ball. Surely the Indian skipper, who had now sped to 53 off 30 balls, would not deny his partner, would he?

Karthik recalled, 'It was only when he'd got to about 160 that it dawned on everyone that there was the possibility of 200. When Dhoni got going, Sachin made it a point to hit those gaps and run but he could be slightly less risky because Dhoni was hitting the boundaries. It was one of those typical Dhoni finishes. He was in a bit of a hurry, playing those big shots, beating the gaps and hitting with power. But we all knew that Dhoni was aware of the milestone and he would make sure that there was enough time for Paaji to do it.'

Langeveldt bowled the final over and Dhoni somehow muscled the ball from near-yorker length over long-off. Finally, Dhoni turned down a second run after playing the ball deep into the leg side and, after watching the previous 10 deliveries, Tendulkar

---

21 Steyn would claim some years later on a Sky Sports podcast that umpire Ian Gould had turned down an lbw appeal around this stage of Tendulkar's innings, telling the bowler, 'If I gave him out, I won't make it back to the hotel.' It seems unlikely, based both on Gould's reputation and the ball-by-ball accounts of the game that record no such incident.

was back on strike. The ball was wide and full, and Tendulkar bent and stretched to guide it behind point for a single. 'The first man on the planet to reach 200 and it's the superman from India,' announced commentator Ravi Shastri as the helmet was removed and arms were outstretched. 'Sachin Tendulkar 200 from 147. Take a bow, master.'

The crowd stood and cheered, conches were blown, and teammates reacted as though they, too, were in the stands as awestruck paying customers. 'It was very apt that a player of Sachin's calibre ended up being the first double centurion,' said Karthik, while Kirsten added, 'You almost thought he would do that at some point. A double hundred in a one-day game had his stamp on it.'

Dhoni, never slow to recognise or enhance the drama of a particular moment, took the rest of the over, realising that for Tendulkar to have to face again would be anticlimax. Arms whirling and the energy in his shots lifting his left leg from the ground, he hit two of the last three balls for four to take India to 401 for 3.

South Africa, of course, had chased more than that to win four years earlier. But not this time; not on Tendulkar's momentous day. An unbeaten century by de Villiers, normally cause for headlines and celebration, would be a mere footnote. India romped home by 153 runs and the images and memories of the occasion would be those of Tendulkar alone. Even for those playing in the game. 'Whenever I watch the match or remember that knock,' said Pathan, 'I can visualise each and every shot he had hit. The way he had batted. You can never forget that innings. You know, I have forgotten my innings but Paaji's innings will forever be etched in my memory.'

Double Centuries in One-Day Internationals (1971-2022)

Date	Player	Score	Match
24 Feb 2010	Sachin Tendulkar	200*	India v South Africa, Gwalior
8 Dec 2011	Virender Sehwag	219	India v West Indies, Indore
2 Nov 2013	Rohit Sharma	209	India v Australia, Bangalore
13 Nov 2014	Rohit Sharma	264	India v Sri Lanka, Kolkata
24 Feb 2015	Chris Gayle	215	West Indies v Zimbabwe, Canberra
21 March 2015	Martin Guptill	237*	New Zealand v West Indies, Wellington
13 Dec 2017	Rohit Sharma	208*	India v Sri Lanka, Mohali
20 July 2018	Fakhar Zaman	218	Pakistan v Zimbabwe, Bulawayo
10 Dec 2022	Ishan Kishan	210	India v Bangladesh, Chattogram

Tendulkar dedicated his innings to 'the people of India who have stood by me no matter what for the past 20 years' and spent most of the next two days responding to messages of congratulations. Having achieved what was considered the ultimate individual accomplishment in ODI cricket, he now focused on rewarding those same fans with the climax to his career that he craved above all else: World Cup victory for India in front of a home crowd in 2011.

Kirsten, whose unbeaten 188 against the United Arab Emirates in 1996 was then still the highest individual score in World Cup history, had been appointed head coach in the wake of India's early exit from the 2007 tournament. Known for man-management and his ability to bring the best out of young players, especially batsmen, he also succeeded in not buckling under the weight of the personalities in the Indian dressing room. His influence, along with home advantage and the Indian public's natural tendency to bestow life-changing importance to every game their team played, meant expectations were higher than ever.

'There was massive pressure because it was 15 years since we had staged the World Cup,' said Karthik, who would miss out on a place in the squad for the tournament. 'Playing in India put more pressure on the team and you could see that people expected India to make it count. Obviously the pressure on Sachin himself was a very integral part of that.'

Kirsten managed to minimise his personal burden by reminding himself that he was still a young, inexperienced coach. 'Your credibility as a coach is always at stake and I had to prove my worth, but because I was young and didn't have any real credibility by then my expectations of my own abilities were quite low, so it made it easier. As a coach you are measured by the wins and losses, but it is not really why I coach. I coach because I love working in a team environment and trying to help people to be the best version of themselves. That is essentially why I coach so even if you lose it can be a good coaching experience.'

That kind of rationalisation – which would have meant little to Indian fans if their team fell short of what the nation demanded – did not mean Kirsten was unexcited about the tournament. 'We lost my first series in Sri Lanka but then we got going and we put a system in place that was foolproof. That's what excites me; when you look at an environment and see what you can create that allows a team to reach its potential. That is where coaching plays a really important role because you have got to facilitate that. You can say this team has got the potential to be a great team, but you have got to put the pieces of the puzzle into place to make sure that the team optimises itself.

'The World Cup was almost the end of a journey of establishing how we wanted to play. We were playing good cricket all around the world, even if we didn't win everything. The important thing about the World Cup was that we didn't play very good cricket in the round-robin stages but when we got to the knockouts we had individuals that proved themselves in those big moments; like Yuvraj Singh, who wasn't playing that well before the World Cup and was on the verge of being left out. Suresh Raina, who had never played a major tournament, had two very important knocks for us. We had guys we knew could win games for us.'

Most notably, Tendulkar – even though he viewed himself as simply part of a collective effort. 'He was a great role model in many ways,' said Kirsten. 'He was very curious around the game. It was great to coach him because he always wanted to share thoughts around his own game and was always wanting my view. He would not necessarily take everything on board but he wanted to improve, he wanted the conversation. You want any senior player in a team to operate the way he operated.

'It had got to the stage where there was nothing more to prove as an individual. That's why I really like Sachin. His behaviour has always reflected that team performance was more important to him. Yes, every player is going for milestones, but he seemed to really get excited when the team did well. And Dhoni was amazing in in that sense, trying to lift up the values of team more than anyone. I have never experienced anyone as good at that in my life.'

As Indian fans and cricket historians know, the pressure was endured and the dream achieved. But as if carrying the expectation of more than a billion Indian citizens was not enough to bear, Tendulkar stuck another weight on the end of his bar when centuries in the group games against India and South Africa left him one away from the unprecedented feat of 100 hundreds in international cricket. It meant that every time he went to the crease in the remainder of the tournament the crowd were in an even more heightened state of frenzy than usual, if such a thing was possible. He made a half-century in the quarter-final against Australia and then fell 15 runs short of making history in the semi-final against the old rival, Pakistan. 'That was maybe the most significant knock of his,' Kirsten suggested. 'He didn't bat that well, but he managed to stay there and work his way to a score that got us to 260.' A century in that match would have been fairytale enough, but now he had the chance to do it in the game that would crown India champions once again.

Sri Lanka won the toss and posted a score of 274 in the final at Mumbai's Wankhede Stadium, a target that was challenging without being daunting, and at least gave fans the knowledge that there were more than enough runs needed for Tendulkar to achieve his milestone. After a couple of early boundaries, he had reached 18. 'Just when the ball had stopped swinging, I was tempted to play a drive outside the off stump,' he recalled. 'The ball from [Lasith] Malinga swung and I edged it to the wicketkeeper.'

Tendulkar ensured a miserable walk back to the dressing room, not because he would have to wait longer – almost a year as it turned out – for his moment of personal glory, but because he had left others with the responsibility of fulfilling his World Cup hopes, and those of the nation.

It was the kind of responsibility, however, upon which the Indian captain thrived. In the history of limited-overs cricket few have matched Dhoni's ability to judge a run chase with such an effective combination of nerveless emotion and calculating brain. Shastri, then a commentator and later to become India's coach, said, 'Captain Cool may sound clichéd now, but in many ways it was an apt description, for nothing could frazzle Dhoni. I've seen him remain steadfast and inscrutable like a monk in victory and defeat.'

On this occasion he displayed boldness as well. When India lost their third wicket for 114 in the 22nd over, the man who had been a motorbike-loving rebel with a long mullet haircut at the time of the 2007 World T20 triumph strode out full of purpose. With the scent of destiny in his nostrils and the crown of leadership sitting comfortably upon his now neatly cut locks, Dhoni had told Yuvraj Singh to stay where he was. Never mind that Yuvraj would soon be named player of the tournament while Dhoni had yet to play a significant innings in the competition. This was a job for the skipper – something the great Sri Lankan spinner, Muttiah Muralitharan, believed Dhoni took on because he knew he could read his doosra better than Yuvraj.

Kirsten explained, 'We had a strong leadership group, so that decision was born out of a conversation with Sachin and Viru [Sehwag] where they felt that making sure we had a left-hand, right-hand combination was going to be very important against Muralitharan. I was sitting outside and Dhoni approached me and said, "What do you think about me going in next if Kohli gets out?" At that point we had a very fluid batting line-up anyway so it wasn't a difficult decision to make. That was the beauty of the leadership around our team; it was very collaborative and we thought about everything together.'

Joining left-hander Gautam Gambhir, who was on his way to scoring 97, Dhoni was the one figure in Indian cricket remotely able to approach Tendulkar's popularity and profile. His penchant for the flamboyant helicopter shot seemed to encapsulate the difference between the two men when set against Tendulkar's classic straight drive. In his study, *The Dhoni Touch*, Bharat Sundaresan suggested, 'In India, Sachin Tendulkar stands for perfection. The perfect 10. The man who could do no wrong. The man who was marked for greatness, prepared for greatness, and achieved greatness beyond anyone's imagination. He was a prodigy who grew up to be a prodigy.' While Tendulkar had followed the path of the likes of Sunil Gavaskar in his traditional cricketing development in Mumbai – with its population 20 times that of Dhoni's hometown of Ranchi – Dhoni was 'the quintessential odd man out. He's as cut off from the system as you can be in the context of Indian cricket … In less than a decade he ended up putting Ranchi on the world cricket map.'

Dhoni's own footprint upon that landscape was about to be enlarged as he played one of the great World Cup final innings, expanding on a characteristically watchful start to score an unbeaten 91 off 79 balls to guide India home with 10 deliveries to spare. Typically, Dhoni sealed victory by clubbing seamer Nuwan Kulasekara into the crowd behind long-on, swirling his bat in one hand above his head like a champion fencer as the stands exploded. 'Forget the fairytale finish that had Sachin Tendulkar or Muttiah Muralitharan contriving a tear-stained swan song,' wrote former England spinner Vic Marks in *The Guardian*. 'The epitome of new India dominated the match.'

Tendulkar missed the winning hit because he and Sehwag were praying in the dressing room. And, in true cricket tradition, once they had taken up such a position there was no moving until the match was won. Sehwag agitated to head back out to the balcony, but Tendulkar recalled, 'I said to him that he could watch the moment 100 times on television if he wanted to but for the time being he should just sit where he was and pray. It was only after Dhoni's shot had finally crossed the boundary that I went out.'

Tears of joy and relief accompanied Tendulkar's embrace of Yuvraj. 'It was one of those life-changing moments and we wanted to live every second of it,' he said. He might not have scored many runs in the final itself, but Tendulkar's contribution to the triumph and to Indian cricket for more than two decades was acknowledged by his teammates when they lifted them on their shoulders and paraded him in front of the people of his hometown as he waved the national flag.

'He had spoken about how it would be the pinnacle of his career to win a World Cup,' said Kirsten. 'To do it at his home ground as well was amazing. Everyone felt that he was the peg in the ground for all of them. He symbolised a lot of what Indian cricket stood for.'

Back in the dressing room, Tendulkar got his teammates to sign the first bottle of champagne to be popped and invited in Sudhir Gautam, the super-fan who became a global figure by painting his body with the colours of his nation's flag and Tendulkar's number 10 and cycled around India to watch every game. After the team bus had taken three hours to make what was normally a 20-minute journey back to their hotel, the Indian players gathered together at 3 a.m. to eat biryani and begin a victory party. All over the country similar celebrations had been in full swing for several hours. India did not sleep that night. Amid the mayhem, Dhoni, who had shorn his flowing locks shortly after the 2007 World T20 victory, found time to shave his head down to crew-cut length before next day's press conferences.

As Tendulkar's teammates spoke to broadcasters, writers, friends and family members, many of them dedicated their victory to 'Paaji', who, during the lap of honour around the Wankhede, had shouted at Yusuf Pathan, 'Don't drop me!'

'We may fall down but we will not let you go down,' was the reply he received. Quite right. The man who had borne the faith, hope and impossible expectation of his nation for so long, who had rewritten the history of ODI batting along the way, deserved to be the one being carried at last.

INDIA v SOUTH AFRICA, 2nd One-Day International

24 February 2010, Captain Roop Singh Stadium, Gwalior

India			Balls	4s	6s
V Sehwag	c Steyn b Parnell	9	11	1	
SR Tendulkar	not out	200	147	25	3
KD Karthik	c Gibbs b Parnell	79	85	4	3
YK Pathan	c de Villers b van der Merwe	36	23	4	2
†*MS Dhoni	not out	68	34	7	4
Extras	(lb 3, nb 1, w 5)	9			
Total	(3 wickets, 50 overs)	401			

Fall: 25, 219, 300.
Did Not Bat: V Kohli, SK Raina, RA Jadeja, P Kumar, A Nehra, S Sreesanth
Bowling: Steyn 10-0-89-0; Parnell 10-0-95-2; van der Merwe 10-0-62-1;
Langeveldt 10-0-70-0; Duminy 5-0-38-0; Kallis 5-0-44-0.

South Africa			Balls	4s	6s
HM Amla	c Nehra b Sreesanth	34	22	7	
HH Gibbs	b Kumar	7	8	1	
RE van der Merwe	c Raina b Sreesanth	12	11	1	1
*JH Kallis	b Nehra	11	13	2	
AB de Villiers	not out	114	101	13	2
AN Petersen	b Jadeja	9	16	1	
J-P Duminy	lbw b Pathan	0	1		
†MV Boucher	lbw b Pathan	14	31	1	
WD Parnell	b Nehra	18	43	1	
D Steyn	b Sreesanth	0	4		
C Langeveldt	c Nehra b Jadeja	12	11	3	
Extras	(lb 5, w 4, nb 8)		17		
Total	(42.5 overs)	248			

Fall: 17, 47, 61, 83, 102, 103, 134, 211, 216, 248.
Bowling: Kumar 5-0-31-1; Nehra 8-0-60-2; Sreesanth 7-0-49-3; Jadeja 8.5-0-41-2;
Pathan 9-1-37-2; Sehwag 5-0-25-0.

India won by 153 runs. **Toss:** India. **Umpires:** IJ Gould, SK Tarapore. **Man of the
Match:** SR Tendulkar.

'FORGET IT, LET'S JUST ENJOY IT'

Royal Challengers Bangalore v Pune Warriors, Indian Premier League, Bengaluru, 2013

In his red and gold uniform, golden pads and green boots, Chris Gayle looked like a 6ft 3in personification of the tri-coloured wristband Viv Richards had worn while brutalising bowlers three decades or so earlier. Completing his deliberately slow journey to the crease in the middle of Bengaluru's M. Chinnaswamy Stadium, Gayle bore the same air of intimidation as his West Indies predecessor but did so with a smiling arrogance absent from the Master Blaster. While Richards carried the nickname he would never have self-bestowed with a knowing, gum-chewing shrug, Gayle had not only awarded himself the title of Universe Boss but lived the persona in the manner of a WWE wrestler. Who else would have decided he could get away with the shirt number 333, his highest score in Test cricket?

By April 2013, the 33-year-old Gayle was in his third season with Royal Challengers Bangalore, for whom he had marked his debut in 2011 with a century against his former team, Kolkata Knight Riders. An innings played after a late call-up and with no meaningful cricket practice for a month while he'd recovered from injury, it was a look-at-me feat typical of a man who rarely failed to deliver against the self-generated hype. Hitting 36 in a seven-ball over (four sixes, three fours) for RCB; being the Indian Premier League's top scorer in his first two seasons with the Challengers; going on to score the 50-over World Cup's first double century in 2015 … all in the line of duty for a man who lived for the limelight and fed off the kind of high stakes that could choke lesser players. 'If you're a star player you will be treated like a Bollywood hero,' he said of his IPL experience. 'And that makes you want to deliver – to stand out by performing as well, to win titles, to live up to the expectations.'

Gayle's first international match in 1999 had been in India and, like so many overseas cricketers, he had allowed the logistical and environmental challenges of playing in that country blind him to the cricketing and off-field opportunities of such an experience.

But now, in the era of the IPL, there was 'no more old India', as he termed it. 'Still the noise and the heat and the chaos, but now something impossible on top of it all,' he wrote. 'Still the stadiums jam-pack *(sic)*, but now the colour and contrast turned up again. Still the madness, but this time you're riding it, riding it. And that wave takes you to places, and those places take you to a whole new world.' He was about to travel to a plane of performance that no cricketer had previously visited.

Five years and five days earlier, Bengaluru's 40,000-seater arena had witnessed Brendon McCullum's pyrotechnic launch of the IPL, and it had quickly become one of Gayle's favourite stages. 'When you see them waving those flags in the stand you get a thrill as a player,' he explained. 'You want to do well, you want to entertain the crowd, the fans. You want to make the most of those particular moments.'

Robin Uthappa, who was on the opposing Pune Warriors team on what was to be an historic night, explained, 'It's a higher altitude place and a nice small ground and once you hit them – and if you hit them as hard as the Universe Boss does – they go all the way.' Gayle was about to benefit from every advantage his Indian home offered, in a manner never before seen in a game of T20 cricket. A couple of hours after his slow march to the middle he would be making the most triumphant of exits, a record-breaking 175 not out against his name.

That his innings began with some careful prods and only a single off the first three balls was not unexpected. 'Having a look – at the pitch, at the bowler, at what the ball is doing' was as important to him in T20 as it was in Test cricket – although not for as long. 'I tear attacks to pieces, but I stalk my prey first,' he wrote in his autobiography, *Six Machine*. As authors Tim Wigmore and Freddie Wilde documented in *Cricket 2.0*, their exhaustive analysis of the 20-over format, Gayle played out more dot balls inside his first 10 deliveries (59 per cent) than any of his contemporaries.

After eight balls of the innings, by which time Gayle had begun to warm up by striking the first two of his eventual 13 fours, the players were forced off the field by rain. 'That wicket is a real belter,' Gayle told his West Indian teammate Ravi Rampaul during the 35-minute delay. 'We need to get at least 170-180 to give ourselves a chance at winning the game.'

Gayle returned to hit medium pacer Ishwar Pandey for three boundaries, two behind square on the leg side and one over mid-off, almost clearing the rope. 'I went back out after the rain interruption and picked up where I left off. I was in that flow, that rhythm. Sometimes as a batsman you know you cannot do anything wrong and that was one of the days. It was remarkable and so funny that I end up with 175 and I was saying that should be the team total.'

He faced only one ball during the third and fourth overs, at the end of which RCB were 33 for 0. Gayle's 21 runs off 11 balls was a smart enough start, but it was just a sighter. He was about to launch a monumental assault that brought him a monstrous total of 17 sixes, the breathless nature of which was captured by ESPNcricinfo's ball-by-ball descriptions (reproduced here with permission):

> **4.1 Marsh to Gayle, SIX runs:** *The first of many? Marsh bowls a length ball on middle and leg and he lofts through the line and clears long-on.*
>
> **4.2 Marsh to Gayle, SIX runs:** *Goes the other way this time! This was wide outside off and he comes forward and scoops it over extra cover.*
>
> **4.5 Marsh to Gayle, SIX runs:** *They're coming! Marsh errs by bowling length again, that too a touch too wide outside off. Gayle lofts over the sightscreen.*
>
> **4.6 Marsh to Gayle, SIX runs:** *Gayle's on 50 already and it's a 28-run over! Marsh pitches it up and with a free swing Gayle takes him downtown, down to the sightscreen. 50 off 17 balls.*
>
> **6.2 Murtaza to Gayle, SIX runs:** *Tossed up on the off stump and Gayle gets on his knee and slogs over deep midwicket, no mercy for the left-arm spinner.*
>
> **6.5 Murtaza to Gayle, SIX runs:** *Can anyone keep him quiet? This was flatter from the bowler. Gayle gets on his knee and slogs it flat over long-on.*

In the commentary box, Sunil Gavaskar, who had seen much of what there could ever be to see in the sport, exclaimed at one point, 'It's over cover,' repeating himself to capture the full impact. 'I can't believe it.'

Warriors captain Aaron Finch had already used five bowlers in the first seven overs. 'Finchy was looking for someone to come on and bowl and everyone had their backs to [him],' Uthappa told ESPNcricinfo. Yuvraj Singh shouted at his skipper, 'Don't you look over here because I am not bowling.' And when Finch, a fellow slow left-armer, made it clear that he would have to take the ball himself, Yuvraj, having seen what he had done to another Aussie, Mitchell Marsh, warned him. 'Finchy, do not bowl.' Gayle added, 'I went berserk in that particular over and Yuvraj said, "See, I told you."'

Daren Sammy, who skippered Gayle for West Indies and against him in many domestic tournaments, explained, 'When I captained against Chris I said, "I will never bowl a left-arm spinner to him." In about 95 per cent of the games I played against him, the left-arm spinners would not be playing or would not be used while Gayle was batting. He was phenomenal. He revolutionised T20 cricket. There is no other person like Chris Gayle. If you mention T20 cricket then he is best batsman that will ever walk this earth.'

> **7.2 Finch to Gayle, SIX runs:** *Finch isn't spared too! He fires that flat and quick and Gayle gets under the bounce and lofts him high over deep midwicket.*
>
> **7.3 Finch to Gayle, SIX runs:** *This goes higher! Flatter one and Gayle stays at the crease and lofts high over long-on, nearly on the roof.*
>
> **7.5 Finch to Gayle, SIX runs:** *Full toss, would you believe it?! Gosh. All too easy for Gayle, those behind deep midwicket had to take cover.*
>
> **7.6 Finch to Gayle, SIX runs:** *29 off this over! Length ball on middle and he slogs it over wide long-on, he's on 95.*
>
> **8.5 Dinda to Gayle, SIX runs:** *Free Hit: It's out of the stadium! Dinda bowls a friendly full toss, Gayle makes room and clubs it straight. It's the fastest-ever IPL hundred, beats Yusuf Pathan's 37-ball ton and Gayle is on his knees! The ball hits the roof.*

With such force did the ball land that splinters of the roof dropped on spectators below. By this time, the opposition were resigned to the magic of the occasion. Deep Dasgupta, head of cricket operations for the Warriors, explained, 'Initially we were looking at those strokes and thinking, "He will get out now. He will get out after five overs, seven overs, 10 overs." But after that you knew where this was heading. Personally, I thought, "Forget it, let's just enjoy it," even though you are on the opposition. Let's just enjoy some real unadulterated power hitting."'

As extreme as this innings might have been, it was by no means out of character for Gayle, who had built himself up in the gym to look like an NFL defensive end since the advent of T20. He had long since decided that swinging for the ropes was more than just a brand-building exercise, it was a calculated risk in search of maximum reward. 'From being regarded as the sport's kamikaze shot, the six is now often viewed as its prudent, percentage option – simply the most effective way to score runs,' Wigmore and Wilde wrote in 2019. And just as the nature of Gayle's attack was in keeping, so was the result. At the time of Wigmore and Wilde's research, he was scoring centuries in T20 – a format designed to prevent such feats – more frequently than all batsmen were reaching three figures in Test cricket (once every 17 innings versus once every 19 innings.)[22]

With his century on the board, Gayle was about to adopt a different mindset. 'I could continue going berserk. I could continue blitzing it. Instead I decide to play it properly. We still have a lot of overs to bat. So I just take my time, and make sure a set batter is there at the end, That's my thinking. I ease off the berserking.' The sixes, therefore, might have slowed a little, but only in relative terms.

> **11.3 Wright to Gayle, SIX runs:** *Even slower balls don't work! Gayle stayed at the crease and lofted it and for a moment it looked like a mis-hit, nope, went a few rows over long-off.*
> **12.6 Marsh to Gayle, SIX runs:** *On the roof! Can we have the ball back please? Marsh bowls another short one, Gayle pulls and it goes into orbit over deep square leg.*
> **14.3 Murtaza to Gayle, SIX runs:** *Outta here! Gives it more air and Gayle gets on his knee and slogs it over long-on. Looked like it cleared the roof.*

---

22 Based on Test matches from 2003 to 2019

14.4 Murtaza to Gayle, SIX runs: *Can't get enough!*
Length delivery on the pads and he bends and mows it
over deep midwicket!
14.6 Murtaza to Gayle, SIX runs: *Gets to 150! Tosses*
it up and Gayle gets down on his knee and slogs it over
deep midwicket. He's just five away from equalling
McCullum's record 158, at this same ground. Virat
Kohli bends and salutes the big man!
19.1 Dinda to Gayle, SIX runs: *Gayle adds to his six*
tally! Dinda errs by bowling length again, Gayle makes
room and smashes it over long-off.

Gayle reached every major landmark of his innings – 50, 100 and 150 – with a six, claiming with some justification, 'I could have had 200 if ABD didn't come in and steal the show as well.' As if the sight of Gayle in full flow was not treat enough, fans and viewers had a glimpse of the genius of South Africa's AB de Villiers, who engineered three sixes and three fours in an eight-ball innings worth 31. To prove his versatility, the first six went over long-off and the second 180 degrees around the field over fine leg.

Yet it was far from being a day of regret for Gayle, whose innings featured the most runs and the record number of sixes in any T20 innings. 'I'm lost for words,' he told the post-game interviewer, who went for looking for clues by asking what he had eaten before the game. 'All I had for breakfast this morning was a plain omelette, two pancakes and a hot chocolate.'

Gayle might have added that, as was customary for him in the inverted day-for-night world of the IPL, he had not been to bed until 7 a.m. He would often be up until that time, playing poker with the younger players who were not accompanied by families, before sleeping during the day, awaking for pancakes, going back to bed for a while, and then drinking of plenty of water to get fully hydrated before the game began.

Finch, whom Gayle had made suffer more than anyone in his one over of left-arm spin, admitted, 'When a guy bats like that there's not a lot we can do. There's no boundary big enough. When you see balls flying over the head it does affect your confidence. Whoever bowled was going the journey. We couldn't stop him.' According to Uthappa, he and his colleague had 'the best seat in the house, although not the nicest', admitting, 'He psyched out the whole team with his intimidation and the way he was hitting the ball.'

One of the surprising statistics of the day was that of the six wides bowled by the Warriors, only one was to Gayle, a man whose presence at the crease was proven to cause bowlers to lose their line in their desire not to be clubbed into the stands. Another revealing element of Gayle's T20 batting unearthed by Wigmore and Wilde was that he received almost twice as many wides as other batsmen, one in 19 deliveries against the average of one in 35. But while slugger Barry Bonds became the most walked batter in baseball history through a deliberate policy of pitching outside the plate and allowing him a free pass to first base rather than risk a home run, Gayle built his statistic through sheer fear and desperation on the bowlers' part. Like the opponents' preference for deliberately putting Bonds where he could do no further damage, most bowlers would happily have given Gayle a single every ball to get him to the non-striker's end if such a law existed in cricket.

Even that tactic would probably have done little to slow Gayle on this day, when he had realised early in his innings, 'Something is happening here.' It took some time for him to fully appreciate exactly what that something had been. Not until he prepared to head to bed in the early hours and saw the hundreds of messages on his phone did he get a true sense of the magnitude of his feat. Two days later he had just about managed to read all of his texts and emails.

* * *

'It was the best of times. It was the worst of times.' That wasn't one of the messages on Gayle's phone, but, of course, the famous opening to the Charles Dickens novel, *A Tale of Two Cities*. Published in 1859, the year that saw the first overseas cricket tour – when a team of English professionals set off for North America – it did rather neatly describe the IPL in 2013. It was a year highlighted by Gayle's personal achievement and a first title for the league's flagship franchise, the Mumbai Indians, but the competition was also undermined by a scandal that might have been expected to threaten its very existence. That it did not says much about how deeply the IPL had become woven into the fabric of India. The sixes that people had been flying onto the roof with their own eyes proved more powerful than secondhand tales of shady bookmakers, greedy players and disgraced owners.

Everything about the IPL had become more bloated since its inaugural season. Two more teams had been added in 2010, and by the following year players such as Rohit Sharma, Gautam Gambhir, Yusuf Pathan and Robin Uthappa were earning more than $2 million a season. It was why Gayle was able to describe the IPL as 'the moment cricket changed forever, when the lifestyle of everyone who took part changed forever'. He wrote, 'What you make for playing seven hours of Test cricket compared to what you earn for playing seven hours of football? Cricketers were underpaid and then suddenly some were earning $1million for just over a month. Whoosh!'

By the time Gayle was playing his record-breaking innings for the Challengers, however, Lalit Modi was long gone from his position as Commissioner, unable to survive the expansion of his personal project. He had clashed with the BCCI when he demanded that bidders for the new teams in 2010 should provide $100 million bank guarantees, a condition BCCI president Shashank Manohar said was not sanctioned and not reasonable. Manohar also accused Modi of trying to cook up a new TV deal with the World Sports Group – despite the rights being owned by Sony – that was designed to defraud the BCCI of $80 million. Immediately after the 2010 final, Modi was suspended from his role at the head of the IPL. Whatever he might or might not have done, few would be able to argue with his claim in 2017 that he had 'unlocked the real potential regarding the commercial value of the game in India'.

The salaries, the global exposure and the sheer excitement of playing on the IPL stage had made the tournament the pinnacle of many players' professional ambitions. One might have expected that it made them more immune than their counterparts of a decade or two earlier to the approaches of bookmakers and match fixers.

Yet three weeks after Gayle's historic knock, Rajasthan Royals CEO Raghu Iyer received a call at dawn on the morning after his team had played in Mumbai. Police officers informed him that they were there to arrest three players on suspicion of spot fixing, Ankeet Chavan,

Ajit Chandila and Sreesanth, one of India's World T20 heroes. The next arrest was that of Vindu Dara Singh, a small-time actor with alleged associations to bookmakers.

A week later Gurunath Meiyappan, team principal of the Chennai Super Kings – and son-in-law of latest BCCI president N. Srinivasan – was taken in for questioning and subsequently arrested. The Super Kings and Srinivasan responded by painting Meiyappan as some kind of super-fan rather than a team official, although a photograph of him wearing an owner's badge quickly went into circulation.

Before an official inquiry could take place, BCCI secretary Sanjay Jagdale resigned, along with treasurer Ajay Shirke, saying he was 'deeply hurt with the recent developments'. A week after the season ended, IPL chairman Rajiv Shukla stood down. Fears that the scandal might have overshadowed the final, or even led to a boycott of fans, proved wildly inaccurate when more than 60,000 saw Mumbai beat Chennai at Kolkata's Eden Gardens. Srinivasan was booed when he presented the trophy, but it all seemed like part of the soap opera drama that was as much an ingredient of the IPL as the action on the field. The IPL was evidently indestructible, and most fans could not have cared less when Chennai and Indian captain MS Dhoni refused to answer questions about the scandal at his press conference prior to the national team's departure for their tour of England. Journalists might have been disappointed by his actions, but it made no dent in the country's love affair with their skipper.

Meanwhile, Srinivasan had stepped down for the duration of the inquiry, the result of which was that the owning companies of the Royals (India Cements) and the Super Kings (Rak Jundra and Jaipur IPL Cricket Pvt Ltd) were cleared of any wrongdoing. However, the findings reported to the BCCI were quickly set aside by the Bombay High Court, which ordered a new inquiry. This time a three-man panel headed by Justice Mukul Mugdal was given free rein to investigate.

According to author Boria Majumdar, fans were finally waking up to the threat to the credibility of their beloved sport. 'Pushed to the brink, the BBCI knew it had to reform itself and its biggest money-spinner – the IPL,' he wrote. 'The spot-fixing scandal helped in bringing about Indian cricket's first mass movement and the impregnable BCCI could no longer stay immune from it. Its bastions had been breached.' At least Sachin Tendulkar's announcement of his impending retirement diverted attention.

In February 2014, Mugdal's committee ruled that Meiyappan had been the principal owner of the Super Kings. The Supreme Court allowed both teams under investigation to play the 2014 season, with Srinivasan asked to step aside from his duties. Finally, in November, Mugdal found Meiyappan and Kundra guilty, with Srinivasan cleared of personal wrongdoing. The Supreme Court gave the task of passing sentence to three of its former judges, led by Justice Rajendra Mal Lodha. In July 2015, he announced that both teams were suspended from the 2016 and 2017 seasons, while Meiyappa and Jundra were banned from cricket administration for life.

Far from being a death penalty for either team, the Super Kings returned to win the IPL in 2018, repeating the achievement in 2021. The vague memory of Dhoni in a Rising Pune Supergiant shirt for a couple of years is virtually the only evidence the wider cricketing world has that the Chennai Super Kings juggernaut was ever knocked off course. For the Rajasthan Royals, the exploits of players such as Jos Buttler and Ben Stokes have, similarly, erased the dark years of exile.

As long as the likes of Gayle and Buttler are swinging for the stands then neither police nor pandemic can halt the march of the IPL.

ROYAL CHALLENGERS BANGALORE v PUNE WARRIORS, Indian Premier League

23 April 2013, M. Chinnaswamy Stadium, Bengaluru

Bangalore			Balls	4s	6s
CH Gayle	not out	175	66	13	17
TM Dilshan	c Murtaza b Wright	33	36	5	
*V Kohli	run out	11	9	1	
AB de Villiers	c Manhas b Marsh	31	8	3	3
SS Tiwary	c Marsh b Dinda	2	2		
R Rampaul	c Marsh b Dinda	0	1		
Extras	(lb 3, w 6, nb 2)	11			
Total	(5 wickets, 20 overs)	263			

Fall: 167, 207, 251, 262, 263.
Did Not Bat: †KBA Karthik, RV Kumar, M Karthik, RP Singh, JD Unadkat
Bowling: Kumar 4-0-23-0; Pandey 2-0-33-0; Dinda 4-0-48-2; Marsh 3-0-56-1; Murtaza 2-0-45-0; Finch 1-0-29-0; Wright 4-0-26-1.

Pune			Balls	4s	6s
†RV Uthappa	c Singh b M Karthik	0	2		
*AJ Finch	c M Karthik b Rampaul	18	15	4	
Yuvraj Singh	c Kohli b Unadkat	16	14	2	
LJ Wright	c de Villiers b Unadkat	7	3	1	
SPD Smith	c Dilshan b Rampaul	41	31	6	
MR Marsh	b Kumar	24	23	2	
M Manhas	not out	11	13	1	
BK Kumar	c KBA Karthik b Singh	6	12	1	
AG Murtaza	st KBA Karthik b Gayle	5	4	1	
IC Pandey	b Gayle	0	2		
AB Dinda	not out	1	1		
Extras	(lb 1, w 3)		4		
Total	(9 wickets, 20 overs)	133			

Fall: 0, 28, 38, 42, 100, 119, 127, 132, 132.
Bowling: M Karthik 3-0-25-1; Singh 4-0-20-1; Rampaul 4-0-21-2; Unadkat 4-0-37-2; Kumar 4-0-24-1; Gayle 1-0-5-2.

Bangalore won by 130 runs. **Toss:** Pune. **Umpires:** Aleen Dar, C Shamshuddin.
Man of the Match: CH Gayle.

23

'REMEMBER THE NAME'

England v West Indies, World T20 Final, Kolkata, 2016

The story of West Indies in Twenty20 cricket is an intriguing one, literally the stuff of documentaries. It ranges from fraud and imprisonment to the embarrassment of England's cricket authorities; the evolution of individual specialisms in the format to team achievement in the face of adversity.

Like it or not – and individuals conned out of savings and Antiguans deprived of a living certainly don't – the off-field and on-field stories are intertwined, with West Indies' period of world domination in the format able to be traced back to the man who fooled the world, at least until the FBI caught up with him.

Allen Stanford was born and raised in Texas, running a chain of gymnasiums into bankruptcy before speculating in real estate with his father. Having opened a bank in Monserrat, he then arrived on the Caribbean island of Antigua in 1990, establishing the Stanford International Bank. By 2006 he was the sole shareholder of the Stanford Financial Group, which comprised 62 companies. He had bankrolled a local hospital, rebuilt a marina, invested heavily in the region's cricket and become one of the island's major employers and economic contributors. For all of that he was given a knighthood by the government of Antigua and Barbuda in November 2006.

A few months earlier, the Stanford 20/20 had been launched, giving the Caribbean its first big competition in the format. With 19 teams it was considered somewhat bloated, but it was a signal of ambition at a time when, according to West Indies batsman Ramnaresh Sarwan, 'we thought cricket was fading away'. A tournament that was staged entirely at Stanford's specially built ground next to Antigua's airport and which ended with Narsingh Deonarine hitting a six to earn Guyana the $1 million first prize changed that perception. Teams had been properly coached and prepared, and granted $280,000 each to spend on players and facilities.

No one knew at the time that Stanford's money was coming from an elaborate Ponzi scheme, where nothing was being done to grow investments and a constant influx of new money was needed to pay those wishing to withdraw their cash. Stanford was using funds deposited in his banks or entrusted to his wealth management company to finance his own whims and lavish lifestyle. He could keep it going only if not everyone wanted to access their money at the same time; and as long as he didn't get caught.

The West Indies Cricket Board (WICB) had never been in a position to fully capitalise on the increased commercialism and professionalism of the sport globally. Its television contracts have historically brought in barely ten percent of what the England and Wales Cricket Board can command, and only a tiny fraction of the amounts banked by India. The decline of the West Indies national team as youngsters in the region became attracted to other sports and recreational options seemed irreversible. But suddenly, thanks to Stanford, players were being treated as elite athletes, not just called professionals while being paid a meagre salary by cash-strapped authorities. 'You could be a cricketer for a living,' recalled former West Indies captain Daren Sammy. 'Until then, only the West Indian international players could have said that.'

'It does come down to economics,' Sarwan told authors Tim Wigmore and Freddie Wilde. 'When I started, my goal was to play Test cricket.' Now the ambition was to land a T20 contract, and players were prepared to work in the gym and in the nets to get to the required level. For a player such as Samuel Badree, pondering his future in cricket at the age of 25, there was a new incentive to remain in the game, a new format in which he could become a master of his trade as a spin bowler.

Sammy explained, 'It was disappointing what happened later, but if you take away all the shenanigans from the cricket you can look back and say, "Wow, Stanford did play a massive role in the turnaround in interest in West Indies cricket." The Stanford T20 was where so many players were discovered, and it gave hope to the fans who started watching cricket again.'

Infamously, it was not only the cricketers of the Caribbean whom Stanford intended to entrance with his – or other people's – millions. Building hospitals might win him the patronage of Antiguan society and politicians, but cricket had the potential to make him a global figure. Which was why, on 11 June 2008, members of the UK cricket media were assembled at Lord's for the bizarre sight of a helicopter landing on the Nursery Ground and Stanford stepping out to announce a $20 million winner-take-all T20 game between England and the 'Stanford Superstars' – West Indies in all but name. The ECB, desperate to appease its players after denying them permission to play in the IPL because it clashed with its own early-season calendar, welcomed Stanford like a child beckoning Santa Claus down the chimney.

The concept of individual players ending a single game with either $1 million each or absolutely nothing was gauche enough. But the levels of tackiness were turned up by the sight of ECB officials gushing while Stanford, flanked by legends such as Sir Viv Richards, showed off a crate purporting to contain $20 million in cash. 'There was a lot of criticism; I guess it did ruffle a few feathers,' Richards told a Sky camera crew many years later, by which time Stanford was almost a decade into an 110-year jail sentence.

'I'm investing in cricket's future in the West Indies,' Stanford declared. 'I have been in the Caribbean for 26 years and when you see something that you love so dearly – it is that glue, that fabric that binds us all together in the West Indies – at the bottom, you want to do everything you can to bring it back up.'

So far, so philanthropic. Unless you knew it was not his money.

Even as Stanford strode around like a man who had just bought the home of cricket, investigators from the FBI, the Department of Justice's fraud squad and the Securities and Exchange Commission were gathering evidence to show he had had stolen $6 billion from 30,000 unknowing investors across more than 100 countries.

They could not strike in time to halt events at the Stanford Super Series, which began in the final week of October. Stanford managed to upset the England players by strolling into their dressing room like he owned the place – which he did, of course – and forcing Matt Prior's embarrassed wife, Emily, to sit on his knee during the warm-up game against Middlesex while the wicketkeeper watched his supposed benefactor's antics being relayed on the stadium screen. When it came to the $20 million match, the West Indian players, battle-hardened and well-prepared, cruised to a 10-wicket victory.

If the week had been embarrassing enough already for the ECB, the size of the hole into which they had dug themselves became evident over the next few months. The global banking crisis led to investors wanting their money back and in February 2009 Stanford's offices in Memphis and Houston were raided and his assets frozen. The subsequent court case revealed the extent of his deceit. Despite Stanford's pleas of innocence, the evidence of former ally Jim Davis led a Houston jury to find him guilty on 13 of 14 counts of fraud.

But while English cricket hoped that the whole episode would be forgotten and was forced to accept the reality of allowing players to participate in the IPL or risk losing them to the national team completely, the West Indies players turned Stanford's on-field legacy into global domination.

It is a dangerous cliché to say that T20 cricket lent itself to the innate Caribbean approach to cricket. But there is no doubt that it was easier for players shaped by flair and fearlessness to adapt than, say, English players, who needed time to unlearn the dread of giving up their wicket. 'If you look back at Sir Garry [Sobers], Learie Constantine, the flair with which they played the game, you would say West Indian players had been playing the T20 style of cricket for a long time,' said Sammy. 'Viv [Richards] scored a Test hundred off 50-something balls in the 1980s.'

Additionally, West Indian players were helped by their grounding in windball cricket, a game of 12 overs, or even less, played on concrete wicket with a tennis ball weighted by sticky tape. It was a format that required batters to attack from the outset and bowlers to seek creative solutions to a constant onslaught. So popular, and lucrative, were such competitions that many West Indian players continued playing long after they had cemented their places in the national team.

Add into the mix the professionalism that came with the Stanford competition then here was a group of players afforded the best possible mix of nature and nurture when it came to readiness for Twenty20. Players saw the advantage of lifting weights in the gym and benefitted from the presence of nutritionists and conditioning coaches at all the island teams competing for Stanford's prizes. It was a level of preparedness that the West Indies team, administered by a permanently hard-up board, was not unable to enjoy.

Darren Ganga, captain of a Trinidad & Tobago side that excelled in T20, described Stanford cricket to Wigmore and Wilde as 'a competition and a format of the game that brought a totally different perspective on our cricket. Our cricket back then was going through a tumultuous time.' He concluded, 'The investment made by Allen Stanford in that format of cricket led to West Indies dominating T20 cricket around the world.' This was true both on an individual and team level.

The approach to T20 had become increasingly forensic after the stakes of the game were raised by the IPL. The realisation had quickly dawned that, far from being an unstructured slog, this was a format where the brevity of the game allowed it to be influenced by planning and tactics to a greater extent than longer matches. With that, the role of the specialist, someone who could fulfil a specific role for a few overs, perhaps only a few balls, became magnified. While there would always be a place for game-changing superstars such as Chris Gayle or Brendon McCullum, the most valuable players in T20 were not always the most obvious or most glamorous names, despite what the cheque books and egos of some franchise owners might have suggested in the early days of the IPL.

Thanks in part to Stanford, a considerable number of these short-format experts emerged from the West Indies. Men such as Andre Russell, Dwayne Bravo, Keiron Pollard, Samuel Badree and Sunil Narine. A mixture of those who had entered consciousness as internationals and found their true calling in franchise T20 cricket – returning to West Indies colours only for the biggest occasions – and others who earned renown in the short game without having yet proved their value to their cricketing nation.

Badree and Narine were prime examples of the latter, not to mention being embodiments of the unexpected importance of spin bowling in T20, an unpredicted phenomenon when the format was first launched.

Badree was part of the Trinidad team that reached the final of the first Stanford tournament in 2006 and, unusually for a leg-spinner, opened the bowling in 80 per cent of the T20 games he played. It is a statistic that, according to Wigmore and Wilde, shows how 'in T20 convention has been challenged at almost every turn'. His professional career might well have ended in his mid-20s but for

288

T20; instead, in 2011 at the age of 31, he found himself representing West Indies.

Not a big turner of the ball nor someone who experimented with different lengths, Badree relied on accuracy and variations in bounce. In the 2012 World T20 final in Sri Lanka, he opened the bowling against the host nation, posting 1 for 24 in his four overs, while fellow-Trinidadian spinner Narine took 3 for 9 as West Indies made a surprisingly easy job of defending a modest 137. 'I believe in T20 cricket you control the powerplay and the last four overs,' recalled victorious skipper Sammy. 'Badree made sure teams didn't get off to a flyer, so even if they scored 60 runs in the last five overs they were still only scoring 170, because you have done so well at the top and in the middle period.'

Sammy reflected, 'The 2012 victory is the one I will forever cherish. I had been made captain just about 18 months earlier. It was real pressure being captain, with some people thinking you shouldn't be in the team. It really tested my mental strength. And no one believed we would win the tournament. We didn't win a game in the first round[23] and we barely scraped through against New Zealand in a Super Over, so the manner in which we got to the final was harder than in 2016. And I probably would have lost the captaincy if we had not won. It solidified me as a leader in that dressing room. I went from being Daren Sammy to Skip.

'My brain was more tired after a T20 game than when I captained in Test cricket. You have got to be thinking every ball, to have plans. You have got to be pro-active and think on your feet. But I really enjoyed captaining West Indies with that calibre of player in the team: Gayle, Pollard, Bravo, Narine, Badree, to name a few. It helps having them at your disposal.'

Influential off-spinner Narine had been a force with both bat and ball in windball cricket, adept at dealing with the bowlers' late movement when batting and developing a variety of deliveries out of the front of his hand when given the ball. His subsequent performance for Trinidad as one of the leading wicket-takers in in the 2011 Champions League helped to earn him both a West Indies

---

[23] After a no-result against Ireland, West Indies finished in the top two of their three-team group by virtue of losing to Australia by a closer margin than Ireland had managed

place and a lucrative IPL contract with the Kolkata Knight Riders, taking 24 wickets as KKR won their first title.

In 2014, Narine topped the ICC's T20 bowling rankings and helped KKR win another IPL crown. He would also find success as a pinch-hitting opening batter. But, as has so often been the case with 'mystery spinners', doubts emerged about the legality of his action on some deliveries, and he received short-term suspensions late in 2014 and in 2015.

By early 2016 it looked like he would be clear to return to international cricket in time for the World T20 in India. Yet on the same day that Pollard pulled out of the West Indies squad because of 'lack of sufficient progress in his rehabilitative work' after a knee injury, Narine also withdrew for what was said to be 'insufficient progress in the rehabilitative work on his bowling action'.

There was suspicion, however, that both withdrawals – followed by that of batter Darren Bravo to focus on Test cricket – were tied into the pay dispute that appeared to be threatening West Indies' participation in the competition. Sammy had written to the WICB saying that the 15 players originally selected for the World T20 'can't accept' the 'huge financial reductions' in their fee for the tournament, said to be an 80 per cent cut compared to previous global competitions. Sammy also argued that the WICB had no right to negotiate those fees with the West Indian Players' Association (WIPA) because 14 members of the squad were not members. In his letter he argued:

> The 2015 World Cup took place with the WI squad remunerated under the terms and conditions that had been in place for the World Cups previous – i.e. that 25 per cent of income received by the WICB for participating in the tournament was distributed to the squad.
>
> We do not understand – nor accept – just one year later being offered contracts to participate in a major ICC World Cup that show such huge financial reductions. We want to represent the West Indies but the financials on offer we can't accept.
>
> Obviously I am not privy to exact numbers paid to the WICB from the ICC, but I understand USD $8m

will be paid to the Board. Traditionally 25 per cent has been paid to the squad. That would equate to US $2m [divided by] 15, therefore approximately US $133,000 per player. Worst-case scenario, the squad would earn $414,000 collectively under the terms of the contract offered by WICB to participate in the T20 World Cup 2016. That is just over 5 per cent. A staggering difference, a near 80 per cent reduction.

Michael Muirhead, CEO of the WICB, said Sammy's calculations were 'totally incorrect' and stated that the WIPA was the recognised representative of West Indian cricketers, regardless of whether they were members or not. Sammy clarified that the team had not threatened to withhold their services, merely that the payment terms were unacceptable. 'That was not going to happen on my watch,' he recalled, 'We knew it was likely to be the last time this group played together. We might not be around in 2020, so we stuck together and went out to entertain the world.'

On the motivation for making his stand, he said, 'That is what a leader does, isn't it? If you don't stand up for something, you will fall for anything. I remember us coming together as a group and saying the only way we can make a stance is if we win. We have to put all these things aside and focus on the cricket.'

Doing so was made tougher by the team's chaotic preparation for the tournament, symbolised by the discovery by team manager Rawl Lewis – a former Test player brand new to the role – that the West Indies jerseys were not ready to be worn. He ended up waiting for two hours at the Kolkata Cricket Association for a man who was able to locate the jerseys. 'He took me downstairs to where we had our kit stored and I took it back to the hotel,' said Lewis, who then had to arrange for the logos and numbers to be applied.

Head coach Phil Simmons added, 'If he wasn't there as manager and doing what he did, we may not have had enough clothes to play in. He had to spend some nights in a lonely place, in a lonely little factory to ensure that all the clothes were printed.'

Meanwhile, Sammy was leading his team into the tournament without having been given a central WICB contract. 'I have not really represented the West Indies,' he said philosophically. 'I ply my trade in different T20 leagues around the world. That is how I provide for my family.'

Which did not mean he did not care. 'Any sportsman, their passion, their desire is to represent their county. That is where your ultimate pride is,' he said, revealing resentment that individual and collective achievements in Twenty20 cricket appeared to be undervalued by the WICB. 'The only team that has shown that they could win cups is the T20 team. They call us all sorts of names, but yes, when selected, we still turn up to play for our country. You cannot ignore the rise of T20 cricket. It is crazy to ignore how T20 cricket has taken the world by storm.'

Sammy questioned how the WICB could compete with the $600,000 IPL contract just awarded to 27-year-old Carlos Brathwaite. West Indies players, he pointed out, did not have the financial option of sitting out a year of IPL to concentrate on international cricket in the manner of an Australian, English or Indian player.

Amid such turmoil, West Indies were not fancied to recapture the title that had been won in 2014 by Sri Lanka, who had beaten India in the final in Dhaka, Bangladesh. Additionally, it was pointed out that West Indies had played only two T20 internationals in the previous year. Yet the more pertinent statistic, as highlighted by Wigmore and Wilde, was that the seven players who featured in the most T20 matches across all competitions in the years 2012 to 2106 were West Indians: Bravo, Pollard, Russell, Gayle, Dwayne Smith, Sammy and Narine.

Similarly, when West Indies won the inaugural World Cup in 1975, they did so with a group of players who were not seasoned in ODIs but had been playing in three different limited-overs competitions in English domestic cricket. For the Gillette Cup and John Player League, read the IPL and the Big Bash League.

According to Sammy, the players themselves were convinced, they would lift the trophy. 'Going through all that before the tournament really brought the team together,' he explained. 'It was really like West Indies versus the world. In all my years in captaining the West Indies I have not seen a more focused and determined West Indies. I was captain and made the decisions out there, but these men we were so focused and we were pulling in the same direction. As a leader in any organisation that is what you want.'

It was why Bravo felt assured enough to say, 'The way West Indies goes about its T20 game, the manner in which we like to dominate the format, is much how we dominated Tests in the 1980s. We see it as our baby, given what West Indies bring to the table in the format.'

Yet commentator Mark Nicholas previewed the tournament by writing, 'West Indies are short of brains, but have IPL history in their ranks.' In the pantheon of provocative remarks it might not come close to the colossus of Tony Greig's 'I intend to make them grovel' before the 1976 Test series in England, but it was enough to wind up the West Indies camp.

According to Sammy, now close friends with Nicholas, 'You have to understand that when you have strong, proud black men you don't make those type of comments. Mark later called me and apologised to me and to the team, but things like that fuel and the fire you, and had us really motivated. All those things played a part in 2016.'

Having won the 2012 tournament after batting first in every game, West Indies reached the 2016 final by winning the toss and opting to chase in all their matches. Sammy explained, 'If you have an opener like Chris Gayle who takes the game so deep – the number of times he would bat until the 16th over was amazing – and then you have guys at the back who can finish games for you ... that is why we were the best during that period 2010 to 2016. We backed ourselves to chase any target.' Topping their group with three wins from four, they overhauled India's 192 in the semi-final, the highest successful chase in a World T20 knockout game.

Badree opened the final at Kolkata's Eden Gardens by beating England's Jason Roy with the first two balls, the second one skidding on to take out leg stump. Alex Hales clipped Russell off his legs into the hands of Badree in the second over. Three fours were taken off slow left-armer Sulieman Benn in the fourth over, but the fifth saw Eoin Morgan failing to pick Badree's googly: 23 for 3.

England recovery tactic was to target Benn, with Jos Buttler dispatching him for back-to-back sixes before holing out in the deep off Brathwaite. When Ben Stokes directed Bravo's slower bouncer into the air, the bowler joined Gayle in a high-stepping, fist-bumping celebration. And after Moeen Ali gloved a second-ball catch down the leg-side and Joe Root's ramp shot failed to clear the considerable figure of Benn, England were floundering at 111 for 7. Even when Willey pumped a couple of sixes to reach a respectable total of 155, it seemed unlikely to be enough – especially with an unbeaten Gayle century having seen West Indies surpass an England total of 182 with almost two overs to spare in the group stages.

Yet England skipper Morgan pulled a masterstroke. After Johnson Charles took a single off the final delivery of Willey's opening over to get West Indies on the board, Root was handed the new ball for the first time in the tournament. Charles's eyes sparkled like the Eden Gardens floodlights, and he greedily swished the first ball into grasp of Stokes on the leg side. Gayle was no more patient, aiming to take Root out of the ground first ball and settling for four off the inside edge. The next ball, he slogged again, putting too much air under his shot and being caught by an ecstatic Stokes running to his right from his station at long-off. 'What a plan this is, from nowhere,' commentator Nasser Hussain purred. There was nothing surprising about Willey's method of attack, but when he swung the ball in at the right-handed Lendl Simmons the batsmen could do nothing to save himself from Rod Tucker's lbw decision. Out first ball and West Indies now 11 for 3.

Marlon Samuels responded gamely until trying to run Liam Plunkett behind square on 27 and under-edging to Buttler. Yet he was stopped short of the boundary by the umpires, unsure if the ball had carried. Television pictures offered a strong enough suggestion that the ball had died just before reaching the wicketkeeper's gloves.

Momentum was building in West Indies' favour, Samuels whipping Stokes's first ball for four. Bravo was dropped by substitute Sam Billings off the same bowler after top-edging a hook to long leg, before sticking Adil Rashid over midwicket for the first six of the innings. But before the end of that over, the 14th, Bravo made a mess of trying to pull the ball and Root accepted the chance at point.

Samuels, his half-century on the board, piled into Plunkett, taking advantage of the short boundary on the leg side to take 18 off the next over, including getting under poorly-executed yorkers to clear the rope on the final two balls.

Willey returned to the attack and Russell pulled the first ball to Stokes, who completed a difficult low catch at deep square leg. The fourth ball saw Sammy fail to clear Hales at deep extra cover, reducing his team to 107 for 6. Willey had taken 3 for 10 in three overs and when Brathwaite ramped the final delivery of his spell for four West Indies required 27 from the last two overs. Samuels drilled Chris Jordan down the ground for four, but the remainder of the penultimate over yielded only four singles. Nineteen needed and Samuels stuck at the non-striker's end on 85 as Stokes went to the end of his run-up.

Gayle turned to Sammy in the dug-out and admitted, 'Wow, 19 in one over is too much.'

Sammy wasn't so sure. 'Not if the first ball goes for six,' he replied. 'Then we only need two more sixes to tie the game.'

'Even with 19 needed from six balls, I still believed we would win,' Sammy recalled. 'It was something we practised all the time. Players get to the end of batting in the nets and you would shout, "Right, we need, 15 off six." But Marlon was the one in form and Carlos had not scored too many runs.'

Brathwaite, who had only been in the squad as Pollard's replacement, remembered, 'I'll be honest, I was nervous. Marlon just said to me, "Swing for the hills."' The all-rounder was calmed by the realisation that even if he was caught in the deep, he would have returned his partner to the strike. 'I had a clear mindset,' he said, remembering his homework; the knowledge that Stokes would probably look for yorkers. It meant Brathwaite would aim for the longer leg-side boundary. 'I just watched the ball and allowed my instincts to react,' he said.

Stokes bowled full and outside leg stump, Brathwaite helping the ball on its way over the boundary behind square leg for six. 'They need a couple more,' former West Indies fast bowler Ian Bishop warned television viewers.

Stokes bowled to the same area. This time Brathwaite got ahead of the ball and sent it on a high arc into the stands behind long-on. Sammy was up on his feet, punching his fist into his palm. The target was now seven from four balls. 'In four balls we we would always back ourselves to clear the ropes with one of them,' Sammy said. Samuels hugged his partner and Bishop declared of the man at the crease, 'This is a glimpse into his future.'

Ball three was straighter but not full enough to be a yorker. Brathwaite swing his bat and the crowd at long-off waited for the ball to land in their midst. Three consecutive sixes had launched West Indies' victory celebrations in their bench area and sent Stokes to his haunches, trapped in a nightmare from which there was no awakening. 'I said he was a superstar under construction,' gushed Bishop. 'The foundation has been laid.'

A mere single was required from three balls. Another leg-side delivery, another flurry of the bat. Brathwaite had his arms horizontal and his jaw wide in a scream of delight long before the ball again landed in the stands. He didn't even realise it had gone for six until told during the team's victory lap. 'Carlos Brathwaite!' was what a hyperventilating Bishop was reduced to shouting. And then, 'Remember the name!' Bishop revealed later that he had said something similar in previewing the competition at a corporate lunch and it was all he could do in the heat of the moment to dredge up the line he'd used earlier.

Lifting the trophy, Sammy could not help but remind people of his team's journey. 'People were wondering if we would play this tournament; we had issues with the board; Mark Nicholas called us players with no brain. But all of us came together. These 15 men put adversity aside,' he said. 'It's something we'll cherish for a long time.'

Years later, his summary was, 'We made history, man. We did it in spite of everything.'

While Brathwaite was basking in the moment that would define what turned out to be a moderate international career, Ben Stokes had been left standing with hands on the back of his head when the winning hit landed in the crowd. It was hard to tell whether he'd felt release from purgatory or slipped deeper into the hell of the moment. 'Every time I went back to my mark, I was trying to remember to bowl a yorker,' he revealed. 'I just didn't execute it. I didn't feel like I composed myself.'

The next time he found himself in the middle with stakes so high he would not be found wanting.

ENGLAND v WEST INDIES, World T20 Final

3 April 2016, Eden Gardens, Kolkata

England			Balls	4s	6s
JJ Roy	b Badree	0	2		
AD Hales	c Badree b Russell	1	3		
JE Root	c Benn b Brathwaite	54	36	7	
*EJG Morgan	c Gayle b Badree	5	12	1	
†JC Buttler	c Bravo b Brathwaite	36	22	1	3
BA Stokes	c Simmons b Bravo	13	8	1	
Moeen Ali	c Ramdin b Bravo	0	2		
CJ Jordan	not out	12	13	1	
DJ Willey	c Charles b Brathwaite	21	14	1	2
LE Plunkett	c Badree b Bravo	4	4		
Adil Rashid	not out	4	4		
Extras	(lb 4, w 1)	5			
Total	(9 wickets, 20 overs)	155			

Fall: 0, 8, 23, 84, 110, 110, 111, 136, 142.
Bowling: Badree 4-1-16-2; Russell 4-0-21-1; Benn 3-0-40-0; Bravo 4-0-37-3; Brathwaite 4-0-23-3; Sammy 1-0-14-0.

West Indies			Balls	4s	6s
J Charles	c Stokes b Root	1	7		
CH Gayle	c Stokes b Root	4	2	1	
MN Samuels	not out	85	66	9	2
LMP Simmons	lbw b Willey	0	1		
DJ Bravo	c Root b Rashid	25	27	1	1
AD Russell	c Stokes b Willey	1	3		
*DJG Sammy	c Hales b Willey	2	2		
CR Brathwaite	not out	34	10	1	4
Extras	(lb 3, w 6)		9		
Total	(6 wickets, 19.4 overs)	161			

Did Not Bat: †D Ramdin, S Badree, SJ Benn.

Fall: 1, 5, 11, 86, 104, 107.
Bowling: Willey 4-0-20-3; Root 1-0-9-2; Jordan 4-0-36-0; Plunkett 4-0-29-0; Rashid 4-0-23-1; Stokes 2.4-0-41-0.

West Indies won by 4 wickets. **Toss:** West Indies. **Umpires:** HDPK Dharmasena, RJ Tucker. **Man of the Match:** M Samuels.

24

'RIGHT, SHIT JUST GOT REAL'

England v India, Women's World Cup Final, Lord's, 2017

Alex Hartley, England's left-arm spinner, could not help feeling a little let down. 'I thought it was going to be a sell-out,' she remarked as she looked out at a half-empty Lord's with the start of the World Cup final against India approaching rapidly. Next to her on the pavilion balcony, opening bowler Anya Shrubsole put her straight. 'Have you seen nearly 30,000 people trying to get into a ground?' she laughed. 'It takes some time.'

At the age of 23 and with only a year of international cricket behind her, Hartley had no frame of reference for what was about to unfold. To be fair, it was to be the kind of day that no one in women's cricket had ever experienced or could have imagined.

Fast bowler Katherine Brunt, who had spent 13 years in the England team and won the World Cup, World T20 and the Ashes, remembered, 'We knew the tournament had brought us some attention, but it was a little bit of a shock when we got to the ground. People had told us before that games were going to be sold out and it had ended up being only our families and the cricket badgers. But when we turned up and saw the ground and they were telling us there might be about 180 million watching on TV we were like, "Right, shit just got real."

'You go out on the balcony and it's, "Oh, fuck. There are a lot of people here to see whether you get it right or wrong and a lot of people behind you to win this game for your country. That was terrifying. It was the moment I knew something had changed.'

Cricket's first World Cup had been staged in England by the women's game in 1973, two years ahead of the men, benefitting from the financial backing of businessman, cricket fan and future Wolverhampton Wanderers owner and knight of the realm Jack Hayward. Rachael Heyhoe Flint's England team were triumphant in the seven-team round-robin tournament, propelled partly by the bat of Enid Bakewell, whose two centuries included one in the opening match against an International XI, recognised as the first official women's ODI. Three years later, the women of England and Australia were allowed on to sacred the Lord's turf for the first time for the second leg of a three-match ODI series that followed three Test matches.

England won the World Cup again at Lord's in 1993, with relatively little fanfare. It was only when the victorious women's team of 2005, celebrating a first Ashes success since 1963, shared the Trafalgar Square stage with the hung over – or, in some cases, still inebriated – heroes of the men's memorable victory over the old enemy that many were reminded of their existence. When they were next playing at cricket's headquarters for the game's biggest prize, in the final of the 2017 World Cup, they were doing so as full-time professionals in front of a live global television audience.

Clare Connor had led the 2005 triumph in the last of her 11 years as an international, five of them as captain. 'Including us in Trafalgar Square was a really good PR move,' she recalled years later as she sat in her office as managing director of England women's cricket. A third World Cup victory in Australia early in 2009 was followed by an English summer in which the team won the World Twenty20 and the Ashes. Further success in home and away Ashes series – now played across three formats of the game, an innovation dreamt up by Connor – brought English women's cricket to the crossroads of professionalism.

It was a journey already undertaken by Australia, where the formalising of women's competition with the inaugural World Cup had led to valuable sponsorship opportunities, allowing for more tours and greater investment in coaching and facilities. When Australia won the 2013 World Cup in India it meant that six of the ten tournaments staged had gone their way. When they were beaten by West Indies in the final of the 2016 World T20 it ended a run of three successive titles in the shortest format.

Australia had been catapulted ahead of all other countries in the late 1990s when a new commercial partnership between the Australian Cricket Board and the Commonwealth Bank included provision for financing the women's team, through kit, equipment and subsidising players for taking time off work. Until then, according to former captain Belinda Clark, 'We would get a dreaded invoice at the end of a tour, anywhere to a couple of thousand dollars.'

Not paying to play was only the first step, of course, and it was a few more years before the introduction of contracts that did more than cover expenses. By 2011, the Aussie women were being recognised as full members of the Australian Cricketers' Association, even though their annual retainers still only ranged between A$5,000 and A$15,000 and vacation time from jobs had to be used to play in state games rather than relaxing on a beach.

A major pay rise in 2013 saw players receiving contracts ranging from A$23,000 to A$52,000. It meant that the 2015 Ashes series in England was not only the first to have full ball-by-ball coverage of every game on TV and radio, but also pitted two fully professional units against each other.

England's full-time status was newly won at that stage, even though the women's game had been administered alongside the men by the ECB since the early 2000s, rather than being subjected to organisational segregation. 'When we've been in a really good place, we've seen the positive spin-offs of being part of the same set up; having the same kit, team sponsorship, being identifiable as part of a strong national brand in terms of Team England,' explained Connor, who moved from a teaching career into cricket administration in 2007. 'Sustained on-field success allowed me to have conversations with the board about professional contracts.'

And when it came to the final presentation of her proposals about professionalism to the ECB board, 'I could have stood there and done a handstand and they would have said yes. It wasn't as though I had to convince hearts and minds; the board were 100 percent behind the agenda item. It needed to happen to go to the next level, being able to ask even more of [the players] and have central control of them as a team. It wasn't some huge masterplan I worked on for two years and had to deliver the world's greatest pitch to make happen. Culturally, within the organisation, there was a sense that this was one of next big things we needed.'

It meant that from 2015 onwards, England's leading players were able to devote themselves without distraction to playing cricket, a situation Connor could never have envisaged when the most she ever received during the latter period of her own playing career was £600 per month from Sport England. 'I really couldn't see professionalism. I probably would have said that by 2015 the England team would be semi-professional.' The inaugural 18 professional deals for England's women consisted of a 'captain's contract' for Charlotte Edwards with three tiers of player deals below.

By the time of the 2017 World Cup, pressure was mounting on England on various fronts. There were those who felt that, since they were now being paid, they should jolly well win – as if it was the critics' own cash that was subsidising the squad's ability to spend their time training and preparing. 'It did feel like overnight we were expected to be so much better,' Shrubsole recalled. 'I remember we played India after turning professional and India won, and all the chat was about this professional team losing to an amateur team. I thought, "If I paid anyone more money to do their job they wouldn't automatically be better tomorrow." That thought process is ludicrous and clearly not how it is going to work.'

There was a sense that an opportunity had been missed two years earlier, when they lost the much-watched Ashes without even taking it to the wire, before their semi-final exit in the 2016 World T20 was seen as further evidence of how far they were falling behind Australia.

The highest profile victim of that latter tournament was Edwards, the team's heartbeat – its leading run-getter for two decades and captain since 2006. New coach Mark Robinson, a former County Championship winner at Sussex, clearly felt that the team needed to step out from her considerable shadow, and she was persuaded to 'retire' – only a year after she'd said, 'I will play for as long as I want to. They all think I am packing up after the 2017 World Cup in England, but I have never said that.' She was left to reflect, 'I have been on this incredible journey for 20 years. Unfortunately, it has had to come to an end.'

Robinson's comment that 'everybody felt it was time for a change' reflected a bold judgement that required others to step forward if it was to be justified. Shrubsole remembered, 'Obviously having a change of captain was big, especially after someone as successful as Lottie. It meant more responsibility on the senior players to step up, as well as Heather [Knight] as the new skipper. But I felt the bigger change was Robbo himself, rather than Lottie. He brought a huge amount of experience as a player and a coach in professional cricket. As a group it hadn't been long since we turned professional and there wasn't really the understanding and knowledge of what being a professional sports person was about and he brought that know-how.'

Robinson also offered a streak of ruthlessness that was alien to his easier-going predecessor Paul Shaw, whose cricketing roots were in Barnsley, as were Brunt's. 'I was feeling very comfortable and sure of myself,' Brunt admitted. 'I was near my prime and playing under Paul, who was a very good friend. For Mark to come in and move on someone on like Charlotte Edwards was an eye opener. Shit, if he can make the best in the word move on just like that, what have the rest of us got in store? Everyone started shitting themselves. None of us could be comfortable anymore.

'Mark knew how to manipulate you to get the best out of you. After Lottie, he was looking to do the same to all the other over-30s unless they could go up a gear. Some people didn't want to do that and find another level. I decided to get more out of myself and find that other 20 per cent. If you tell me that I can't do something there is a side of me that says, "I can give you more. I will do it." Mark was good at knowing how people tick.'

Yet when England lost their World Cup opening game against India it sounded echoes of the disaster of the men's performance when they had last hosted the tournament in 1999. There was no panic in the camp, however. According to Brunt it was a 'huge slap around the face' but was 'what we needed at the time'. Shrubsole added, 'In many respects, losing wasn't a bad thing and it took more expectation off us. With the nature of the tournament, it was never likely to be disastrous. In tournament cricket you want to be playing your best cricket at the end.'

England duly reeled off six wins to top the round-robin stage. Nat Sciver scored two centuries, while Tammy Beaumont – who had replaced Edwards in the batting line-up – and Sarah Taylor both reached three figures in a partnership of 275 against South Africa. 'Heather and Mark encouraged us to be more on the front foot,' said Shrubsole.' Heather took to [captaincy] like a duck to water. It felt like she had been in the job for years.' Most significantly, a total of 259 proved enough to secure a three-run victory over Australia, who beat everyone else. 'The Aussie game gave us all the confidence we needed,' said Brunt. 'Beating Australia like that on a good surface would help you believe you can do anything.'

The semi-final against South Africa at Bristol turned out to be a thriller, although Shrubsole described it as a 'pretty ugly game of cricket'. Looking to overhaul their opponents' 218, England needed two off three balls when Shrubsole arrived at the crease with eight wickets down and thrashed her first ball to the boundary through point. 'Any time I am striding out to the middle isn't ideal,' she recalled, 'but I got lucky in terms of where the ball was. If I was to ask them to bowl a ball for me to hit it would be exactly where that one was; outside off stump.' The most relieved person in the ground might have been England's number 11, Hartley, who owned up to tears of relief that it was not left up to her to go in search of the winning runs.

At Derby two days later, Harmanpreet Kaur made a brilliant unbeaten 171 in a rain-reduced 42 overs – the highest score by a woman in the World Cup's knockout stages – as India upset the Australians by 36 runs. It was one of the most significant results in the history of women's cricket, leaving India one victory from a global triumph that might truly unlock the full potential of the women's game in the sport's modern epicentre. 'It showed that everyone else is catching up,' said Brunt. 'People were realising there were more than two teams in the tournament.'

Having missed the first World Cup in 1973, the year their Women's Cricket Association was formed, India played their first ODI when hosting the 1978 event, which they were awarded on the strength of strong attendance for Test matches and domestic competition. Thrashed by Australia when they reached their first final in South Africa in 2005, this was their first time back. One more good performance could mark the end of the Australia-England duopoly that had accounted for nine of the ten previous World Cups.

Every one of the 26,500 tickets for the final was reported to have been sold. 'We know Lord's has been one of the last bastions of male superiority,' Connor said on the eve of the match. 'We should see this game as unbelievably symbolic and use the power of that to drive the changes that are needed for the sport to grow.'

Anticipating his team's presence in the tournament's climax, Robinson had taken his players to Lord's to practise and visit the Long Room and changing rooms several weeks earlier. 'We had some players who had never played or been there before,' said

Shrubsole. 'We didn't want the first time someone turned up there to be the World Cup final. The weather was dodgy we ended up training indoors, but it was worthwhile.'

Yet even some of those who had seen it all before could not avoid being affected by the occasion. 'I honestly don't like talking about it,' Brunt admitted. 'It was a fucking difficult period for me. That four-year cycle was so hard, and I gave all of me, emotionally and physically. The tournament itself was like an out-of-body experience. It was so hard; there was so much more to be afraid of. Most of the time in the past you would not be challenged, but now every single game, every single batter, was an event. It used to be that you would worry about playing against Australia and no one else. Now there were three or four people in every team to be afraid of. Every day was stressful or something to lose sleep about.'

Brunt, who would marry teammate Sciver in 2022, also had intensely personal reasons for another sleepless night before the final. 'My mum is really religious and has a problem with me being gay,' she explained. 'She blames sport for making me that way. She still watches me on TV but won't come to our games. The night before the final, I begged her to come. I said, "If you are ever going to come to a game and never again, please can it be this one?" I begged her to come, but she said she couldn't. It really upset me, and I couldn't sleep. I have had to go through a whole load of stuff in my career, and that was sad and shit.'

To a certain extent Lord's felt like it had for most of the numerous one-day finals it had been hosting since 1963. Excitement, anticipation and tension wrapped itself around the capacity crowd. Yet if anything, the gender of the players intensified the atmosphere, recapturing the air of special occasion that characterised earlier finals before they became more commonplace. That the audience was not typical of a Lord's big-game gathering was evidenced by the amount of tea and cake sold on the day. And the greater number of young fans and women meant that the old ground even sounded different to normal. For the ECB, in particular, it offered a glimpse of a new kind of audience that could be attracted to the sport.

Certainly, no one was taking issue with Alison Mitchell when she welcomed TV viewers to 'the biggest game in the history of women's cricket'.

Knight confessed it was 'a day when I felt nervous the whole time' and was clearly emotional when the pre-match anthems were preceded by an on-screen tribute to pioneer Heyhoe-Flint, who had died six months earlier. 'I got a real sense of what this game meant for women's cricket, not just for us,' she explained. 'The players that had gone before us and led to that point.'

Even the laid-back Shrubsole would admit, 'I was grateful we were batting first because it allowed me to sit out on the balcony and take it all in.' And opening bat Beaumont revealed that after the first ball she had to 'slap myself and pull myself round'.

Having won the toss, England's final hopes of a big score disappeared when Sciver played across Jhulan Goswami, the long-time linchpin of India's attack, and was given out for 51, making the score 164 for 6 in the 38th over. Goswami's burst of three wickets helped restrict England to 228 for 7. 'India will be ecstatic with their bowling efforts,' noted former Australian international Lisa Sthalekar on commentary.

Yet Brunt recalled, 'We know that finals add a lot of stress that can make people do stupid things. We knew were 100 short, but we thought 80 of them are based on nerves so we didn't feel too stressed about it. Me and Natalie had brought momentum back towards us at the end and we felt like it was back in our favour.' As it had been in the group game against Australia, it was down to England's bowlers. Shrubsole reckoned 'in a final you can always add 15 or 20 to the total because of the pressure' and immediately got a tentative Smriti Mandhana to play around a floaty full ball.

Punam Raut demonstrated her intent by stepping down the wicket to Shrubsole and Sciver, while Mithali Raj favoured more classical cuts, flicks and cover drives, It needed an ill-advised attempt at a quick single to bring to the second wicket with the score on 42 in the 13th over, Raj giving herself up for dead when Sciver threw to Taylor.

Kaur picked on the left-arm spin of Hartley; six over long-on and another over midwicket into the Grand Stand, going on to reach 50 off 78 balls. Raut had already reached the landmark off three fewer deliveries and India were clear favourites at 136 for 2 after 33 overs.

The scream of relief from Hartley when Kaur swept her into the hands of Beaumont at deep square leg felt like the cry of an England uprising. 'We knew Harman would go after Alex,' said Brunt. 'She would fancy herself to clear the fielder and if Alex got it just right she wouldn't get it. If she had just played a smart innings we would have lost, we needed her to put her chest out.'

New batter Veda Krishnamurthy's foot movement against the slow bowlers and the continued force of Raut kept India moving towards apparent victory. Taylor's uncharacteristic failure to pull off a stumping, Knight's dropped catch at extra cover, and Krishnamurthy's successive fours off Shrubsole left England's hopes looking as dark as the clouds that had begun hovering over the Lord's pavilion. Shrubsole admitted, 'When you drop a catch and miss a stumping you think this is just not going to be our day.'

Brunt saw it differently. 'Because those things were happening, we were thinking, "Right, if we are doing that then anything can happen." We only needed a couple of wickets and we were into the players who hadn't batted in the tournament. It wasn't like facing Australia who had 11 batters.'

Shrubsole found the ball back in her hands. 'I struggled early in the tournament,' she remembered. 'I wasn't bowling where I wanted to be or getting the wickets I wanted. On reflection, I probably wasn't bowling as badly as I thought, but you always want to get a wicket early and you search a bit more when you don't. It took a bit of a chat from Robbo, who sat me down and said, '"Things aren't as bad as you think they might be. Just try and reset." That chat helped me turn things around.'

The pay-off was on its way. With two balls left in the 43rd over, Raut offered an indecisive push at England's seamer and was equally hesitant in her use of the review system, allowing time to run out before attempting to challenge the lbw decision. The next over saw Sushma Verma bowled behind her legs by Hartley; the next found Krishnamurthy swiping Shrubsole to Sciver at midwicket. Two balls later, Goswami was yorked. Four wickets in three overs had seen India slide from 191 for 3 to 201 for 7. Now they needed 28 in five overs.

Shrubsole continued, 'I executed my plan in terms of where I was bowling. Then there was the pressure on the people coming in late in a final with runs still to get. That does funny things to you.' If the 17 runs scored off the next 14 deliveries put India in control once more it was obviously not enough to calm the jittery Shikha Pandey, who set off on a non-existent run and had no chance of getting back to her crease.

It was 11 runs to win with two wickets left as Shrubsole began the 49th over, bowling round the wicket from the Pavilion End. The left-handed Sharma tried to manoeuvre the first ball over midwicket but chipped it into the air for Sciver to take an easy catch moving to her right.

Facing only her second delivery, the advancing Poonam Yadav tried to lift Shrubsole over mid-off, only to dolly an easy catch to Gunn. The World Cup was about to fall into England's grasp. Yet, quicker than expected, the ball's trajectory dipped. Instead of finding it landing safely and simply in her hands, Gunn, the quiet veteran of the England team, had to reach forward. As her right knee touched the grass the ball slipped from her grasp and the batters took a single. Television replays showed the faces of celebration among the England fielders turning to Munch-like masks of horror.

English viewers who had never paid much attention to women's cricket yelled at their screens. In India, where the ICC reported that 126 million had tuned in for the final, hopes were rekindled. In the middle of it all, the aggrieved bowler might have been the calmest person of all, turning to her teammates and assuring them, 'It's OK. I've got this.'

Brunt recalled that 'I was mortified for Jenny', while Shrubsole said, 'I felt absolutely fine. They still needed nine to win and we had just taken six wickets in no time whatsoever. If you are not confident about getting the number 11 out at that point, then you are never going to be. They still had a huge amount to get.'

Shrubsole approached the crease once more, sending down a ball full of length. Rajeshwari Gayakwad played down the wrong line. The ball struck off stump. Shrubsole stopped in her tracks, head thrown back, arms outstretched – an image that would come to symbolise an historic moment in the growth of women's cricket and be used in numerous TV sizzle reels in the ensuing years. Then she was swamped by teammates, whose bouncing up and down was mirrored by fans in the stands. Lord's had experienced few more joyous moments.

'It's difficult to put into words,' was Shrubsole's response to the request to describe the moment. 'Pure elation. To have the opportunity to play in a World Cup final at Lord's in front of friends and family is one thing, and to be able to win it is amazing, It kind of all comes at you at once. You celebrate the moment; you celebrate with the team and then you look around for your family. And I spent a lot of time in disbelief at the way India just folded in that last half an hour. It all happened so fast I remember thinking. "What the bloody hell has just happened?"'

Brunt, who was proud of 'batting my arse off' in the tournament and had bowled more dot balls than anyone, was overwhelmed by the release of pressure, finding herself on her knees while teammates leapt about her. 'The days leading up to that had taken its toll. I just wanted to relax and not feel anything again. Not have to worry about running in and bowling, not having to worry about putting my pads on. It just hit me all at once. Everyone was jumping around, and you want to scream but you are not allowed to, so the next thing is just to cry. And there was a box right up above us where are families were, but I didn't have my mum there…'

The emotion of the day was not over for Brunt and Sciver, long-time housemates near England's training base in Loughborough. 'Every summer, we come together as a team and watch *Love Island*,' Brunt explained. 'It is the only thing to watch and chat shit about the next day. It is a subject where we all bond. One of the lads in it had asked one of the girls to be his girlfriend by getting all his lad mates to lie down on the floor in an "I love you" symbol. So in a jokey, cringe way I got the girls to lie on the ground at Lord's and then I took Nat up to the changing room balcony. It was really awful but quite funny and I asked her to be my girlfriend. I would have done it whether we had won or lost. I thought that if we lose it will make me feel better about the day and if we won it would make it even better. It was a win-win.'

It was a couple of years before the pair publicly announced their relationship and their engagement, and not until the worst of the Covid pandemic had passed were they able to stage their wedding day. The heightened public profile that the pair achieved through England's World Cup win made them important role models and powerful spokespeople for the LGBT community.

'I have never enjoyed being ashamed of who I am,' said Brunt. 'I always have to try to be better with being me, and being comfortable with being me with other people there. It has always been a challenge. It was more about showing other people they are not alone. You do feel alone and like an alien and feel other people are looking at you. Now I have a platform to help other people, so why wouldn't I? I don't like speaking publicly about it or crying on TV or radio, but it is important and it feels necessary. It is not anything I can't handle, and I am happy to do it.'

The importance of the World Cup final – not just in what England had achieved and what it meant on a personal level, but what the day represented for women's cricket – quickly revealed itself. 'It hits you the next day,' said Shrubsole, 'when you come down for breakfast and see the front, back and middle pages of all the papers; then going to Lord's for interviews. That was when you realised the impact that game could have.'

Further realisation came the way of winning coach Robinson. 'I met the chairman of the MCC [Gerald Corbett] the next day and he said they had blown their budgets,' he explained. 'He said, "We didn't do any of our budgets for alcohol. We hardly sold any alcohol; it was all coffee and tea. We had to shut half the male toilets down to open them up for women because of the queues." He said it was just a completely different audience. It was women, children and families, which is what the game is trying to attract.'

* * *

Soon after the World Cup, Australia's women were included for the first time in the ACB's revenue sharing model, taking the minimum retainer for a centrally contracted player from A\$40,000 to A\$72,000, with players earning an average of A\$180,000. The new pool of money for female players, which had risen from A\$7.5 million to A\$55.2, also included a minimum A\$35,951 for domestic players holding both state and Women's Big Bash League contracts – a near 100 per cent increase.

When the next big event in the ICC women's calendar, the T20 World Cup, arrived in Australia early in 2020 it was clear that the bar had been raised; from the expectation of victory for the well-resourced hosts to the predictions that Melbourne Cricket Ground could be almost full for the final. India, who almost pooped on England's party in 2017, were again the biggest threat to Anglo-Aussie dominance. 'I am just hoping we can inspire young girls to take up cricket and to go forward thinking there is a profession out there, a career to be made,' said Veda Krishnamurthy, a typical and sincerely-held desire among players of all nations, who might have been excused for voicing entirely parochial goals.

India began by beating Australia by 17 runs in the opening game at the Sydney Showground, after which events built towards a rematch in front of a women's record 86,174 at the Melbourne Cricket Ground. The only unsatisfactory chord in the tournament was struck by the rain that washed out the India-England semi-final, meaning the former went through to the final by virtue of winning their qualification group.

'Everyone's pinching themselves,' tournament CEO Adam Hockley said before the final, which was being staged on International Women's Day. 'It's nothing less (sic) than the players deserve.'

American chart-topper Katy Perry, who would perform the pre-game ceremony in the late stages of pregnancy, might not have known Meg Lanning from Meg Ryan before boarding the plane for Australia, but captured the mood when saying, 'It's going to be a game about empowered women and strong women and hopefully it inspires and empowers all the women of every age that are watching.'

The game itself could not come close to the drama of Lord's two and a half years earlier, Australia winning by a comfortable 85 runs. It was a sign of the progress of women's cricket that no one used the one-sidedness of the contest to denigrate the overall product; or trot out the old complaints that the players didn't hit the ball hard enough or bowl fast enough. Or if they did, their voices were lost amid the roars of 84,000, the post-game fireworks and the vocals of Perry, who seemed genuinely chuffed to end up on the victory podium with the victorious Aussies. 'We never thought we'd experience anything like this throughout our career,' said Alyssa Healy, whose innings of 75 had decided the match.

Lord's 2017 and Melbourne 2020 rewrote the norms of expectation for women's cricket. When the ECB's inaugural Hundred tournament in 2021 saw crowds taking advantage of the double-header format of the fixtures to get there early enough to watch – and demonstrate genuine excitement for – the women's matches that preceded the men's, there was no feeling of incongruity. No one had boycotted the 2018 *Wisden* when Shrubsole was pictured on the cover; nor was anyone storming the barricades at Lord's when it was announced that Clare Connor would become the first female president of MCC in October 2021, barely two decades after women were still banned from the pavilion.

'Potentially you wouldn't have the record crowd at the MCG without Lord's in 2017, although Australia have been leading the way,' said Shrubsole. 'There were so many things that come off the back of that World Cup that you didn't ever think about happening. It's been incredible.'

ENGLAND v INDIA, Women's World Cup Final
23 July 2017, Lord's

England			Balls	4s	6s
L Winfield	b Gayakwad	25	39	4	
TT Beaumont	c Gosmami b Yadav	23	37	5	
†SJ Taylor	c Verman b Goswami	45	62		
*HC Knight	lbw b Yadav	1	7		
NR Sciver	lbw b Goswami	51	68	5	
FC Wilson	lbw b Goswami	0	1		
KH Brunt	run out	34	42	2	
JL Gunn	not out	25	38	1	
LA Marsh	not out	14	11	1	
Extras	(lb 3, w 1, nb 7)	11			
Total	(7 wickets, 50 overs)	228			

Did Not Bat: A Shrubsole, A Hartley

Fall: 47, 60, 63, 146, 146, 164, 196.
Bowling: Goswami 10-3-23-3; Pandey 7-0-53-0; Gayakwad 10-1-49-1; Sharma 9-0-39-0; Yadav 10-0-36-2; Kaur 4-0-25-0.

India			Balls	4s	6s
PG Raut	lbw b Shrubsole	86	115	4	1
SS Mandhana	b Shrubsole	0	9		
*MD Raj	run out	17	31	3	
H Kaur	c Beaumont b Hartley	51	80	3	2
V Krishnamurthy	c Sciver b Shrubsole	35	34	5	
†S Verma	b Hartley	0	2		
DB Sharma	c Sciver b Shrubsole	14	12	1	
JN Goswami	b Shrubsole	0	1		
SS Pandey	run out	4	8		
P Yadav	not out	1	5		
R Gayakwad	b Shrubsole	0	1		
Extras	(lb 3, w 1, nb 7)	11			
Total	(48.4 overs)	219			

Fall: 5, 43, 138, 191, 196, 200, 201, 218, 218, 219.
Bowling: Brunt 6-0-22-0; 9.4-0-46-6; Sciver 5-1-26-0; Gunn 7-2-17-0; Marsh 10-1-40-0; Hartley 10-0-58-2; Knight 1-0-7-0.

England won by 8 runs. **Toss:** England. **Umpires:** GO Brathwaite, S George.
Player of the Match: A Shrubsole

'BY THE BAREST OF MARGINS'

England v New Zealand, World Cup Final, Lord's, 2019

Lord's had seen everything limited-overs cricket had to offer. From Ted Dexter daring to put fielders on the boundary in the inaugural Gillette Cup, to the sport's first global tournament, the music and fireworks of Twenty20 and even packed stands for a women's game. But never this.

One over to decide the World Cup.

A tournament lasting more than six weeks had seen its 48th and final match produce eight hours of tense, taut and dramatic cricket; a throwback to the days when scores of 400 in one-day games were mere fantasy. On this day, New Zealand and England had managed only 241 runs each. As the 30,000 spectators at Lord's, the millions watching around the world – and even the players and umpires in the changing rooms – made sure they understood the rules of the Super Over that would determine the destiny of the World Cup, nobody was complaining that they had been shortchanged.

The way it worked, it was explained, was that the team batting second in the main game now batted first. 'There was panic,' recalled Jonny Bairstow. 'No one knew the Super Over rules.' As regular opening batsman Jason Roy scurried to borrow a protective box from bowler Mark Wood, an exhausted Ben Stokes, who had just finished unbeaten on 84, found a quiet spot at the back of the pavilion to compose himself before being asked to go out to bat again. Jos Buttler, who had made a half-century, would join him.

'People who scored runs in the game were probably the best to send straight back out,' captain Eoin Morgan explained. Roy, it was originally planned, would be the third permitted batter, only for Morgan to decide after a couple of balls that he would rather be the one to go in if fellow left-hander Stokes was dismissed.

In the end, no one else was needed. Stokes and Buttler took 11 runs from the first five deliveries by left-arm paceman Trent Boult, and Buttler punched the final ball into a gap at midwicket for a total of 15 for 0. 'When Jos hit that four, I thought we had won the World Cup,' remembered Stokes.

England, the birthplace of professional limited-overs cricket, had been close to winning the World Cup before – falling at the last hurdle in 1979, 1987 and 1992. But never had they been *this* close. And never had their journey to the final been so long, so painful and, at times, so downright inept. Victory in the World T20 of 2010 had given their senior men's team a taste of triumph in a global tournament for the first time. But in the 20 years since fumbling their most recent turn at hosting the 50-over championship, they had suffered further early exits and been beaten by supposedly minor nations. The 1992 event was still the last one at which they had been a competitive presence. At the most recent World Cup, in Australia, their only wins in six matches had been against Afghanistan and Scotland. Reaching the final of the ICC Champions Trophy in 2003 and 2014 didn't count for much when set against the disappointments in the premier 50-over competition.

Alongside, and contributing to, the poor results had been a litany of strange selection decisions; last-minute, largely unrehearsed, moves to use the likes of Nasser Hussain, Kevin Pietersen and Ian Bell as opening batsmen at various tournaments included in the prime exhibits.

Among the moments that came to symbolise the chaos of England's 50-over selection was the NatWest Series final against India at Lord's in 2002, when skipper Hussain completed his first ODI hundred at the 72nd attempt. Having been batting, mostly unproductively, at number three for the previous year and been criticised by eminent observers for his stubbornness in doing so, he turned towards the media centre, made a show of pointing to the No 3 on his shirt and then raised three fingers, accompanied by various expletives.

'I was an average white-ball cricketer,' Hussain recalled. 'For about a year, [Bob] Willis, [Ian] Botham and [Jonathan] Agnew had gone on, saying Hussain shouldn't be batting at three. And it did wind me up.'

Teammate Michael Vaughan, who led the unsuccessful 2007 World Cup campaign in the West Indies, remembered, 'He did get the piss taken out of him for his celebration.' But he came to recognise how the job could drive its holder to such extremes. 'You wanted to do it on regular basis. Even when you have won a game you have to deal with a certain amount of adversity as a skipper. And when it's personal, about your place in the side, it is very frustrating that people can't see what else you are doing.'

By the 2015 World Cup, any sense of English underachievement had all but disappeared, buried under the acceptance of years of ineptitude. During their campaign, New Zealand took fewer than 13 overs to chase a paltry 123; Sri Lanka reached a 300-plus target with one wicket down; and Bangladesh rubber-stamped England's early exit. This time it was the coach – and a national cricketing structure that seemed to care little about winning the World Cup – that was held accountable. Morgan was excused, having only been made captain when England's make-it-up-as-we-go-along strategy saw Alastair Cook removed from the post two months before the tournament after a heavy series defeat in Sri Lanka.

Peter Moores, in his second stint as England head coach, was the individual held most responsible. England were already being criticised, from the press box and from those who had recently stepped out of the dressing room, for being too data-driven in their approach to one-day cricket; a method that erred towards caution and stifled freedom of expression. So, when it sounded as though Moores told BBC Radio, after the Bangladesh defeat, that 'we'll have to look at the data' the walls of ridicule came crashing down upon him. A poor line obscured that he'd said 'we'll have to look at it later' – for which the BBC apologised. But given the apparent insistence on letting numbers rather than instinct drive tactics, and the fact he then told Sky Sports, 'We'll have to analyse the game data a bit later,' the damage was done.

It was not so much that data did not have a place in the game; more that Moores had stumbled onto the wrong side of the fine line between embracing the kind of analytics that were becoming such a force in franchise Twenty20 cricket, and allowing natural talent to have its head. In a much more simplistic way, Dexter – whose beloved Sussex had later been captained and coached by Moores – had achieved success in the early days of limited-overs cricket because he mastered the balance of pragmatism, intuition and flair.

Paul Farbrace, assistant to Moores, would admit to Nick Hoult and Steve James, authors of *Morgan's Men*, 'Even leading into the World

Cup we knew we that we had players who were not necessarily playing the modern one-day game. We weren't scoring the big runs.'

Joe Root identified that Sri Lanka defeat as the moment of 'realisation that a lot of teams were so far ahead of us in that form.' Identical comments had accompanied a heavy defeat against the same team in the 1996 tournament. Two decades on, nothing much had changed.

England ended the 2015 tournament with a suitably chaotic and acrimonious team meeting in which most players appeared keener to point fingers at others rather than look at their own contribution. And then the revolution began. Managing Director of Cricket Paul Downton was the first to go, replaced by former Test captain Andrew Strauss, who immediately removed Moores. Australian Trevor Bayliss, who had led Sri Lanka to the 2011 World Cup final and won a couple of IPL titles with Kolkata Knight Riders, was appointed head coach, reflecting the emphasis that was to be placed on white-ball cricket with the next World Cup being held in England and Wales. Farbrace remained as his assistant.

Bayliss immediately made it clear that he wanted a specialist white-ball captain and identified Morgan as the man for the role. Having felt that 'my influence on the team was minimal' during the World Cup, Morgan had made extensive notes about what he felt would be required should he retain the captaincy and was excited about bringing them to life alongside a man he'd enjoyed working for at Kolkata.

Those plans took shape quickly, with nine of the 11 who would play in the World Cup final appearing in the first 50-over series after the World Cup – a brilliantly unpredictable five-match contest against New Zealand. Morgan's view was that his men should 'not worry about batting 50 overs', believing it 'makes guys hesitate and question their natural way of playing.' The result was a score of 408 in the first match, 300-plus in the next three and a successful Duckworth-Lewis chase of 192 in only 26 overs to win the decisive final game.

The series established a new opening partnership of Surrey's Jason Roy and Nottinghamshire's Alex Hales, two players whose preferred method of seeing off the new ball was to whack it into the stands. But Roy's loss of form cost him his place to Bairstow during the 2017 Champions Trophy, only to have it handed back to him by events outside a nightclub in Bristol later that summer.

Stokes was arrested – eventually being tried and acquitted on a charge of affray – while Hales was also embroiled in the events. Like his teammate, who missed out on an Ashes tour, Hales faced a spell out of the England team, allowing Roy and Bairstow to form their country's best-ever ODI opening partnership.

Morgan and Test captain Root encouraged their players to see the three lions on their badge as symbols of the courage needed to play bold cricket, the unity required to bring the country together behind a diverse team; and the respect due to teammates, opponents and the sport itself. When Hales was revealed to have a failed a test for the use of recreational drugs a few weeks before the 2019 World Cup, there was no room for compromise on those standards.

'We have worked extremely hard over the last 18 months to establish our culture and work towards values that everyone across all three formats could adhere to, respect and relate to,' Morgan told a press conference. 'There has been a complete disregard for those values. There has been a complete breakdown in trust between Alex and the team. Everybody in the senior players meeting agreed that the best decision for the team and the culture moving forward was for Alex to be deselected.' England's team management concurred with Morgan and his men. Even the fact that a change in powerplay rules since 2015 had placed even greater emphasis on scoring runs up front – with the first 10 overs now the only period when all but two men had to be inside the 30-yard circle – there were to be no concessions for the sake of keeping Hales's big bat in the team's armoury.

Such had been the progress made by the England ODI team since 2015 that Morgan had earned the right to guide such decisions in order to protect the chemistry of what was now a winning team, rated among the favourites for the World Cup. The statistics stacked up to support their status. They had scored a world-record 418 against Australia at Trent Bridge a year earlier; no team had scored more runs against spin bowlers in overs 11 to 40 over the previous two years; and no one hit more boundaries in the final ten overs. Even Liam Plunkett, batting at number 10, had hit the final ball of an ODI against Sri Lanka for six to achieve a tie in 2016.

And, by the time the tournament started, they had the most talked about fast bowler in the world in their ranks. Jofra Archer, who had made his Sussex debut in 2016, had proved himself one of the world's most lethal white-ball exponents in two years in the IPL (Rajasthan Royals) and Big Bash League (Hobart Hurricanes). Now, thanks to a lowering of the ECB's residential requirements to three years from seven, the man born in Bridgetown, Barbados – holder of British citizenship through his father – was eligible to play for England, just in time for a summer that would feature the World Cup and an Ashes series.

Archer's gentle, almost benign, approach to the crease gave little hint of the potential dismantling of dignity that confronted every batter to whom he bowled. The prospect of a ball delivered in excess of 90mph from close to the stumps that could arrive as a yorker or spit from short of a length and undermine any attempt at evasive action made him one of the most feared pacemen in the world before he had played international cricket. There had to be a place for him in England's 15, and it was the misfortune of the left-arm seamer David Willey that he was the one to be sacrificed. England had spoken for years about the need for mystery spin, express pace and a left-arm variation in their attack. Adil Rashid provided the former; the latter was happily foregone for the opportunity to have both Archer and Mark Wood launching rockets at the opposition.

The big difference in this England team compared to previous versions was that, rather than shying away from their status as tournament favourites, they took pride in it, felt they deserved it, and were happy to defy anyone to dispute it. It was 'something to be embraced', according to wicketkeeper-batsman Buttler, one of several England players who had benefitted from the ECB finally allowing its players to mix in the rarefied company of the world's best in the IPL.

It meant that England went into the opening match against South Africa at The Oval giddy with excitement rather than weighed down by the expectation that they undoubtedly felt. Even the loss of Bairstow, who edged his first ball to the wicketkeeper, could not derail them. The batting of Root and Stokes, who later pulled off a circus-act one-handed catch, proved more than enough, while Archer announced himself with a menacing spell memorable as much for the blow he struck on Hashim Amla's helmet as his three wickets.

Yet even though this was a new England, the old frailties in tournament play suddenly began to emerge. Dropped catches undermined centuries by Root and Buttler and led to defeat against Pakistan. Against West Indies, Roy – who had just belted 153 in a victory over Bangladesh – pulled a hamstring while fielding, placing his participation in the rest of the competition in doubt. Root scored a century as an emergency opener to win the match, but the long-term loss of someone 'who breathes confidence in our changing room', according to Morgan, would be a blow, especially with the self-inflicted absence of Hales as back-up.

Morgan seemed unaffected by such worries as he struck a world-record 17 sixes to demolish Afghanistan at Old Trafford, but then England fell short of Sri Lanka's measly 232 at Headingley. A performance that Buttler described as 'a little bit lazy, a little bit complacent' was followed by a 64-run defeat against Australia at Lord's. All the pre-tournament optimism and bravado was in danger of being buried under the pressure of knowing they now needed to beat India, still undefeated, and New Zealand to squeak into the top four and a semi-final berth.

There were even conspiracy theories emerging that the slow wickets predominant in the competition – which made England's hit-it-hard and bowl-it-fast brand of cricket more difficult to execute – had been prepared at the behest of the ICC to benefit its supposedly favourite Indian sons.

It was at this point that England team psychologist David Young staged a meeting aimed at having players confront their fears. When Stokes – the alpha-male of the squad, who bore scars of the 2016 World T20 final – discussed his own nerves and doubts, it served as a comfort to others experiencing similar stress. 'I thought Stokesy was bullet-proof,' recalled Wood.

Roy returned to face India at Edgbaston, and England were back to their gun-slinging best. An opening partnership of 160, with Bairstow ending up with 111, led to a total of 337. It proved 31 too many for India, despite losing only five wickets – three to Liam Plunkett – and Rohit Sharma reaching three figures. Another century by Bairstow at Chester-le-Street, and what Morgan felt was England's best bowling performance of the tournament, delivered the required victory over New Zealand, setting up a return contest against Australia in the semi-final.

The last time England faced their arch-rivals at home in a World Cup knockout game, they had crumbled in the inaugural tournament at Headingley. It was a different story at Edgbaston in 2019, Archer removing Aaron Finch first ball, Chris Woakes giving a man-of-the-match performance with three wickets on his home ground and the batters making light of passing Australia's 223 with almost 18 overs left and only two wickets down.

Morgan thought it the best his team had played throughout his reign as captain. Head coach Bayliss loved the manner of the victory more than the way the players celebrated excitedly in the dressing room. 'This is why the Aussies think you don't win anything,' he barked. 'You have won nothing. The final is the one to celebrate.' Suddenly, the champagne lost its fizz.

Three days later, England played in their first final since 1992; their first on home soil since surrendering to West Indies in 1979. The MCC members seemed to offload their 40 years of hurt as the players filed past to take the field. 'The lining of the stairs as we walked down to go into the Long Room and when we stood in the Long Room before game was without doubt the loudest that I have heard,' Bairstow would tell Sky Sports' *The World Cup Through Their Eyes* documentary. 'It was spine-tingling, It was something that I will never forget.' Meanwhile, millions in the United Kingdom were able to watch in excited anticipation after Sky's decision to allow its coverage to air for free on Channel 4, the first time in 14 years that England's players had performed on terrestrial network TV in their own country.

That England were taking the field first was down to Morgan having lost a toss about which he was uncertain after rain had left the surface slow and tacky. 'It's a World Cup final, it's going to feel different,' Morgan told his men. 'Embrace it, lads.' It was certainly different from much of the cricket his team had been involved in for four years, the surface playing its role in producing what seemed like an old-fashioned Lord's final. When New Zealand were restricted to 241 for 8 by England's bowlers, many observers, putting parochial bias aside, feared a straightforward victory for the hosts and a wasted opportunity for cricket to sell itself to that new, subscription-free audience suddenly given access to the sport.

They need not have worried.

England had bowled well, particularly Woakes and Plunkett, three wickets apiece, and Archer, who went for only two boundaries, despite operating at both ends of the innings. It was a statistic to prove more important than first thought.

Plunkett had become England's go-to bowler in the traditionally dead middle overs, thanks to his ability to fire the old ball hard into the surface. 'Whenever he played in the tournament, [he] was exceptional,' related Morgan after the Durham man claimed the prized wicket of Kane Williamson and half-century maker Henry Nicholls in quick succession to destabilise the New Zealand innings,

But, as Root recalled, England were 'still not quite sure of the wicket', and New Zealand's bowlers had proved in previous matches their ability to hold on to whatever their batsmen had given them. When Morgan was fourth out in the 24th over, England were only 86 runs towards their target. Bairstow had gone for 36, and Stokes and Buttler faced the task of rebuilding. Colin de Grandhomme, remover of Root, was in the midst of bowling his seemingly unthreatening medium pacers unchanged for 10 overs, conceding only 25 runs and proving how difficult it was to score runs quickly, especially when the batsmen were new to the crease.

'It was going to take something special from one or two guys to get us close to the score,' said Root. Even Archer, who had quickly impressed his teammates with his ability to doze off in the dressing room while his colleagues batted, admitted he found it difficult to 'have a good nap' on this occasion.

Stokes and Buttler proceeded with caution. Both had reached 22 and the score 129 by the end of the 33rd over, the former having taken 45 balls to get there. Advancing down the wicket he began the next over by taking Matt Henry for three consecutive twos, the noise from the crowd increasing with each shot to levels not usually associated with Lord's – at least not since the West Indian fans had colonised the place for the first final. Stokes could not help but comment on it when he met Buttler in mid-pitch. 'I had never heard noise like that at Lord's before,' he said, laughing as he urged his partner, 'Come on, let's get back on it.'

Buttler responded by taking advantage of Lockie Ferguson's width and Jimmy Neesham's length to collect a couple of boundaries, and Stokes swivelled to pull Ferguson to the ropes again. A scoop for four by Buttler off Henry and England needed 72 from 10 overs.

Only 13 came from the next three, before Buttler released some of the tension by firing Boult to the midwicket boundary to reach his half-century. Three balls later, Stokes achieved the landmark, but it was the Kiwis who were celebrating in the 45th over when Buttler sent Ferguson's slower ball flying towards the cover-point boundary, where substitute fielder Tim Southee made a late adjustment and held a sliding catch. 'I tried to finish it a little too early,' admitted the batsman, whose uncharacteristic shouting and punching of objects in the dressing room revealed his frustration. Ferguson then induced a top-edged hook from Woakes.

By the time the final two overs began, boundaries by Plunkett and Stokes had reduced the target to 24. Plunkett attempted to loft Neesham's third ball over long-off, only to drop it into the hands of Boult, who found himself under the very next ball after Stokes went down on one knee to swing for deep midwicket. Again, he held the catch, but this time he took one step back, only flipping the ball to Guptill when he felt the rope below his heel. Stokes joined the umpire in signalling six.

Another single, and Archer faced the final ball of the over with 15 needed. He had joined Stokes in a similar situation in an IPL game for Rajasthan and now, as then, he received advice from his partner. 'It's a free hit, mate.' He was clean bowled.

Boult began the final over to Stokes, who could only dig out the first two balls to extra cover, turning down singles. 'We were gone, we were down, we were out, we were done,' Bairstow would recall. And then Stokes nailed the third ball. 'Is it out of the ground?' was the cry from Ian Smith, the former New Zealand wicketkeeper, on commentary. 'It is!' he confirmed as the ball landed in the Grand Stand. And then … 'You couldn't write the next ball,' said Morgan.

Stokes drove Boult's full toss toward the same area of the field, along the ground this time. Guptill fielded and threw towards the Nursery End, where Stokes was diving in to complete a second run. To the fielders' horror, the ball struck the bat that had already produced 78 runs and shot off to the boundary at the end of the ground for four more. Had it stopped short of the rope, Stokes would happily have followed protocol and declined the opportunity to run any overthrows. All he could now was put up his arms, say 'sorry' and accept the gift. The England dressing room, out of view and feeling no need for such restraint, celebrated wildly. 'Can you believe this?' roared Smith. 'I do not believe what I have just seen,' – which, coming from a man involved in the final over of the infamous 'underarm' match, was quite a statement.

As was later pointed out, umpire Kumar Dharmasena actually made a mistake according to Law 19.8 in awarding six runs in total – the two that had been run, plus four overthrows. The law states that the run in progress only counts if the batsmen had crossed 'at the instant of the throw', which TV footage confirmed they had not. Therefore, one run plus four overthrows should have been the call and Adil Rashid should have faced the next ball instead of Stokes. Not one person suggested as much at the time, demonstrating how impenetrable the laws of cricket can be, especially when needing to be applied in the heat of the moment.

So, three needed from two balls. Stokes lost his footing as he pumped Boult's full delivery to deep mid-off, and Rashid gave himself up getting back to the bowlers' end. Two needed from the final ball with Wood coming to the crease, wearing chest guard and thigh pad, even though all that was required of him was to run like crazy. 'When I looked up and saw what he had on, I was like, "What are you doing?"' said Stokes.

A full toss on leg stump. Instead of aiming for the ropes and risking defeat by being caught, Stokes pushed to long on, ensuring at least a tie and hoping that Wood could get back for a second run. It wasn't even close. At 241 for 9, the game was tied and the World Cup was heading for the first Super Over in tournament history. 'I still ask why Ben didn't hit that ball for six,' said Morgan.

* * *

Archer had known what was coming. No other bowlers were warming up or putting on their boots. 'Morgs, it's me, isn't it?' he asked his captain as England's batsmen were scrambling to get ready to bat in the Super Over.

While Stokes and Buttler were batting, Archer warmed up with bowling coach Chris Silverwood. 'Fifteen is a great score in the Super Over, especially when you have one of the best yorker bowlers in the world at your disposal,' said Morgan. Having shed his pads,

323

Stokes wondered whether he should say anything to Archer, whom everyone recognised as being 'chilled', even in the most intense heat of battle. He went for it. 'Whatever happens here is not going to define your career,' Stokes told him, liberating the trauma of that last over in the World T20 final from the place he'd locked it away for three years.

New Zealand sent out the free-swinging, left-handed Neesham and the clean-hitting, but out of form, Guptill. It was 16, the world learned, that they required to avoid defeat in a second successive final, thanks to a somewhat random rule that felt like it had been added as an afterthought in a tournament committee meeting in the knowledge that it would never need to be applied. In the event of a tied Super Over, the team having scored most boundaries in the main game would win. Remarkably, the World Cup might be decided by an arbitrary law that virtually no one – either watching or playing – had known about until a few minutes previously. England had hit 22 fours and two sixes, against New Zealand's 14 fours and two sixes.

Archer, informed that he had to bowl from his less favoured Nursery End because that is where Boult had operated from for New Zealand, began full and wide outside off – too wide to be deemed legal, even though it appeared to be right on the permitted limit. The bowler told his captain he wanted to review it. 'No, Jofra, this is not how it works,' was the skipper's patient reply.

Neesham sent the first legal delivery, another wide yorker, to long-off for two runs; then swung a straight, good-length ball over midwicket for six. 'Boom!' Smith exclaimed. 'That's seven [needed] from four.' Another hit to leg, and Roy's fumbled pick-up in the deep allowed them back for a second. Next ball, same outcome. This time Roy fielded cleanly, but threw to the bowler's end, where the speedy Guptill was home comfortably. Twenty-two yards away, Buttler was vainly yelling 'my end' over the maelstrom inside the old ground. Three needed off two balls.

'Right, it's gamble time,' Morgan said as he approached his bowler. 'What are we going to do to get a wicket or a dot ball?'

Archer announced that he was going to bowl a bouncer, reasserting that intention when his skipper challenged him.

'OK then. Let's set a field for it.'

Neesham swiped, but the ball plopped on the strip in front of him and the batsmen crossed for a single. 'Although it turned out to be the right delivery in costing just one run, looking back I think I might have done things differently,' Archer would admit. 'The reward is not enough when you consider the risk of being hit for a four or six.' It said everything about Morgan's enlightened, intuitive captaincy that he sensed it was better to have Archer feeling comfortable bowling what was possibly the wrong delivery, than impose on him a plan he did not go along with. When Morgan stood down as England's white-ball captain in 2022, Archer would describe him as 'someone who believed in his players; someone who was prepared to risk things'.

One ball to win the World Cup. Two runs for New Zealand; anything less and England's 44-year quest to win what they started out believing was 'their' tournament would be complete. Stokes, fielding at long-on, noticed the New Zealand commentator and former seamer Simon Doull on the other side of the boundary – 'a nervous wreck'. Root remembered how quiet it went inside Lord's when Archer reached the end of his run up, only to explode into life again as he approached Guptill, who had last faced a ball well over eight hours earlier. 'Here it is, folks,' chirped Smith. 'This is the moment,'

It was outside leg stump; wide enough that a batsman without the weight of the World Cup on his shoulders might have calmly stepped inside the line and accepted the extra run. Guptill dug it out to deep midwicket, where Roy had become a magnet for the ball. Again, all the hours of fielding practice – attacking the ball, picking up cleanly, making the right decision about where to throw and delivering with accuracy – should have made it an automatic exercise for the Surrey man. 'It's going towards Jason. Yes, our best fielder,' was the reaction of Stokes. But after what had happened earlier in the over, every one of the millions of England fans held their breath and squinted nervously through almost closed eyes.

The throw was good enough. Buttler had to reach back, swing his arms from right to left and reach out to break the stumps, but Guptill was nowhere near completing the second run. 'He's got it! England have won the World Cup,' Smith shrieked. 'By the barest of margins.'

In unison with Smith's now immortal words, Buttler raced in the direction of the pavilion, tossing his gloves as players chased after him. 'All your dreams come true in that one moment,' he explained.

Bairstow jumped on the nearest person he could find and then Root jumped on him; Stokes slipped and lay on his back with arms outstretched; Archer knelt in relief; Plunkett and others cried. When the initial, climactic burst of energy had calmed, players went to console opponents who had lost via the application of an obscure note in the tournament playing conditions and perhaps the umpires' failure to observe the laws of the game in England's last over. To their eternal credit, the New Zealanders made a big deal of neither.

The chaos in the stands reflected the mayhem of the players' victory celebrations. 'Lord's has never been like it,' ventured Stokes. 'I don't think the crowd would ever have expected to be watching something like they did that day.'

And then, in the moments before the trophy presentation, a chance for the England men to reflect on achievement, to acknowledge family and loved ones in the stadium, and in the case of Bairstow, to think about those not present. David Bairstow, his father, had played four Tests and 21 ODIs as England wicketkeeper – most famously being placed on the boundary by Mike Brearley at the end of a game in Australia – before taking his own life when he was only 46 and his son eight years old.

In the most moving moments of Sky Sports' *The World Cup Through Their Eyes*, an emotional Buttler recalls, 'I just said his old man would be so proud looking down on him. It hit him a bit hard, I think, that I even said it.' Bairstow, of course, had been thinking it. 'It was a special day for me, for family that were there, family that could not be there.' When recalling Buttler's words as they waited to receive their medals, he manages to force out, 'Jos basically said, "Your dad would be proud as hell,"' before turning from the camera with a deep exhalation of breath that betrays the effort of the memory.

For most, there were no conflicting emotions. 'If I could bottle a feeling it would be the ten seconds when Morgs lifts the trophy and we were all together,' said Wood. Under the ticker tape and the fireworks, below the gold being held aloft, stood the men who had banished the World Cup ghosts of Gary Gilmour, Viv Richards, Allan Border, Imran Khan, Sanath Jayasuriya and others. A group of men from differing nations and cultures who had, in the eyes of the English at least, brought cricket home.

By the barest of margins.

ENGLAND v NEW ZEALAND, World Cup Final

14 July 2019, Lord's

New Zealand			Balls	4s	6s
MJ Guptill	lbw b Woakes	19	18	2	1
HM Nicholls	b Plunkett	55	77	4	
*KS Williamson	c Buttler b Plunkett	30	53	2	
LRPL Taylor	lbw b Wood	15	31		
†TWM Latham	c sub (Vince) b Woakes	47	56	2	1
JDS Neesham	c Root b Plunkett	19	25	3	
C de Grandhomme	c sub (Vince) b Woakes	16	28		
MJ Santner	not out	5	9		
MJ Henry	b Archer	4	2	1	
TA Boult	not out	1	2		
Extras	(lb 12, w 17, nb 1)	30			
Total	(8 wickets, 50 overs)	241			

Did Not Bat: LH Ferguson

Fall: 29, 103, 118, 141, 173, 219, 232, 240
Bowling: Woakes 9-0-37-3; Archer 10-0-42-1l; Plunkett 10-0-42-3l; Wood 10-1-49-1; Rashid 8-0-39-0; Stokes 3-0-20-0.

England			Balls	4s	6s
JJ Roy	c Latham b Henry	17	20	3	
JM Bairstow	b Ferguson	38	56	7	
JE Root	c Latham b de Grandhomme	7	30		
*EJG Morgan	c Ferguson b Neesham	9	22		
BA Stokes	not out	84	98	5	2
†JC Buttler	c sub (Southee) b Ferguson	59	60	6	
CR Woakes	c Latham b Ferguson	2	4		
LE Plunkett	c Boult b Neesham	10	10	1	
JC Archer	b Neesham	0	1		
Adil Rashid	run out	0	0		
MA Wood	run out	0	0		
Extras	(b 2, lb 3, w 12)	11			
Total	(50 overs)	241			

Fall: 28, 59, 71, 86, 196, 203, 220, 227, 240, 240.
Bowling: Boult 10-0-67-0; Henry 10-2-40-1; de Grandhomme 10-2-25-1; Ferguson 10-0-50-3; Neesham 7-0-43-3; Santner 3-0-11-0.

Match Tied (Super Over: England 15-0; New Zealand 15-1. England won on boundary countback). **Toss:** New Zealand. **Umpires:** HDPK Dharmasena, M Erasmus. **Man of the Match:** BA Stokes.

327

AFTERWORD

Aside from the discovery that a full one-day game sits more comfortably within a 100-over structure than the bloated 130 used for the first Gillette Cup in 1963, it has been a tribute to cricket's multi-layered texture that various formats of the short game have managed to coexist for so many years without any becoming entirely obsolete. As the authorities battle with a more complicated calendar and greater demands on the players, this may not always be the case.

'The schedule for me feels unsustainable,' Ben Stokes, England's still new Test captain and hero of the 2019 World Cup, warned in July 2022 when announcing that he would no longer play one-day internationals for his country. 'I want to play as long as I possibly can,' he added, before signing off against a South Africa team whose most celebrated batsman, wicketkeeper Quinton de Kock, had not long made his own compromise by stepping out of Test cricket.

Stokes's statement of intent was quickly followed by Pakistan World Cup winner Wasim Akram creating headlines by arguing for the scrapping of ODIs. 'In England you have full houses,' he said. 'In India, Pakistan especially, Sri Lanka, Bangladesh, South Africa; [in] one-day cricket you are not going to fill the stadiums.'

Wasim was promptly bombarded by fans citing examples of packed crowds in most of those places. He had perhaps been guilty of what others within the game have been accused of in the past: using their own fatigue with certain amounts or formats of cricket to ignore the special event that those games still represented for many fans in the stadium or in front of TV screens. If broadcasters continue to feel that ODIs offer enough eyeballs to justify their rights fees they will remain cemented in the calendar.

Yet there is, as I write this, no ignoring the threat to the continued existence of multiple formats; a peril that comes chiefly from the demands and choices in front of the players. Some, like Stokes, will continue to drop certain types of cricket from their résumés in order to maintain health and fitness. Others will make decisions based on finances, especially those from outside England, India and Australia who cannot afford to miss out on lucrative franchise tournaments in order to be paid relatively low amounts for playing for their impoverished countries. With the same ownership groups now beginning to control teams in multiple domestic competitions, a player signing for, say, an IPL team may in future find himself with the option, or obligation, to represent the same franchise in various countries over the course of several months.

The solution to that, many believe, is to protect the primacy of international cricket by playing less of it, giving more players the chance to have their cake and cash it in. That the 50-over version is the most vulnerable and may face a future that includes little more than a World Cup every four years – despite how dearly bi-lateral series matches may be held by many fans – was made clear by South Africa's decision to pull out of a three-game ODI series in Australia early in 2023 in order to use that period of time to launch a new Twenty20 tournament, featuring many IPL owners.

In England, the 50-over county competition, the bloodline of the original Gillette Cup, was downgraded to a virtual second eleven event at a time when the nation was at last world champion in the format so as to offer The Hundred the prime spot in the summer calendar and the pick of the players.

I did not include as a main game in this book anything from the ECB's new made-for-TV format launched in 2021. Not for reasons of bias against the competition but because, at the time of writing, its long-term impact – especially with no other countries yet to adopt it – remains uncertain, despite the obvious elevation it has offered to the women's game. Maybe The Hundred, rather than more 50-over games, will form the bulk of the fresh content should this book be updated for the 70th anniversary of limited-overs cricket.

Mind you, I am writing in the wake of a 2022 English summer in which the approach and success of the home country's Test team began to change the perception of the longest version of the game and its potential to draw in non-aficionados. While it is the development of the short formats that has characterised cricket's changing face over six decades, it is suddenly possible – when intoxicated by the fumes of another successful English fourth-innings chase – to envisage a time when shrinking its fixture list is not considered the only way to intensify its drama. Who knows where the sport might be in ten years' time?

If the past 60 years have proved anything it is that cricket will keep evolving, sometimes at what seems like a revolutionary pace and, probably, one day at a time.

ACKNOWLEDGEMENTS

A book such as this, encompassing an extended timespan, inevitably relies heavily on the authors and broadcasters who have previously chronicled various elements of the story. My thanks, therefore, are due to those responsible for the works appearing in the list of sources that follows this section. In particular, I welcome any opportunity to recognise once more Gideon Haigh's *The Cricket War*, still my favourite book about the sport; and to highlight Tim Wigmore and Freddie Wilde's *Cricket 2.0*, their brilliantly insightful study of the Twenty20 game, which has been of great benefit to some of the latter chapters of this book.

Thank you to the players, coaches and administrators with whom I have spoken for this and other work. At the risk of omissions, I have also listed them among my sources.

As always, there are those whose contributions have earned my gratitude rather than a mention anywhere else in the narrative of the book. This time they include Claire Furlong at the ICC; Edward Griffiths; Bryan Henderson at Sky Sports; Andrew Miller at ESPNcricinfo; Will Quin; Tom Skinner and Stephen Martin at Derbyshire CCC; Nick Pike; Ann Ridley; Matt Sherry; and Jon Surtees at Surrey CCC.

It has been my great fortune – although perhaps not his – to have had Richard Whitehead as editor for several of my titles. His thoughtful and assiduous work has again been a great asset, along with the sound sense and advice he places at my disposal at all hours and on all topics.

Once more, I am grateful to my agent David Luxton, and his associate Rebecca Winfield, for their diligence in bringing this book to a publisher and pulling together all the contractual stuff. Having worked with Matt Thacker on a range of previous projects, it is very exciting to be part of his new venture at Fairfield. I hope this book will add to the history of exceptional chronicling of cricket for which Fairfield has become known and for which Matt has boldly taken on responsibility.

As always, my final thanks are reserved for my family for their love and support: including daughters Amy, Sarah, Laura and Karis, grandsons Jacob and Oscar, and granddaughter Heidi. To my wife, Sara, all I can offer in return for everything that she brings to my life is the promise that, one day at a time, I will keep trying to repay her.

SOURCES AND BIBLIOGRAPHY

Interviews (conducted for this and previous titles)

Dennis Amiss, Geoff Arnold, Mickey Arthur, Bill Athey, Katherine Brunt, Ian Chappell, Clare Connor, Charles Dagnall, Paul Davey, Geoffrey Dean, Frank Duckworth, Bruce Edgar, Ross Edwards, Steve Elworthy, Graeme Fowler, Peter Graves, Peter Griffiths, Jamie Grove, Vanburn Holder, Alvin Kallicharran, Dinesh Karthik, Gary Kirsten, Peter Kirsten, Alan Knott, Clive Lloyd, David Lloyd, Brian McKechnie, Niall O'Brien, Chris Old, Pat Pocock, Derek Pringle, Ramiz Raja, Ian Redpath, Daren Sammy, Anya Shrubsole, Jack Simmons, Gladstone Small, John Snow, Alec Stewart, Derek Underwood, Michel Vaughan, Mike Veletta, Ian Ward, Barry Wood, and the late Tony Greig, Jim Parks and Bob Willis.

Newspapers, magazines and annuals (including their websites)

Daily Mirror, Indian Express, India Today, Manchester Evening News, Melbourne Age, Sydney Morning Herald, Sydney Morning Telegraph, The Cricketer, The Daily Telegraph, The Independent, The Observer, The Times, Time (Australia), *Wisden Cricket Monthly, Wisden Cricketers' Almanack.*

Other online sources

Ashwin (Ravi Ashwin's YouTube channel); AsiaNetNews.com; BBC Sport website; BharatArmy.com; Cricket Couch (podcast); Cricket.com.au; CricketArchive.com; CricketCountry.com; Dawn.com; ESPNCricinfo.com; FirstPost.com; Following On (podcast); HowStat.com; LancashireCricket.co.uk; Lessons Learned from the Greats (podcast); Papare.com; Sportscafe.in; Stumped (BBC podcast); Supersport.com; The 80s and 90s Cricket Show (podcast); The Final Word (podcast); The Scoop (podcast); TheHindu.com; TheNational.ae; WalesOnline.com

Broadcasts

Bad Sport: Fallen Idol (Netflix); *Beyond Boundaries* (Netflix); *Black Armband: The Full Story* (BBC Radio); *Breaking Boundaries: Ireland's Extraordinary World Cup* (Zanzibar Films); *Captain's Log* (Sky Sports); *Capturing the World Cup*, various episodes (ESPN Star for ICC); *Cricket in Colour – The Story of the 1992 World Cup* (Sunset and Vine/Kingsdown TV for ICC); *Cricket in the 80s: Rookies, Rebels and Renaissance* (ABC TV); *How the World Cup Was Won* (ICC); *India-Pakistan: Unforgettables* (unknown); *Sportsworld* (BBC World Service); *Test Match Special* (BBC Radio); *That Wining Feeling* (Times Now); *The World Through Their Eyes* (Sky Sports); *Underarm: The Ball That Changed Cricket* (Gordian Media); *Viv Richards Through His Eyes* (Sky Sports); *Winning Over the World* (Sky Sports).

Bibliography

Amiss, Dennis, with James Graham-Brown, *Not Out at the Close of Play: A Life in Cricket* (The History Press, 2021)

Addison, Vernon and Derek Bearshaw, *Lancashire Cricket at The Top* (Stanley Paul, 1971)

Badale, Manoj, and Simon Hughes, *A New Innings: How the IPL's Reinvention of Cricket Provides Lessons for the Business of Sport* (Clink Street Publishing, 2020)

Berry, Scyld, *Cricket Wallah: With England in India and Sri Lanka* (Hodder & Stoughton, 1982)

Birley, Derek, *A Social History of English Cricket* (Aurum Press, 1999)

Bose, Mihir, *A History of Indian Cricket* (Andre Deutsch, 1990)

Boucher, Mark with Neil Manthorp, *Bouch: Through My Eyes* (Jonathan Ball, 2013)

Brearley, Mike and Dudley Doust, *The Ashes Retained* (Hodder & Stoughton, 1979)

Cashman, Richard, *'Ave a Go, Yer Mug!'* (Harper Collins Australia, 1984)

Chappell, Greg, with Malcolm Knox, *Fierce Focus* (Hardie Grant, 2012)

Duncan Isabelle, *Skirting The Boundary: A History of Women's Cricket* (Robson Books, 2013)

Donald, Allan, *White Lightning: The Autobiography* (Willow, 1999)

Fletcher, Duncan, *Behind the Shades: The Autobiography* (Simon & Schuster, 2007)

Gavaskar, Sunil, *Sunny Days: The Sunil Gavaskar Omnibus* (Rupa and Co, 1999)

Gibbs, Herschelle with Steve Smith, *To The Point: The No-Holds-Barred Autobiography* (Zebra Press, 2011)

Gouws, Deon, '...And Nothing But The Truth' (Struick Publishers, 2000)

Griffiths, Edward Glory Days: Forty Years of One-Day Cricket (Penguins Books South Africa, 2003)

Haigh, Gideon The Cricket War: The Inside Story of Kerry Packer's World Series Cricket (The Text Publishing Company, 1993)

Hindley, Martyn, Crash! Bang! Wallop! Twenty20: A History of The Brief Game (Know The Score, 2008)

Hussey, Michael, Underneath The Southern Cross (Hardie Grant Books, 2014)

Johnston, Trent and Gerard Siggins, Raiders of the Caribbean: Ireland's Cricket World Cup (O'Brien Press, 2007)

Laker, Jim, One-Day Cricket (Batsford, 1977)

Lee, Alan, A Pitch in Both Camps: England and World Series Cricket in Australia 1978-79 (Stanley Paul 1979)

Lee, Alan, Lord Ted: The Dexter Enigma (Gollancz/Witherby, 1995)

Lee, Christopher From the Sea End: The Official History of Sussex County Cricket Club (Partridge Press, 1989)

Lillee, Dennis, Menace: The Autobiography (Headline, 2003)

Majumdar, Boria Eleven Gods and a Billion Indians: The On and Off the Field Story of Cricket in India and Beyond, (Simon & Schuster India, 2018)

Meyer, Barrie with Andrew Hignell, Getting It Right (Tempus, 2008)

Miandad, Javed with Saas Shafqat, Cutting Edge; My Autobiography (Oxford University Press, 2003)

Miller, Peter and Dave Tickner, 28 Days' Data: England's Troubled Relationship with One-Day Cricket (Pitch Publishing, 2016)

Northall, Jonathan, Ruling the World: The Story of the 1992 Cricket World Cup (Pitch Publishing, 2019)

Oborne, Peter, Wounded Tiger: A History of Cricket in Pakistan (Simon & Schuster, 2014)

Olonga, Henry, Blood, Sweat and Treason: My Story (Vision Sports Publishing, 2010)

Parks, Jim, Time to Hit Out (Stanley Paul, 1967)

Ponting, Ricky, At the Close of Play (HarperSport, 2013)

Procter, Mike, Mike Procter And Cricket (Pelham Books, 1981)

Ray, Ashis, One-Day Cricket: The Indian Challenge (Harper Collins Publishers India, 2007)

Richards, Viv, *Hitting Across the Line: An Autobiography* (Headline, 1991)

Richards, Viv, *Sir Vivian: The Definitive Autobiography* (Michael Joseph, 2000)

Richards, Viv with David Foot, *Viv Richards* (World's Work, 1979)

Ross, Gordon, *The Gillette Cup 1963-1980* (Queen Anne Press, 1980)

Salve, NKP, *The Story of the Reliance Cup* (Vikas Pub. House, 1987)

Samiuddin, Osman *The Unquiet Ones: A History of Pakistan Cricket* (Harper Sport, 2014)

Snow, John *Cricket Rebel* (Hamlyn, 1976)

Srinivas, Alam and TR Vivek, *IPL: An Inside Story, Cricket and Commerce* (Roli Books, 2009)

Sundaresan, Bharat, *The Dhoni Touch: Unravelling the Enigma That is MS Dhoni* (Penguin Ebury Press, 2018)

Tharoor, Shashi and Shaharyar Khan, *Shadows Across the Playing Field: 60 Years of India-Pakistan Cricket* (Lotus/Roli 2009)

Tossell, David, *Grovel! The Summer and Legacy of 1976* (Know The Score, 2007)

Tossell, David, *Sex and Drugs and Rebel Tours: The England Cricket Team in the 1980s* (Pitch Publishing, 2015)

Tossell, David, *The Girls of Summer: An Ashes Summer with the England Women's Cricket Team* (Pitch Publishing, 2015)

Tossell, David, *Tony Greig: A Reappraisal of English Cricket's Most Controversial Captain* (Pitch Publishing, 2011)

Waugh, Steve, *Out of My Comfort Zone: The Autobiography* (Penguin, 2005)

Waugh, Steve, *No Regrets: A Captain's Diary* (HarperCollins Publishers, Australia, 1999)

Wigmore, Tim and Freddie Wilde, *Cricket 2.0: Inside the T20 Revolution* (Polaris, 2019)

Wooldridge, Ian and Ted Dexter (editors) *The International Cavaliers' World of Cricket* (Purnell, 1970)

Woolmer, Bob, *Woolmer on Cricket* (Virgin Books, 2000)